Surreal
Spaces

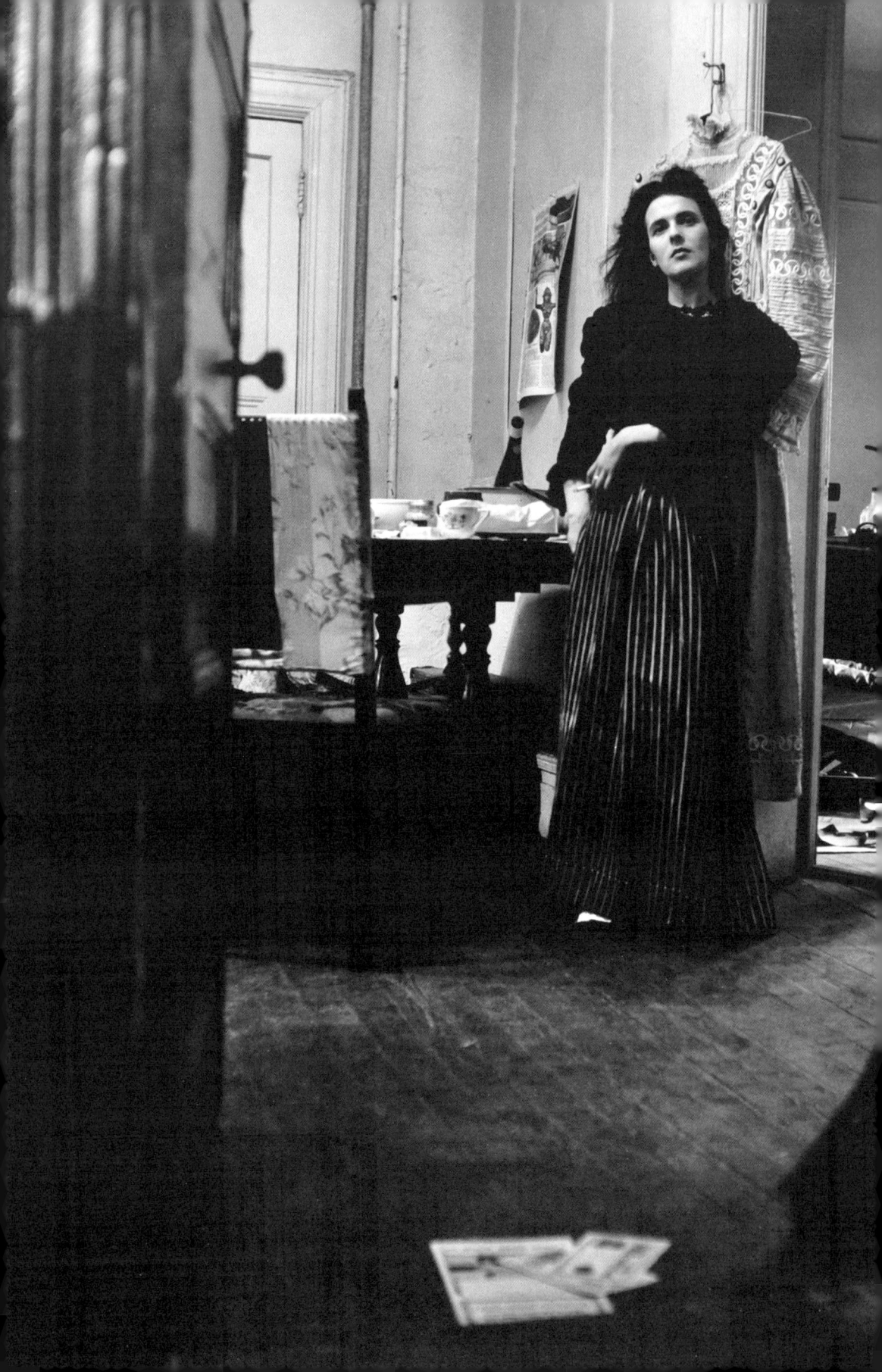

Surreal Spaces

The Life and Art of
Leonora Carrington

JOANNA MOORHEAD

Princeton University Press
Princeton and Oxford

Published in the United States of America and Canada in 2023
by Princeton University Press,
41 William Street, Princeton, New Jersey 08540
press.princeton.edu

Published by arrangement with Thames & Hudson Ltd, London

First published in the United Kingdom in 2023
by Thames & Hudson Ltd,
181A High Holborn, London WC1V 7QX

Designed by P D Burgess

Library of Congress Control Number 2022951503

ISBN 978-0-691-25448-7

EBOOK ISBN 978-0-691-25449-4

Printed and bound in China by C&C Offset Printing Co. Ltd.

FSC
www.fsc.org

MIX
Paper | Supporting
responsible forestry
FSC® C008047

Frontispiece: Leonora Carrington in her Greenwich Village
apartment, *c.* 1942. Photograph by Hermann Landshoff

10 9 8 7 6 5 4 3 2 1

Contents

Introduction   6

1   **Beginnings**   1917–1927   12

2   **Adolescence**   1927–1935   38

3   **Debutante and Art Student**   1935–1937   56

4   **Cornwall**   1937   68

5   **Paris**   1937–1938   78

6   **Saint-Martin-d'Ardèche**   1938–1940   94

7   **Santander and Lisbon**   1940–1941   114

8   **New York**   1941–1942   134

9   **Mexico**   1942–1968   150

10   **New York and Chicago**   1968–1992   176

11   **Mexico City**   1992–the present   190

Notes   208

Further Reading   213

Acknowledgments   214

Credits   216

Index   219

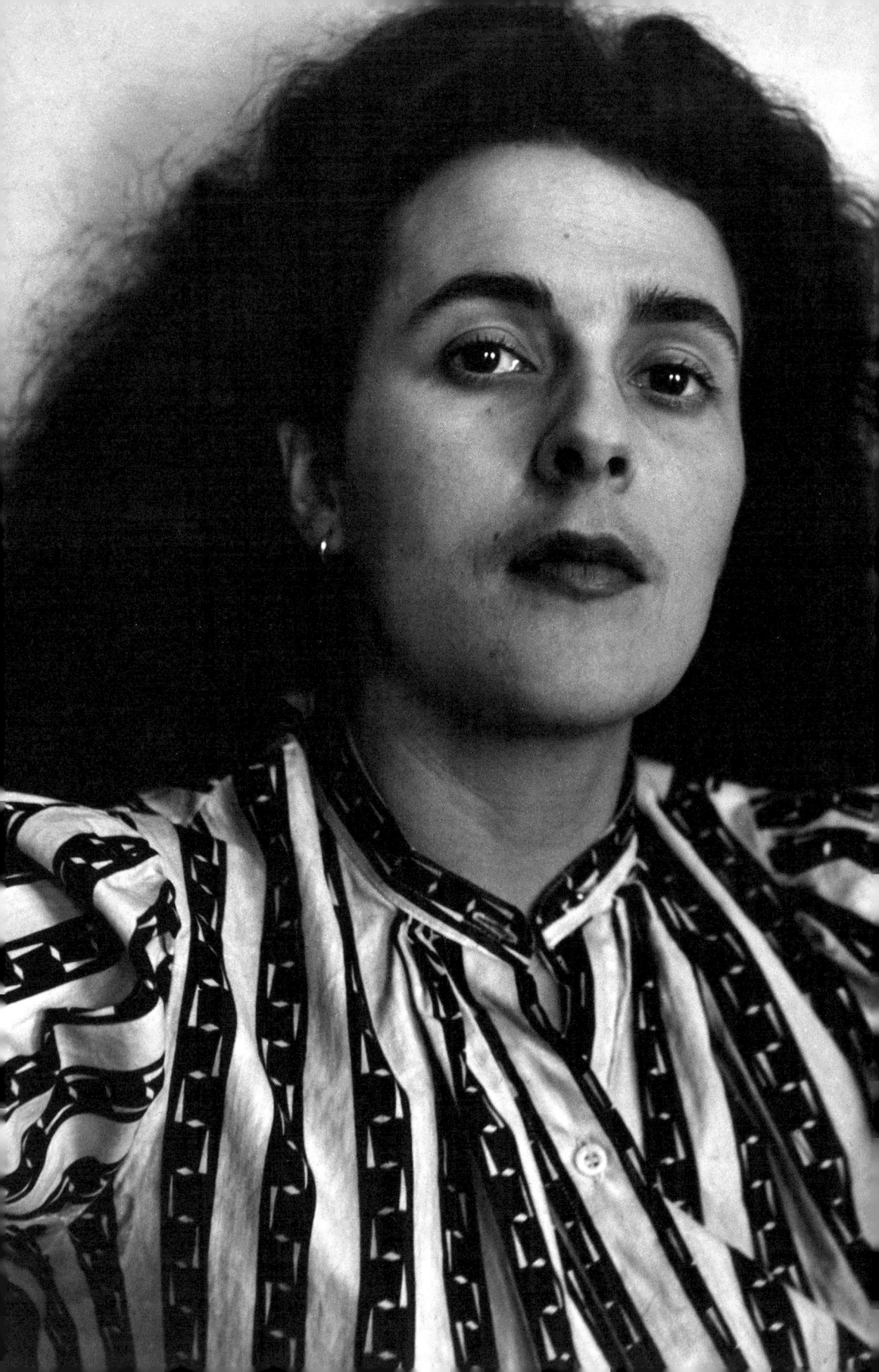

Introduction

One day in late autumn 2006 I took a flight from London to Mexico City, a piece of paper with a telephone number on it in my pocket. My luggage didn't make it to Mexico – not for a few more days, anyway – but that didn't matter, because the piece of paper was the only baggage I needed. The number scribbled on it was my route to my father's cousin, the surrealist artist Leonora Carrington.

A few months earlier, I'd discovered during a chance conversation that the woman I had only ever known of as the black sheep of our family was, in fact, Mexico's most famous living artist. Now I was determined to find out more. I was a journalist; I knew a good story when I stumbled across one, and the piece I planned to write had been commissioned by the *Guardian*.

At that point, most interviewers who wanted an audience with Leonora were told it wouldn't be possible. She was in her late eighties; she shied away from publicity, as she always had, and she had little time for art historians. But I was hoping my credentials would give me access. I knew she'd be familiar with my surname because her mother, Maurie (my great-aunt), had been a Moorhead. I had made indirect contact via the gallery that represented Leonora in Mexico City and a tentative yes had come back via its owner, Eva Marcovich. 'No promises,' Eva told me, over a crackly line to London. 'But as you're going to be in Mexico City anyway [I wasn't, of course], do give her a call. If she's feeling up to it she'll probably invite you over for a cup of tea.'

Eva said not to try Leonora before ten a.m., so I called her at a minute past on my first morning in Mexico. She answered immediately – a very English, mannish-sounding voice – and invited me straight over.

I remember walking along Calle Álvaro Obregón towards her house in the neighbourhood of Roma Norte and thinking, this is

Leonora Carrington, 1942. Photograph by Hermann Landshoff

7

going to be an interesting article. Leonora had, I knew by now, been at the heart of the surrealist movement in prewar Paris. She'd known everyone – Picasso, Dalí, Duchamp, Breton, Miró – and Max Ernst had been her lover. The turbulent 1930s had whisked her from Lancashire to London and Paris before transporting her to a house surrounded by sun-drenched vineyards in the South of France. There had been a series of thrilling wartime adventures that I was keen to hear about, and then the seismic move from Europe to Mexico. At that point Leonora had put her country, her continent and her family behind her; she'd been based in Central America ever since. And in Mexico she had become (I'd been informed by the Mexican art historian who first told me about her) a national treasure. This was quite a story, one that had transported her across Britain, Europe and the world, and she had created a body of work that drew on all the places and spaces she had inhabited in the course of almost ninety years.

A few minutes later I was ringing her doorbell. A woman I would come to know as Yolanda, Leonora's housekeeper, opened the door; then she stood aside to let a diminutive figure, dressed entirely in black, approach along the corridor.

'Prim?' I ventured, using the family nickname, the only name I'd ever known our relatives to use.

'Not Prim now,' she answered. 'I'm Leonora.' And then she invited me in. Yolanda closed the door behind us and we went into the kitchen for tea and, later, tequila.

This was my initiation into Leonora's private world. It was clear from the start that it was largely sealed off from the Mexico in which it was physically situated. In this house, at 194 Calle Chihuahua, she had lived for more than sixty years. The kitchen, with its Liberty print tablecloth and fridge magnets recalling the England she had left behind, was its epicentre: it was where she held court for the few visitors she did allow and it was also, by that time, where she often sat alone. Only one of her two sons lived in Mexico and most of her grandchildren were in America. There was space at her table for a new friend – and if it was ironic that this friend came from the family she had bid farewell to so many decades earlier, Leonora wasn't fazed by it.

And so we talked. She told me the story of her life and I told her about the family she had left behind (she was surprisingly, or perhaps not so surprisingly, interested in what had happened to them all). We talked all the rest of that day, and when I left she asked what time I'd be coming over the next morning. I spent the entire week with her, ensconced in her kitchen, talking. On my penultimate day in Mexico I remembered with a jolt that I still had a piece to write, and no official interview had yet taken place. The next day when we sat down I got my notebook out of my bag and put it on the table.

'What's that?' asked Leonora, a little sharply. I explained it was my notebook, that I was here to interview her and write a story about her, that I needed some notes. 'Well, you can put it away,' she said. 'Write your story if you want, but you're not interviewing me. You're not a journalist here.'

She was right, and I'd realized the same thing. It was clear that our relationship was about something more than work, either hers or mine. We had bonded over our shared roots and I could see, from the first day I spent with her, that I had a huge amount to learn from her. What she would ultimately teach me was the most precious gift of all: how to be the best version of myself. Through our conversations I came to understand that the world is limited only by our own ways of seeing it; that each of us is as big as our own imagination. I also learned that there is more to life than the here and now; and I learned the value of being humble, of admitting what I did not know. Although Leonora was almost ninety and had experienced enough to fill many lifetimes, she often remarked on how little she knew. All it came down to, she would say, was that she was a human, female animal, and that she would one day die.

I loved her honesty – she once told me that the most important thing she'd learned in the course of her long life was to be honest: 'To be authentic. To be true to oneself.' I loved the breadth of her vision. I loved her unexpected, sometimes completely left-field points of view on all sorts of topics. And I appreciated how generous she was in welcoming me into her world, how freely she shared her insights and ideas.

After that I began to visit Leonora twice a year, usually in spring and autumn, a pattern that continued until her death in May 2011. During all of the hours I was fortunate enough to spend with her, I never again took out my notebook. I did, however, keep a diary of our time together: each night, before I went to sleep, I'd write about the day we'd shared.

I've returned to those diaries while writing this book, working some of the things Leonora said into its pages. I hope her words convey a sense of her, of the human animal she was; and that they help to evoke the important places in her life, what they meant to her and how they shaped her work.

Leonora always resisted being pinned down. She was a free spirit and hated to be the centre of attention; she was the antithesis of the 21st-century artists to whom courting the media comes naturally. She would go out of her way to avoid publicity, and if that affected how well known her work was, so be it. Revisiting the interviews she did occasionally give – some of which read like masterclasses in avoiding the question – has made me realize what a gift she gave me in refusing to approach our conversations the same way. Her interview with Hans Ulrich Obrist, now artistic director at the Serpentine Galleries in London, is festooned with Leonora gems. When Obrist asks if, given the prevalence of animals in her work, she has been surrounded by animals in life too, she responds: 'I don't think so. I think that a lot of things occurred, but I don't know why.' And in response to a question about the relationship between her painting and her writing: 'It's always been a puzzle to me,' she says. 'The relationship between language and image. I find it very difficult, but you can tell me...'

This is the stuff of journalists' nightmares. But Leonora was being honest: she didn't know the answers and wasn't prepared to pretend that she did, or to concoct an artificial narrative that would come to define her. So on it went: when Obrist asked her how much meaning the idea of space occupied in her work, she replied: 'So what do you think?' Asked about her move to the US, she said: 'Why did I go to Chicago? It's a very nice city, Chicago.'

Finally, the coup de grâce. Interviewers invariably flatter interviewees in the hope of coaxing out information. Obrist mentions a 1948 quote of Leonora's – 'I am armed with madness for a long voyage' – and tells her he thinks it is beautiful. Leonora's reaction? 'I think it was a very stupid thing to say.'

Reader, I was blessed: there would be no interviews with Leonora for me. Instead, she invited me to be close to her and to share her world. That was infinitely, immensely preferable because it allowed me to discover her by osmosis, by an emotional connection, by what I felt rather than by what she said. And that was one of her most significant pieces of advice: to gauge the world not by what was said, but by how I felt.

The other thing I came to realize was that Leonora was setting me a puzzle, or in fact a series of puzzles, to solve if I wanted to understand who she was and what she believed in. She was never going to simply tell me what she knew (although she would be honest about what she didn't know); instead she would give me clues, and it would be up to me whether or not I followed up on those and learned more.

I cherished the time I spent with Leonora. I knew she wouldn't be around forever, and that whatever happened afterwards wouldn't be as wonderful as those absorbing days in Mexico. But after her death in 2011 I set off on another journey: to the houses, landscapes and countries she had inhabited. I knew there would be fragments of her that remained; I knew there would be clues and signposts, if I was open to seeing them. I knew I would find more of her if I travelled hopefully.

As it turned out, many of the places Leonora had inhabited were exactly as she had left them, so much so that it sometimes seemed like more than a coincidence. Crookhey Hall, her childhood home was virtually untouched; Hazelwood Hall, her next home, restored to exactly as it was – externally, anyway – in the years she spent there. The block of flats where she met Max Ernst: still just as she would have known it. The house in France where they lived together felt as though she had only recently closed the door for the last time, although that had been seventy years earlier. Then there was the park where the sanatorium had been in Santander, which still matched the map she had drawn. And finally, the house in Mexico City where I had spent so much time with her was restored to exactly as it had been in the final years of her life – it is now open to the public as a museum.

I pondered as I travelled on how the truth about all of us is contained in many layers: some historical, some spiritual, some genetic, some related to particular places and times. Leonora's art was about trying to separate those layers out from one another so as to better understand ourselves. Wherever I went, things fell into place and I was able to understand a little more about who she was, what she was about, and why.

I realized, too, that I would be able to find Leonora wherever I might go – because, as all the people we have loved live in our hearts, she lives in mine. I appreciate what it means to have her there more than I can say. I know I am fortunate to have spent time with her, and to have had the chance to explore the history and geography of her life after she was gone. This book is my attempt to share what I found out about the influences, stories and places that helped to make Leonora Carrington who she was, both as an artist and as a woman.

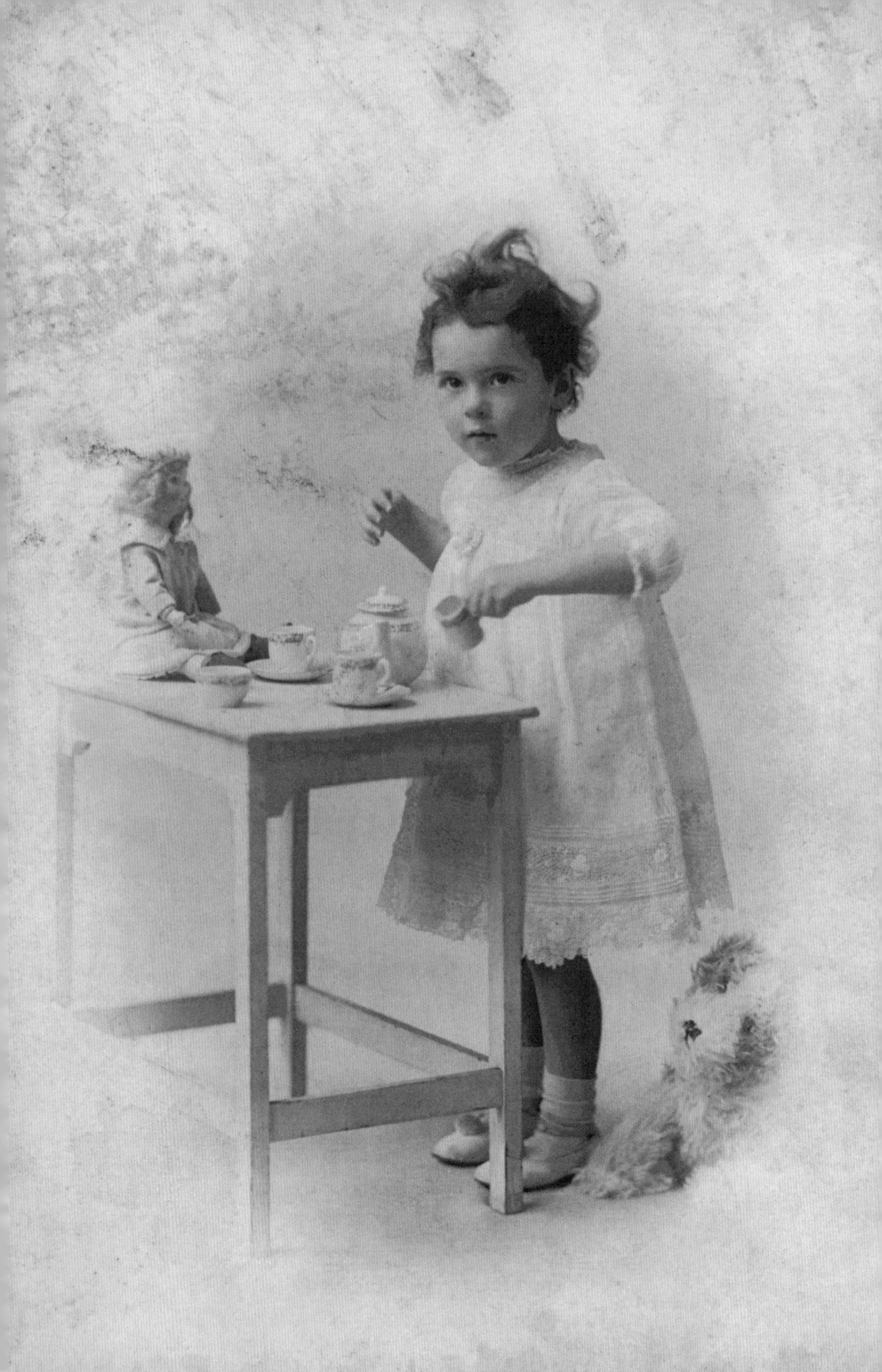

1
Beginnings
1917−1927

Crookhey Hall was the home Leonora Carrington spent a lifetime trying to escape; but did she ever truly want to leave it behind? Her work was infused, throughout her long career, with references to and memories of the house in which she had spent the formative years of her childhood. When I met Leonora for the first time in Mexico City, eight decades after her family moved out of Crookhey, recollections of the turreted Gothic mansion came easily and quickly to her mind. It was much more than the dwelling-place of her youth: it was the launchpad for her imagination, the genesis of a bank of visual and emotional memories that would sustain her direction and her art for the rest of her days.

Leonora wasn't born at Crookhey. Her birthplace was a mansion, now demolished, called Westwood House, in the village of Clayton-le-Woods near Chorley in Lancashire. She arrived there on 6 April 1917, which that year was Good Friday, the most sombre date in the Christian calendar. She was to be raised in her mother's faith, as a Catholic, and the visual, narrative and magical qualities of Catholicism would play out across her work throughout her life.

Leonora's parents had come from very different backgrounds. Her paternal grandfather was a self-made industrialist, a man of humble roots who transformed himself into the managing director of the Carrington and Dewhurst textile company. Harold Carrington, Leonora's father, inherited the business during a boom period: textiles were a huge growth industry in the early years of the 20th century, and money was quickly made.

Photograph of Leonora as a child

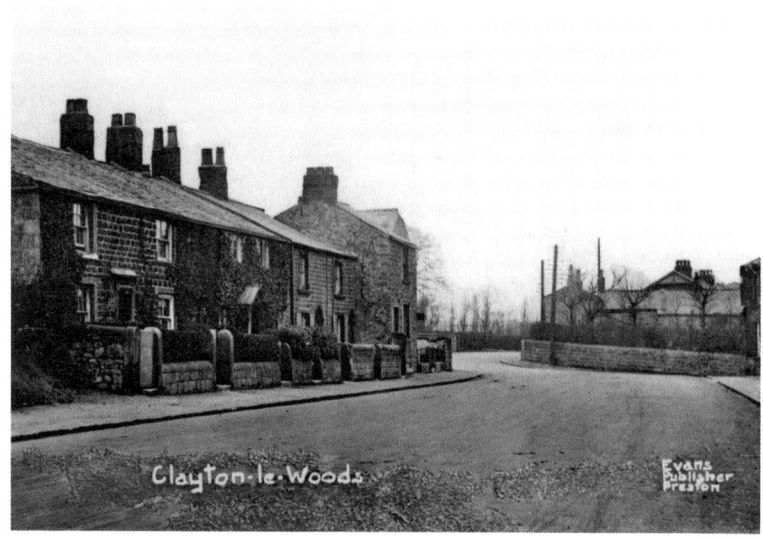

View of Clayton-le-Woods village, 1900s

Her mother, Maurie Moorhead, was from Moate in County Westmeath, Ireland. She was the eldest of five siblings, one of whom was my grandfather George; the sibling closest in age to Maurie was a sister, Leonora. By the time Maurie and Harold met, at a cricket match in Ireland in 1907, Leo (as she was always known in the family) had entered a convent in Dublin and become a Sister of Charity. But the two women remained close, so it would have been no surprise that when Maurie gave birth to a daughter, she named the baby after her own sister. In line with Catholic tradition, Mary was the first given name on the child's birth certificate, but it was always intended that the name which followed – Leonora – was the one by which she would be known.

Given that there was already one Leonora in the family, it was inevitable that a nickname would come into use. Sure enough, by the time the family left Westwood and arrived at Crookhey, the three-year-old girl with her mane of tight black curls was already known by everyone as 'Prim'. How or why this came about is lost in the annals of time, although there's a vague family story about a business colleague of Harold's who remarked, upon meeting the little girl, that she seemed very prim. Perhaps its irony partly explained the gusto with which it was taken up; perhaps even in the nursery she was defying convention.

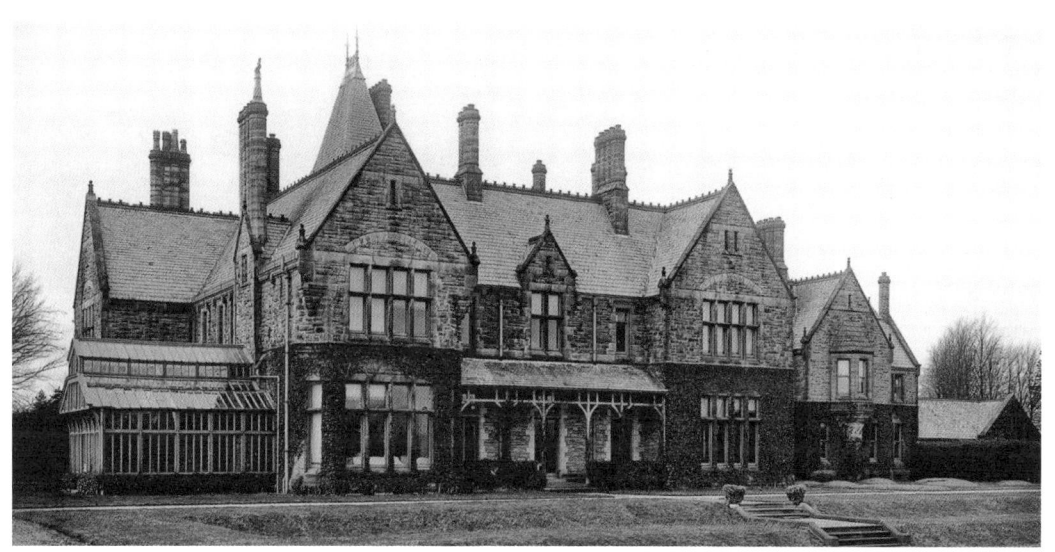

Crookhey Hall, exterior

When the Carringtons arrived at Crookhey Hall in 1920, its Victorian splendour was still less than a century old. It was the work of architect Alfred Waterhouse (1830–1905), who also designed London's Natural History Museum as well as Eaton Hall in Cheshire, seat of the dukes of Westminster. Crookhey was completed in 1874, as a stone inlay on one of its eaves testifies. It is a Gothic-inspired construction of grey sandstone with a large porch under which, in the days of carriages, people could disembark without encountering the full force of the Lancashire weather. Atop the porch stands a stone bird. Birds are very much the emblem of the house: its first owner was one Colonel Bird, who made his name synonymous with his branding. In his day, staff at Crookhey wore uniforms whose buttons carried an avian motif. By Leonora's time this had changed, but the imagery of birds remained strongly represented in the fabric of the building.

Her painting *Bird Bath II* (1978) shows a building clearly inspired by Crookhey, with its large portico to one side, exactly as it is at the Lancashire house. A large red bird in the foreground is being bathed, in what looks like a cauldron but is also reminiscent of a baptismal font, by a black-clad woman not dissimilar in appearance from Leonora herself at sixty, the age she was when she created this work. The woman is assisted by a sinister figure wearing a Venetian-style plague mask; in the background, another individual holds a second bird. Dominating

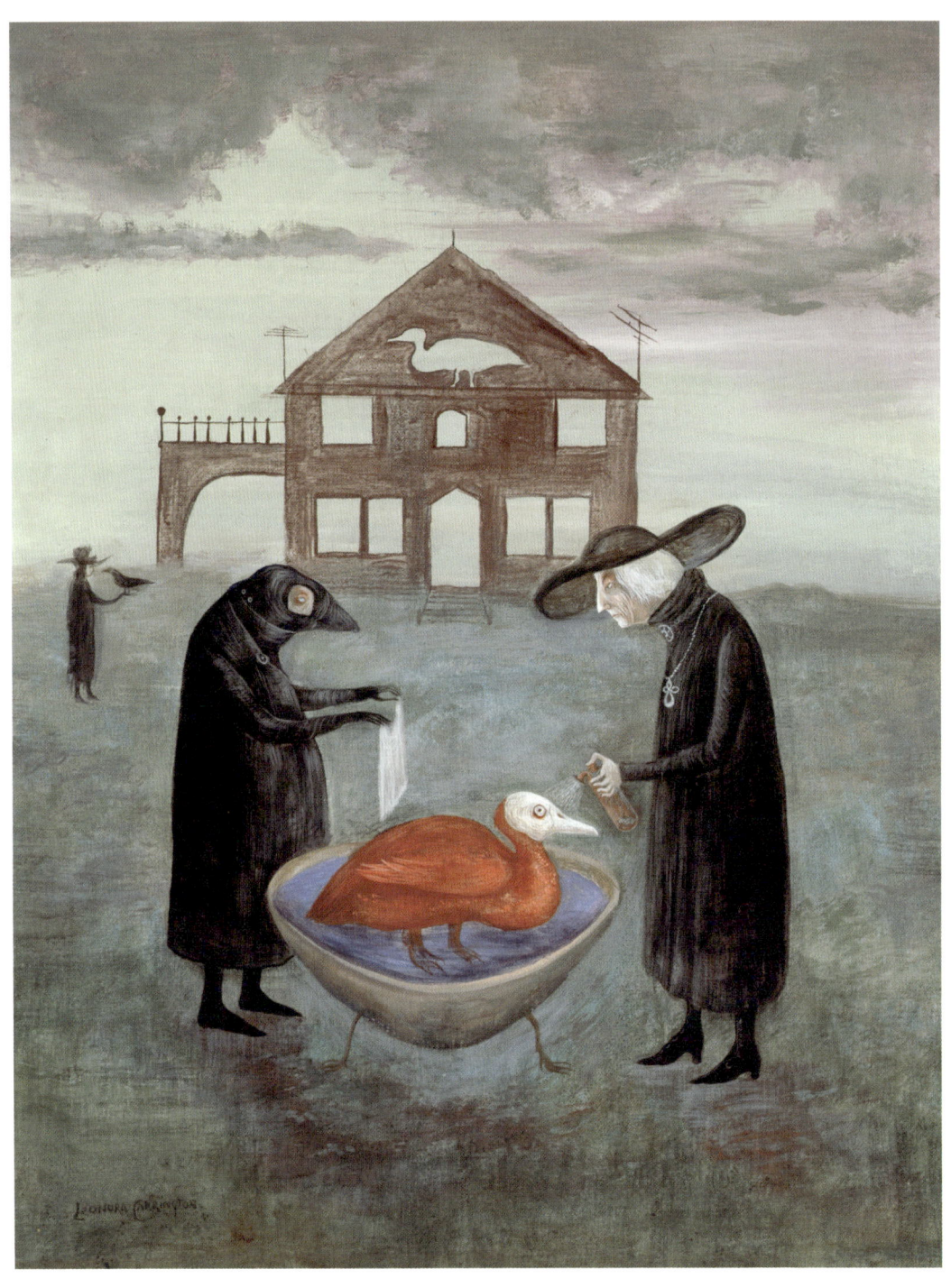

Bird Bath II, 1978

the structure of the house is a form that mirrors that of the bathing bird, carved into the fabric of the building, exactly as at Crookhey. The painting is a commentary on Leonora's own relationship with the house that had always occupied the hinterland of her own canvas. She is washing the bird that represents Crookhey out of her life; the building, though prominent, is merely a shell; there are no longer any rooms behind that door and those windows, and instead we can see the sky through the apertures. Leonora is attempting, as she had for so long attempted, to leave Crookhey behind – but she would never be able to shake off its influence.

'Do you think anyone escapes their childhood?' she asked, aged seventy-five. 'I don't think they do.'[1] While she could reduce Crookhey to an edifice, as in *Bird Bath II*, and take the power of the birds for herself, she could not cancel out its impact on her life or her work – it was folded into who she was, connected to her in a spiritual sense as firmly as it was connected in a physical way to the stone bird. As she wrote in her novella *The Hearing Trumpet*, 'Houses are really bodies. We connect ourselves with walls, roofs, and objects just as we hang on to our livers, skeletons, flesh and blood stream.'[2] To the end of her life, Crookhey was as much a part of Leonora as her flesh or her liver.

The skies over Crookhey are often grey and cloud-filled, mirroring the heavy gloom of the house below. From the gate, it resembles a building glimpsed at the opening of a horror movie: all turrets and chimneys, sharp eaves and narrow windows. There's a sense of foreboding – it is cold, a house of secrets, a place of chilling mystery. You'd be forgiven for turning back.

For Leonora, though, there was no turning back. However off-putting, however frightening, this pile was her home. Surely it was the place she had in mind when writing her 1938 story 'The House of Fear', which features a castle 'built of stones that held the cold of winter'; inside – even chillier than outside – is a great hall 'decorated with mushrooms and other fruits of the night', and there, 'reclining in the Roman fashion on a very large bed, lay the mistress of the house – Fear. Her dressing gown was made of live bats sewn together by their wings: the way they fluttered, one would have thought they didn't much like it.'[3]

Through a young child's eyes, Crookhey's canopied porch must have felt enormous; still more the galleried hallway with its glass roof in the centre of the house. Leonora's favourite room, she told me many

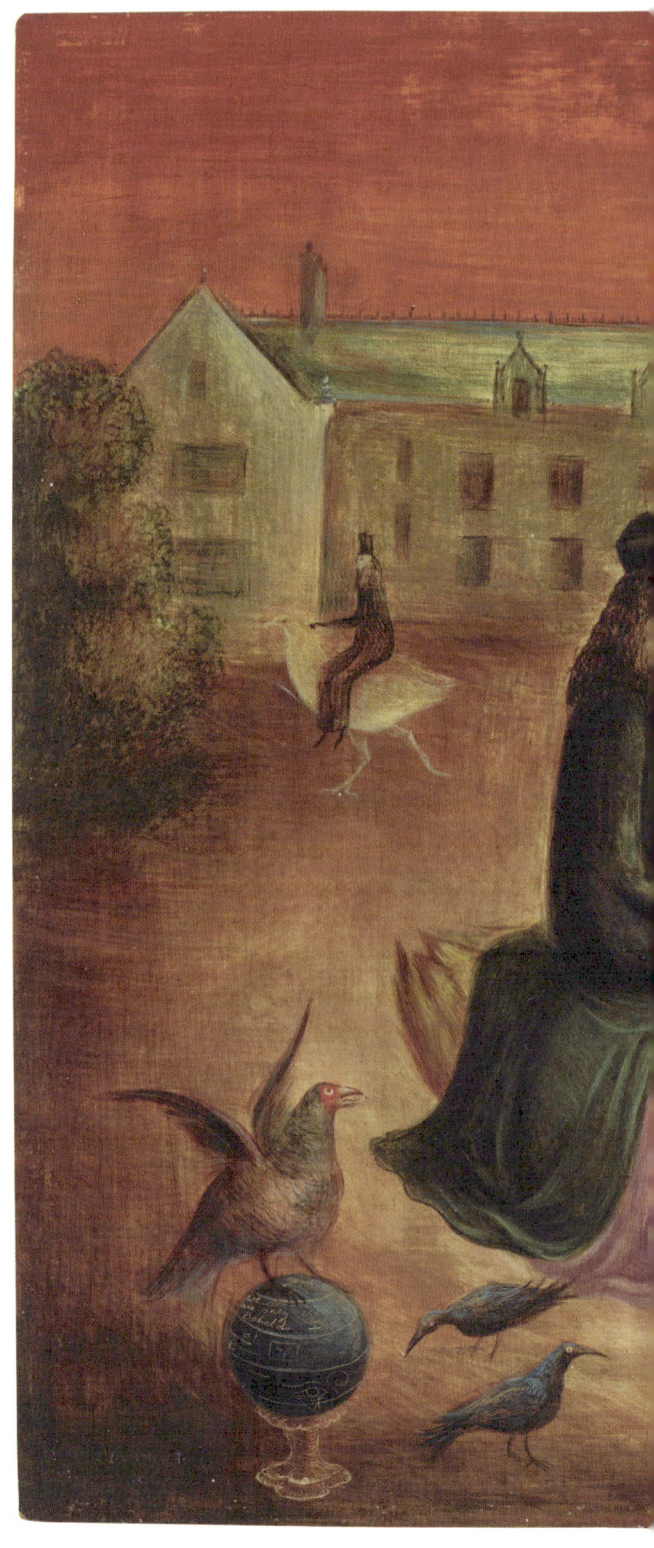

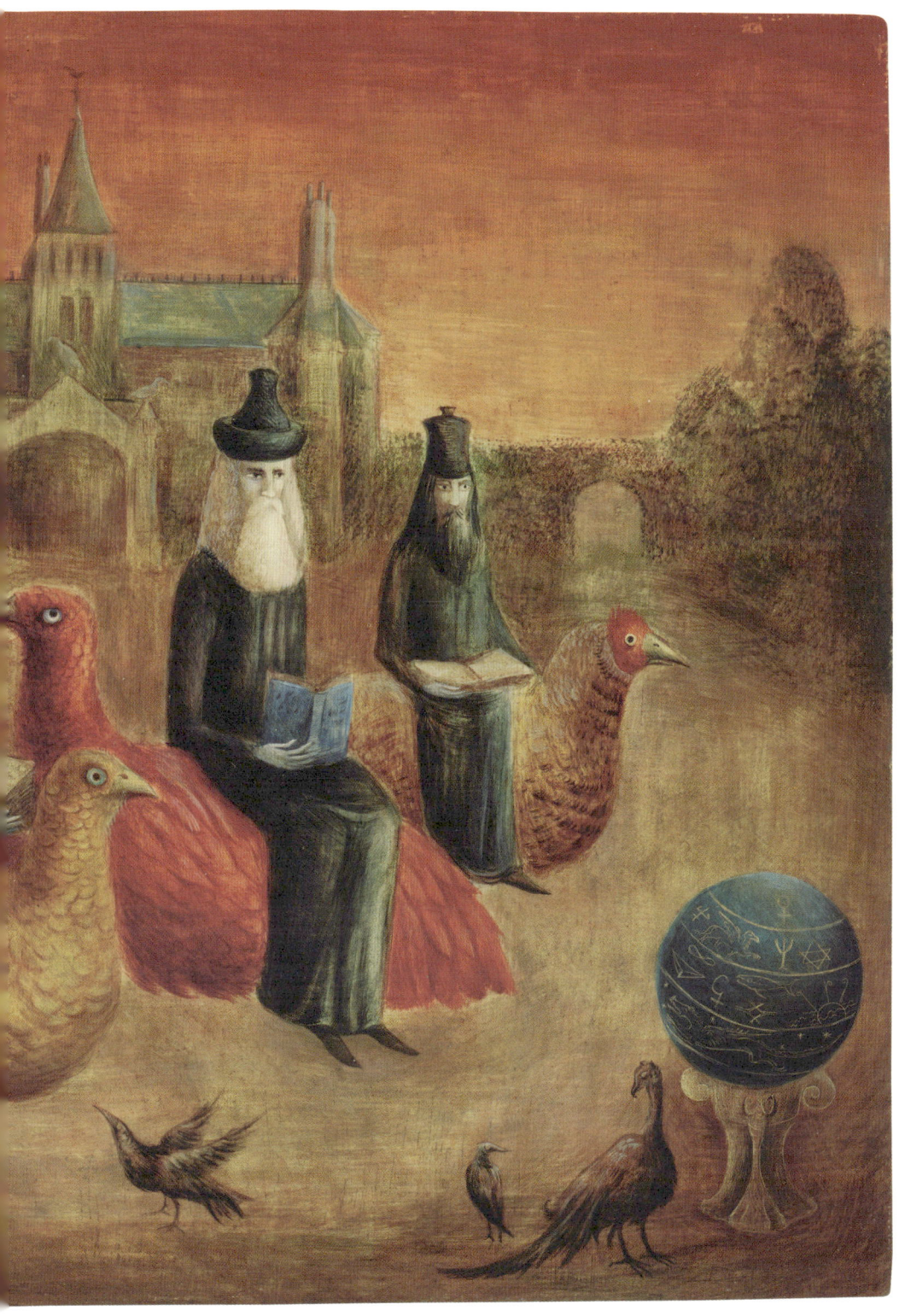

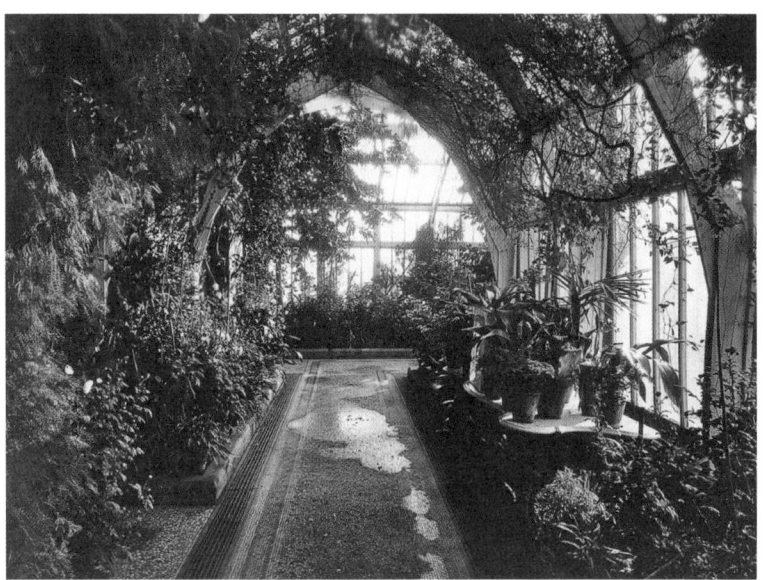

Crookhey Hall, interior

years later, was the conservatory. Sadly, or perhaps fittingly, that's the one part of the place that's been pulled down.

She remembered other rooms well, especially the nursery; she also spoke of a cabinet in her mother's room, in which Maurie kept a collection of small model animals. 'When I was a little girl I loved taking the animals out and playing with them,' Leonora recalled. 'I've always liked small things, I like them better than big things.' For Maurie, the family didn't live in Lancashire. 'She thought that made us sound common. She would always say we lived in "the north of England".'[4]

Today, Crookhey Hall is a school. Much of the building is unmodernized, so the interior space remains similar to the way it was in Leonora's time. There's a very thorough description of the house as it was in July 1926, when it was sold at auction, with the Carringtons (who had rented the house and park) as sitting tenants. In the particulars, the estate is described as 'standing in well laid out Grounds, with a picturesque two-storied Lodge, and about two miles of Brown and Sea Trout Fishing in the River Cocker'.[5] As well as the hall there were twenty agricultural holdings, cottages, the Lord or Manorship of the village of Cockerham, and even a fully licensed inn. Mention is also made of the fact that both the Oxenholme Staghounds and the Vale of Lune Harriers met regularly nearby, and also that 'other hounds meet

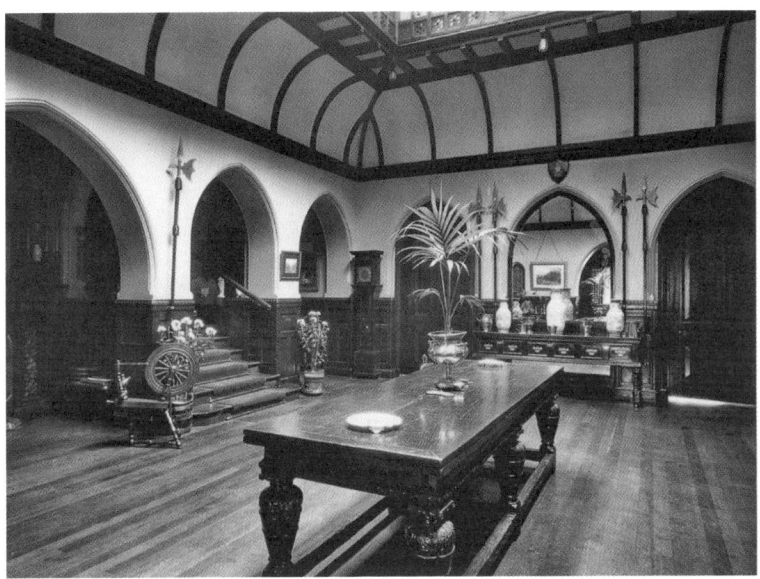

Crookhey Hall, interior

in the neighbourhood, and occasionally by permission on the estate'. Partridges, hares and pheasants are described as plentiful for shooting.

According to these records, Harold Carrington paid £245 10s annual rent for the hall and its three-bedroomed lodge at the gate. The public rooms included a drawing room with French windows, a library, a boudoir, and a billiard room whose carriage clock I have inherited. It sits on my mantelpiece today, as it once sat on the mantelpiece there, and chimes every quarter.

The hall had six main bedrooms, five dressing rooms, a five-bedroomed bachelors' wing and a similar-sized area for the maids. The grounds included tennis and croquet lawns, terraces and summerhouses, a lake and bridge, glasshouses and potting sheds. The stables (where Leonora had her own pony) included a harness room and a two-bedroomed flat for the chauffeur.

The wider Crookhey estate offered rich pickings for Leonora's imagination. Hunting scenes appear in a number of her paintings, including *Edwardian Hunt Breakfast* (1956), while horses would be a recurring theme throughout her career. *The Horses of Lord Candlestick* (1938, pp. 84–85) recalls the stables at Crookhey; 'Candlestick' was a pseudonym for 'Carrington'. This would be the first work Leonora would ever sell, in Paris in the same year it was painted.

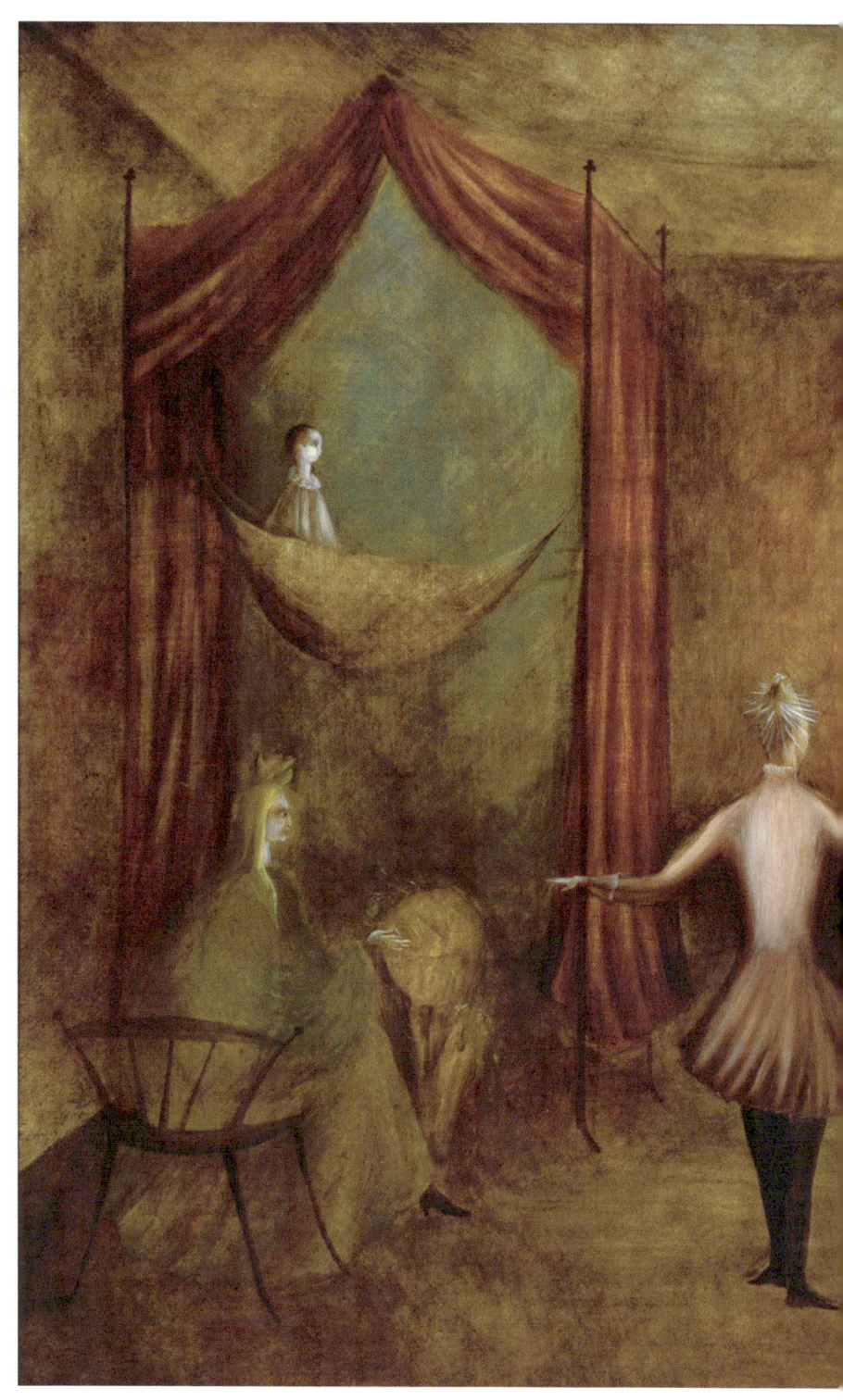

Night Nursery Everything, 1947

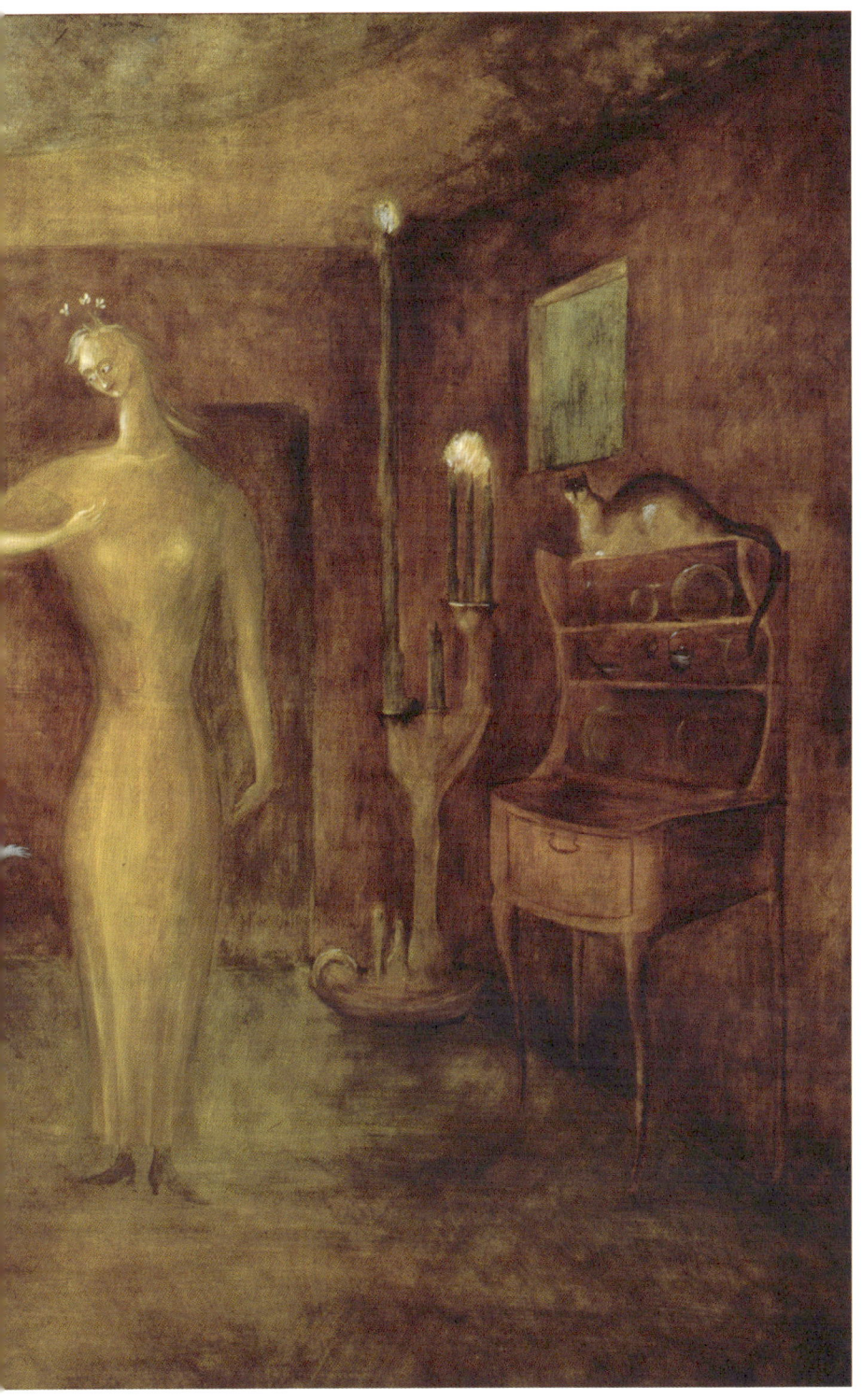

Domestic interiors also feature regularly in Leonora's work, and the art historian Whitney Chadwick is among those who have written about their significance and meaning. Several early paintings that draw on memories of Crookhey – *The Old Maids*, *Night Nursery Everything*, *Neighbourly Advice* (all 1947) – 'use the image of the house and the domestic activities that take place within its walls as metaphors for women's consciousness';[6] they also, Chadwick has noted, root female experience and awareness in the real world. *Night Nursery Everything* was painted to honour the arrival of Leonora's second son, Pablo. Like many parents, she found that the arrival of offspring transported her back to her own childhood, 5,000 miles from Mexico, where she was then living. The nursery she was recalling was at Crookhey.

As Chadwick also points out, many of Leonora's paintings and some of her writings make reference to a white rocking horse. It turns up in her epic survey of womanhood *The House Opposite* (1945), and it's there most famously in her *Self-Portrait/Inn of the Dawn Horse* (*c*. 1937–38), in which it symbolizes the rigid, stultified, unyielding life she associated with Crookhey, the life she might have gone on to live had she not found a means of escape. At Crookhey Hall today, staff say that this painting (probably the best known of all her works, it now hangs in New York's Metropolitan Museum of Art) is a scene imagined in a room at the top of the house, above the nursery, in the eaves. The brown-tiled floor echoes that of other rooms at Crookhey to this day, and may have been the floor covering in that room in the 1920s. The view across the tops of the trees is certainly reminiscent of the painting, as is the shape of the window. Was this, then, the room that for Leonora came to symbolize her family's attempt to crush her spirit and curtail her freedom – to prevent her from being the artist she knew she had been born to become?

The story of Leonora's life at Crookhey is told most graphically in *Crookhey Hall* (1947). Like so many of her works, this one draws on other worlds and other narratives, on things that happened in her physical life as well as her spiritual and psychological life, and experiences that might be taking place in other lives, human and animal, as well. The palette is mossy green and there is a greyness to the sky. Figures float, run, sit and stand in the landscape around the house; the building is solid bricks and mortar but the figures are ethereal, transitory, otherworldly. The figure that surely represents Leonora herself is in the foreground: entirely white, with long hair flowing out behind her like a jet stream as she races out of the frame. This

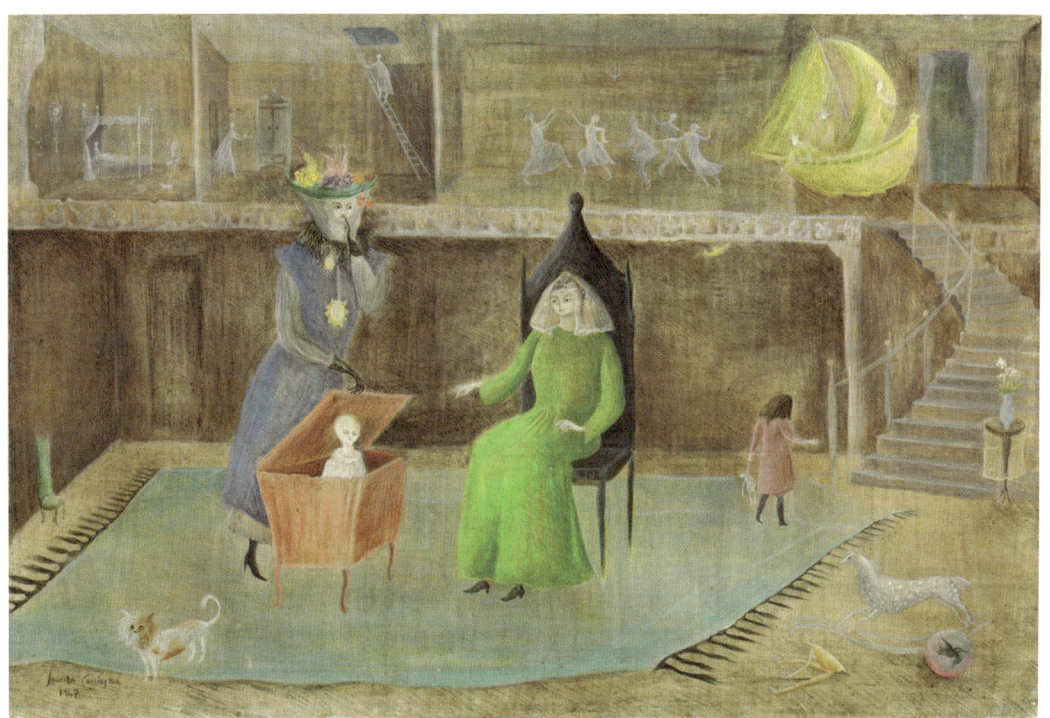

Neighbourly Advice, 1947

individual doesn't want to spend another second in this picture: you feel that if you glance away, she'll have gone by the time you look back.

By chance, many aspects of Leonora's life seem to have combined to perfect her surrealist sensibilities in a way that would have been impossible to design, and her time at Crookhey was the first of these. Where one lives as a child is down to luck (or lack of it); but where better for this particular child than a house that was often terrifying, and unsettling – a house that remains to this day a maze of turrets and passageways, secret doors and tucked-away attics? To a three-year-old it would have seemed like a vast and mysterious kingdom; a kingdom, Leonora later recalled, where the children (by 1923 she and Pat had been joined by two younger brothers, Gerard and Arthur) were mostly confined to the nursery. There they were cared for by a nanny, Mary Kavanaugh, who had grown up, like Maurie, in Westmeath.

Two elements of nursery life in particular would shape Leonora's art as well as her character. The first was the influence of Kavanaugh, known in the family as Nanny Carrington, whom Leonora recalled

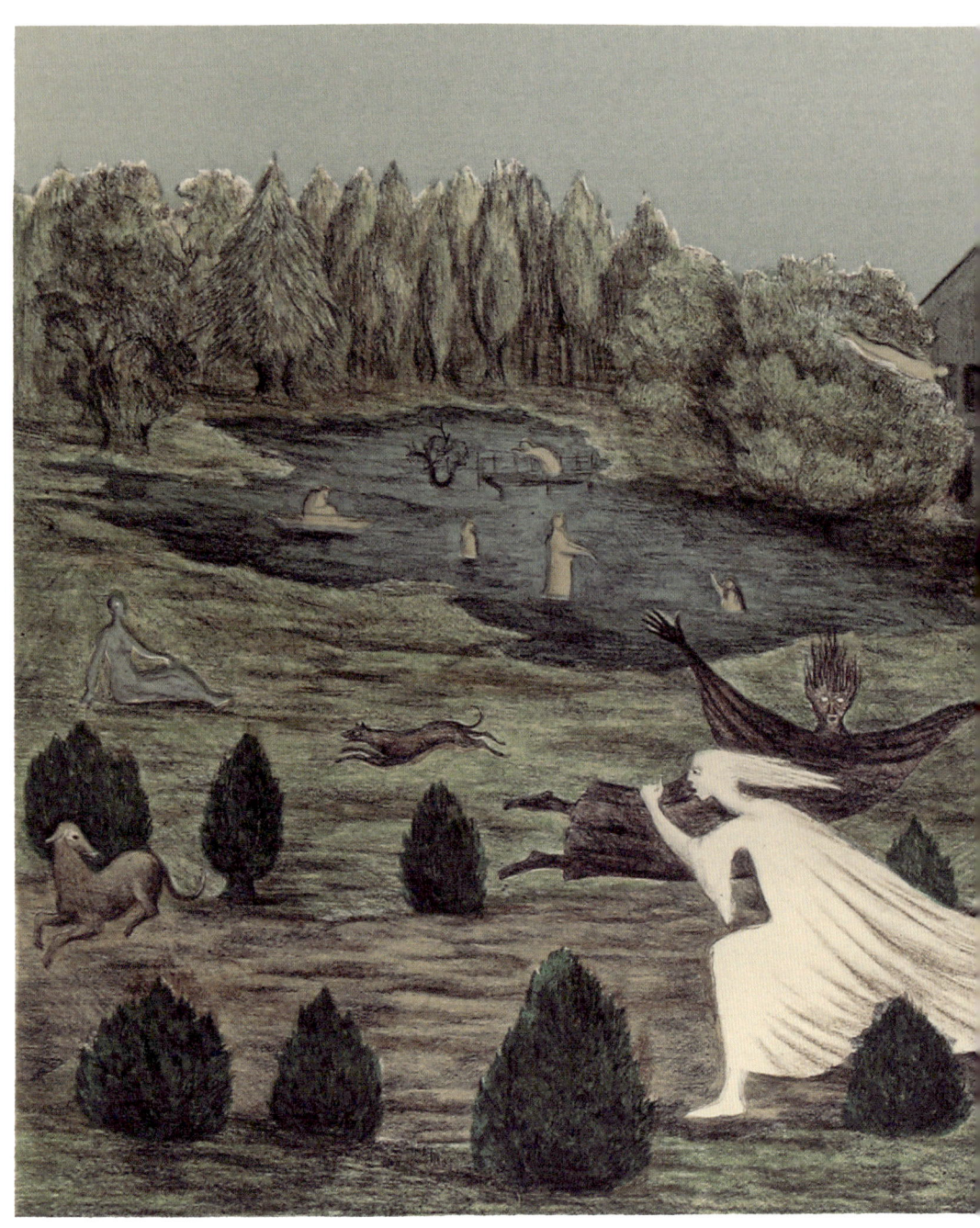

Crookhey Hall, 1947 (lithograph, 1987)

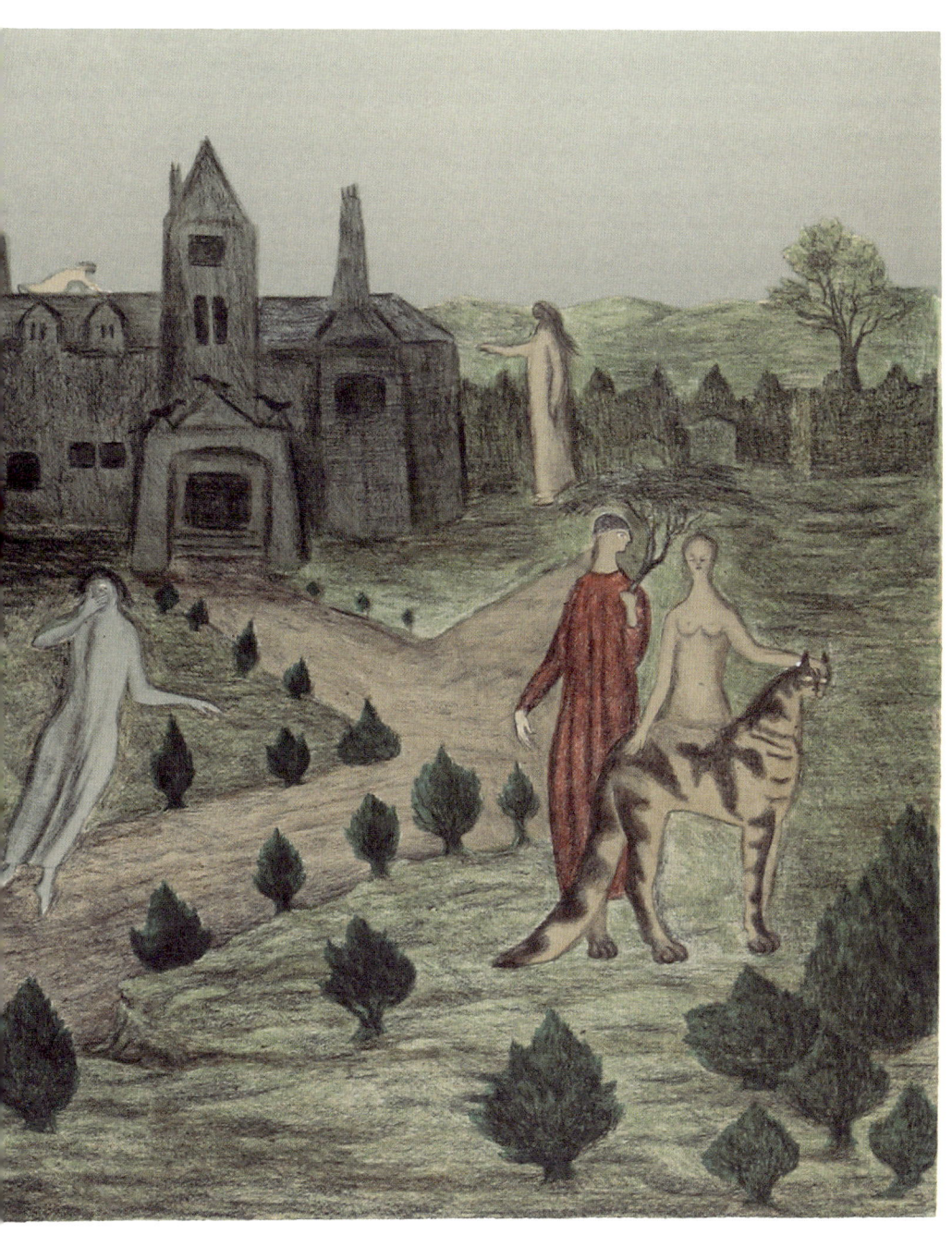

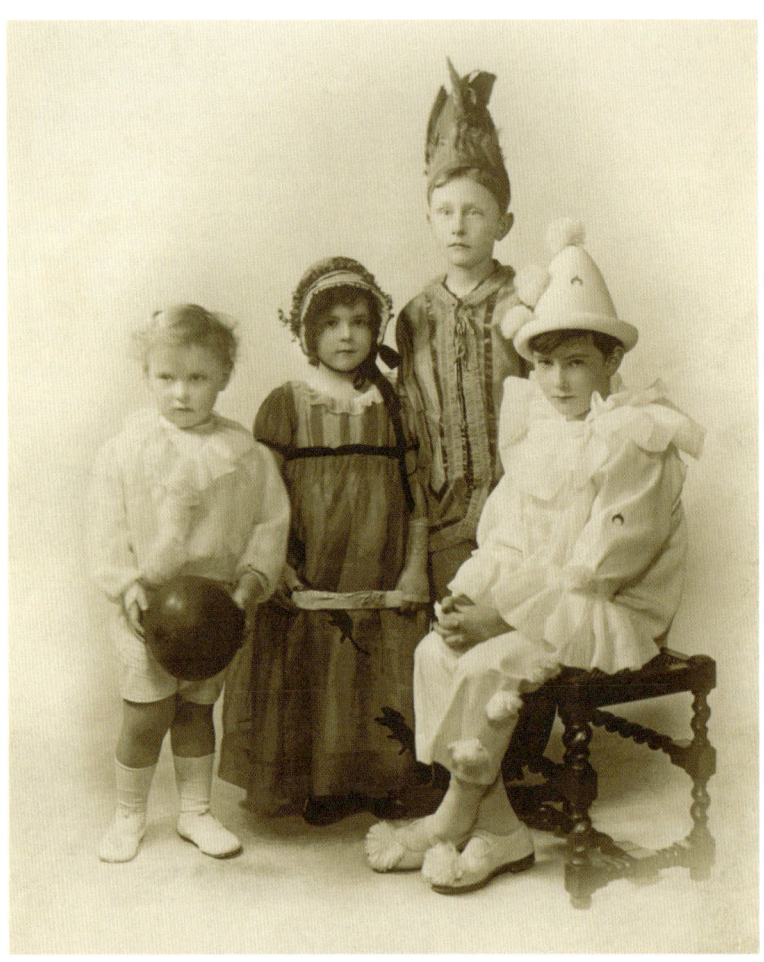

Photograph of Leonora and children

many years later as an indefatigable source of stories. These stories had their roots in the richly mythologized landscape of County
Westmeath, which, of course, was also entirely familiar to Maurie.
Between them the two women created a fabulous, colourful and magical hinterland to Leonora's life. There were stories of travellers (much
later, Leonora claimed the Moorheads had themselves been travellers); stories of fairies; stories of kings and princes, queens and
princesses. There were legends about Irish saints like Saint Brigid and
Saint Patrick; legends of birds and horses, deer and eagles; legends of
war, and others that centred on inexplicable happenings and events.
There was a telephone at Crookhey with a handle that you turned to

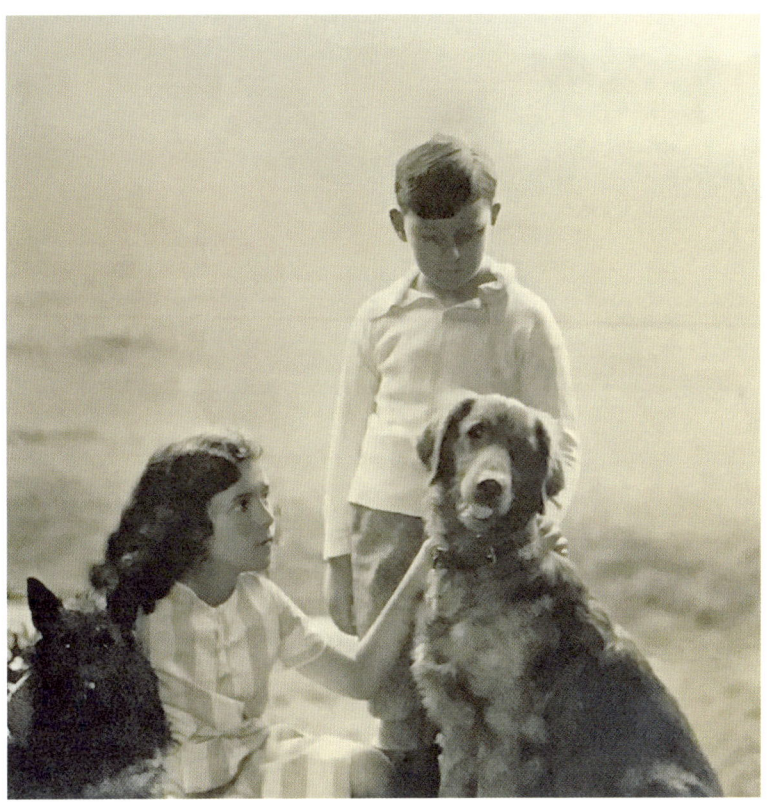

Leonora as a child with her brother Gerard and dog, 1926

call the local exchange if you wanted to place a call – Nanny Carrington, Leonora remembered, would tell the children this was a direct line to Jack Frost. It was a childhood where the veil between what was real and what was fable was often very fine indeed, especially in Kavanaugh's province, the nursery.

There was another significant storyteller in Leonora's life, too: her maternal grandmother, who was born Mary Monica Somers in 1865 in Offaly and married Henry Moorhead, a doctor and later justice of the peace. Mary believed that her family was descended, like Saint Brigid, from the Tuatha Dé Danann, a matriarchal, supernatural line that preceded Christianity and had its roots in the ancient world of the Celts. This was no mild boast: it associated the women in the Somers line with a deep-seated strength and power. And it wasn't the only feminist heritage Mary Monica laid claim to. She was also related, she said, to Maria Edgeworth (1767–1849), a novelist sometimes

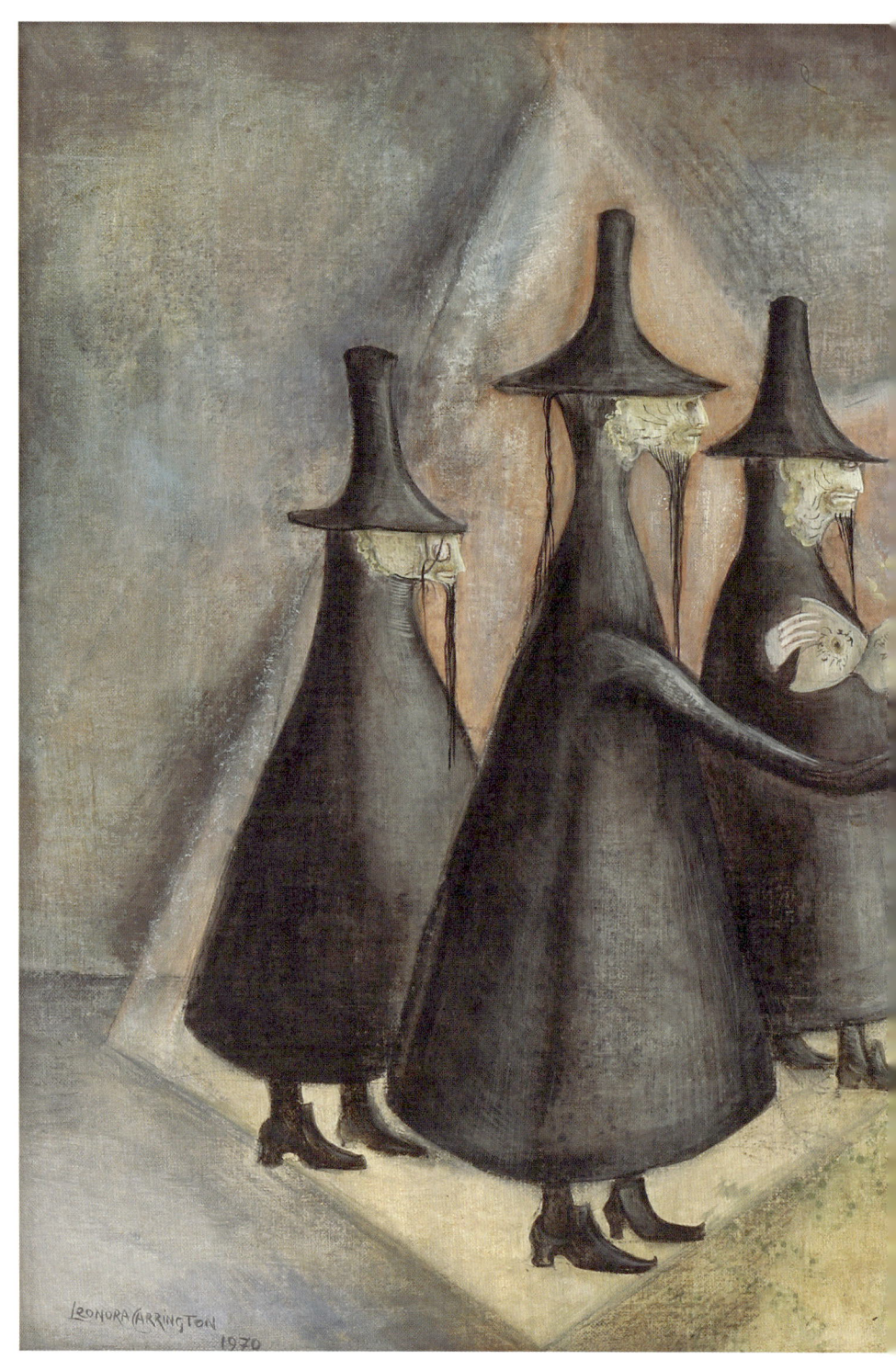

The Bird Men of Burnley, 1970

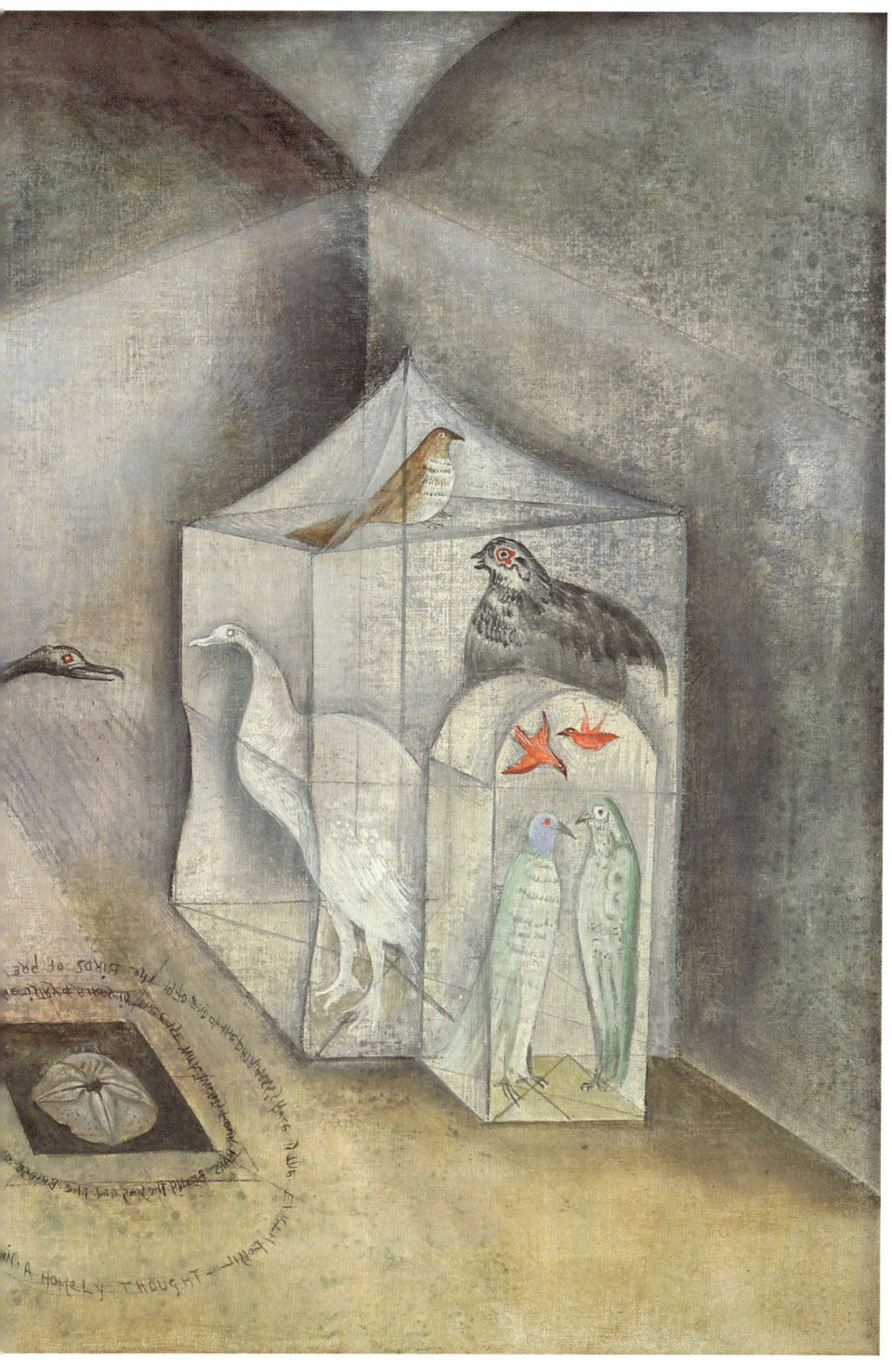

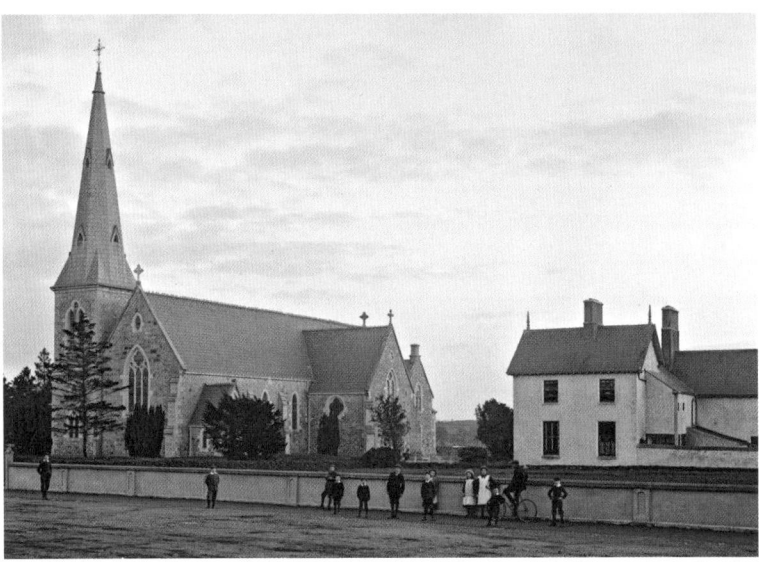

St Patrick's Church, Moate

described as the Jane Austen of Ireland. Edgeworth's 'Essay on the Noble Science of Self-Justification' (1795) argues that women should use their wit and intelligence to continually challenge the force and power of men.[7]

Leonora's Moorhead grandparents lived in a whitewashed house at the top of the drive of St Patrick's Church in Moate, where her parents had been married in 1904. (Because Harold was not Catholic – which must have seemed shocking in that place and time – he and Maurie were not allowed a nuptial mass and had to make do with the lesser, shortened marriage ceremony instead.) As children, Leonora and Gerard, the brother she was closest to in age and most fond of, were taken to Ireland by Nanny Carrington to stay with their grandparents. The cavernous kitchen of their home, dominated by a vast range, would later become the setting for her 1975 painting *Grandmother Moorhead's Aromatic Kitchen*.

It's a work that suggests, in its fiery redness, the fusion of the various worlds of Leonora's childhood – a fusion over which countless layers of experience would accumulate as her life stretched out across its ninety-four-year canvas. Grandmother Moorhead's kitchen is rooted in a space Leonora recalled accurately decades later (the range is also remembered by other members of our family, and was faithfully reproduced in scale and shape). Into this setting that existed in her childhood memory, Leonora has overlaid other worlds: the world, firstly, of those stories, those fables, those tales. Who is the giant goose dominating the scene? Is she, perhaps, a figure from one of the stories told by Granny Moorhead, Maurie, or Nanny Carrington? Why is the horned creature holding a broomstick? What are the three hooded figures doing at the table – or the figure with a hat and dark glasses at the stove, or the red-robed figure at their feet? Look more closely and there are other worlds, too: the world of Leonora's home in Mexico is referenced in the peppers on the table, in the corn lying on the floor and being ground on a Mexican stone called a metate. To one side is an open door, through which there is the merest glimpse into another world. Past, present, future; mystery, fable, suspense; family, strangers, animals; familiar, unknown, fantastical: all these layers coexist in Leonora's brushstrokes. Perhaps her grandmother's kitchen was the first magical space in her life, the first place where she experienced these interwoven worlds she would forever flit between. The only element she couldn't convey on the canvas, she has gifted us in her work's title: we are invited to savour the smells and flavours of Grandmother Moorhead's kitchen while we ponder its myriad inhabitants.

Time and again throughout Leonora's life, the kitchen would be central to everything, and her grandmother's kitchen in Moate seems to have been her first taste of what this room would always represent to her. At Crookhey, the kitchen was the servants' domain; in Ireland, Mary Monica's kitchen was the family hub, a place of stories and mystery, food and chatter and gatherings. The holistic nature of the kitchen, the way it seemed to extend beyond the domestic here and now into mystical, unseen worlds; the kitchen as a meeting-place, a venue for the exchange of stories; the kitchen as a place that could be both safe and edgy – all these ideas and more sprang from the time Leonora spent in Ireland. And in Moate, as at Crookhey, it was the women who were present and the men who were absent. Henry Moorhead, like Harold Carrington, was a busy man with much to occupy him outside the domestic sphere; that was the province of wives, servants and children.

As with Crookhey and later with Mexico, Ireland brought important vistas and perspective into Leonora's life – if she had added it to her map by design and not random chance, it would have been a genius move. Like Mexico, Ireland was embraced by the original surrealists as a place they felt connected naturally with their viewpoint. Both

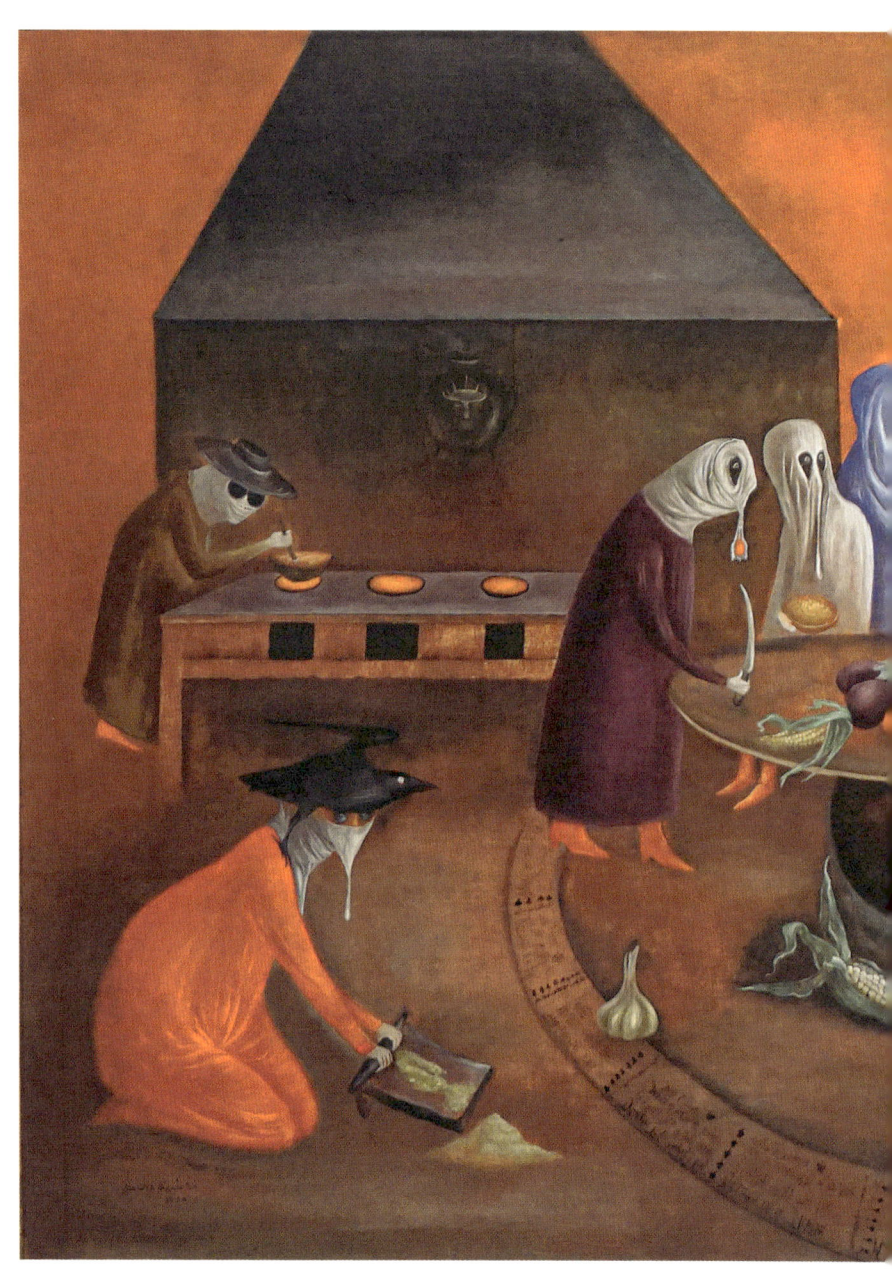

Grandmother Moorhead's Aromatic Kitchen, 1975

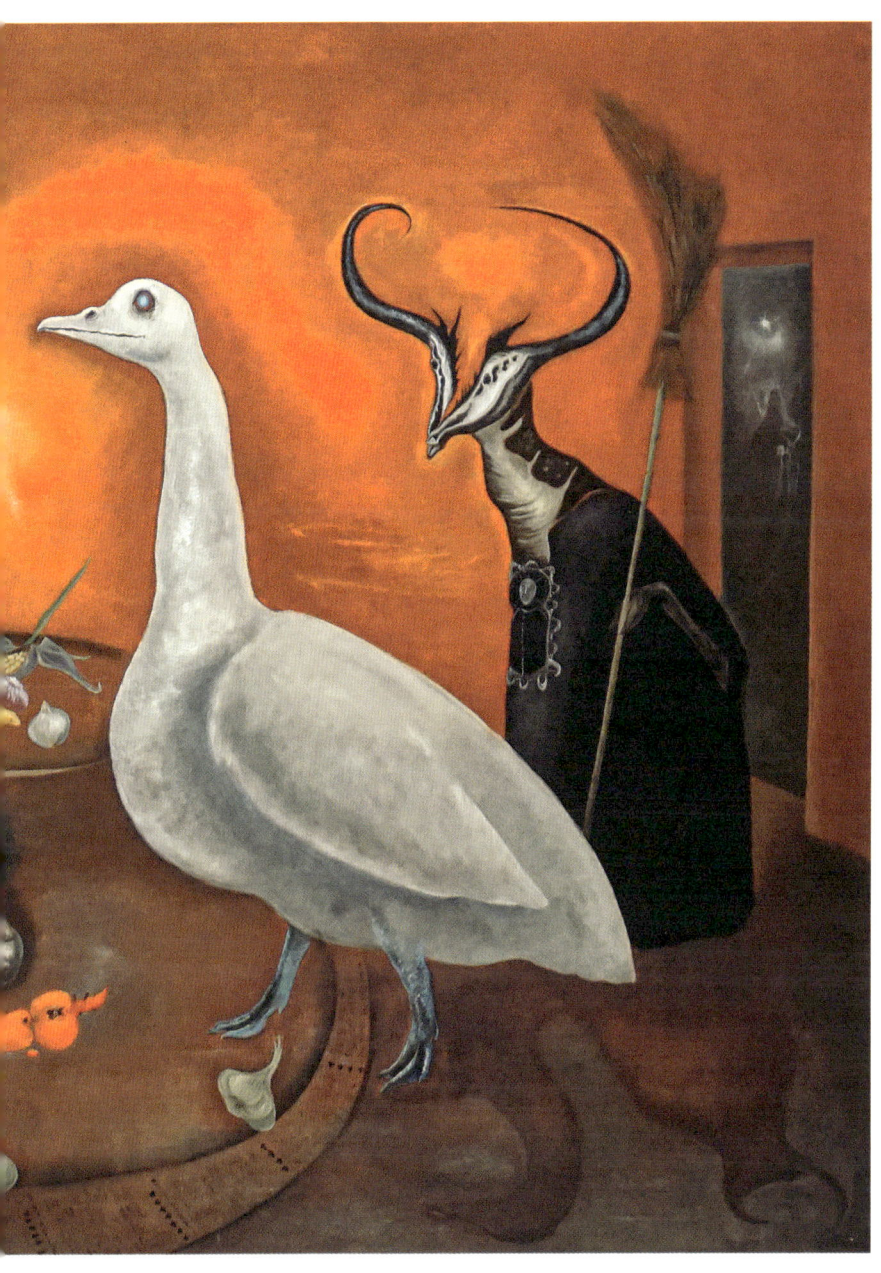

cultures gave equal weight to past, present, fact and fiction; in the land of the Day of the Dead, like the country of the Sidhe, the fantastical was woven seamlessly into the everyday.

There was another ingredient that the nursery at Crookhey provided for Leonora's development: the presence of her three siblings, all brothers. Leonora found them difficult, in particular the eldest, Pat. In one of her childhood notebooks she wrote: 'Pat is going to the dentist. I hope he enjoys himself. HA! HA! HA! HA!'[8]

From earliest childhood, the boys had been treated differently from their sister. They were allowed more freedom, encouraged to play outdoors and to engage in rough and tumble; and their lives were expanded early on when, at the age of seven, each was sent to St Mary's, the prep school of Stonyhurst College. It seemed as if the boys were being readied for adventure and excitement, but while their horizons were opening up, Leonora felt hers were being closed down – or more specifically, never explored. Her role, which was clear even when she was in the nursery, was to keep safe: not to rock any boats, not to take any chances. What they sought to teach her was that she should sit a certain way and behave a certain way: she should be supportive, helpful, polite. She should listen, especially to men; she should hone traditional skills, such as playing music and speaking French. Drawing and painting, for which she showed aptitude from an early age, were fine within reason. What harm could there be in Prim creating pictures? Especially if those pictures were of flowers and trees, family members and characters from fairy stories.

But art was Leonora's secret weapon – and she hid it in plain sight, because her parents did not have the faintest idea where her talents might lead. Art, for them, was unthreatening and pretty. They had no idea that this skill their daughter was developing would become the key to another life entirely; still less that art could never be a validation of the status quo, but meant a radical reappraisal of everything in the artist's sight.

So what Leonora practised in the nursery at Crookhey was the subversive silence of smouldering rebellion. Sparked by the inherent unfairness that gave Pat, Gerard and Arthur so much more freedom; stoked by the growing realization that she had a talent that would lead, eventually, to liberty. 'I always painted, and I always knew it was what I would do,' she said many years later.[9] As the Jesuits who educated her brothers at Stonyhurst might have said (but didn't): show me a girl aged seven, and I will show you the woman.

In 1926, there was an important development in the Carringtons' family life: Crookhey, which they had been renting for seven years, was put up for sale. Harold appears not to have been interested in bidding for it – as a man of means but not family wealth, raising very large amounts of capital may have been difficult for him – so, in 1927, the family moved to a new home twenty miles to the north, which again they rented (and did eventually buy). Hazelwood Hall was about as different from the Gothic gloom of Crookhey as it is possible to imagine. Where Crookhey was slate-grey, Hazelwood was cream; where Crookhey was forbidding, Hazelwood was friendly; where Crookhey was sharp-edged, Hazelwood was rounded, its bay windows undulating towards the lawn.

This new home seemed far more welcoming, but although Leonora enjoyed living there, she would not spend as much time in it as she had at Crookhey. In 1926 she was enrolled at her first school, New Hall, run by the Canonesses of the Holy Sepulchre, originally a Belgian order whose nuns had moved to England after the French Revolution. New Hall was a magnificent Tudor palace that had once been home to the family of Anne Boleyn and was later acquired by Henry VIII, who knew it as Beaulieu. To this day, Henry's coat of arms hangs in the school chapel. During her few years there, that was a place where Leonora, increasingly reluctantly, would spend plenty of her time.

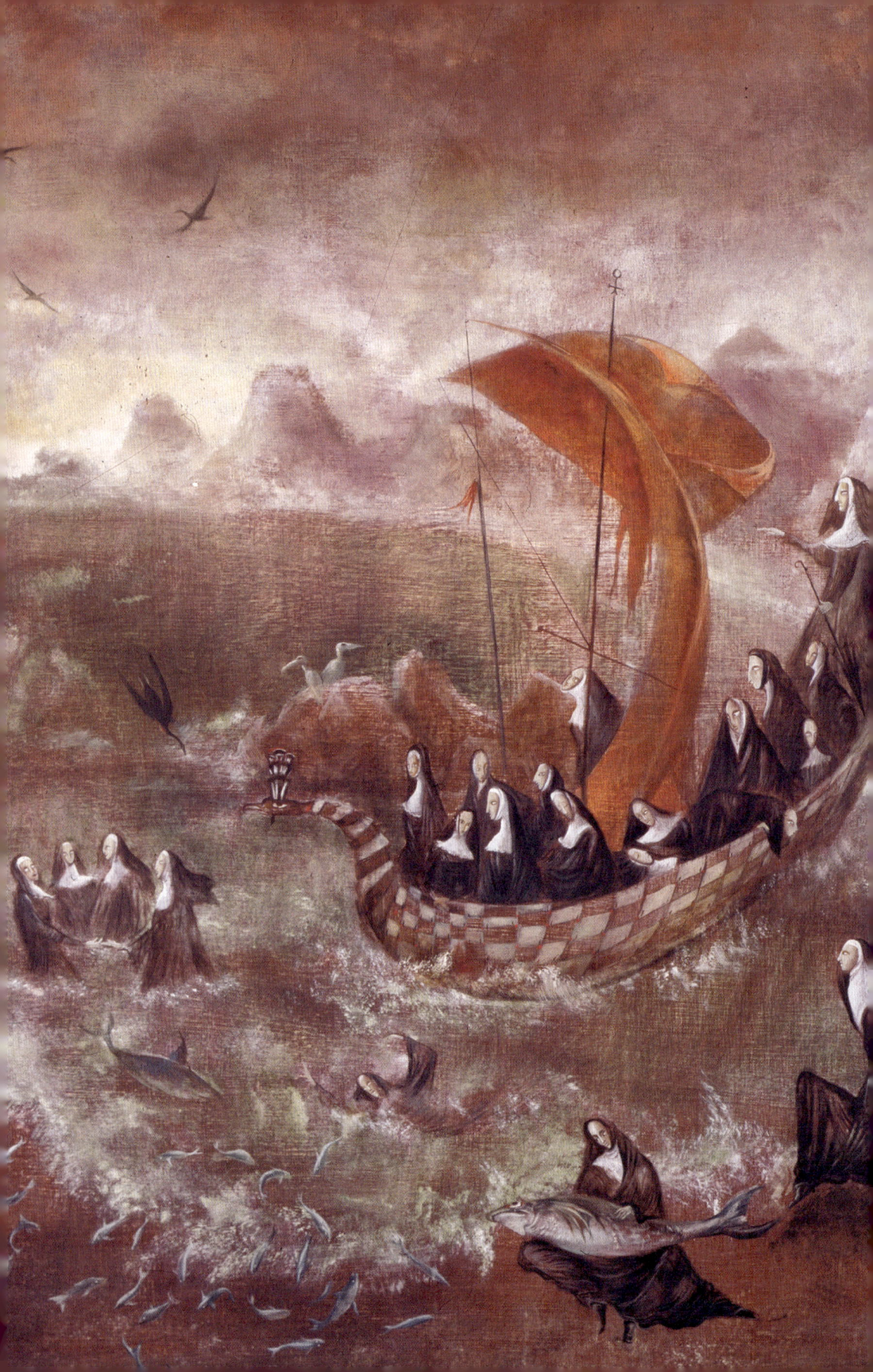

2
Adolescence
1927–1935

Hazelwood Hall has never captured the imaginations of art historians in quite the same way as Crookhey. Probably this is because one of Leonora's most important works features Crookhey's eponymous edifice, and her story – of running away, of her relationship with her family and her feelings about being hemmed in – is woven into the fabric of that piece. Hazelwood is not documented so directly in her art, yet its influence is every bit as significant to her story, and to her work, as that of the earlier home.

Hazelwood is tucked away in a village called Silverdale. It feels like an outpost, hidden away behind a country lane on an often-overlooked area of no man's land between Lancashire and Cumbria. But for anyone who wants to taste the Lancashire of Leonora's time, the Midland Hotel in the seaside town of Morecambe, fifteen miles to the south, is a good place to start. This magnificently restored modernist gem has snow-coloured seahorses by Eric Gill carved on the outside of the whitewashed building; a ceiling medallion painted by him at the top of a circular staircase celebrates Neptune and Triton, and there's an Eric Ravilious painting titled *Day and Night* on the wall of the tea room. A map of the area, also by Gill, has Arnside (where Hazelwood stands) clearly marked and shows a fast train steaming through the area. It was this train, with the excellent transport links it provided, that drew Harold Carrington to make his home here.

When the Midland opened in 1933, it brought glamour as well as cutting-edge art to the Lancashire seaside. People who had only ever associated the area with shrimp fishing were suddenly aware of

Nunscape in Manzanillo, detail, 1956

a 'glittering white building built in a wide curve to conform to the line of the promenade [and] illuminated by concealed flood lights at night [that dominate] the whole of the sea front. Inside you will look up in wonder at its magnificent circular stair case and then gaze at the lighting effects, striking colour schemes and decorations of the hall, dining room, cocktail bar and lounge.'[1]

The hotel fell into disrepair in the 1960s and '70s, and its registers went missing. But it's said that Edward VIII and Wallis Simpson, Winston Churchill, Coco Chanel, Noël Coward and Gloria Vanderbilt were among the beautiful people who took the train or motored up from London to spend a few nights in one of its spacious, airy suites, with their balconies overlooking the sweeping bay. It's hard to imagine the Carringtons weren't at least occasional visitors to the hotel *Country Life* called 'the most beautiful contemporary building in this country'.[2] Undoubtedly, in the 1930s North of England, it was *the* place to see and be seen.

But it was less the bright lights of Morecambe and more the natural beauty of Arnside that most impressed Leonora during these years. Hazelwood, a mansion with around fifteen bedrooms (now converted into apartments) is situated in what has become a designated Area of Outstanding Natural Beauty. It was granted this status in 1972, long after Leonora's time there; but the rich beauty of the area, which took in woodland and coastline, would have been, if anything, even more glorious in the late 1920s and early 1930s than it is today. The wide diversity of types of land – woodlands, wetlands, grasslands – in a relatively small space, supports a huge variety of trees and flowers. The woodland is dominated by ash, hazel and oak trees; the flowers include colourful primroses, harebells and orchids.

There's a wealth of bird life, too. Among the many species are curlews with their haunting call, white-bellied lapwings, and redshanks, known as the sentinels of the marshes because of the way they pipe to warn other birds of danger. You see the birds chasing the line of the tide on Morecambe Bay, which is a few minutes' walk from Hazelwood. The bay is as wide as the eye can see and entirely flat; it's also dangerous, as numerous signs warn, criss-crossed as it is with ever-changing channels of water and treacherous quicksands. And when the tide comes in, it comes quickly: it's said that the incoming wave, known locally as the bore, travels as fast as a galloping horse across the sands.

That Hazelwood retained a special place in Leonora's heart is evidenced by her son Gabriel's memories of the time they spent there

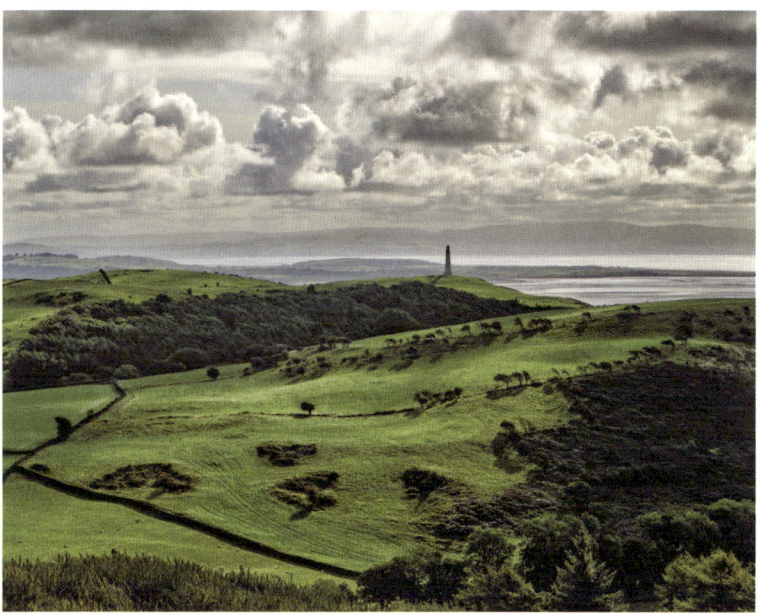

Morecambe Bay

together in the early 1950s. Leonora had taken both her sons to Europe and the first stop on their tour, he remembers, was to see his grandmother Maurie, by now widowed and still living at Hazelwood. 'The property's large gardens, which gave way to surrounding forest, promised a whole slew of adventures,' writes Gabriel. 'While we were there Leonora and I took frequent walks. She would point to a pile of rocks and set off talking about the fabled community of elves and fairies that belonged to our family's Irish and Celtic history – creatures that would hide behind trees and take refuge in little burrows. The whole forest area seemed to me enchanted, and it remains a place I think of often.'[3]

Frequent downpours, Gabriel continues, left rainbow-coloured patches on the roads, which Leonora called 'witches' pee'. Leonora 'adorned everything with her imagination, allowing the fantastical to triumph over reality. Her way of looking at the world allowed the forest to be transformed, for me, into an ancient, magical land.' He wonders whether their visit has reminded Leonora of her own time there as a child – times when she would play 'solitary games...inhabiting mythical places'.

The importance of this place in Leonora's memory is evidenced in *The Hearing Trumpet* (first published in 1974), in which her heroine

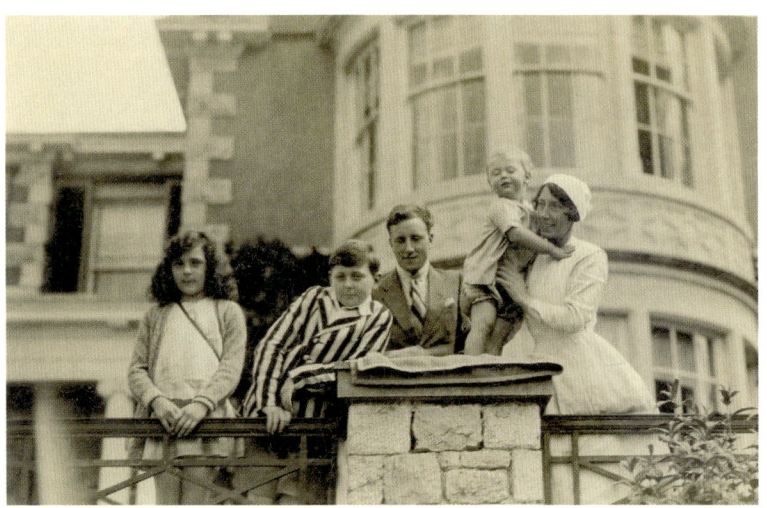

Leonora Carrington with her brothers Gerard and Arthur, her uncle
George Moorhead and her nanny Mary Kavanaugh at Hazelwood Hall

Marian Leatherby, Leonora's projection of herself in the future, is
transported in her mind from her life in a far-away Spanish-speaking
country, back to England. On a Sunday afternoon, she writes, 'I was
sitting with a book on a stone seat under a lilac bush. Close by a clump
of rosemary saturated the air with perfume. They were playing tennis nearby, the clump clump of the rackets and balls was quite audible.
This was the sunken Dutch garden, why Dutch I wonder? The roses?
The geometrical flower beds? Or perhaps because it is sunken? The
church bells ringing, that is the Protestant church, have we had tea
yet? (cucumber sandwiches, seed cake and rock buns). Yes, tea must
be over.'[4]

This description is immediately recognizable as Hazelwood. The
tennis court was below the main façade of the house, and there is a
sunken rose garden to one side of the building. The gardens had been
redesigned by the Edwardian landscape gardener Thomas Mawson,
and have now been restored to how he left them: there are indeed geometrical flower beds, box hedges, steps and pergolas.

Marian makes an important discovery on her journey back to the
garden at Hazelwood – perhaps because it was while sitting on a bench
in that place that the teenage Leonora made the same discovery. Her
long, dark hair, she writes, is soft like cat's fur. And that is when it
dawns on her: she is beautiful. 'This is quite a shock because I have just

realized that I am beautiful and there is something that I must do about it, but what?' Beauty, she goes on, is 'a responsibility like anything else, beautiful women have special lives like prime ministers but that is not what I really want, there must be something else...'.[5]

A few paragraphs later, she returns to the natural beauty of Hazelwood and what it means to her. 'The woods are full of wild anemones now, shall we go...hundreds and thousands of wild flowers all over the ground under the trees all the way up to the gazebo. They have no smell but they have a presence just like a perfume and quite as obsessive. I shall remember them all my life.'[6]

Leonora certainly did remember Hazelwood all her life, and some-times spoke of it; but it wasn't where she spent the majority of her time during this period, because between the ages of nine and fifteen, her life was dominated by school. Until 1926 she had been educated at home, at Crookhey, by a French governess; but when her younger brother Gerard joined his older brother Pat at Stonyhurst prep school, it was felt the young Prim would be lonely at home. The choice of the girls' school at the Convent of the Holy Sepulchre in Essex was no doubt influenced by Harold and Maurie's close connection with the Jesuit school at Stonyhurst to which they sent their sons, because there were strong links between the two. One of the Stonyhurst Jesuits, Father Robert de Trafford, was a good friend and fishing companion of Harold's and a frequent visitor to the Carrington home.[7]

School was a new world for Leonora. Like the world of Crookhey, it was cushioned and privileged but also full of a kind of Gothic Catholic drama. Faith was centre stage: the nuns were cloistered, and each day mass was celebrated in the convent chapel, with the girls in their section of the church and the nuns, who wore the traditional habit, behind their grille. The chapel was at the centre of the nuns' exist-ence, and the girls – known, for reasons rooted in the school's history, as 'fishes'[8] – also spent lots of their time there. The nuns said or sang Divine Office seven times each day, and on feast days and every day in May (the month dedicated to the Virgin Mary) there was Benediction, which the girls attended.[9]

Like all convents, New Hall was a place of much bell-ringing. The Angelus bell, which prompted the saying of the thrice-daily recitation of a prayer to the Virgin, was rung at six a.m., midday and six p.m. And the main convent clock was unusual: as well as the hours, the half and the quarter hours, it for some reason also struck seven minutes past the hour and the half hour. Leonora was almost certainly remembering

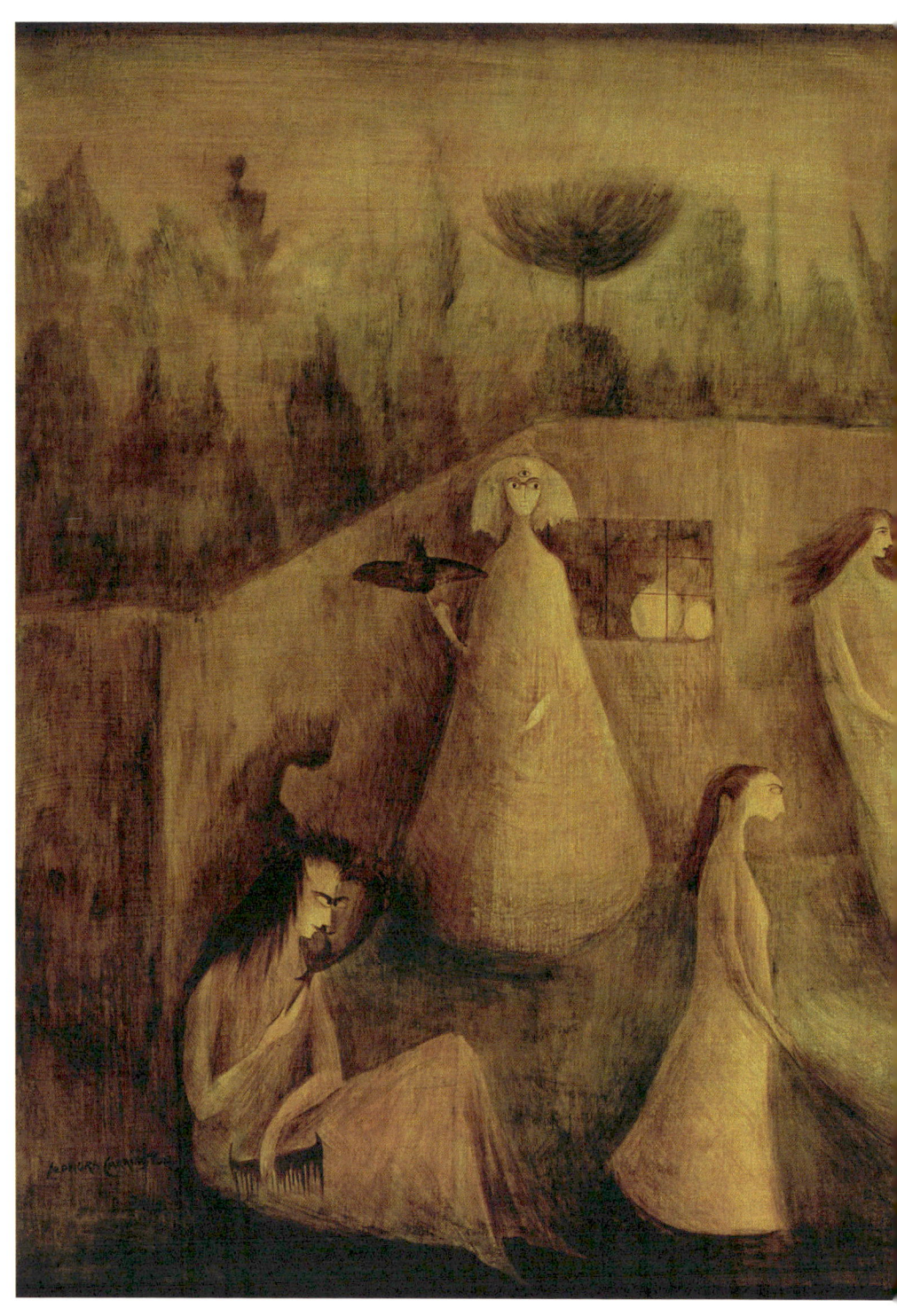

The Hour of the Angelus, 1949

44

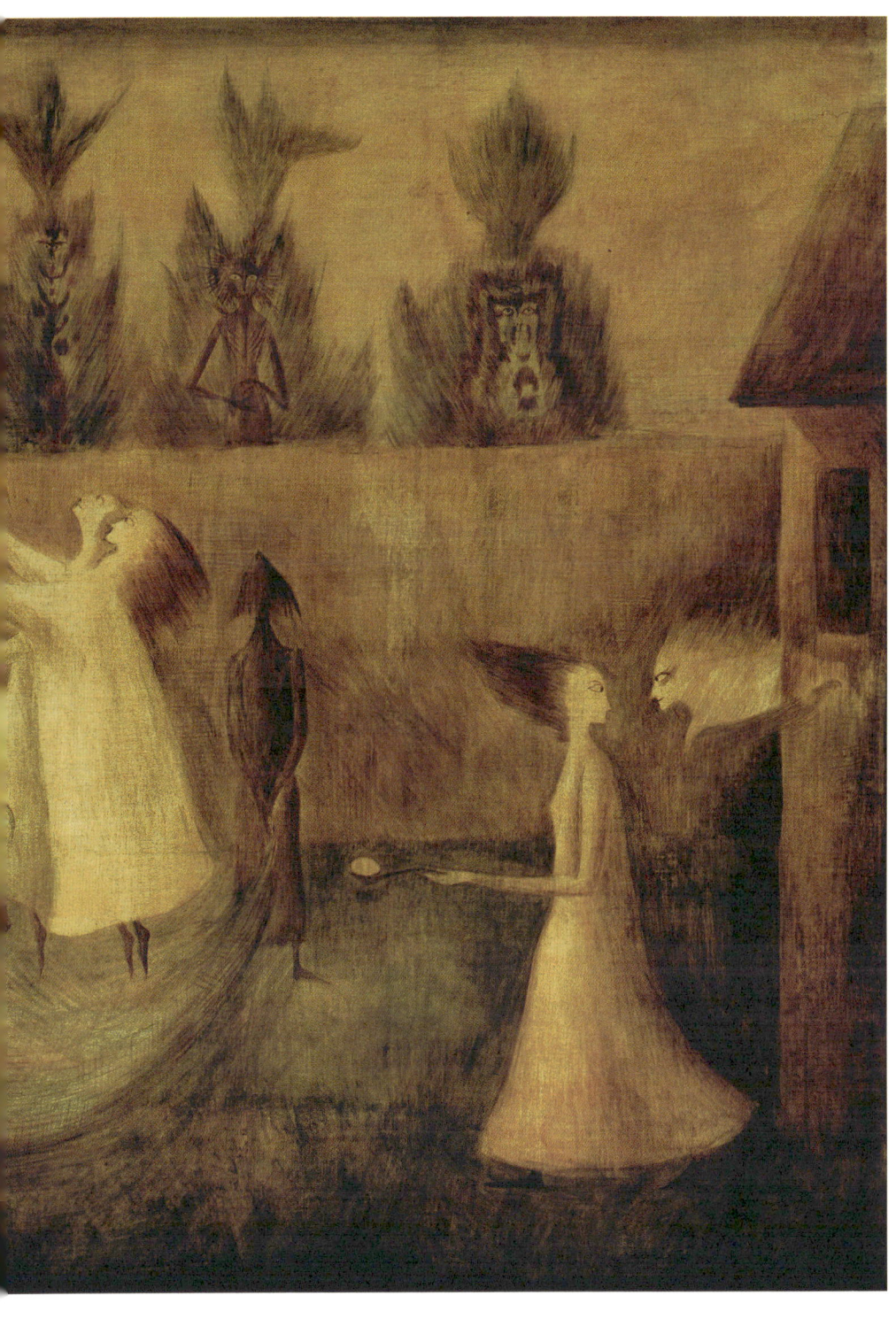

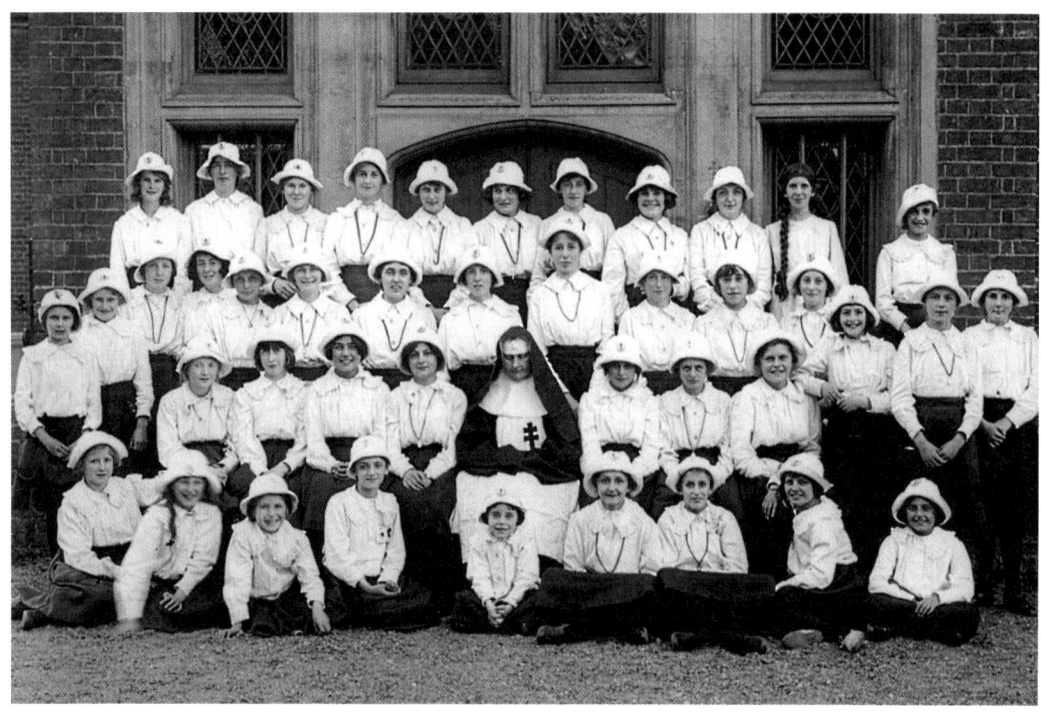

Students at the New Hall School, Chelmsford. Headmistress Sister Mary Dismas Weld is at the centre, with Leonora Carrington to her right, 1920s

the ubiquitous bell in her painting *The Hour of the Angelus* (1949), which depicts a number of girls playing out of doors while various strange and sinister figures look on, partly hidden by trees. One girl is carrying a lacrosse net; the game had recently replaced hockey at New Hall. The other school games were netball and tennis. The girls in the painting wear long, shapeless shifts although in fact the school uniform was a striking bright scarlet, with silk shirts. For weekday mass the girls wore black mantillas, with a white replacement for Sundays. And it was after mass on Sundays that the tuck shop was opened and they could buy treats such as peppermint creams. On Sunday evenings there were sometimes concerts, with performers including a Jesuit priest who sang African American spiritual songs.

The nuns were rather otherworldly. Sister Mary Dismas Weld, the nun sitting beside Leonora in the school photograph, apparently never lifted her eyes 'so as not to see the world'.[10] Academic achievement seems to have been fairly low on the priority list: in 1927 the school had a visit from His Majesty's Inspectors of Schools, and while they offered 'encouragement and advice on the standards of work', a certificate of efficiency was not granted, as improvements were needed to the curriculum.

In 1928, the school was reorganized with three boarding houses: seniors, intermediates and juniors. Seniors were allowed a wireless set, but intermediates – of whom Leonora would have been one – had to make do with a gramophone. Each section had a 'house mother' who was a nun, but in general the nuns lived out of sight of the fishes, in their own separate area of the building. There was an art club, known for some unknown reason as 'the parrot pot'.

Leonora does not look particularly happy in the school photograph in which she appears, and indeed she reported many years later that she had not enjoyed her time at New Hall. She was not the first fish to disobey the rules – there was an account of one girl, from before her time, who climbed onto the school roof and was severely reprimanded – but in a way Leonora's misdemeanours were worse, because she wasn't just unruly, she failed to engage. 'The nuns always said I would collaborate in neither work nor play,' she said. By the summer term of 1930, Harold and Maurie had received a letter asking them not to return Leonora to school in the autumn. The nuns felt she was not suited to the school, and would do better elsewhere.

The truth was that New Hall was just the second, after her family home, on what would become a long list of places where Leonora failed to fit in. Like all artists, she was a natural outsider. Wherever she found herself, she remained on the margins, looking in from the outside, never seeking membership or belonging.

She was now thirteen and her parents wanted her to continue in education. They enrolled her in another convent, St Mary's Ascot, run by sisters of the Institute of the Blessed Virgin Mary, a teaching order founded by a 16th-century champion of female education called Mary Ward. According to the school's records, Leonora arrived there in September 1930 as a pupil in Form III and was registered to take extra subjects in Italian, cooking, dancing, drawing, painting, elocution, golf, tennis and riding. She is also recorded as having achieved a higher piano certificate. She left at the end of the Upper IV in July 1932 and although the school does not have a record of her being asked to leave, that was certainly Leonora's recollection. She had been no happier at St Mary's than at New Hall. In 2009 she told me: 'I only ever wanted to murder one person: Mother Ignatius [Beveridge, who was head teacher of St Mary's from 1921 to 1949]. My room looked over

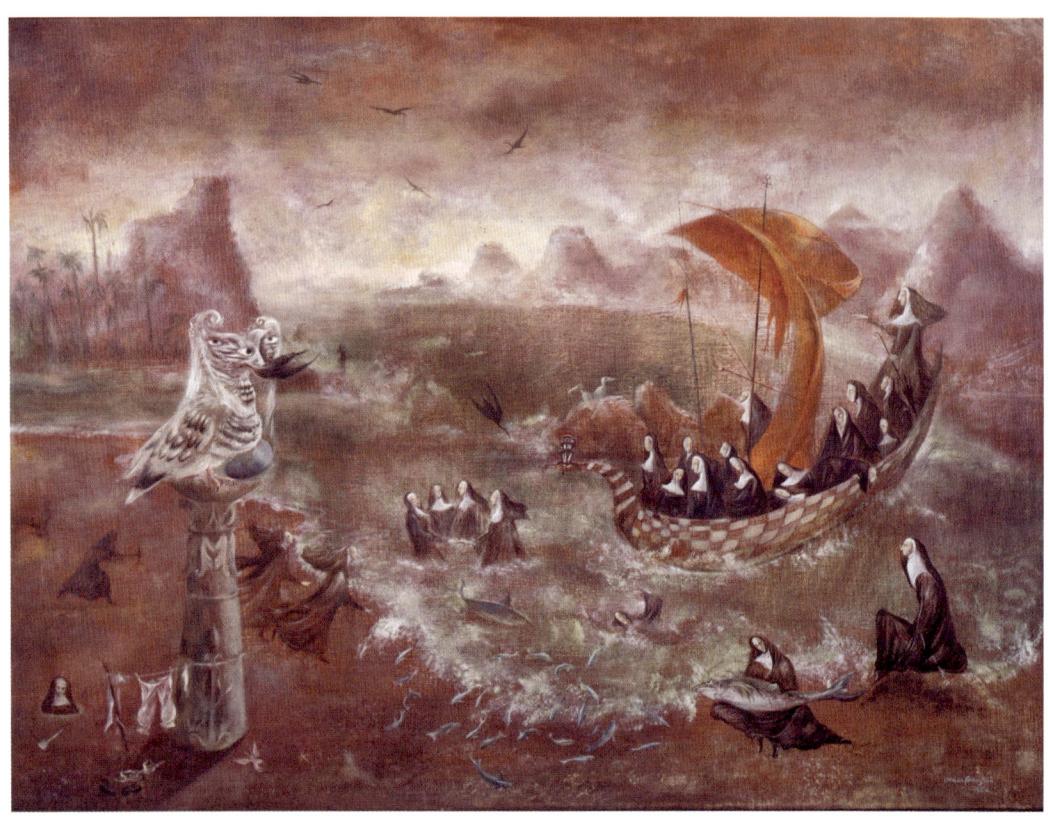

Nunscape in Manzanillo, 1956

her study and I used to look down on her and I used to think, I wish I had a gun so I could kill her.'

Leonora had never forgotten her embarrassment when Mother Ignatius upbraided her for what Leonora said was a simple mistake. 'She once said, in front of the whole school when I accidentally put on shoes that didn't match: "Leonora Carrington. Desperate to be different."'

Another alumnus of St Mary's, a contemporary of Leonora, remembered Mother Ignatius as a disciplinarian who insisted on long periods of silence and standing in line. As at New Hall, religion played a huge part in the pupils' lives, with daily mass, Benediction twice a week, and prayers in chapel every evening. The same pupil recalls that independent thinking was not encouraged, and although there were art classes, these were not designed to lead to self-expression of any kind. It's easy to imagine Leonora's relief as she left St Mary's, aged fifteen, for the final time.

The Leonora I knew in Mexico City seventy years later was very like the teenage Leonora, as evidenced by one of her old notebooks dating from that final term at Ascot. Dated 'Summer Term 1932', it's full of the same humour, the same interests she had in her nineties. There are sketches of horses, snatches of poems and verses she's enjoyed by Shelley and Milton, and short stories she's written.[11]

Leonora's departure from St Mary's was to be the end of her formal education. Not that 'formal education' mattered much to her: she would often talk about how all of life is an education, and how learning continues right through one's life. In fact, on occasion she referred to her time at the convent schools as 'dis-education', because she saw it as a negative rather than a positive learning experience – although there were certainly lessons to be learned, and she learned them.

After Ascot there was a different kind of school, in a different country: a finishing school in Florence. Based in a house in the Piazza Donatello, this establishment was run by a Miss Penrose and focused on guiding young women from well-to-do British families towards knowledge of the things that mattered most, such as 'how to behave socially'.[12] The idea of basing the school in Florence, a destination beloved of the British upper classes, was to impart some basic cultural knowledge to these young women. This would turn out to be another moment in Leonora's life when she found herself in the right place at the right time by chance rather than design. Her parents sent her to Italy to hone her into a good bet for a 'suitable' marriage, but there could have been no more useful place for this fifteen-year-old to find herself than the birthplace of the Renaissance.

An appreciation of the art of the Renaissance greats was part of the course at Miss Penrose's Academy, as evidenced in another of Leonora's notebooks from the time. This blue book, with 'History of Art – Leonora Carrington' written on the front page, contains jottings on the history and art of Florence, with drawings of horses dancing around the words. Horses had long been important to Leonora; at Crookhey she had had a Shetland pony, Black Bess, and later another pony called Winkie. She found horses, she said later, to be more dependable than humans. From her earliest years she felt a special affinity with them, and throughout her life they remained a recurring feature of her canvases.

The notebook contains snippets of detail about what she was learning on tours of the great galleries of Florence. Looking back on that time, she told me that the Uffizi was one of the museums she

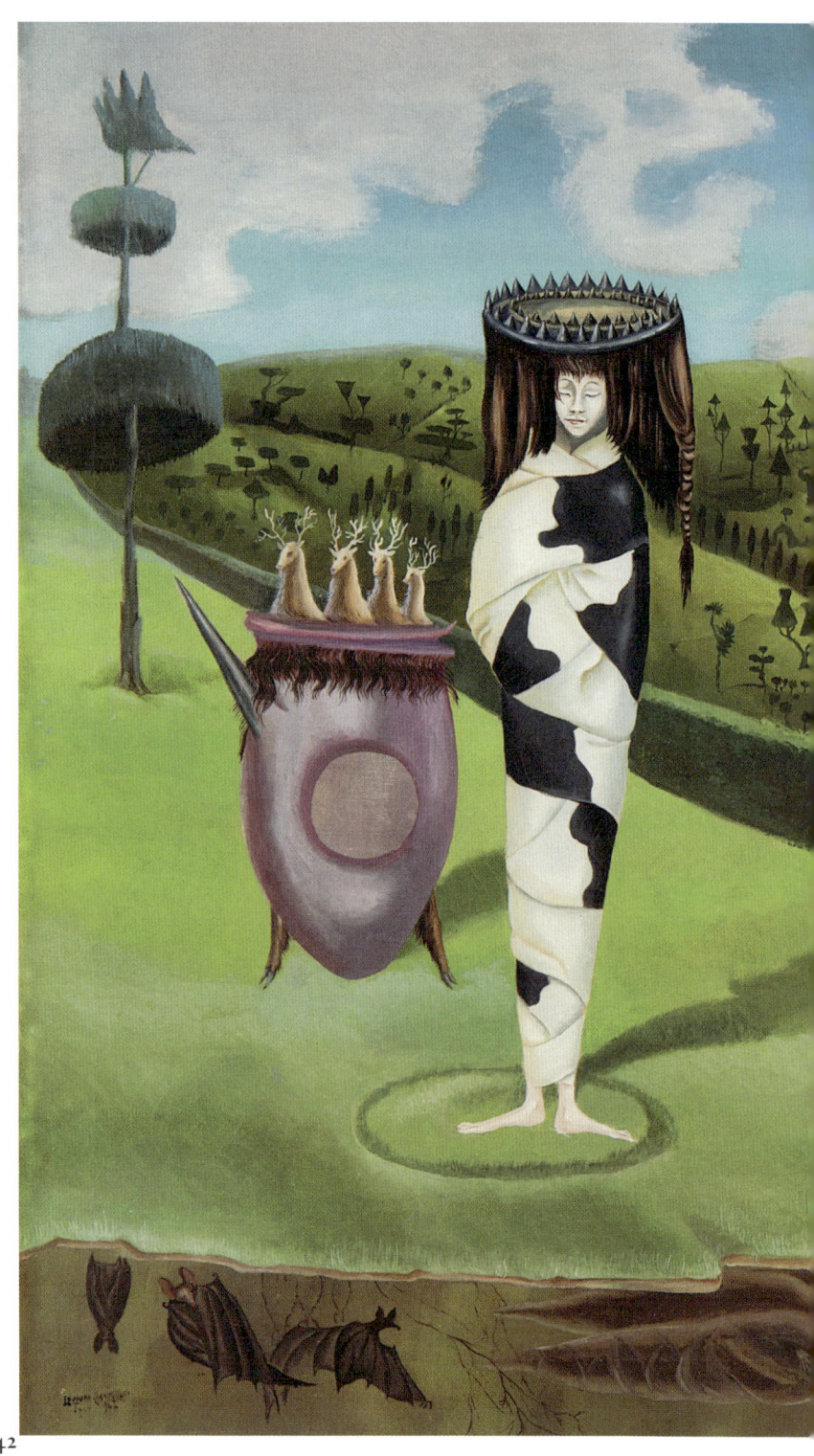

Green Tea, 1942

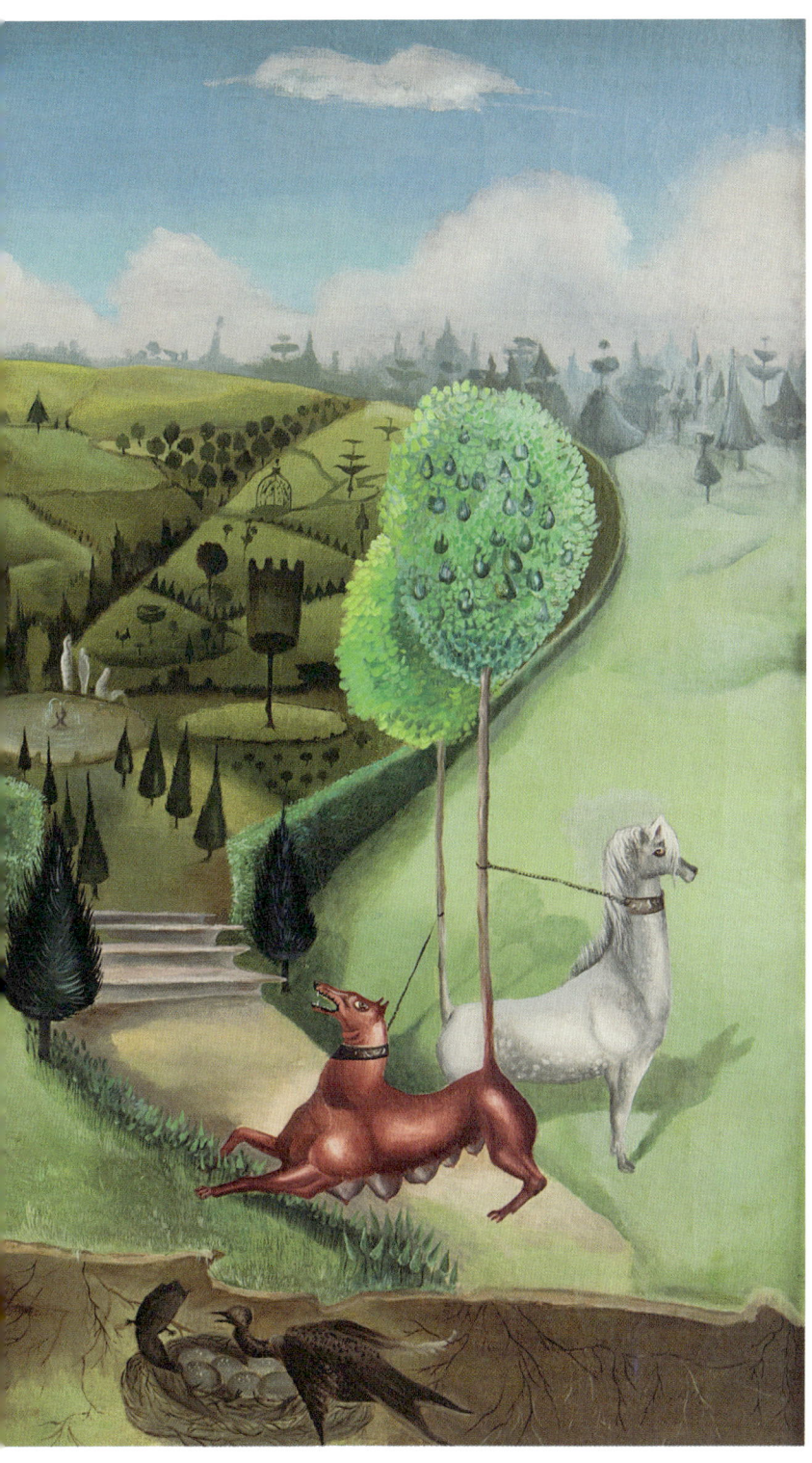

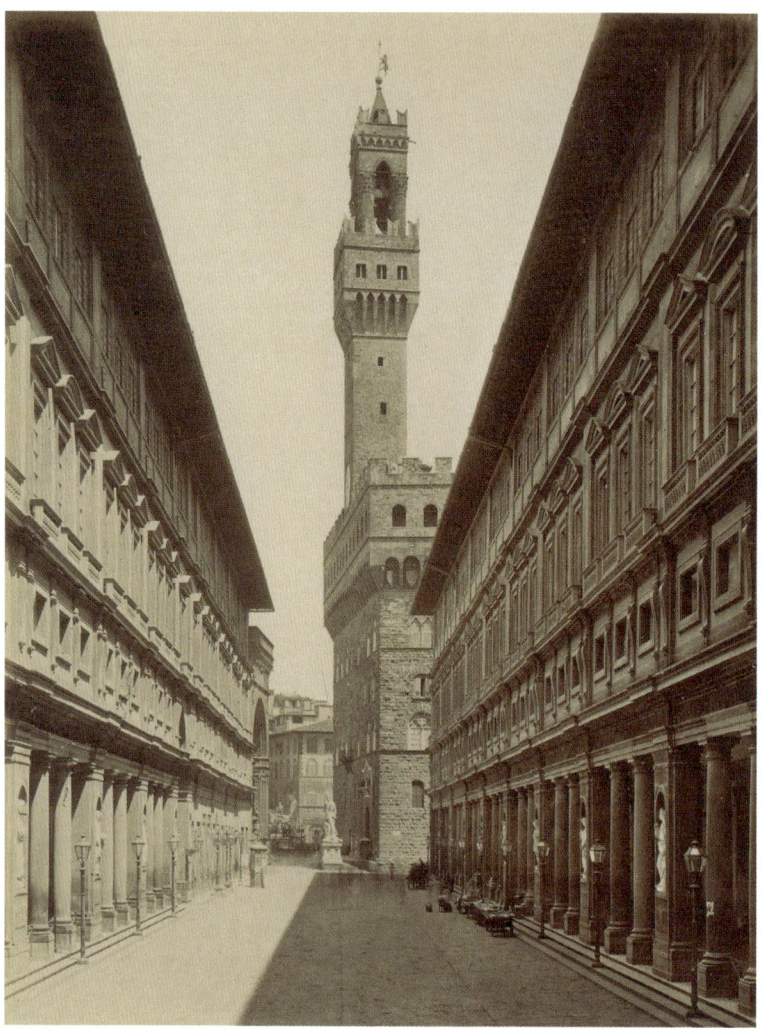

The Uffizi and Palazzo Vecchio, Florence, late 19th century

remembered best and had enjoyed the most. Uccello's 'best pictures are battle pieces with large subjects'. Her notes on Michelangelo are particularly interesting: 'He always desired to be an artist, but his father opposed him,' she writes. 'At 16 he quarrelled with his master [Ghirlandaio] and then he never had another lesson' (her underlining).

In an interview with Silvia Cherem, Leonora would later say of her time in Florence: 'Everything seemed impressive to me. My eyes were opened. I was as impressed by the crucifix of Cimabue in the Galleries of the Uffizi as with the frescos of Piero della Francesca in Arezzo, the art in Bologno, or the work of Leonardo. I consider Cimabue as one of the first modernists, and he lived in the 13th century.'[13]

After returning home for Christmas in 1931, she travelled with her parents to Switzerland, intending to return to Florence at the end of the trip. They went to the town of Mürren and stayed at a ski resort, where 'my mother skated and my father practised curling, which consists of pushing enormous rocks over the ice. I was awful at sports; the only thing in which I halfway excelled was riding a horse.'[14]

The return to Florence though was not to be. Leonora developed appendicitis, for which she was operated on in Bern; and then a fellow pupil at Miss Penrose's came down with scarlet fever. Leonora's time there was at an end. But the paintings of the Renaissance, the Italian masters' use of tempera (which she would use in her own work for many years), the echoes of the predella in her paintings, and her use of the most-loved colours of the Renaissance greats – sultry golds and brilliant blues, mellow yellows and mossy greens – would grace her pieces until the end of her days.

Marina Warner notes the way the storytelling nature of many Renaissance works left its mark on Leonora. 'The composition scheme of *The House Opposite* and *A Winter Fairy Tale* (undated) as well as many other pictures, refashions the narrative sequences of Sassetta or Matteo di Giovanni or Francesco di Giorgio; they unfold a tale in a journey across the image, with simultaneous incidents represented in demarcated antechambers and chambers of a palace or other edifice seen in section, so that time flows in the stasis of a painted moment.'[15] In New York in 1948, a dealer called Kirk Askew made the same point when he saw her work, saying that the paintings reminded him, also, of Sassetta, leading artist of the Sienese School.[16]

As well as exposing her to a pivotal moment in European art history, her time in Florence gave Leonora a lifelong friend in Joan Powell, goddaughter of Miss Penrose. Joan was seven years her senior and her job in Florence, as her son Adam Hogg later recalled, 'was to protect the girls from the amorous intentions of the Italian youth'. Joan was charged, he said, with escorting Leonora around Florence. But many years later, Prim (as Hogg always called her) remembered: 'I thought Joan was very fierce and was terrified of her, but no sooner were we out of sight of the school she spotted a bar and said "let's have a drink".'[17] Powell was one of the first people whose portrait Leonora painted; and also, as she recounted over tea in Mexico City during the last years of her life, the first person she ever heard use the word 'fuck'.

In autumn 1933 Leonora was dispatched to another finishing school, this time in Paris. In a 1991 interview she remembered her time there: she was expelled, she said – 'I only lasted a couple of months.'[18] The story of what happened to her seems to have been the inspiration for a short story she wrote in March 1934 about a character called Mary Anne, aged sixteen. Mary Anne is asked by another character, the Prince, whether she ever thinks; she is puzzled, then responds that she doesn't think she does – she only dreams or feels.

'Feel what?' asks the Prince. 'Oh, pain mostly – sometimes love. But I like imagining things best,' says Mary Anne. 'Ah – so you have loved?' asks the Prince. 'Yes,' Mary Anne replies. 'I think so. But it always eludes me after a little while and the person gets kind of too real.'

By the end of the story, Mary Anne is facing expulsion from her French school. She tells her friend that she's afraid she'll be sent back to her parents – 'oh my God, life will be finished if I have to go' – and sounds off about the unfairness of it all. All she was doing wrong, she says, was smoking, and walking along the ledge outside her window.

Her friend Noona says the real reason she's being sent home is 'they just don't like you because you look remarkable'. Mary Anne/Leonora replies darkly that if she's sent home she'll 'break up the whole damn place'; she doesn't care about the consequences, she says, 'because there won't be anything left to live for'.[19]

In the 1991 interview Leonora describes how, after she was expelled from the finishing school, her father decided she had to go 'somewhere really tough'. She was billeted with a Miss Sampson in the 14th Arondissement: 'I had a little room over a churchyard, a graveyard.' In the notebook she gives her address as 3 bis, Rue Cassoni; if she had a room at the top of that house she would have been looking over the graveyard of Montparnasse, burial place of Guy de Maupassant. In the interview she says that she didn't like Miss Sampson's, 'so I escaped at night' and took herself off to a family she'd never met but heard of through a friend of her family. Their name was Simon, and M. Simon was a professor of beaux arts. This was probably Lucien Simon (1861–1945), who was elected to the Académie des Beaux-Arts in 1929 and remained there for thirteen years.

The Simon family took Leonora in and she remained with them at their home in Paris for some months. In *The Hearing Trumpet*, Leonora remembers 'the Luxembourg Gardens and the smell of chestnut trees, Paris. St Germain des Prés, having breakfast on the terrace of a café with Simon, whose face was as clear and solid as if still full of life, but

Simon must be dead for thirty years now, there is nothing left of him as far as I know.'[20] It's clear from the way she continues how much she loves Paris: she writes of the joy she would feel if she could walk again along the quais and admire the books there, and how much she'd like to gaze at the Seine from the Pont Neuf. She would walk up the Rue Saint-André-des-Arts to the market – she always adored markets – and buy red wine and Brie for lunch.

After Paris Leonora returned to Hazelwood; and it is there, retracing her journey, that I feel a sense of how it perhaps felt to her. Sitting on the rocks at the bay near her home, I'm struck by how flat the horizon is, and I wonder whether that vista echoed her views on what her future in England might hold. The landscape here is acres of sameness: the tea parties, the hunt balls, the shopping expeditions, all mirrored by her view of these long, low, relentless sands. Mile after mile of damp, brown ground, broken up here and there by small, half-hearted channels of water that don't go anywhere. The rocky shores with an occasional windswept tree clinging to a stone. The quicksand: how easy would it be to lose your footing? You could go under, and you'd be lost forever.

Above all this, though, is a huge, wide sky, full of promise. Sitting where I am right now, Leonora would have seen that horizon: surely she thought about the opportunities it represented. They were there if you looked for them – now that she had travelled she knew this to be true. Whatever life held for her, it would be far away from Silverdale.

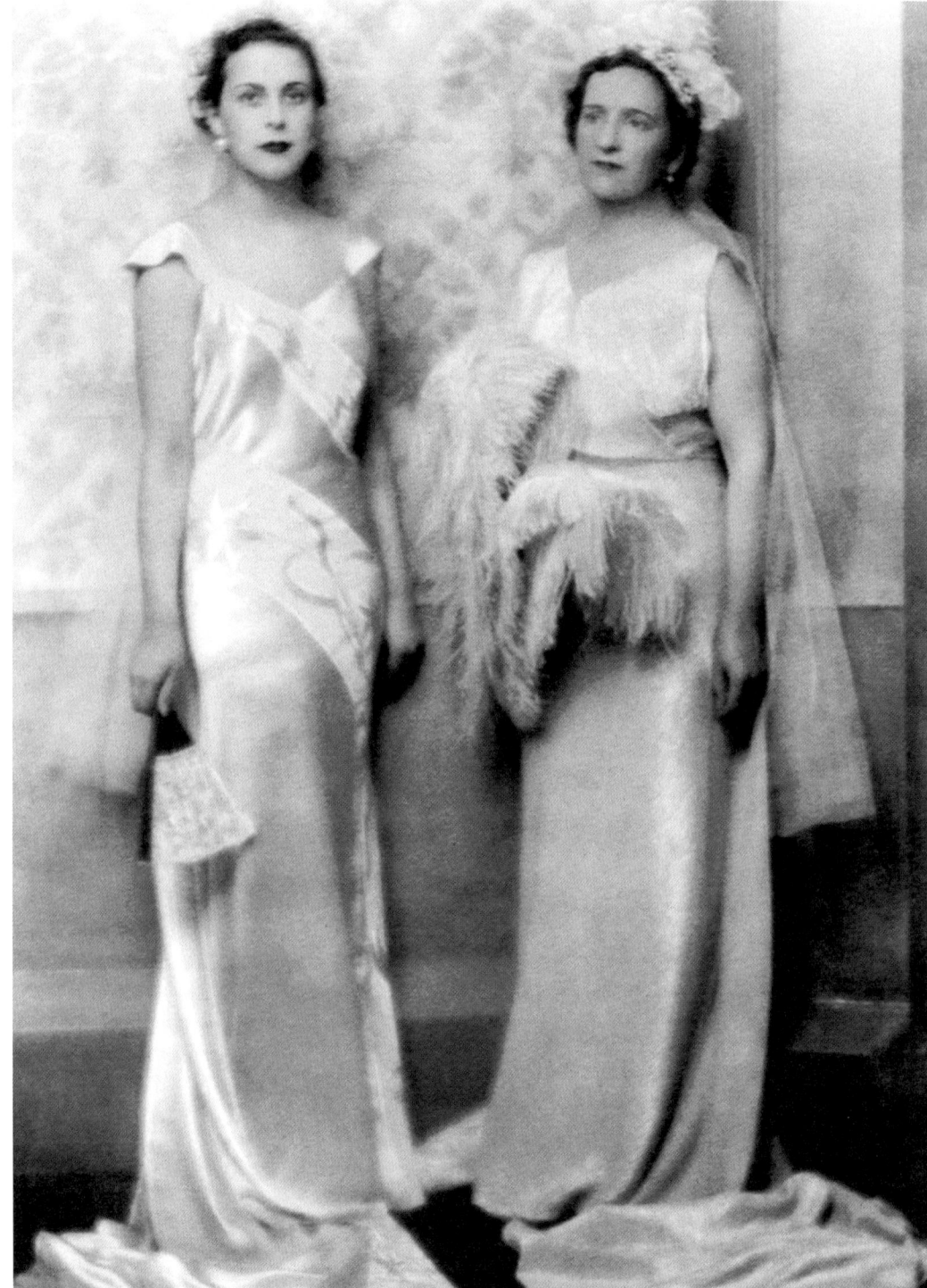

3
Debutante and Art Student
1935–1937

By the start of 1935 Leonora, still aged seventeen, was by the standards of the day a well-travelled young woman. She had tasted life in Florence and Paris and visited other cities and countries in Europe including Rome, the South of France, and Switzerland. In *The Hearing Trumpet* she pays tribute to Maurie's role in all of this – 'thanks to my mother I did see most of Europe during my youth' – and describes some of the highlights, including Monte Carlo ('Mother found her home in the casino') and Sicily, where a waiter sold them a painting by Fra Angelico 'which did not turn out to be authentic and was therefore not as cheap as we thought'.[1]

And while the family had always been based in Lancashire, Leonora had also lived in Essex and Berkshire, at her convent boarding schools. London, though, was a city she was less familiar with, and that was about to change. Harold and Maurie, disappointed at their daughter's inability to fit in at any of the schools to which they had sent her, had decided to up the tempo on getting her married off and settled down. Given her consistent refusal to conform in a variety of settings, it seems extraordinary that they still hoped she might comply with this; but hope they did, and plans were made for her to have a season as a debutante in the capital. It was an experience that would be filled with garden parties, balls, expensive outfits, an overload of other people of privilege and – crucially – opportunities to become acquainted (but not too well acquainted) with desirable young men interested in finding themselves a wife.

Leonora as a debutante and her mother Maurie, *c.* 1935

If it's hard to imagine – and it is – why Leonora allowed herself to be recruited into the ranks of debutantes, it's worth remembering that from her point of view, 'coming out' meant the chance to taste London. The family took an apartment in town and the rigmarole kicked off in March that year with a presentation at Buckingham Palace. Maurie accompanied her, and the entire occasion meant a great deal more to her than it did to Leonora. 'Ever since she left Ireland at the age of eighteen Mother had lived a constant round of dizzy pleasure,' Leonora writes in *The Hearing Trumpet*. 'Cricket matches, shooting parties, jumble sales, shopping in Regent Street, bridge parties and face massage at Madame Pomeroy's, an unfashionable beauty parlour just off Piccadilly Circus.'[2]

A *Times* report of the presentation gives a flavour of all that it entailed: 'Victorian frocks for debutantes and long classical gowns for older women were worn at their Majesties' First Court of the season last night. Frilled tulle and net and taffeta or ciré made most of the dresses for the young girls, the bodies sloping off the shoulders and finished with tiny puff sleeves or epaulettes. In striking contrast were the older ladies' slim-fitting, severe gowns of lamé and tissue in rich colours, cut with short trains to the skirts. Embroidery was an important feature of all the dresses; heavy incrustations of sequins, pearls or diamanté weighted the hems of many skirts and trains, and the design of most lace frocks was outlined with dainty beading.'[3] Queen Mary wore 'a gown of opalescent paillettes embroidered with crystal and diamante'; the Duchess of York wore a gown of gold and white with a lace train. Some paragraphs later, we are told that Mrs Harold Carrington wore 'a gown of rose and silver lamé' with a train of the same material lined with rose romaine, and a diamond tiara. Miss Leonora Carrington wore 'a gown of citron satin embroidered with the reversed side of the material. A train to match. A petit-point dentelle fan.' Both dresses were by the designer Victor Stiebel of Bruton Street, Mayfair.

Leonora referred to the debutante season as 'a cattle market', and it's clear that it epitomized everything she had come to loathe about the society in which she found herself: snobbery, fixed expectations, lack of spontaneity, sexism. As Maurie became more and more excited by the prospect of an 'advantageous' marriage that would change her daughter's life – perhaps even opening doors into the world of old-money aristocrats for herself and Harold – Leonora was becoming more and more appalled by how limited her horizons would be if she were to buy into that world. The truth was, the Carringtons were arrivistes: they had plenty of money, and Harold was one of the most successful businessmen in northern England, but both he and Maurie came from humble stock. His background was working class – his grandfather had been a stationmaster – and she came from rural Ireland. The whirl of the London season was a window on a world Maurie had long hoped to inhabit, and which at last seemed within reach. But it all rested on her daughter's marriage; and she had only one daughter.

Harold Carrington was less fixated on Leonora's marriage prospects than Maurie but he shared his wife's sentiment. He might have been a pioneer in the textile industry, but he was a conventional thinker when it came to social mores. Leonora said he 'lived tied to rationality and did not know how to understand me. When I would say to him how much I was bored in the house, he would say: "Breed fox terriers," as if breeding dogs would have been of my interest; or "Learn to cook," when I was not even interested to know if to fry an egg I had to put in the pan the egg first or the oil! He was a man without pretensions. Perhaps it would have made him happy if only I would have married a wealthy man and become a dignified society lady.'[4]

In an interview many years later, she remembered – with a sense of irony, and still shocked at the sexism – how it had felt to be a debutante. The royal garden party, she said, was 'tea in a tent at Buckingham Palace, and you go around with a teacup. You have a different dress for that, very expensive. Then you go to Ascot, the races, and you're in the royal enclosure. And, if you please, in those days, if you were a woman, you were not allowed to bet. You weren't even allowed to the paddock, where they show the horses. So I took a book. I mean, what would you do? It was Huxley's *Eyeless in Gaza*, which I read all the way through.'[5]

Many years after she was a deb, Leonora still remembered 'the tiara – biting into my skull'. But her 'season' provided rich material; not, on this occasion, for a painting, but for a short story written a couple of years later. 'The Debutante' is a glorious mixture of fact and fiction, the actual and the imagined, events real and events surreal. Leonora describes how, as a debutante, she often visited the zoo: 'I went so often that I knew the animals better than I knew the girls of my own age. Indeed it was in order to get away from people that I found myself at the zoo every day.'[6]

The animal she came to know best, she writes, was a hyena, who was very intelligent. 'I taught her French and she, in return, taught me

INTERNATIONAL SURREALIST EXHIBITION

NEW BURLINGTON GALLERIES
BURLINGTON GARDENS

The Committee have the honour to announce that

M. ANDRÉ BRETON
WILL OPEN THE EXHIBITION
on THURSDAY, JUNE 11th

MM. HANS ARP, SALVADOR DALI, MAX ERNST,
MAN RAY, and other distinguished members of the
Surrealist Movement abroad will be present

The Committee hope to have the pleasure of your company at 3 p.m.

Exhibition announcement, International Surrealist Exhibition,
New Burlington Galleries, London, 1936

her language.' When Leonora's mother organizes a ball in her honour ('I've always detested balls, especially when they are given in my honour'), Leonora complains about it to the hyena, who replies that she would love to go. Why doesn't she go in her place, Leonora suggests – and after a quick murder, which means the hyena can disguise herself with the face of a sacrificed maid ('a brief cry, and it was over' – she would never have done it, Leonora assures us, if she hadn't hated the idea of the ball so much), the camouflaged creature takes her place at the sumptuous event, leaving Leonora to sit alone in her room reading *Gulliver's Travels* by Jonathan Swift.

In life as in her story, Leonora rejected the debutante experience. But it had given her, as she had hoped it would, an introduction to life in London and to the expanding art scene it had on offer. Indeed, the following year, 1936, would see a pivotal event in the story of surrealism in Britain: the first International Surrealist Exhibition, held at the New Burlington Galleries from 11 June to 4 July. This show brought to London the work of artists including Giorgio de Chirico, Salvador Dalí, Marcel Duchamp, Leonor Fini, Paul Klee, René Magritte, Joan Miró and Meret Oppenheim. Pablo Picasso, Francis Picabia and of course Max Ernst were also in the line-up. British artists represented

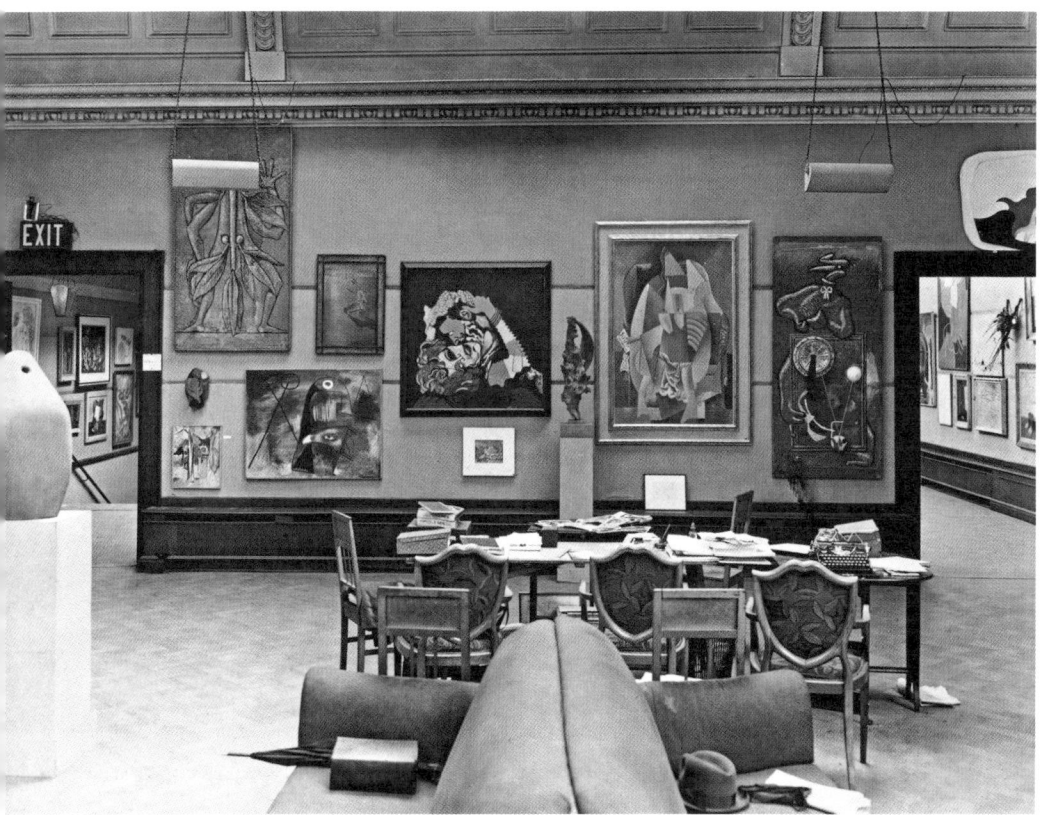

Interior view of the International Surrealist Exhibition,
New Burlington Galleries, London, 1936

included Roland Penrose, Eileen Agar and Edward Burra; and there
was (according to art historian Herbert Read, one of the exhibition's
organizers) much to be excited about in terms of the British contribution to the movement. In his introduction to the catalogue, Read
wrote: 'A nation which has produced two such superrealists as William
Blake and Lewis Carroll is to the manner born. Because our art and
literature is the most romantic in the world, it is likely to become the
most superrealistic. The English contribution to this Exhibition is
comparatively tentative, but our poets and painters have scarcely
become conscious of this international movement. Now that it has
been revealed in all its range and irrationality, they may recover, shall
we say, the courage of their instincts.'[7]

Read's optimism for the future of British surrealism was, it would
turn out, misplaced; the 1936 exhibition was the movement's last,

as well as its first major hurrah on its territory. But for Leonora it brought what would turn out to be a crucial introduction to the work of the German surrealist Max Ernst. 'I fell in love with Max's paintings before I fell in love with Max,' she told me in 2006. And her first sight of his work was contained within Read's book *Surrealism*, published to mark the 1936 exhibition. Her copy was given to her, she remembered, by the unlikeliest of people: her mother, Maurie. The work that particularly appealed to Leonora was *Two Children Are Threatened by a Nightingale* (1924), a mixed-media piece that Ernst later said was the product of a 'fevervision' he had experienced while sick with measles as a child. It shows a haunting image in which a tiny nightingale, barely a speck in the sky, appears to be somehow endangering the lives of two young girls. One of them brandishes a knife in the bird's direction; the other is in the arms of a man who seems to be trying to take her to safety across a rooftop.

The painting spoke to Leonora. Indeed, in one interview she said it totally shocked her.[8] 'I thought, ah, this is familiar: I know what this about. A kind of world which would move between worlds. The world of our dreaming and imagination.'[9]

Leonora dispensed with being a debutante as briskly as she had dispensed with being a convent schoolgirl and a finishing-school pupil; but giving up the frivolity of the season didn't mean giving up the artistic opportunities London had to offer. Somehow she persuaded her parents (who perhaps continued to hold onto the slender hope that if they played along, she would eventually acquiesce and settle into conventional upper-class life) to allow her to enrol at the Chelsea School of Art. 'I had scrambled eggs on a gas range, and I did a lot of painting. But my father had a spy there, in London, who used to see me weekly, Serge Chermayeff,' she remembered. Chermayeff was the designer, with his partner Erich Mendelsohn, of the De La Warr Pavilion in Bexhill, East Sussex. They probably got to know Harold Carrington because Mendelsohn was involved in the construction of the ICI Dyestuffs Laboratory at Blackley, Manchester, which Harold would have known through his work in the textile industry.[10]

It was certainly Chermayeff who got Leonora into the Ozenfant school, as she remembered later. '(He) said, you'd better at least try and learn to draw. Go to Amédée Ozenfant.'[11] So she left the Chelsea School, and signed up for the Ozenfant Academy of Fine Arts.

Ozenfant was a fifty-year-old French cubist painter who had recently moved to London. The name of his art school was rather grander than its humble location, which Leonora described as 'a barn in west Kensington'.[12] The venue was a mews block on Warwick Road, round the corner from Kensington High Street tube station. Leonora went along to see Ozenfant, taking some work she'd done already. He replied that she could start the following day and warned that she was about to do some real work. 'Then he made me work like bloody hell. You had to know the chemistry of everything you used, including the pencil and the paper. He would give you one apple, one bit of paper, and one pencil, like a 9H, which was like drawing with a bit of steel. And you had to do a line drawing, with one line. I was drawing the apple for six months, the same apple, which had become a kind of mummy.'[13]

Like the Renaissance masters whose work Leonora had come to know during her time in Florence, Ozenfant worked alongside his small number of pupils. According to the school's prospectus (a few sheets of printed paper), the Master, unlike in other schools, would almost always be present while his pupils worked. The philosophy was 'to create for the benefit of his pupils a technical, theoretical and empirical spirit, which constituted the value of studios of the past, where the master worked in company with his novices'.[14]

The importance to an artist of being connected to the surrounding world is also underlined in the Ozenfant manifesto. 'To be an artist of one's time it is not sufficient to declare oneself modern. An artist is capable of creating works necessary to his epoch only if he lives fully the life of his time. Too many artists isolate themselves from life, and ignore precisely that which imparts originality to their age. Living fossilized, how should their works be modern, to interest, to be useful to, to be in accord with the active men of the time?'[15]

The document gives an outline of a typical day at the academy, which was open daily (except Saturdays) from ten a.m. until four p.m. A life model posed for students each morning between ten and one, and in the afternoons students could either continue on their study from the morning or pursue a personal piece of their own. M. Ozenfant gave a course, and correction, every morning. Fees were five guineas a month, thirteen guineas a quarter, or thirty guineas a year; pupils were welcome to join for a month, a quarter or a year, and could begin on any day.

There were, Leonora remembered later, no more than about ten students at any one time. These included, in her day, the painter, photographer and collage artist Stella Snead, whom she would later meet again in New York. But it was another fellow pupil whose presence was to have the longest-lasting impact on Leonora's life: Ursula Blackwell, whose antecedent had been one-half of the founding duo behind the food brand Crosse and Blackwell. Ursula herself was now known by her married name, which was Goldfinger. Her husband was Ernő Goldfinger, who would in time, after a falling-out with the writer Ian Fleming, lend his name to James Bond's adversary, the gold smuggler Auric Goldfinger.

Ursula and Ernő, who had been born in Hungary and would later design buildings including London's Balfron Tower and Trellick Tower, lived with their two young children in a building often described as the first piece of modernist architecture in England: a tall, whitewashed block at the top of Highgate Hill in north London called Highpoint. It had been designed by the Georgian émigré Berthold Lubetkin, who was himself a resident of the block. The Goldfingers lived at Number 3 Highpoint, a three-bedroomed first-floor dwelling with concertina windows along the sitting-room wall, opening onto a narrow balcony. This room would be the setting for a small gathering that had a profound effect on Leonora's life: in early June 1937,

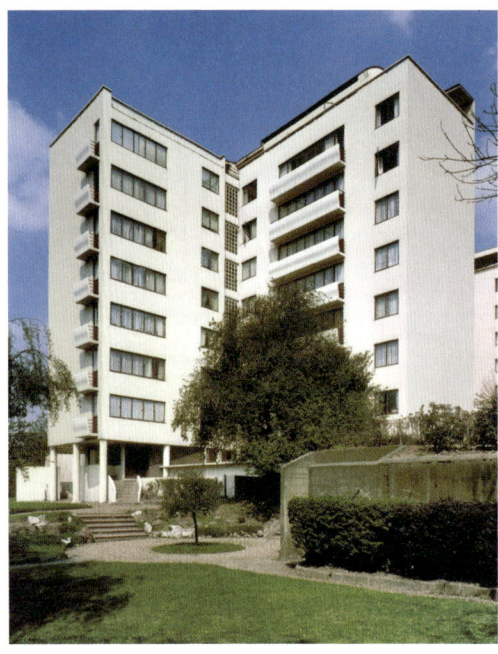

Highpoint One, Highgate

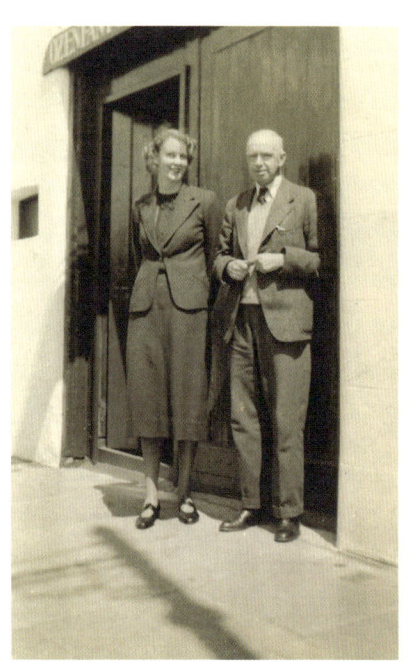

Amédée Ozenfant with Ursula Goldfinger outside the Ozenfant Academy of Fine Arts, London

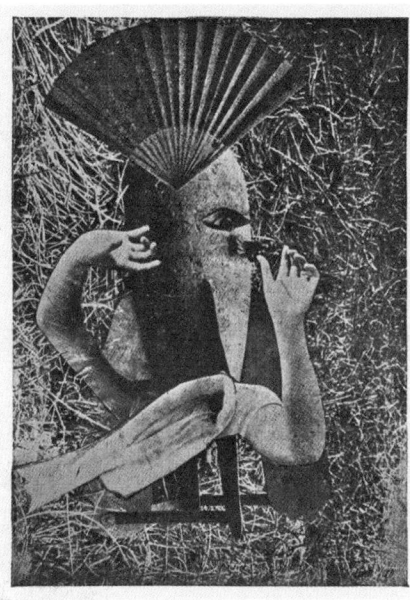

EXHIBITION
OF SURREALIST
PAINTINGS BY
MAX ERNST

JUNE 3rd to 27th, 1937

**THE MAYOR
GALLERY**

19 CORK STREET
LONDON, W.1

Poster advertising the Max Ernst exhibition at the Mayor Gallery, 1937

Ursula invited her to come to supper at the Goldfingers' flat and meet Max Ernst. Ernst was in London for his first ever solo show in Britain, which would take place that month at the Mayor Gallery in Mayfair.

Leonora's friend Joan Powell gave her a lift to Highpoint that evening but didn't go in,[16] and there were just four people around the table: the Goldfingers, Max, and herself. Did she, she was asked, know in advance that Max would be coming to supper that evening? 'Oh yes, yes, yes,' Leonora replied. 'And I was very, very excited. I was thrilled. I mean, this was the big, I don't know what. Ursula thought that I was a good-looking young woman, and that this would appeal to Max.'[17]

The attraction between Leonora and Max, who at the time was married to his second wife, Marie-Berthe, was instant and mutual. The couple got together 'immediately, immediately. I remember we spent a day in the country, and this for me was a whole world opening. He showed me how he did what he called a "frottage" [a rubbing] with a pencil and paper, grass and whatnot, leaves and such.'[18]

Leonora could hardly have found a man more unlike the imagined one her parents had hoped she would marry. At forty-six, Max was old enough to be her father (that was no doubt part of the attraction). German-born, by now he had left his homeland out of contempt for

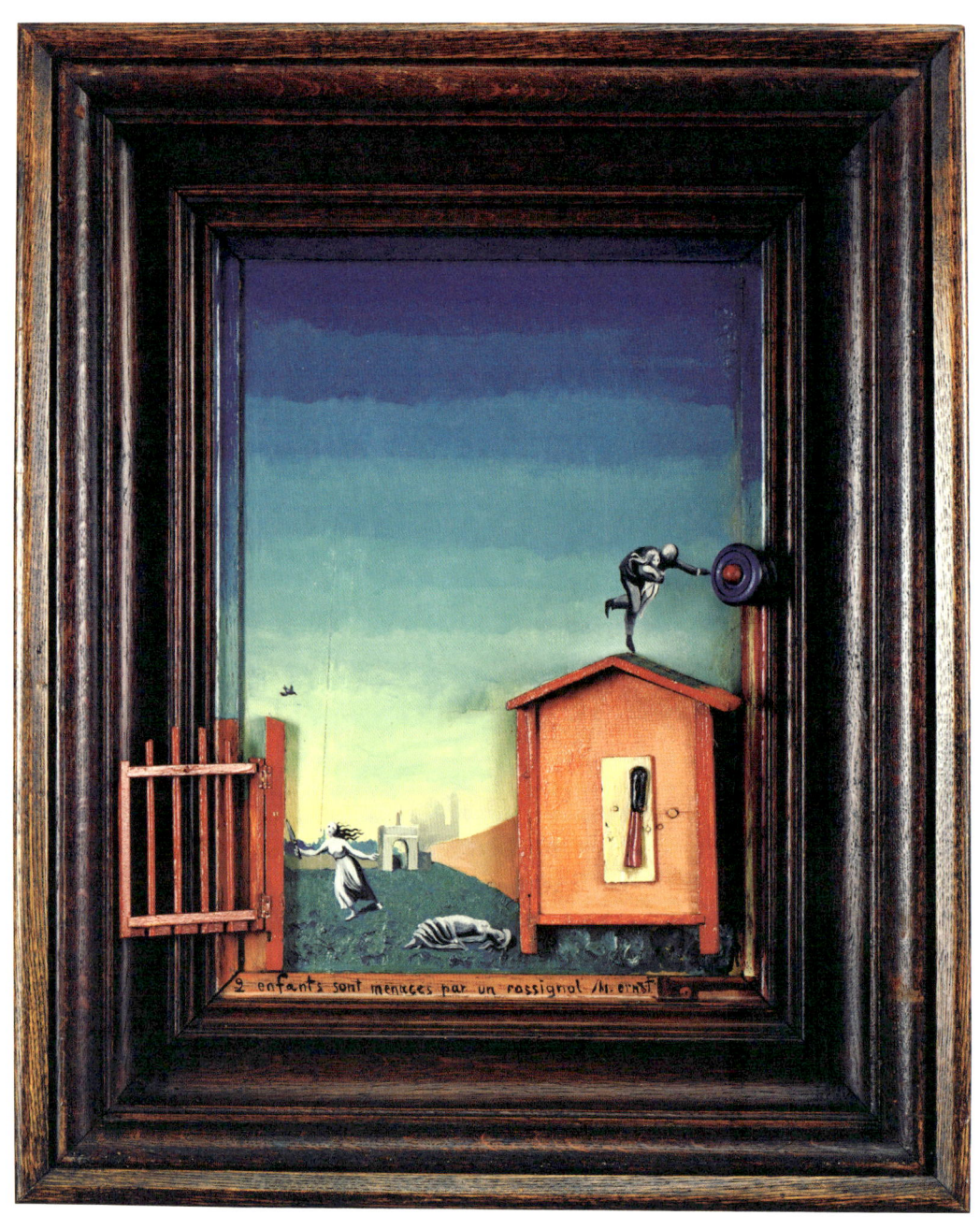

Max Ernst, *Two Children Are Threatened by a Nightingale*, 1924

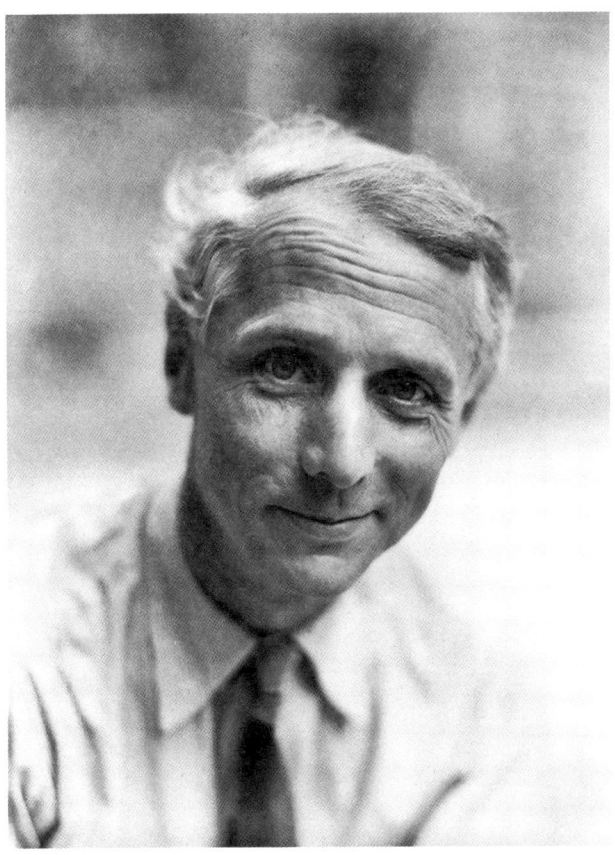

Max Ernst, 1933. Photograph by Anna Riwkin

the rise of Hitler and was living in Paris with Marie-Berthe; his former wife, Louise, and their young son were still in Germany. He was
at the heart of a group of surrealist artists and writers that included
Duchamp, Dalí, André Breton, Paul Éluard and Yves Tanguy. A man
more than twice her age; a father; a divorced man, married to another
woman; a foreigner; and an artist, with nothing like the wealth of the
Carringtons. Harold and Maurie, when news reached them, were
horrified, but Leonora was smitten. Max was about more than his art,
more than his fatherly affections, more than his politics, so different
from those at home. He was also about the future, about the fact that
a door was opening for Leonora in a way she had always hoped for and
believed in, but hadn't quite known when to expect. Here, suddenly,
it was: she was on a threshold, and all she had to do was embrace the
thrilling uncertainty of what awaited her.

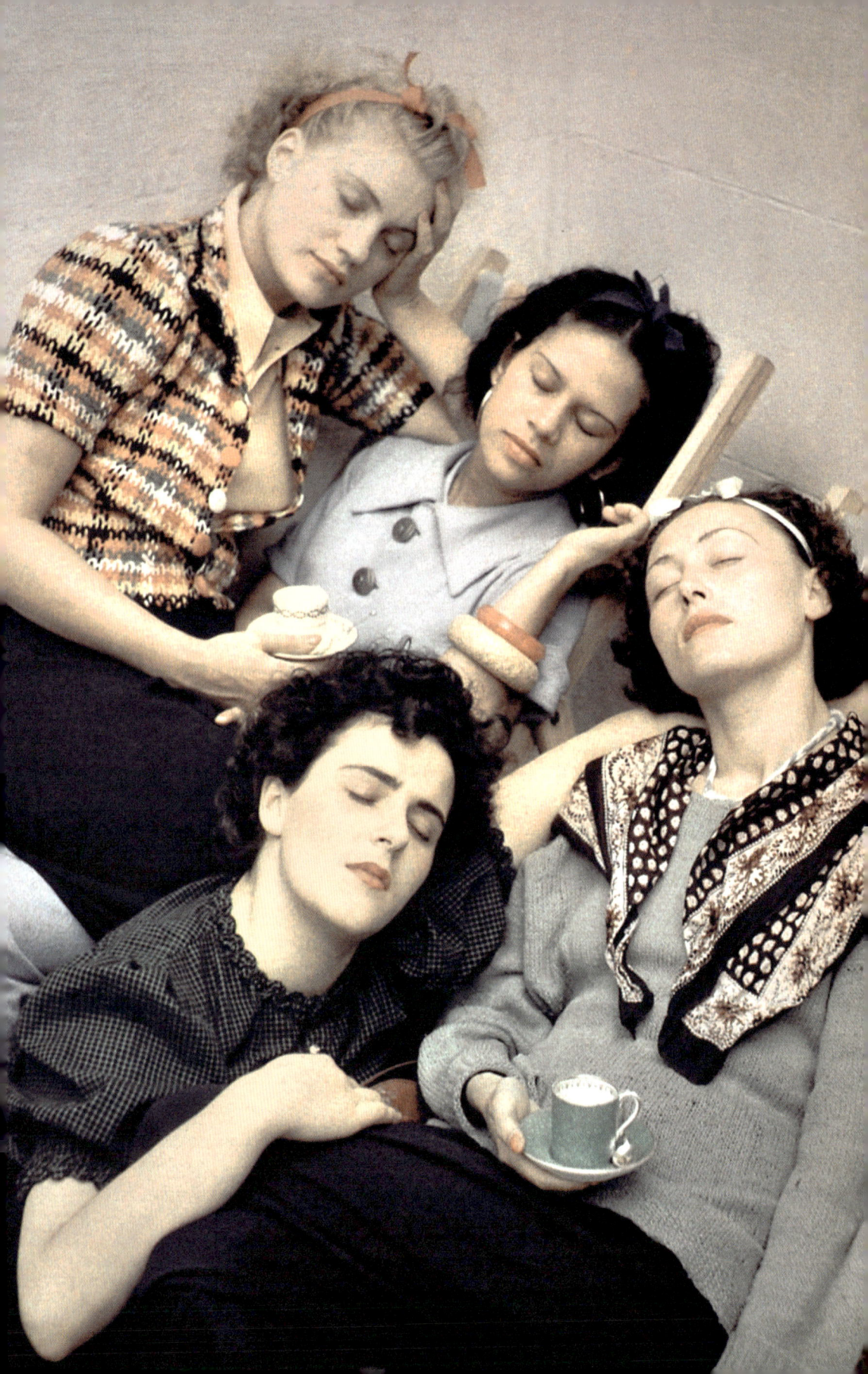

4
Cornwall
1937

The International Surrealist Exhibition had put the art movement on the map in stiff-upper-lip 1930s Britain, but it was a holiday in Cornwall that revealed its true spirit and potential in Leonora's own life. That holiday took place in summer, 1937, as a direct result of the love affair now in full swing between Leonora and Max Ernst.

The couple were enjoying life in London and days out of the capital, while doing nothing to hide their relationship; so it would not have been long before someone, probably Serge Chermayeff, passed on the news to Harold and Maurie Carrington, who were back at Hazelwood. Maurie was devastated, but Harold was incandescent – unable to cope with the idea that his only daughter was now openly having a love affair with a man so unsuitable, a man of almost his own age.

Harold was a powerful figure in his professional life and did not take well to being disobeyed or, worse, ignored; but Leonora was the one person in the world he could never control. Maybe she had more of his single-mindedness, his determination to be successful, than anyone else in their family. But the prize on which her sights were set was a universe away from Harold's conventional ambitions.

Faced with the possibility of public embarrassment as well as domestic defeat, Harold decided he would stop at nothing to end the affair between his daughter and Max. He contacted, or got some-one else to contact, the Metropolitan Police, informing them that the exhibition of the German artist Max Ernst currently showing at the Mayor Gallery in Cork Street was pornographic. The police needed

Four women asleep [Lee Miller, Ady Fidelin, Nusch Éluard and Leonora Carrington], Lambe Creek, Cornwall. Photograph by Roland Penrose

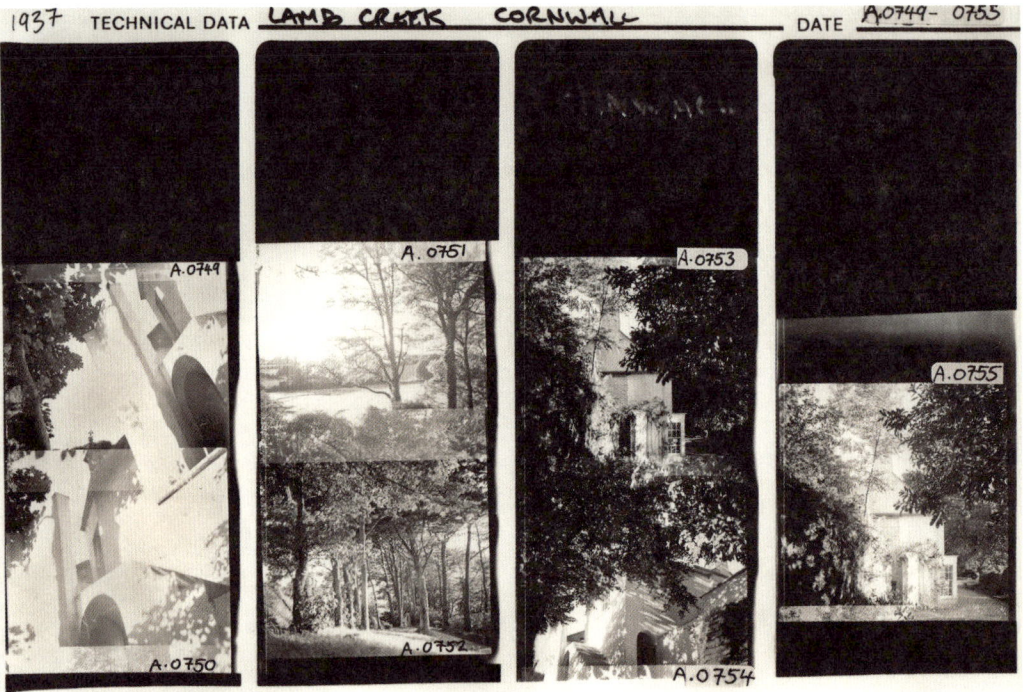

1937 TECHNICAL DATA *LAMB CREEK CORNWALL* DATE A.0749 – 0755

A.0749 A.0751 A.0753 A.0755

A.0750 A.0752 A.0754

Lambe Creek, Cornwall. Photograph by Lee Miller

to investigate, he insisted, because the work was filthy. It's difficult now to know which specific pieces he had in mind; reviewers, including Anthony Blunt in the *Spectator*, spoke only of Max's dream creations and his central piece in the gallery window. This featured an upside-down table set for a surreal dinner party, its legs facing up rather than down and the chairs covered with broken glass.

Whatever evidence he had for his accusations, Harold was successful in persuading the police to look into the matter and even to issue a warrant for Max's arrest. The situation escalated into something truly worrying: as a German citizen, Max was now at risk of being returned to the country he had left because he didn't agree with its politics, and where he would almost certainly have been in danger. His friend Roland Penrose, to whom he had been close since they met in Paris in the mid-1920s, came up with an idea. Penrose had recently begun a relationship with the photographer Lee Miller, and they had the use of his brother Beacus's house in Lambe Creek, Cornwall. How about if all of them – Roland and Lee, Max and Leonora – were to motor down to the west country and lie low for a while?

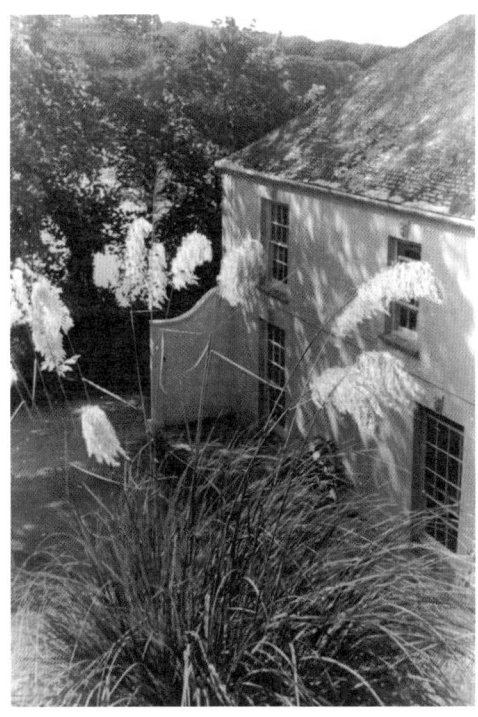

Lambe Creek Cottage, Lambe Creek, Cornwall. Photograph by Roland Penrose

They left without a word to anyone. As a hideaway, the place could hardly have been more perfect: tucked away on an inlet of the River Truro, close to a village called Kea, it sits at the end of a series of winding lanes with high hedges on either side. 'Tall trees hang low over the water's edge and cling to the steep slopes of the little peninsula that shelters the house from south-easterly gales. The formal but kindly 19th-century white painted front of the house overlooks a sloping lawn and the drive that curves away to the distant road. The afternoon sun streams straight in through the big windows, or warms those who want to doze outside after lunch.'[1]

The two couples were joined by Lee's former partner Man Ray and his new partner, Ady Fidelin. Ady was just two years older than Leonora, and they got on well. She had been born into one of Guadeloupe's oldest Creole families and moved to France after a cyclone devastated the Caribbean in 1928, becoming part of the Black Jazz scene in Paris. She probably met Man Ray – a fan of Black music and dance – at a club like the city's Bal Blomet. The couple were at the heart of the surrealist art set in Paris, and in the same year as their

Cornwall sojourn Ady posed for Picasso (*Femme assise sur fond jaune et rose, II – Portrait de femme*).

In 2006, on my first visit to Mexico to meet Leonora, she remembered Ady and talked about how much she'd liked her; however, she was less keen on Man Ray. 'What she saw in him I'll never know,' she told me. 'It certainly wasn't his looks.' Man Ray was a year younger than Max, so the two couples had a similar age difference in common. Born into a family of Russian Jewish immigrants in Philadephia, Man Ray had moved to Paris in 1921 and, after a love affair with the model Kiki de Montparnasse, had met and fallen in love with Lee Miller, who became his photographic assistant. Together, the pair reinvented the photographic technique of solarization. Their romantic relationship had ended five years earlier but, as was common in surrealist circles, they remained good friends and befriended one another's new partners.

Another member of the Lambe Creek house party was the French poet Paul Éluard, then in his early forties, who had been part of the surrealist movement from its earliest days. His first love had been a young Russian woman, Elena Diakonova, whom he called Gala; the pair were married for a time. Gala would go on to become the muse *par excellence* of surrealism and the inspiration for works by Salvador Dalí (to whom she was married twice), as well as André Breton and Louis Aragon. Gala, Max and Éluard had been in a ménage à trois for three years during the mid-1920s. Now, though, Éluard was married to Nusch (Maria Benz), an actress and singer he had met through Man Ray, and she accompanied him on the trip to Cornwall.

These eight – Leonora and Max, Lee and Roland, Ady and Man Ray, and Nusch and Paul – were the core group for the Lambe Creek holiday, but others visited as well. They included the sculptor Henry Moore and his wife, Irina; along with Roland, he had been involved in the organization of the International Surrealist Exhibition in London the previous year. At various points they were also joined by the Belgian surrealist poet and art dealer E. L. T. (Édouard) Mesens; the Hungarian writer Joseph Bard; and his partner, the British surrealist Eileen Agar, one of the few women to have been involved in the 1936 show. The Moores came for lunch, as they were on their way to another part of Cornwall; Édouard, Joseph and Eileen all stayed for a few days. It seems likely that Eileen's visit didn't coincide with the time when Leonora and Max were there, because there is no mention of them in her memoirs. She does, however, describe Max at another

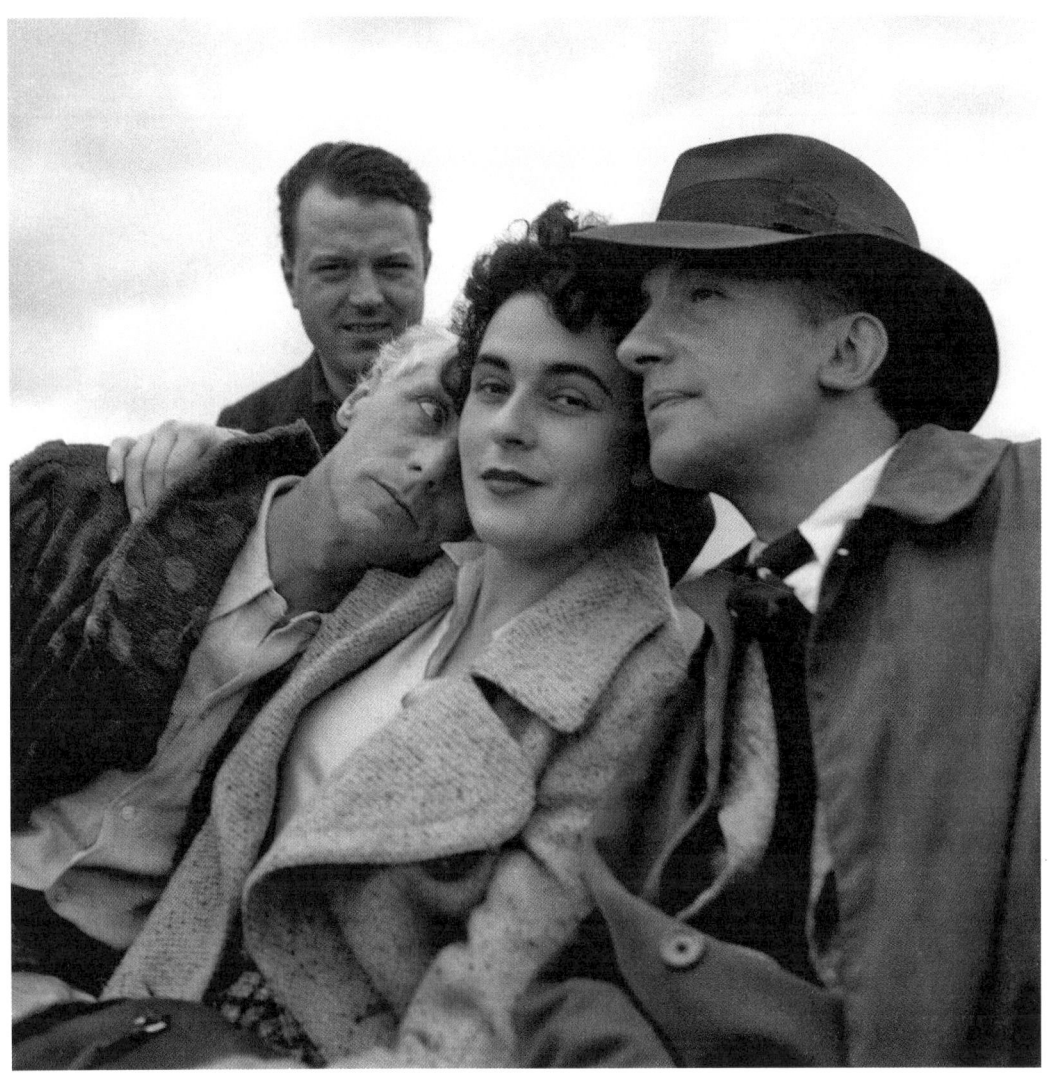

E. L. T. Mesens, Max Ernst, Leonora Carrington and Paul Éluard, Lambe Creek, Cornwall.
Photograph by Lee Miller

point in her book: he had 'a startling bird-like face, eagle presence and blue eyes'. And she gives us a flavour of the holiday, reporting that it was 'a delightful Surrealist houseparty…with Roland…ready to turn the slightest encounter into an orgy'.[2]

It was an overcast summer, but what the holiday lacked in sunshine was more than made up for by the sparkle and gleam of the participants. Days were spent hanging out at the house, swimming in the River Fal, rowing across to the Heron Inn at Malpas, and exploring the church and graveyard of Old Kea. Roland had a Ford V8 and as many of them as could cram into it enjoyed outings further afield, including to Land's End.

The holiday was documented in photographs taken by Lee Miller that capture a spirit of determined enjoyment, an almost defiant sense of fun and love of life, set against the backdrop of a country already preparing for war and very conscious of the conflict already in progress in Spain. (Roland, a supporter of the Republic, had already visited Spain to see what was happening there for himself.) The Second World War would catapult Lee's career to new heights – her bold images of Germany in the wake of defeat, and of the newly liberated concentration camps at Buchenwald and Dachau, would become her most powerful work. Portraits of her in Hitler's Munich apartment, taken by her friend David E. Scherman, show her washing off the dirt of Dachau in the dead dictator's own bathtub.

But all of that still lay ahead. For now, in Cornwall, Lee's photos showed that she had more than made the transition from her early career as a model and was becoming a versatile and talented photographer. Just as she would later be in Germany, she was present on both sides of the lens: in one Lambe Creek image she leans, bare-breasted, out of an upstairs window. She has composed the shot and Roland has pressed the shutter. Lee's hair is lit up, halo-like, by the sun behind her, and sheets of fabric fluttering in the breeze reinforce the sense that we are glimpsing through the curtains into another world.

And another world it truly was for Leonora: a world where surrealist values ruled, where the absurd brushed up against irony and sexuality, where experimentation was celebrated. Another of Lee's compositions – perhaps the most famous image of the Cornwall trip – shows four of the women seemingly dozing, teacups in hand. Lee is on Ady's knee, her head resting on her hand; Ady's arm is curled up next to her face as though she is lying in bed. Nusch's head falls to one side and Leonora is on the floor beside her, her hand resting on Nusch's

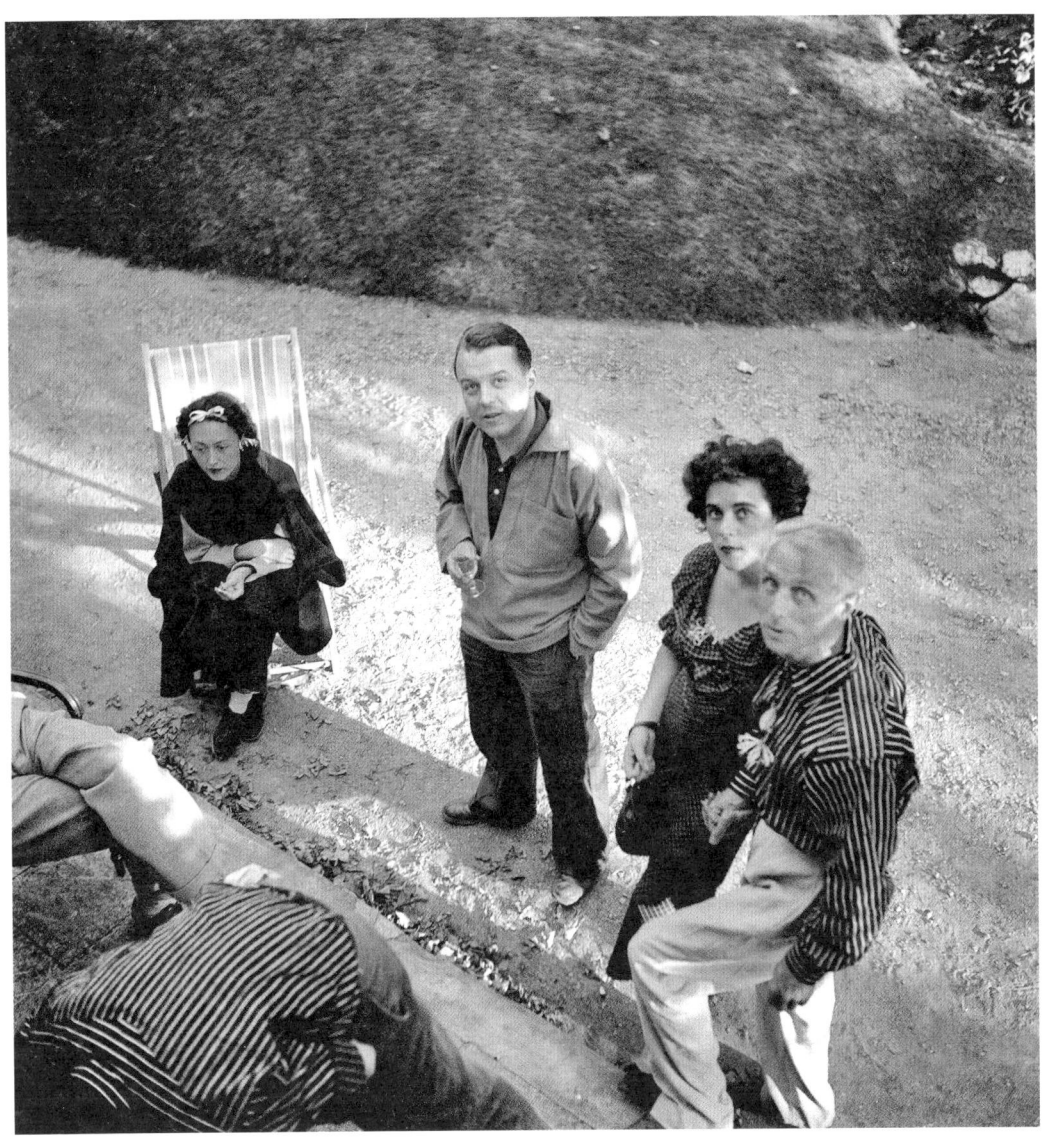

Nusch Éluard, E. L. T. Mesens, Leonora Carrington and Max Ernst, Lambe Creek, Cornwall.
Photograph by Lee Miller

lap. The muses are asleep. Perhaps they are no longer playing ball, and instead are connecting themselves with another power.

Certainly for Leonora, Lambe Creek was a place where her eyes were opened, not shut. Max had told her about the reality of surrealism, but it was in Cornwall that she truly began to feel it – and feeling, as she told me many times, was always the mechanism by which she made sense of the world. It must have seemed as though the strictures of her old life, against which she had fought for so long, were finally falling away. Here at last was a group of people for whom convention and expectation were unimportant. They were as prepared as she was to tear up the rule book and live by a different credo. In 2006, on my first visit to see her in Mexico, I asked Leonora what surrealism meant to her. 'It's the belief,' she told me, 'that nothing is ordinary; that everything in life is extraordinary. And being old is no more, no less, extraordinary than being young.'[3]

When it came to relationships, too, the surrealists had a different approach from most people, and it was one that made sense to Leonora. As Max, Paul Éluard and Gala had shown while they were together in Paris, the Cornwall group was flexible about reimagining their boundaries. During the holiday Eileen Agar embarked on a passionate affair with Paul, and Nusch Éluard with Joseph Bard. 'I think if love comes your way you should accept it, as I did with Paul Nash and Paul Éluard,' Eileen wrote later.[4] Leonora told me: 'It certainly wasn't about marriage, for us – we weren't concerned with bits of paper, it didn't bother us whether people were married or not.'[5]

'There was a strong hedonistic belief in sexual freedom, based on the idea that sex and love were separate and being in love with a person did not confer ownership of them,' writes Antony Penrose, son of Lee and Roland. The switching of partners, he says, 'occurred quite naturally, as an expression of their sense of freedom and their genuine affection for each other. The seclusion of the house and an instinct for discretion protected this microcosm of Surrealism, and the neighbouring farmers and the regulars in the Heron pub at Malpas probably got nothing more than mild amusement from the visit of these strange foreign people.'[6]

Various objects that appear in Lee's photographs seem to serve as talismans of the holiday. One recurring item is a model of a naked woman, hands clasped above her head: this was a ship's figurehead discovered by Roland in Falmouth and brought back to Lambe Creek to be painted and photographed. In one image Lee is seen holding it, her hands on the model's breasts. Like the mannequins so beloved of the surrealists, the figure represents both a flight of fantasy and the object-ification of the female body. As in the 'sleeping women' photograph, Lee is heralding a shift in the traditional relationship of male artist and female muse. The role of women was changing, and the women at Lambe Creek recognized that. Rather than objects of the male gaze, they were becoming creators of their own art, and both Lee and Leonora would be in the vanguard of this transformation.

Another object that recurs is a glass gun. In one photograph Lee is holding it to her head in the foreground, while behind her a sunbath-ing Leonora is locked in a passionate embrace with Max. Their love affair is the focus for another image that shows Max's hands spread across Leonora's bare breasts; he gazes dreamily into the distance while she smokes a cigarette, eyes firmly shut. One arm rests on the window ledge behind her, the other is balanced on her leg. Leonora owns the scene: she is confident and in control, and she, Max and Lee are all completely aware of where the power lies.

The group sent postcards to their friends: one to Gala, by now liv-ing with Dalí, and another to Monsieur Pablo Picasso, Rue des Grands Augustine, Paris VI. It was, they reported to Gala, 'very healthy in this wonderful country, but not too hot'.[7]

Afterwards, Paul Éluard wrote a poem about the holiday entitled 'The Last Letter to Roland Penrose'. It seems to reference the ship's figurehead that came to symbolize so much:

I have put my hand in the nudity of the waves
Outside my boat and inside my boat
To operate the double union
Of the intimate world and the public world
In the nets of adventure
Of disordered life
I am very amiable
And the very obstinate guardian of weightless fire
The reflection of a body naked and hard calms the flood tide.[8]

'We were all invited to Cornwall, and we had a wonderful time there,' Leonora remembered many years later.[9] The trip had fuelled her journey, and its destination was now within her reach.

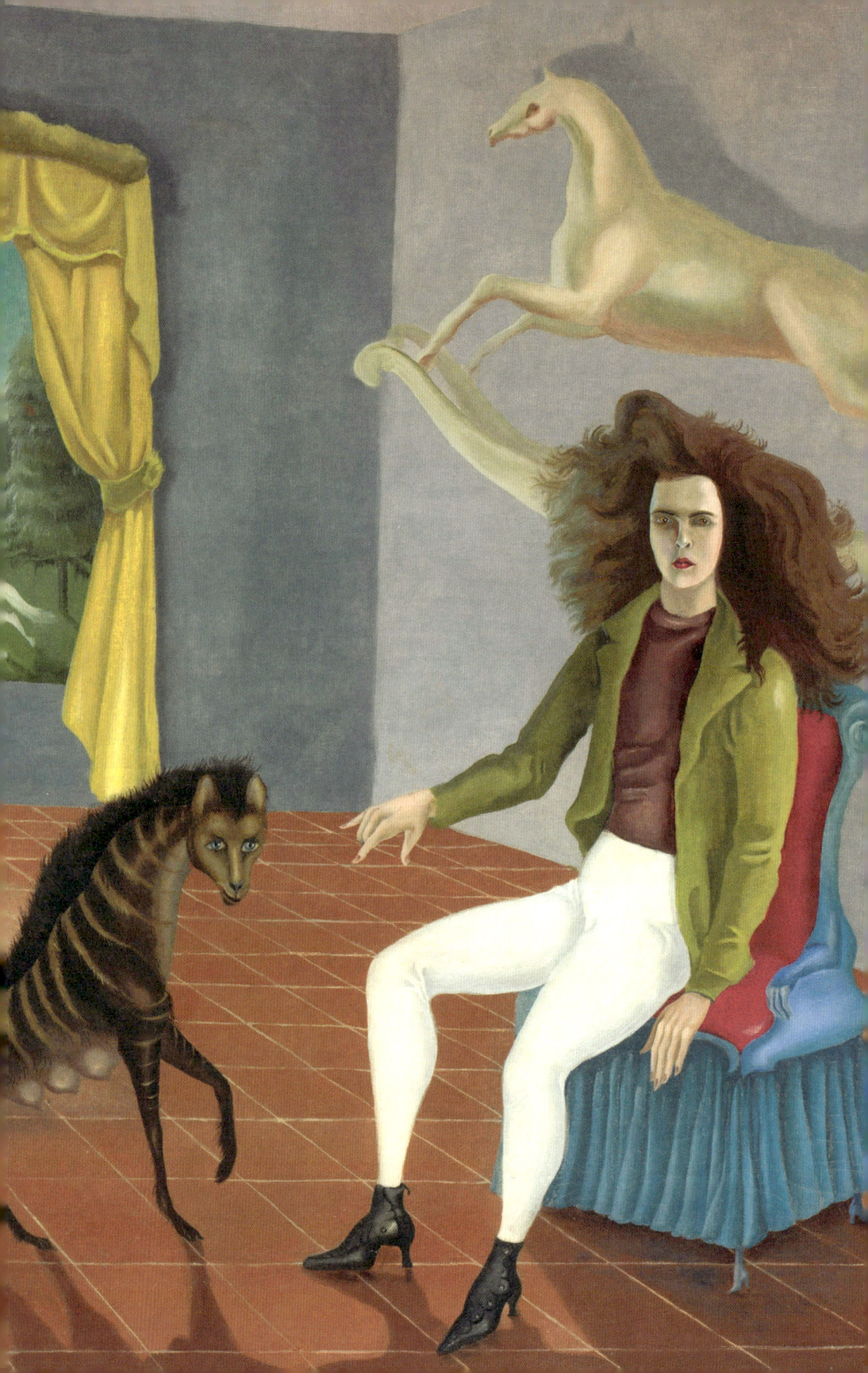

5
Paris
1937–1938

'I moved to Paris.'[1] This was Leonora's typically understated recollection, many years later, of her relocation across the Channel in the autumn of 1937. She did indeed move to Paris, but in doing so she was effectively saying a final goodbye to her family, her country and many of her friends, not to mention a life of immense privilege.

Meeting Max had opened a door into a new world; their summer in Cornwall had allowed her to experience that world; and now, for the first time, she had a focus. Not for her the country house parties and hunt balls of the Lancashire gentry, nor the dizzy, see-and-be-seen London society landscape. What Leonora had longed for was a way of living that felt congruent to her, a way of being where she could learn what she needed to know, and where she would have the psychological and physical space to practise the art that was in her soul.

Some commentators and art historians have described Leonora's flight as an elopement, but that seems to imply she was leaving for love, and there was a lot more in the mix. Although she did love Max – who, as a father figure, could hardly have been more different from her actual father, making him all the more appealing – she also loved the idea of what life with him could offer. 'I always did my running away alone,' she told me; but running away alone is much easier when you are heading towards someone, or something.

Max left for France soon after their return to London from Cornwall. Before Leonora could follow, there was a conversation she needed to have with her parents. She went to see them to tell them she was leaving, that she was going to live in Paris to become an

Self-Portrait/Inn of the Dawn Horse, detail, *c.* 1937–38

artist. Her father observed that artists lived in garrets, and she would not be happy in a garret. Leonora told him she was going anyway. Harold replied that in that case, she need not return. He was speaking in anger, in the heat of the moment, but sometimes angry words shape the future.

Although Leonora knew Paris well, she was about to experience it in a completely new way. She and Max rented an apartment on the Rue Jacob, a short walk from the cafés of Saint-Germain-des-Prés, where the surrealists gathered. Max had lived in the area since leaving his native Cologne in the early 1920s, when André Breton and the other Paris surrealists were working on their first manifesto, published in 1924. He was at the heart of a movement that now reads like a roll call of the great men of 20th-century art. There was Pablo Picasso – 'He looked like a Spanish shopkeeper,' Leonora remembered[2] – and also, 'he thought all women were in love with him'. When I asked her whether *she* had been in love with him, she said absolutely not – but she had liked his art. There was Salvador Dalí, who she told me 'certainly wasn't extraordinary then – he looked like everyone else. It was only when he went to America that he started looking extraordinary.' Dalí liked Leonora, calling her 'a most important woman artist'. Joan Miró was another regular at their gatherings. 'He gave me some money one day and told me to get him some cigarettes. I gave it back and said if he wanted cigarettes, he could bloody well get them himself,' she recalled. 'I wasn't daunted by any of them.'[3]

This was a movement that, for all its revolutionary talk, was dominated by a patriarchal viewpoint, and by men – most of them a great deal older than Leonora, who was still just twenty. Did she, I asked, feel nurtured by the established members of the group? 'No, not really. They were doing their own thing. With Max I did a bit, yes. But he was doing his own thing as well. They weren't that interested in me.'[4] There were a few, some women on the scene, and their presence was critical. Meret Oppenheim, who had created her *Object (Breakfast in Fur)* the previous year, was an important influence. The Argentine-Italian Leonor Fini, an ex-lover of Max's who was ten years older than Leonora, would be another significant figure in her life over the next few years. Whitney Chadwick writes that after the end of Leonor and Max's affair the two 'had settled into a close and affectionate friendship' and when Leonora arrived in Paris, this expanded to include her. She was dazzled by the older woman's intelligence and independence, and Leonor made clear her respect for Leonora, whom she regarded

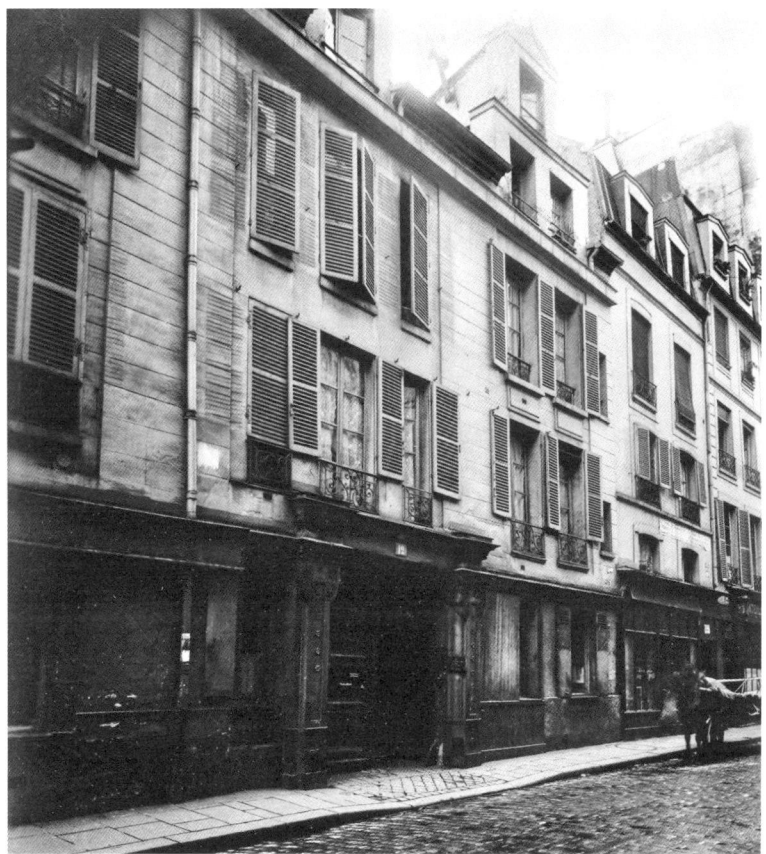

Rue Jacob 12, *c.* 1910. Photograph by Eugène Atget

as not truly surrealist but certainly a revolutionary. Chadwick believes Leonora had never met a woman as independent, confident and passionate as Leonor, and that Leonor saw something of herself in her young friend's freshness and beauty – as well as in the black sense of humour that led Breton to describe Leonora as 'superb in her refusals, with a boundless, human authenticity'.[5]

Breton held court in the Café Deux Magots, while Leonora and Max spent more time at the Café de Flore next door. Together, these two venues were the beating heart of the Paris surrealist group. Everyone gathered there to discuss the things that mattered, from Picasso's latest painting to the rise of Hitler, the growing inevitability of war in Europe, how art could and should be changed, what they needed to do to challenge the status quo, and how to make a splash in the world of ideas and decision-making. Unlike many art movements, surrealism was never defined by a particular visual style: ideas, rather than form or artistic technique, were its bedrock. It had its own manifestos, but Leonora told me she was never interested in these. 'I didn't read the surrealist manifesto. I think a lot of other people [in the group] did, but I didn't. Why should I read it? I didn't want anyone else to tell me what to do or what to think. I've never had anyone tell me what to do or what to think.'[6]

This focus on ideas inevitably led to frequent arguments between members of the group. Many decades later, in Mexico City, Leonora still remembered the constant rows and fallings-out, and she was pleased to have escaped them through the choices she made down the line. One reason why she and Max had veered away from the Deux Magots and towards the Flore was that Max and Breton, around this time, weren't getting along, and each preferred to have his own space.

But the volatile relationship with Breton wasn't the only problem in their lives. Even more significant was the presence in Paris of Max's wife, Marie-Berthe, who was understandably far from happy at her husband's return from London with a new paramour. Their situation is reflected in Leonora's short story 'Little Francis', written around this time, although the people involved are lightly disguised. A young boy called Francis (Leonora) loves his uncle Ubriaco (Max); but he is usurping Ubriaco's daughter, Amelia (Marie-Berthe), who wants her father to herself. In a remarkably honest parallel to the real situation, the narrative makes it clear that Amelia has a stronger claim to her father – she is portrayed as highly strung and difficult, but absolutely not unreasonable.

'Little Francis' includes what may have been a real-life incident: Amelia arrives at the flat where Ubriaco and Francis live, and goes out for a walk with her father. On their return, she announces that she and Ubriaco will be leaving Paris the following day and that Francis should go straight back to England. Francis retorts, tongue in cheek, that he will only leave if Ubriaco tells him to, and goes on to say that Ubriaco is bored with Amelia. On another occasion, as Leonora recalled many years later in Mexico, Marie-Berthe appeared at the Café de Flore and caused a scene involving thrown cups and saucers: 'she gave me a huge blow in the face in the café, which I returned later'.[7]

It was around this time that Leonora first met the American collector Peggy Guggenheim, who was in Paris trawling for new works. This search took her one day to visit Max, who, she noted, was 'still very good looking in spite of his age'. At his feet 'sat Leonora Carrington, his lady love. I had seen them around Paris and thought how intriguing they appeared together. She was so much younger than Ernst: they looked exactly like Nell and her grandfather in *The Old Curiosity Shop*.'[8]

Peggy wanted to buy a painting by Max, but the one she liked belonged to Leonora and was not for sale. However, she didn't leave empty-handed – another work, Leonora's *The Horses of Lord Candlestick*, took her fancy. This exchange was notable for both buyer and seller: it was the first painting Leonora ever sold, and the first by a female artist ever purchased by Peggy (who would include Leonora in one of the first all-women shows at her New York gallery, Guggenheim Jeune, a few years later). Peggy wrote that the work 'portrayed four horses of four different colours in a tree'; Leonora was 'not very well known but very good and full of imagination in the best Surrealist manner and always painted animals and birds'.[9]

Its title, like *The Meal of Lord Candlestick* (both 1938), uses Leonora's nickname for her family. The latter is a shocking composition featuring an orgiastic feast in which a human baby (is he the Christ child, whose real body Catholics believe is being consumed at mass?) is offered as a dish alongside a roasted bird. The diners are five bourgeois dames who seem to be gesturing and chatting among themselves as though at a perfectly normal dinner party. This is Leonora at her most surreal, and its themes aim at the heart of her family. The genteel ladies are cannibals, and their dark dresses contrast with the colourful array of bizarre foodstuffs on offer. Food would continue to be a theme in Leonora's paintings throughout her career.

But another ongoing theme was horses, and the painting Peggy bought heralded Leonora's identification with these animals, which she had drawn obsessively from a young age and saw as her alter ego. As Whitney Chadwick notes, 'The horse...became for her a metaphor for transcendent vision and a symbolic image of the sexual union which the surrealists believed would resolve the polarities of male and female into an androgynous creative whole.' Chadwick believes Leonora was refocusing the lens: while male surrealists had seen women as 'the mediating link between men and the Marvellous', here she explored the powerful role of nature in the female artist's creativity.[10]

In an interview many years later, Leonora recalled attempting to visit Germany with Max during this period. From Paris they went first to Alsace, where they saw the German Renaissance artist Matthias Grünewald's altarpiece exhibited in the Musée Unterlinden in Colmar. Their plan, apparently, was to go on from there to Max's home city of

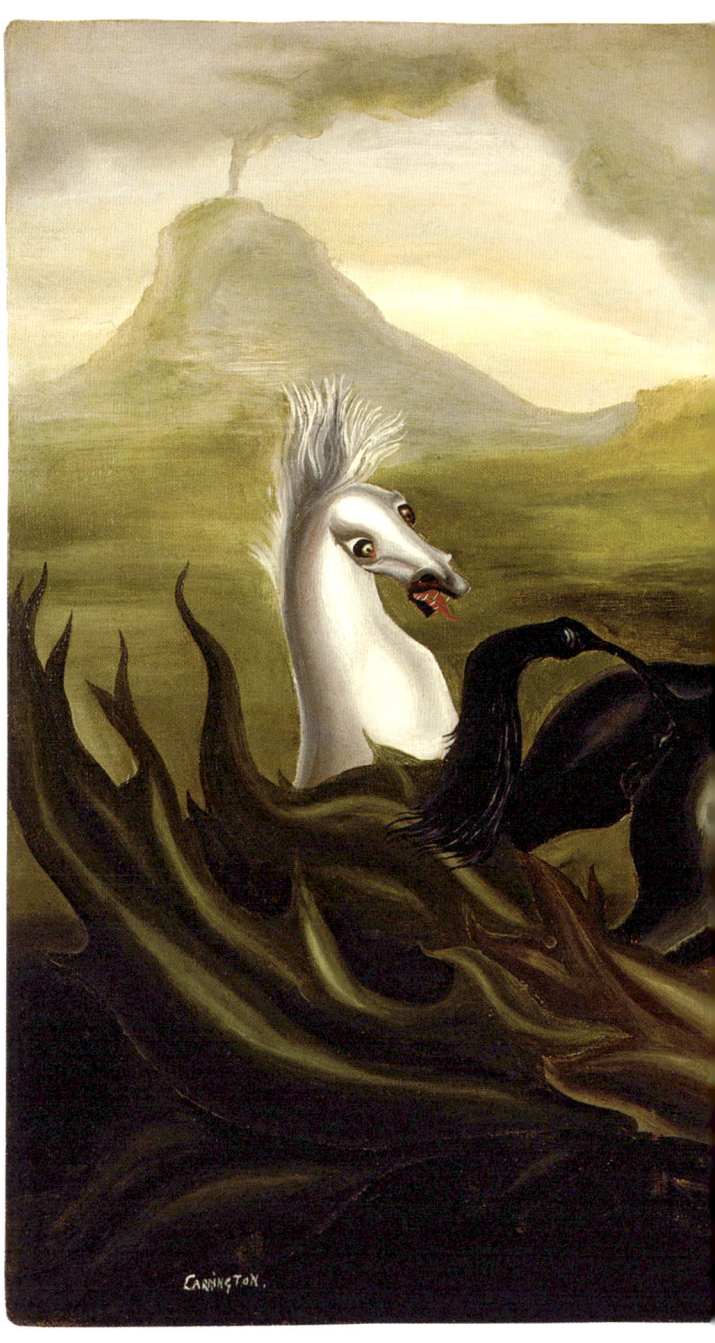

The Horses of Lord Candlestick,
1938

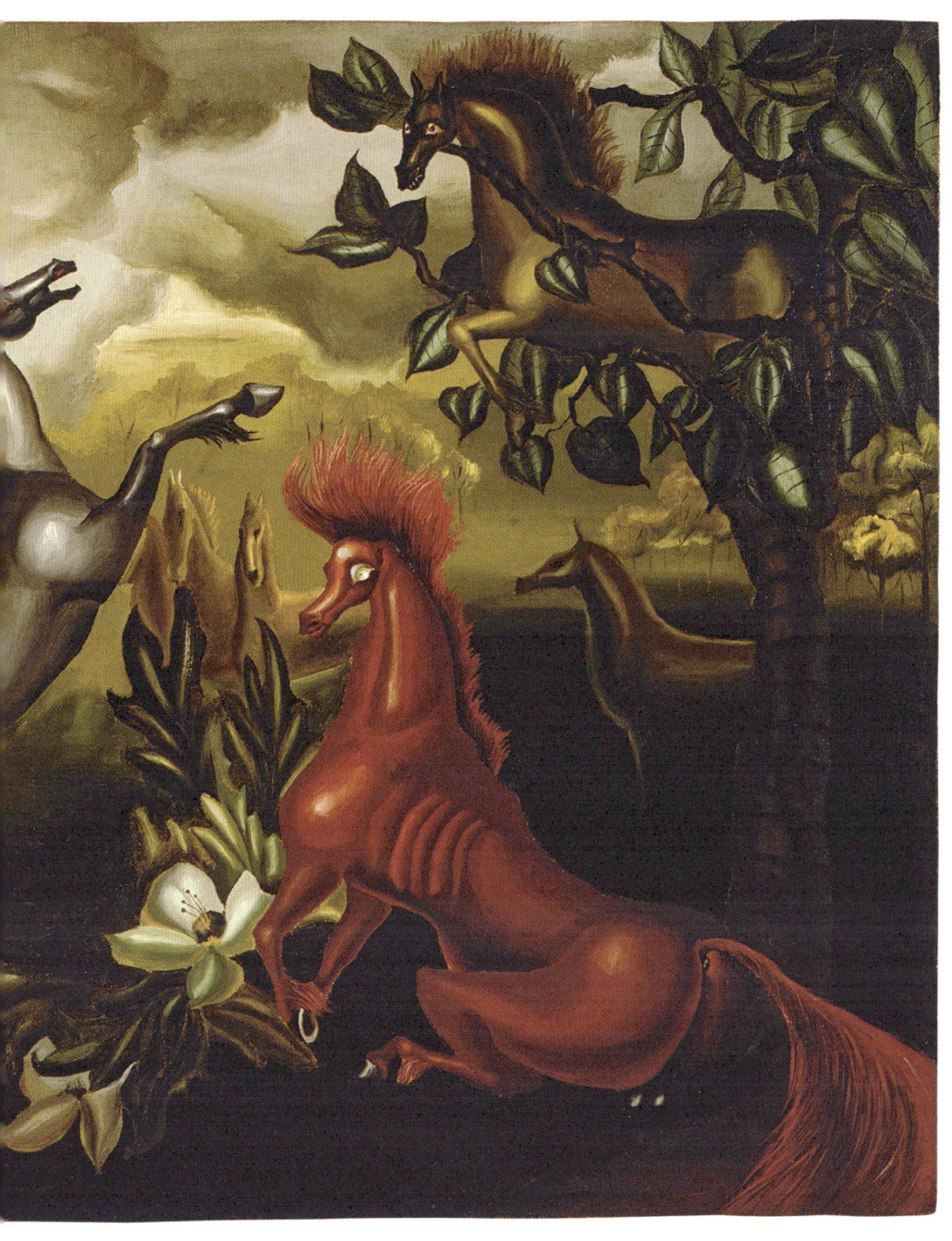

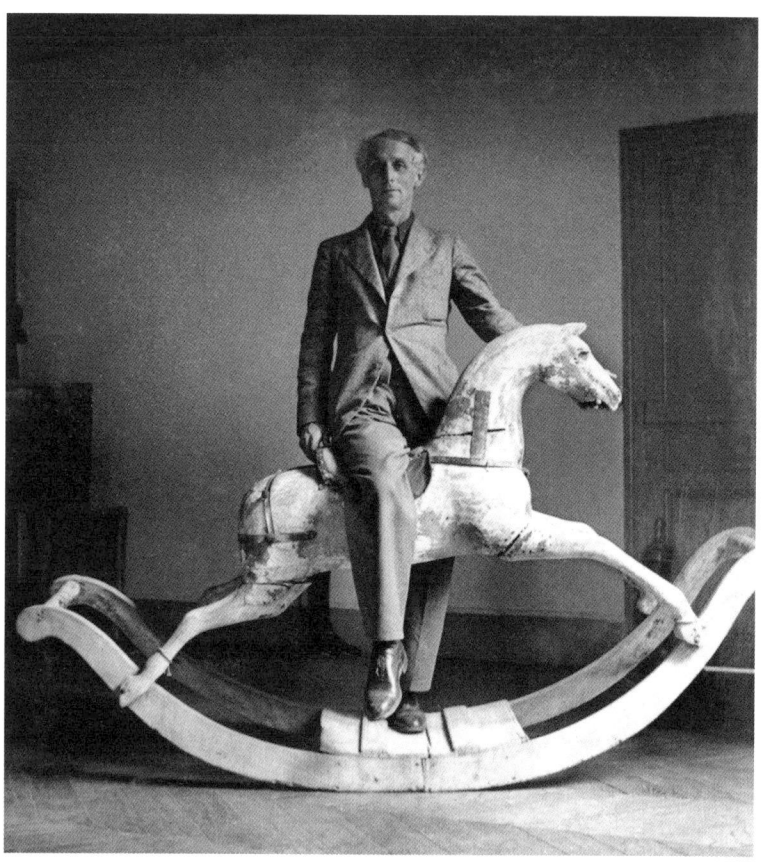

Max Ernst on a rocking horse, Paris, 1938

Cologne; but when they crossed the Rhine, they saw a sign with red letters that read *Ein Volk, ein Reich, ein Führer* – one people, one order, one leader. 'We didn't want to go on,' said Leonora. 'Before staying in Paris, I didn't know social or racial discrimination. It was Max who spoke to me with clarity about the goals of Nazi antisemitism and of Hitler's evil.' She had never, she said, known prejudice growing up: 'My parents had friends of all religions and that seemed perfectly natural.' Her father, she said, was 'a just man' who had actively opposed the British fascist leader Oswald Mosley.[11]

That positive characterization of Harold is fascinating, given that he has generally been presented as Leonora's nemesis and the central reason for her seismic decision to leave both her family and her country. It hints at the truth of the matter, which is that the

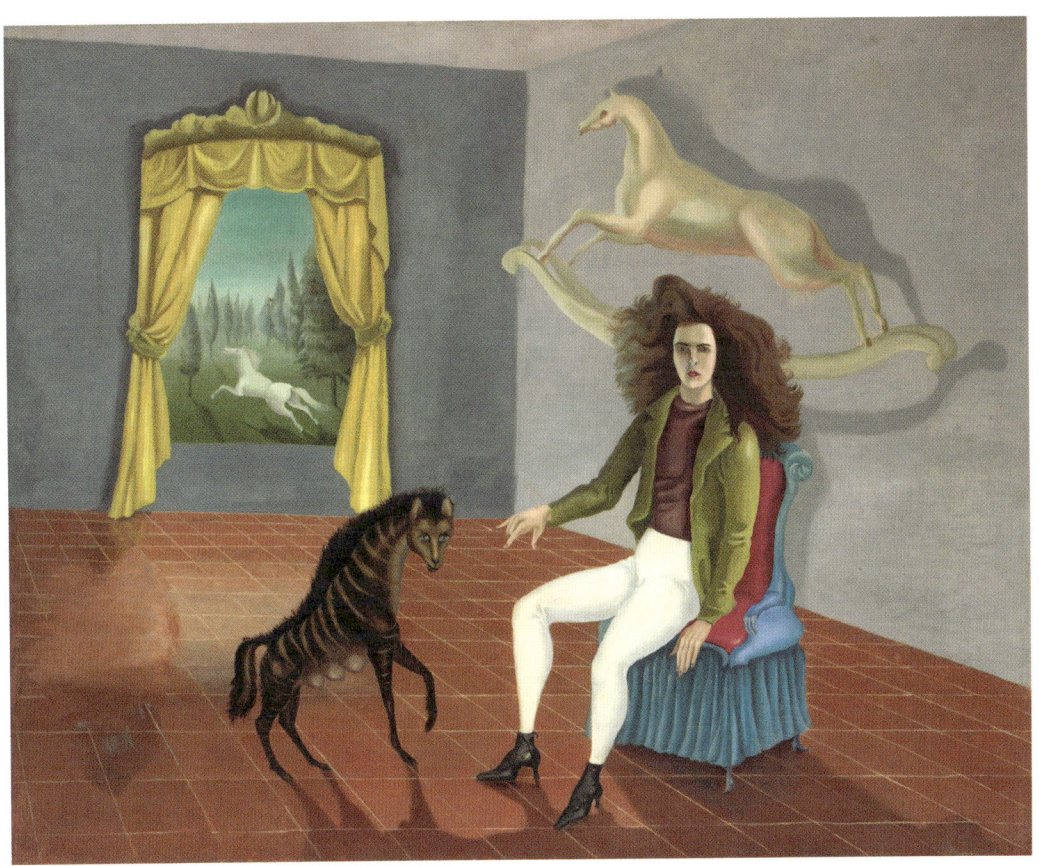

Self-Portrait/Inn of the Dawn Horse, c. 1937–38

relationship between father and daughter was more complicated and more nuanced than some art historians have suggested. Later, there would be further evidence that, however difficult things had been between them, Leonora retained a respect and even an affection for her father. Family relationships, as she would have been the first to admit, are far from linear or straightforward.

Leonora seems to have bought a rocking horse for the Paris apartment, rather like the white one from the Crookhey nursery that some members of our family remember from the Hazelwood days. Max sits astride it in a 1938 photograph and it is centre stage in Leonora's self-portrait, alternatively titled *Inn of the Dawn Horse* (*c*. 1937–38), which she began in Paris and continued to work on when the couple moved south. There are two horses in the painting. The rigid, wooden version behind Leonora's head is usually taken to represent her life before she escaped, first to Cornwall and then to France. The other horse is a real one, running free outside the window. Leonora herself sits in the centre of the room, reaching out to a hyena (the same animal that features in her story 'The Debutante'). She wears white jodhpurs that match the horses, a brown top that matches the floor tiles, and a moss-green jacket that matches the trees and grass around the galloping horse. She cuts an androgynous figure, deliberately desexualized: this isn't about how beautiful or fascinating the surrealists think she is. It is about her self-determination, her story, her life choices.

Leonora was in Paris for the 1938 International Exhibition of Surrealism, which opened on 17 January at the Galerie des Beaux-Arts, organized by Breton, Duchamp and Éluard with the help of Max, Dalí and Man Ray. The show was designed to discombobulate its visitors, beginning with its launch. The invitations said that it would open at ten p.m., but in the event the gallery stayed locked until midnight, leaving a confused crowd milling around on the Rue du Faubourg Saint-Honoré.

When they were eventually admitted, the first thing visitors saw was a Fiat taxi parked in the forecourt, inside which rain was pouring down on two mannequin occupants. The one in the front seat wore a peaked hat and dark glasses and was holding the steering wheel; the other, female, reclined in the back, covered in slimy trails left by a procession of live snails. Next came an avenue of variously costumed mannequins, each designed by a different artist, lined up like the prostitutes on the Rue Saint-Denis. Max's surely referenced his relationship with Leonora: it featured a female figure in a black dress with a veiled face, a white-haired man lying prostrate at her feet.

Adding to the atmosphere, visitors were told the lights had failed and issued with torches; and in the central gallery, carpeted with moss and dead leaves, 1,200 coal bags hung threateningly from the ceiling. The entire show 'was much more than a simple juxtaposition of works of art. [It] was "staged" in such a way as to forge relationships between the works themselves, and between the art and the spectators, thereby creating added levels of meaning.'[12] For Leonora, this was a first taste of being included in a major exhibition, her work displayed alongside not only Max's but that of Duchamp, Dalí, Oppenheim, the Czech painter Toyen and the Spanish artist Remedios Varo. Later, Varo would become one of Leonora's close friends, but for now she was merely a passing acquaintance.

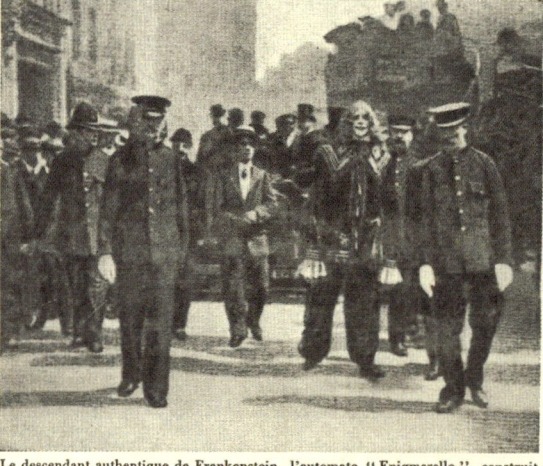

INVITATION
pour le
17 Janvier 1938
TENUE DE SOIRÉE

EXPOSITION INTERNATIONALE
DU
SURRÉALISME

A 22 heures
signal d'ouverture
par André BRETON

APPARITIONS
D'ÊTRES-OBJETS

L'HYSTÉRIE

LE TRÈFLE
INCARNAT

L'ACTE MANQUÉ

PAR

Hélène
VANEL

COQS ATTACHÉS

CLIPS
FLUORESCENTS

DESCENTE
DE LIT
EN FLANCS D'
HYDROPHILES

LES
PLUS BELLES
RUES DE PARIS

TAXI PLUVIEUX

CIEL DE
ROUSSETTES

Le descendant authentique de Frankenstein, l'automate " Enigmarelle ", construit
en 1900 par l'ingénieur américain Ireland, traversera, à minuit et demi, en fausse
chair et en faux os, la salle de l'Exposition Surréaliste.

GALERIE BEAUX-ARTS, 140, RUE DU FAUBOURG SAINT-HONORÉ — PARIS

Invite advertising the International Exhibition of Surrealism, Paris, 1938

From the beginning, Leonora's strongest motivation had been a longing to communicate her own interior reality – her experience of the different worlds jostling for space within her psyche – to something outside of herself. And apart from that desire to communicate, the experiences themselves demanded detachment from her in some way. That is what she meant when she told me that for her, art was not a choice; it was a need, which manifested itself not only in painting, drawing and works of visual art but in her writing.[13] From childhood, as her adolescent notebooks show, Leonora had been using words as well as images to explore the world inside herself. Now, in Paris, she became for the first time a published author, with her short story 'The House of Fear'.

This story, like the painting she had sold to Peggy Guggenheim, is populated with horses. All the horses in the world, the narrator says at one point, are at the party she is attending, in a castle whose stones

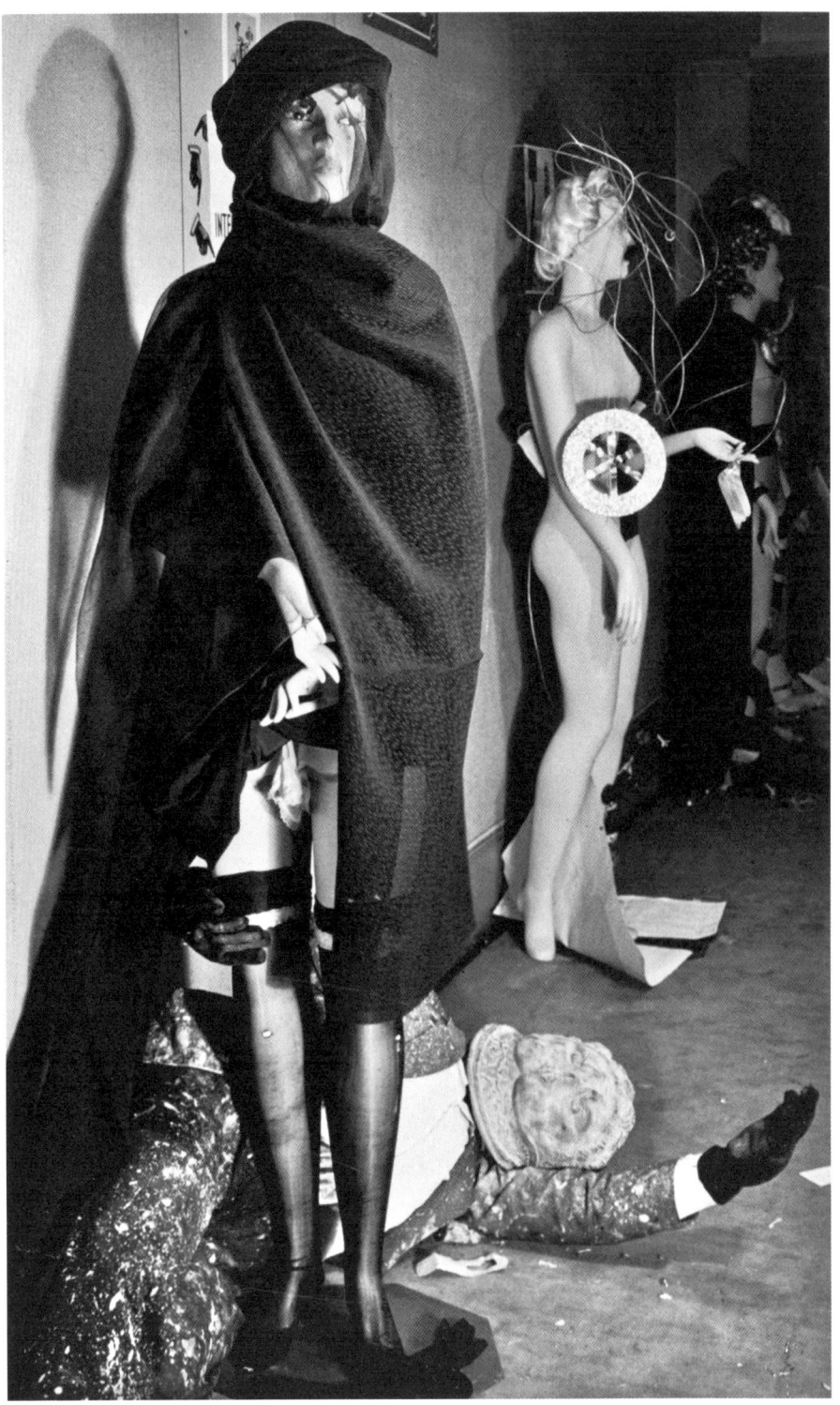

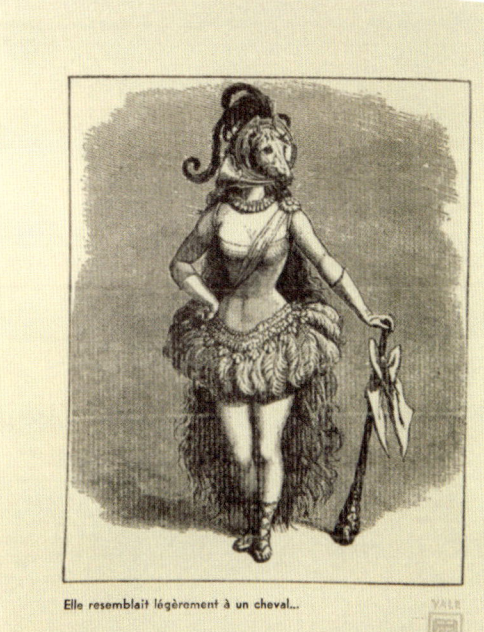

PREFACE
OU
LOPLOP PRESENTE LA MARIEE DU VENT

Couchés sur le seuil de la maison unique, mais de dimensions impo-
santes, d'une ville construite en pierre de tonnerre, deux rossignols
se tiennent étroitement enlacés. Le silence du soleil préside à leurs
ébats. Le soleil se défait de sa jupe noire et de son corsage blanc.
On ne le voit plus. La nuit tombe d'un coup avec fracas.
Voyez cet homme : dans l'eau jusqu'aux genoux, il se tient fière-
ment debout. De violentes caresses ont laissé leurs traces lumineuses
sur son superbe corps nacré. Que diable fait cet homme, au regard
turquoise, aux lèvres empourprées de désirs généreux? Cet homme
égaie le paysage.
Que diable fait ce nuage blanc ? Ce nuage blanc s'échappe en
sifflant d'un panier renversé. Il anime la nature.
D'où sortent ces deux étranges personnes qui s'avancent lentement
dans la rue, suivies d'un millier de nains ? Est-ce l'homme qu'on
appelle Loplop, le supérieur des oiseaux, à cause de son caractère
doux et féroce ? Sur son énorme chapeau blanc il a arrêté dans son
vol un extraordinaire oiseau au plumage émeraude, au bec crochu,
à l'œil dur. Il n'a pas peur. Il sort de la maison de la peur. Et la
femme, dont le haut du bras est cerclé d'un mince filet de sang, ne
serait donc autre que la Mariée du Vent?

Elle resemblait légèrement à un cheval...

Interior spread from *La maison de la peur* ('The House of Fear'), with Max Ernst illustration, 1938

hold the cold of winter. The mistress of the house is Fear, and Fear, in her dressing gown of live bats, has devised a complicated dance routine that the horses must attempt to follow 'while thinking of your own fate and weeping for those who have gone before you'. Upon hearing these instructions, 'the horses began to beat the floor with their hooves as if they wanted to descend to the depths of the earth'. As an allegory of patriarchy it could hardly be bettered.

'The House of Fear' was published in 1938 with a preface by Max – a preface that exposes the deeply patronizing attitude of this established artist, in his late forties, towards his partner, an emerging artist barely into her twenties. The story is Leonora's but the first character Max introduces is himself ('behold this man...he stands proudly upright'). The man has no fear; he has left the house of fear behind. With him is a woman, 'none other than the Bride of the Wind', who

Max Ernst and Joan Miró mannequins at the International Exhibition of Surrealism, Paris, 1938. Photograph by Raoul Ubac

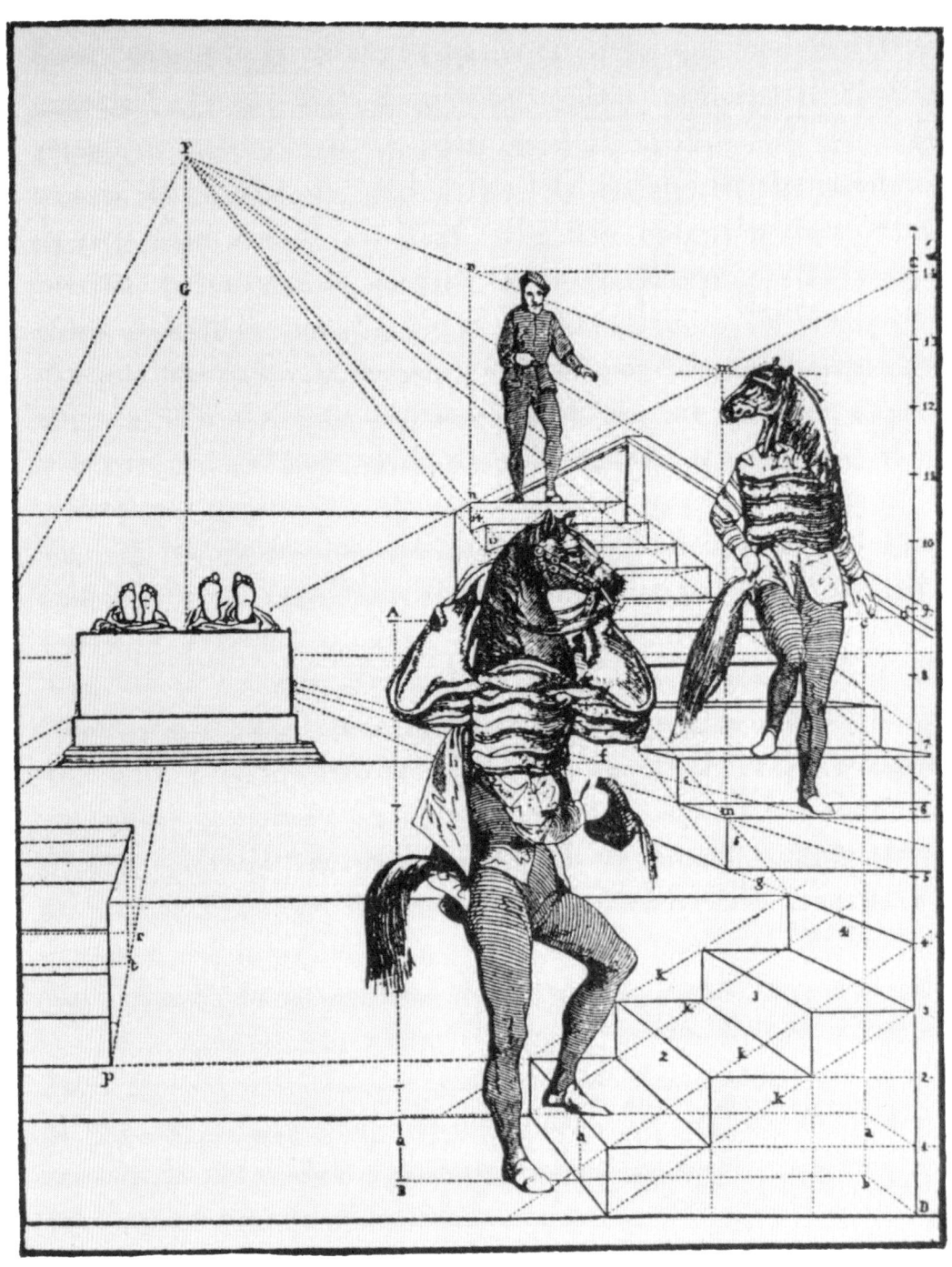

Max Ernst illustration from *La maison de la peur* ('The House of Fear'), 1938

is acknowledged by the horses that stand in the windows of all the houses in the street along which they are walking. She 'has read nothing, but drunk everything'. She cannot read, and yet she has written 'The House of Fear', 'truthful and pure'.

The debt Leonora the artist owes to Max Ernst has been much discussed, especially since the 1980s, when the women of surrealism were brought to centre stage by Chadwick and other feminist art historians. Some have expressed discomfort about his role in Leonora's development, but she herself was quite open about it. She often acknowledged that their relationship had opened up her path to a new future. But she also made it very clear that when it came to her work, she had found everything she wrote and painted within herself: 'It is obvious that I did not write my books under the influence of Max. It is obvious, I expressed in them my own way of thinking. I do not understand why people want to think that I was a little girl under Ernst's spell. It is true, I learned much from him, I liberated myself and I became free, but I painted and wrote since I was five years old, surely horrible things, but finally I was born with my vocation and my works were only mine.'[14]

As in all truly creative relationships, the connection between Leonora and Max was a two-way street. There is plenty of evidence of her influence on his work as well as vice versa, and this dynamic would become increasingly evident as their affair played out.

For now, though, they were about to make a move. Paris was fascinating in so many ways, but it had its problems. First and foremost, the presence in the city of Marie-Berthe, which wasn't a happy arrangement given that her husband and his new lover were living together openly, down the road. Then there were the issues between Max and the surrealists. Jimmy Ernst recalled that his father 'was tired, he told, that minor squabbles within the group were constantly being blown up into major confrontations with their conscience, André Breton'. There was also disagreement over Russia's leadership, with Paul Éluard far less enthusiastic about Trotsky than was Breton. 'All I want to do,' Max told Jimmy, 'is to leave Paris for a long time and live with Leonora in the Ardèche…and to love her…if only the world will allow it.'[15]

For a while, it would. The next – and most fulfilling – chapter of the relationship between Leonora and Max was about to begin.

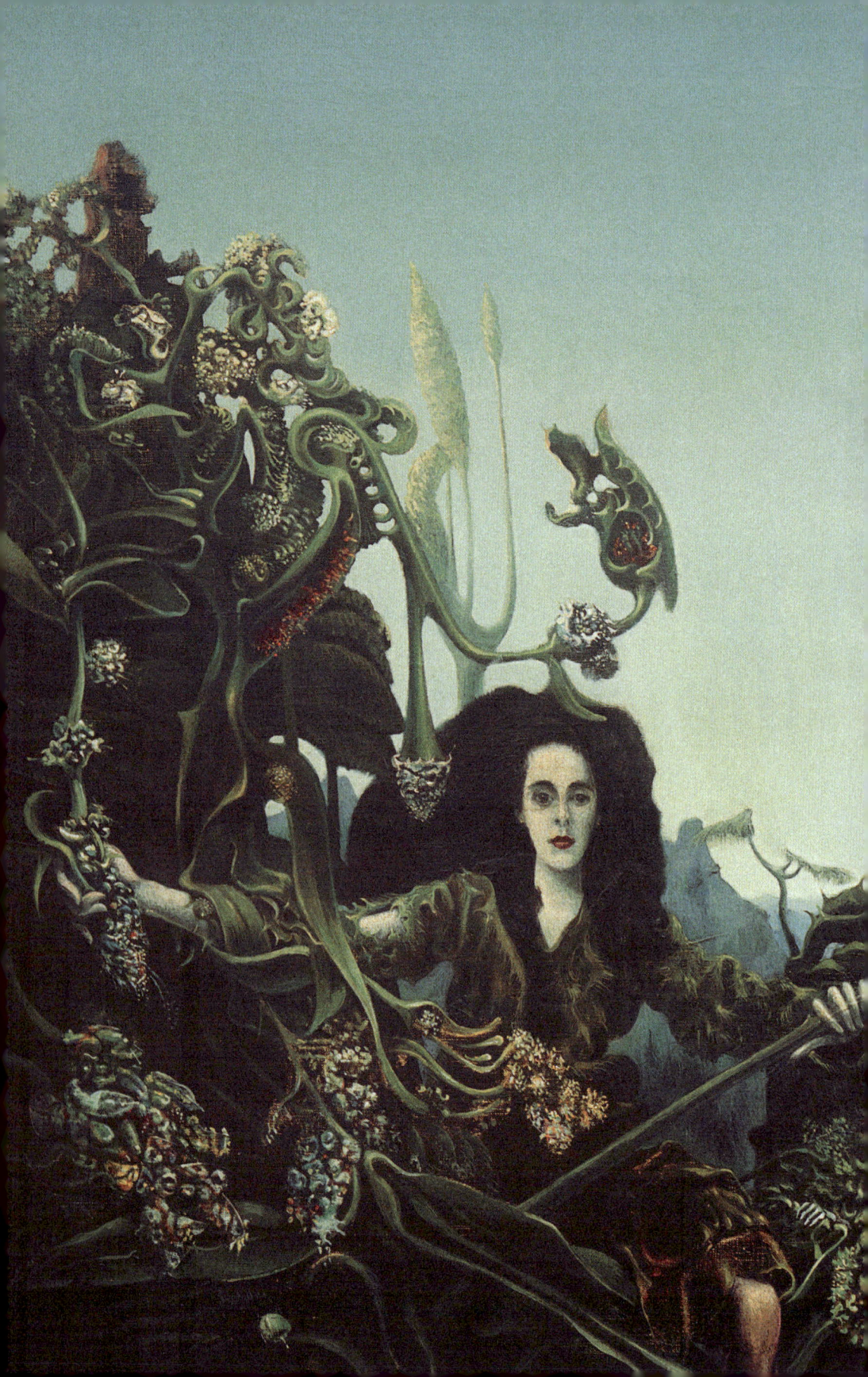

6
Saint-Martin-d'Ardèche
1938–1940

The journey south was punctuated with efforts by Max to improve Leonora's French. He got her to sing the verbs 'to be' and 'to have' to the tunes of 'Rule, Britannia' and 'Onward, Christian Soldiers'. In the evenings, he read her poems by Jean Arp and the novels of Rabelais.

Leonora's story 'Little Francis' again brings to life some of her impressions of this time. Through the characters of Francis and Ubriaco (a drunk, which is what the word means in Italian), she describes her trip with Max: 'the weather became slowly warmer, and one evening in a mounting thunderstorm they came upon the South: announced by an agitated chorus of crickets trilling and chirping, the air was alive with noise, yet it did not disturb the heavy silence of the approaching night. This is me, I must be careful, thought Francis. The next day they went over the hills and down into a plain and rode all through the day, coming up on a river with a white stony shore. Francis had never seen such water, so brilliant and deep and green.'[1]

Saint-Martin-d'Ardèche, the village to which they travelled, was at that time the end of the road. Beyond it, limestone cliffs cut into the landscape, huge and dramatic. Now, as I write, it's morning in that same village, which is named after a 4th-century bishop of Tours who later became patron saint of the Third Republic. A bird perches comfortably on the crozier of the stone sculpture commemorating him in the main square.

I'm waiting for the church bells to strike seven. There's a hint of chill in the air, but this will be the only cool time of this late May day,

Max Ernst, *Leonora in the Morning Light*, detail, 1940

and the village is already awake and making the most of it. Earlier I passed the boulangerie and saw the baker loading his oven, and caught the scent of deliciously cooking bread. Another clock strikes – there seem to be many clocks here, many bells.

I'm standing by the river, in a little pool of sunshine flooding through the trees. The morning light falls straight onto the limestone cliffs on the far side of the water, showing them at their magnificent best, rising towards the pure blue sky. Trees cling to the cliffs and spread out along the top, their deep green foliage a sharp contrast to the chalky white rock. At this hour the cliffs look particularly dramatic, with swirls of shade spilling from rounded inlets: Leonora and Max used to personify these, imagining what they might say if they could speak. The river is almost still, only the faintest hint of a ripple, so the entire panoply is reflected in its surface, a double palette of whites and creams and greys and greens on the land and in the water. Where do the rocks end; where does the river begin?

This is the dawn Leonora knew when she lived here. She listened to the same symphony of birdsong and crickets I am hearing now; she smelled the ancestors of those baguettes. She heard the voices: morning talk, errand news, things to do, deliveries to organize. She was warmed, as I am being warmed, by the strengthening sun. She looked out at these cliffs; she swam, as I have swum, in this gentle water.

When she and Max came here they stayed first at the nearby Hôtel des Touristes. Within a few days, they had bought a tent and moved across the river to camp on the stony white shore directly opposite. Local people warned them that if there was heavy rainfall in the mountains, the water level could swell quickly and wash them away; but it was summer, and they decided to take their chances. That spot is where the morning sun hits and that's when you'd want the sun, if you were under canvas.

I'm imagining Leonora waking up, emerging from her tent, stretching her arms above her head, contemplating the swim she will shortly take. Max is still inside the tent; is he going to make a fire for some coffee, or will she? The day stretches out languorously ahead: a day to talk and to laugh, a day to make love and to sunbathe, a day to wander along the river shore, a day to simply be. How different from Lancashire it all was; but this was the prize, this was what she had won for herself, by simply daring to be different.

It was like the nun had said at school: *Leonora Carrington, desperate to be different*. Leonora had been offended by that; she wasn't desperate to be different at all, she explained to me. She just *was* different. She dared to hope for something better; and not only that, she dared to do something about it. That boldness was what had brought her to this cliff-fringed village with its warm river and its hot sunshine, where she could sit and enjoy and love and dream. Or perhaps she no longer needed to dream, because this *was* the dream. Maybe she knew that, even as she was living it. This was the high point.

The Saint-Martin Leonora describes in 'Little Francis' is very much the Saint-Martin I am standing in today. In her day, it was quieter – the population was around 150, while today it's more like 1,000. But the geography and scenery are now as they were then. A few yards from Leonora and Max's tent, to their left, the river 'rushed white over the stones, broke into a deep green pool, and sailed on smooth and wide. The pool was the deepest point on the river for a hundred yards. A rock like a big mushroom stood in the middle, sinking into the stones beneath.'[2] Max would sit under this rock – the base is just below the water line. I swam out to it myself, in the sunshine.

Camping was marvellous, but when they realized Marie-Berthe was on their tail, the couple left town for a few days. When they returned to Saint-Martin, though, Max's wife was still there. He went to talk to her, and then told Leonora he was going to accompany her back to Paris. At this point Leonora moved back into the Hôtel des Touristes, where she 'was left bereft, angry and afraid'.[3] But while in the story she/Francis ends up being destroyed by her rival, in reality it was Leonora who won the battle for Max. He seems to have oscillated between Paris and Saint-Martin until the early months of 1939; then, when he at last left Marie-Berthe behind, he assured Leonora that the relationship with his wife was properly over.

By that point, Leonora had bought a group of dilapidated farm buildings on a hillside above Saint-Martin. Later in life, Max gave his son Jimmy the impression that it was he who had made this purchase; in fact, it was certainly Leonora. 'I bought a little house in Saint-Martin-d'Ardèche,' she said later. 'I forget where I got the money from. Most likely I conned my mother.'[4]

Over the next few months the couple hired workers from the village to make some alterations to the buildings, especially the main house in which they slept. But more significant was the art they created here, most of which they embedded into the fabric of the building. Remarkably, this work – and in fact the entire house – remains intact, almost exactly as it was when they lived in it more than eighty years ago.

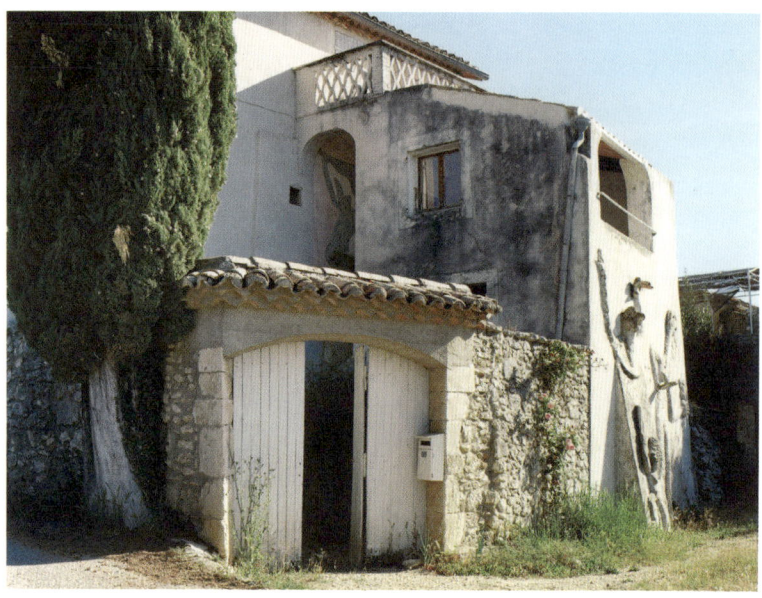

Leonora's home at Saint-Martin-d'Ardèche, exterior.
Photograph by Tim Beddow

Now I walk up the lane Leonora walked up so often, to Les Alliberts, the farmhouse on the hill. I've left the village behind and climbed quite steeply, passing olive groves and fields of long green grass. Approaching the building, it strikes me that if you were to glance at it quickly, you might think it was an ordinary, if characterful, small farmhouse. The bas-reliefs on the exterior wall that mark it out manage to be exceptional and unobtrusive at the same time. They are by Max, and he has woven a character that represents him – 'Loplop' – into an existing buttress. Max/Loplop is, as so often in his work, two figures: a large central figure with arms above his head and a beak-like nose, and a smaller figure with wings, dancing at his feet. Leonora, beside him, is naked, with apple-round breasts. She is bending slightly to one side, looking at a creature perched on her hand. Her other hand is perpendicular to the wall, casting a shadow onto the ground that looks like a bolt from heaven.

The bas-relief is stunning, but it is only the beginning. Inside, the house bursts with the couple's artwork. Along with cooking, drinking wine, entertaining their friends and making love, Leonora and Max found plenty of time to paint and to sculpt, and their canvas was all around them. When you enter through the main door a few metres

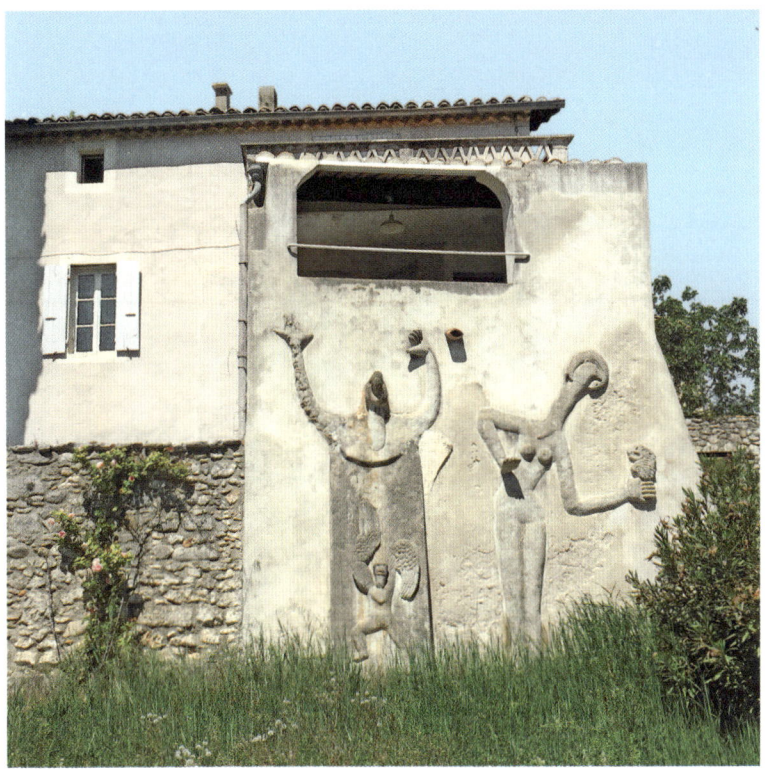

Leonora's home at Saint-Martin-d'Ardèche, exterior

along from the wall sculptures, you find a small courtyard leading to an open staircase, on the wall of which is painted a chalk-white giant with a head that might be a horse or a devil. This creature, reminiscent of a painting by Max from the previous year called *L'Ange du foyer*, seems benign rather than menacing; his arms – or wings – could even be outstretched in welcome. But he is very big, and very present. Just in front of the mural is a horse's head sculpture, also white, its head held quizzically to one side. The white horse, of course, was Leonora's alter ego. Who are you? I wonder as I look at her; and she seems to ask in turn, who are *you*? What brings you to my house? From across the room, three other silent figures watch us, one with its head adorned with the spikes from a pitchfork.

This room is a lantern: the wall facing out across the valley has been cut out to create a glassless window. Even on the hottest summer's day, this was always a cool spot in the house, and it was the best place to look out over the vineyards and lush green fields running down to

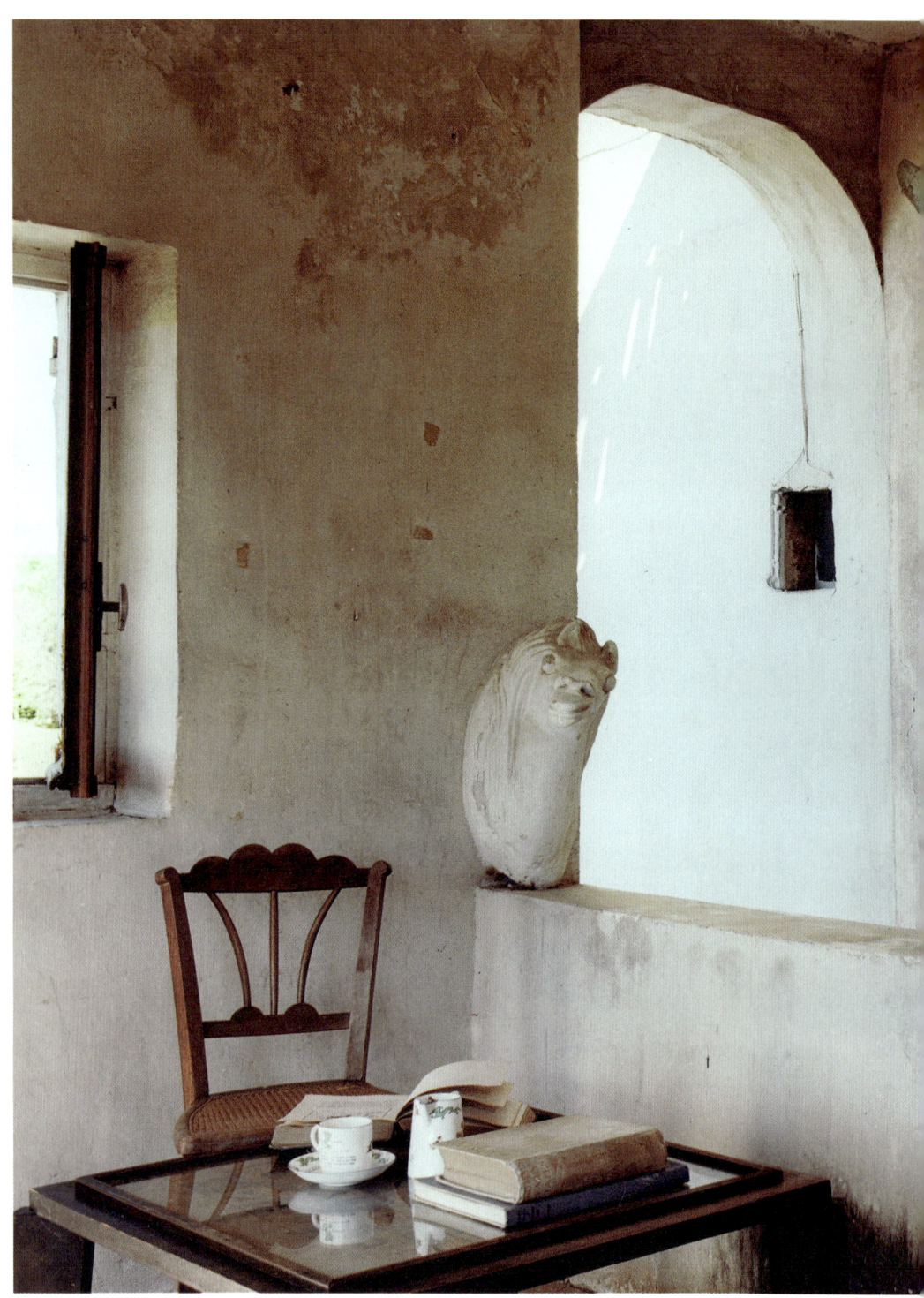

Saint-Martin-d'Ardèche interior, with work by Max Ernst on the wall.
Photograph by Tim Beddow

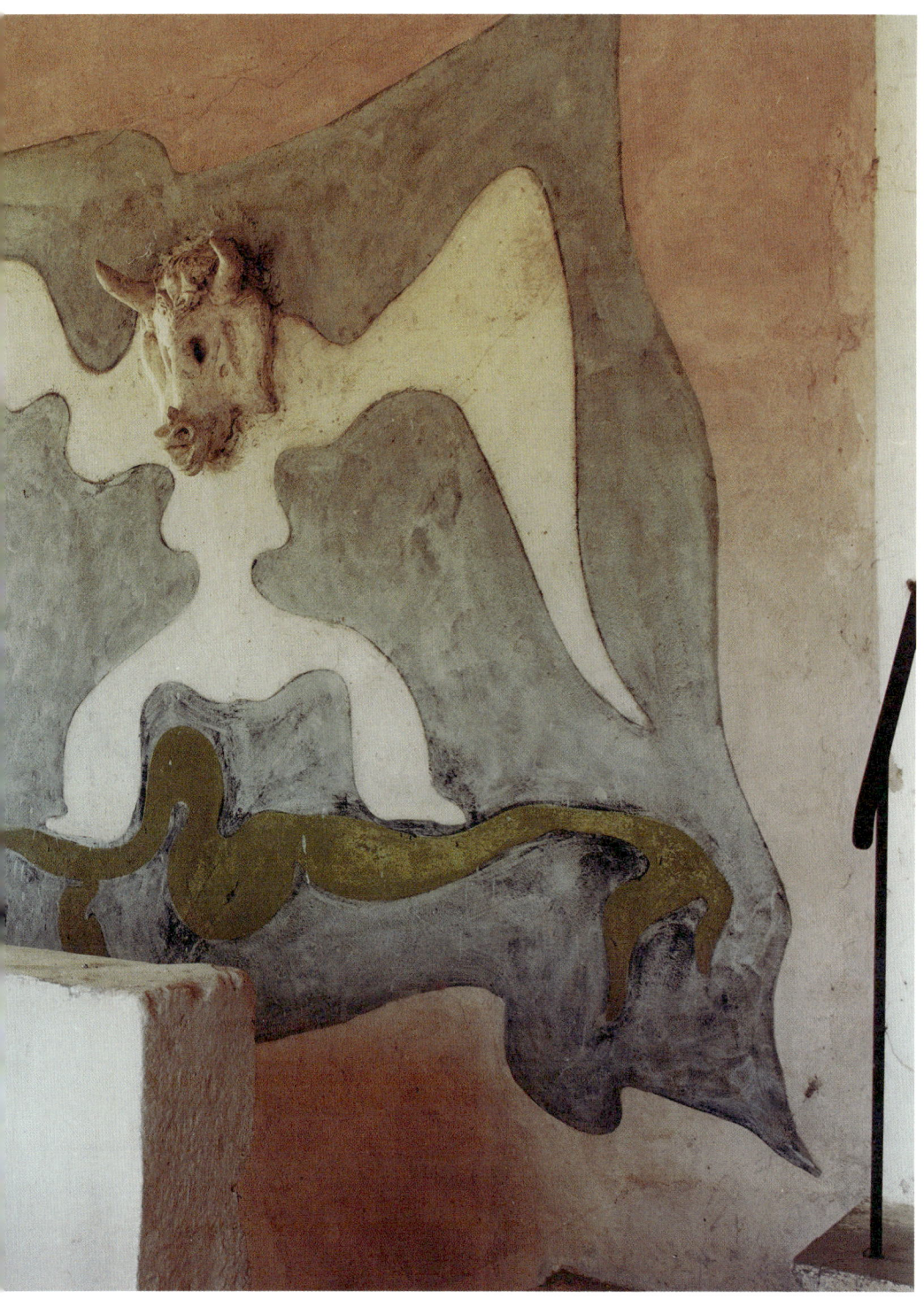

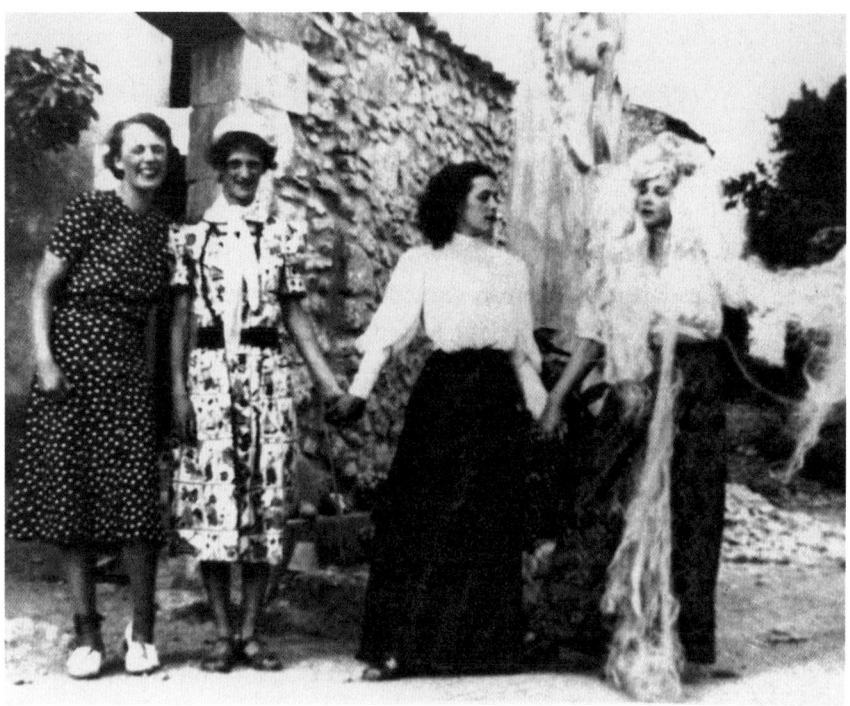

From left: Joan Powell, Philip Powell, Leonora and Leonor Fini,
Saint-Martin-d'Ardèche, 1939

the river. Here Leonora and Max sat with their visitors during that
prewar summer – Lee Miller and Roland Penrose; Leonora's old friend
Joan Powell and her brother Philip; Leonor Fini.

There was a spirit of playfulness, of fun, a fusing of the worlds
of real and make-believe, at the house in Saint-Martin. Some of
the atmosphere from the sojourn in Cornwall two years earlier was
recaptured here in the South of France, and as before, Lee Miller's
photographs convey the feel of the place. There is Leonora in what
looks like a matador's jacket, embellished with tiny bells; Leonora
again in a lace jacket, with a faraway look in her eyes; and Leonor Fini,
wearing a creased white shirt with a high neckline and what might be
a feather threaded through her hair on a stick. Other images show
Leonora and Leonor hand in hand, with both of them wearing long
skirts and Leonor a wispy veil; Leonora, wearing what appears to be
an oversized bikini and cape and carrying a stick, sunning herself flam-
boyantly at the main door; and Philip Powell in drag, holding hands
with Leonora. The house at Saint-Martin was a kingdom unto itself
– the rules of elsewhere didn't cross the threshold.

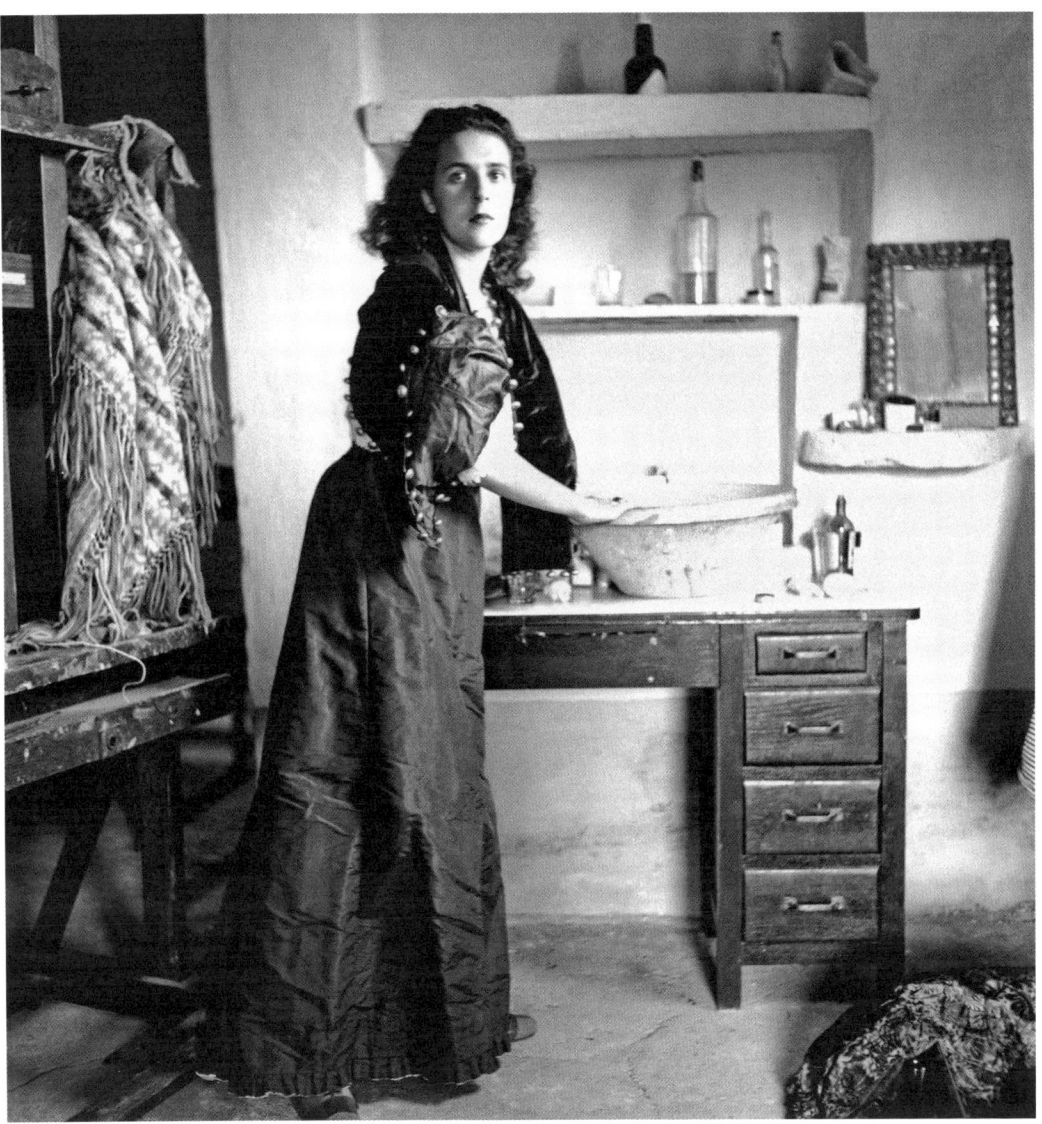

Leonora Carrington at Saint-Martin-d'Ardèche, 1939. Photograph by Lee Miller

That spirit was sustained by the art inside the house. Leonora created a series of colourful images, mainly on the doors of rooms and cupboards. In the main room there is a striking horse/woman/bird wearing a pinky-red dress; she is a voluptuous female figure with a horse's head and wild mane, and a flowing yellow wing where her arm might be. This is surely a self-portrait, as is the seated female figure with a horse's mane, human breasts, a horse's hooves and a fish's tail, executed on the outside of what is today the bathroom door (in Leonora's time it was the cellar door). But was there horror even in heaven? This figure has a tortured face with red pupils, white lips and sharp teeth.

Some of the images are funny: there is a burlesque figure with generous buttocks, a horse's face and long blonde hair, wearing nothing but a tiny pair of pointed black boots. Elsewhere a flame-red unicorn, with a yellow and orange mane and a goatee beard, surveys the scene from behind the frame of a cupboard door. Upstairs, in the airing cupboard, a painting Max exhibited in his 1937 Mayor Gallery show has been used to form part of the structure: amid the sheets and pillowcases

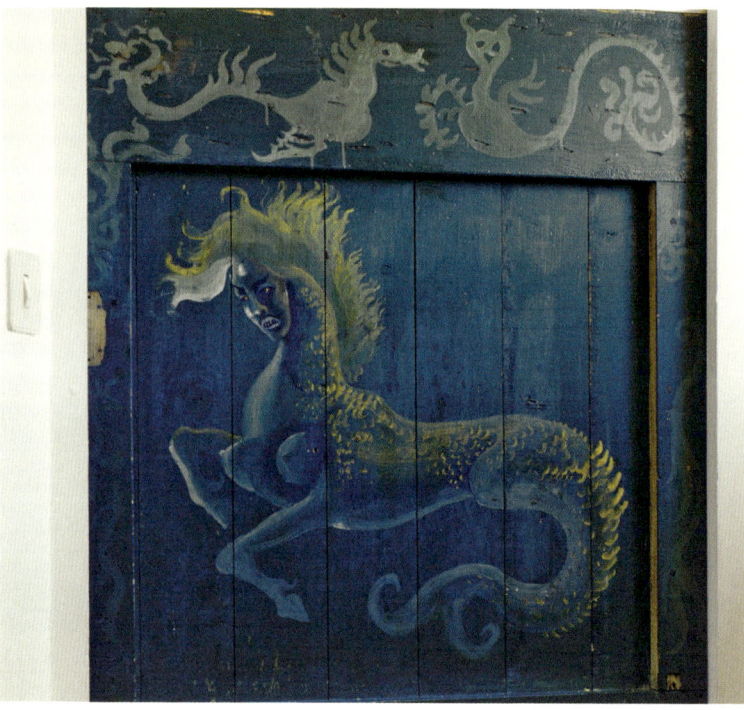

Saint-Martin-d'Ardèche interior, with work by Leonora Carrington.
Photograph by Tim Beddow

is the reverse of the piece, with his signature and the date clearly visible. Downstairs in the cellar there's a magnificent bat mosaic set into the floor, surrounded by the usual basement clutter – including the golf clubs Leonora brought with her from Lancashire, still in their bag marked 'LC'.

That this period in the Ardèche had its idyllic moments is beyond doubt. Later in life, Leonora remembered it as perhaps her happiest time. There was a harmony, a balance to her existence: she and Max had time to be together, and time to be alone. They had time to work on their separate projects – as well as painting, Leonora was writing stories, including 'Little Francis'. But, as that ghoulish face on the bathroom door hints, trouble eventually came, and it arrived in various different guises.

First there was a row, which originated with the Paris surrealists but was played out in the relationship between Leonora and Leonor. During the period in summer 1939 when Leonor was staying at Les Alliberts, the poet Tristan Tzara decided to pay a visit. Tzara's

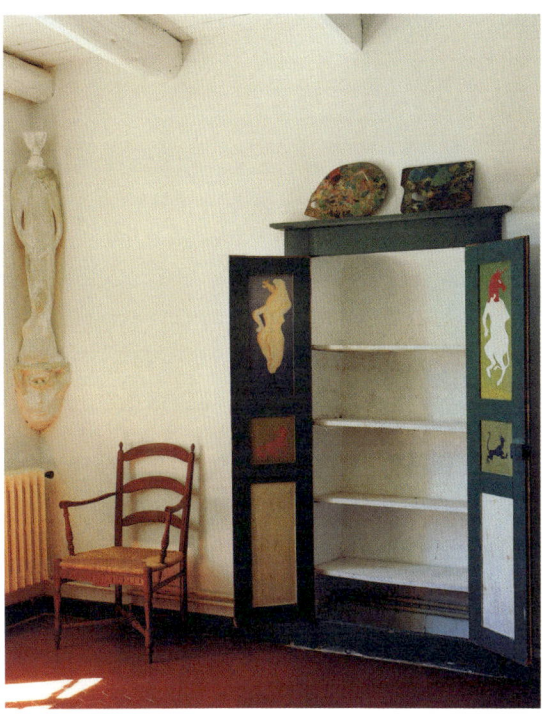

Saint-Martin-d'Ardèche interior, with work by Leonora Carrington.
Photograph by Tim Beddow

political sympathies lay with Stalin (unlike Leonora, Max and Leonor, all of whom favoured Trotsky's philosophy) and he had not been invited; but despite their incompatible views, Leonora and Max allowed him to stay. 'Leonor, disgusted at what she saw as her friends' "hypocrisy", responded with rage and attacked an unfinished portrait of Leonora with a palette knife. Only the face, a delicately drawn portrait now surrounded by a sea of scratched and scumbled paint, remained.'[5] Then she and the two companions she had arrived with – the writer André Pieyre de Mandiargues and the painter Federico Veneziani – bundled their possessions into Federico's Buick and drove away. Later, Leonora wrote to Leonor that she had 'forced me to choose between you and Max' and that she 'did not want a quarrel between the two friends I love'.[6]

According to Whitney Chadwick, Meret Oppenheim then intervened, trying to smooth the waters between the two women. But it was now September 1939, and worse things were happening in the world. Germany had invaded Poland, Britain had declared war, and a few hours later France had done the same. Leonora's mother Maurie, despite the row over Leonora's department had visited the couple in Paris the previous year, had suggested to them that Max should seek French citizenship to protect himself in the event of war – but he hadn't taken her advice and was still a German national. Consequently, once the war began he was detained as an enemy alien and taken away to prison in the town of Largentière, fifty kilometres to the north. Leonora went with him and stayed at an inn not far from the jail. Her summer of delight had imploded, and when Leonor wrote to her in conciliatory tones later that month, Leonora responded that 'your letter was the first good thing to happen to me for a long time. I'm deprived, tortured, and half mad...'[7]

She was, said Leonora, in a terrible situation. Not allowed even to see Max (although this later changed), she hardly spoke to anyone. In a prescient aside, she expressed her fear that 'if things continue [as they are] I will end up in a madhouse' – a sentiment echoed in a further letter in which she confessed to having 'noticed signs of madness in myself'.[8]

Her anguish is also captured in a letter she wrote to Max while staying at the inn. According to Chadwick, who has seen and written about it, this letter makes clear how much Leonora feels she owes to Max and how bereft she is without him. She refers to herself as the 'property of Max Ernst', without whom she is 'losing my sense of life, of poetry, of everything that I owe to knowing you'.[9]

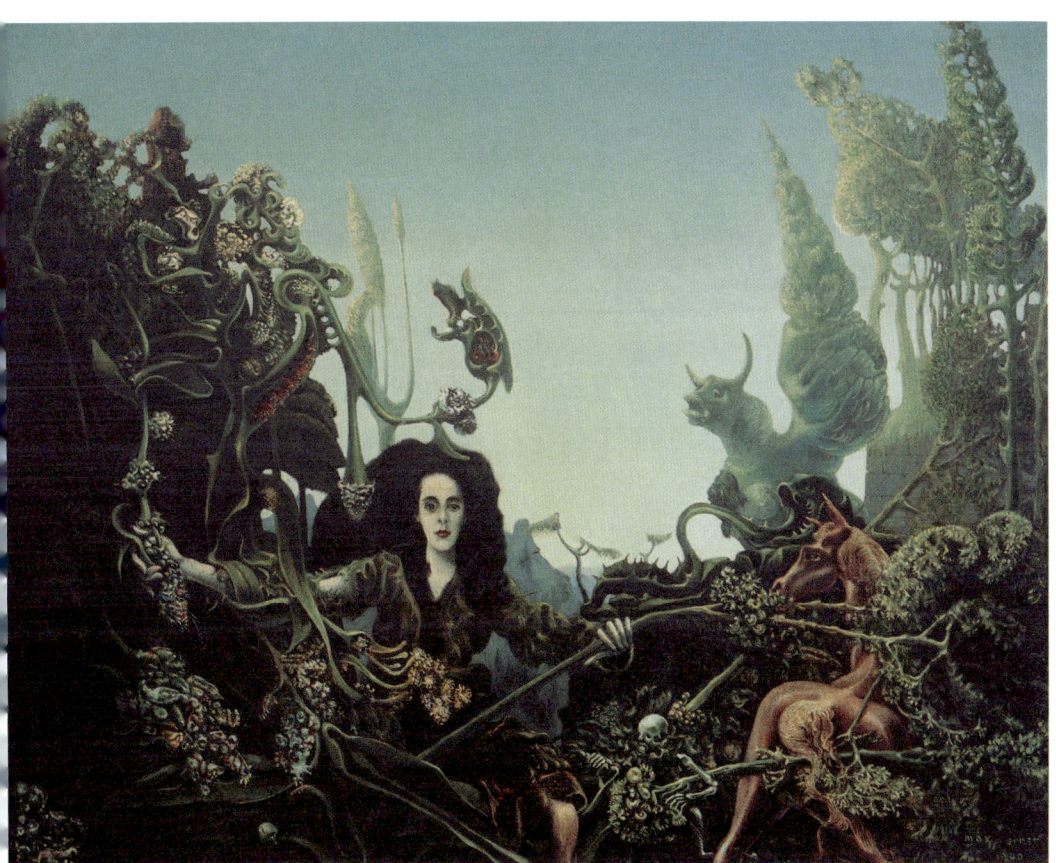

Max Ernst, *Leonora in the Morning Light*, 1940

Things would get worse before they got better. In November, Max was moved to another detention centre further away, a former brick factory at Les Milles near Marseilles. The weather was cold and the air in the centre was thick with dust; the only consolation was that one of his old friends, the painter Hans Bellmer, was a fellow internee. To pass the time, the two made portraits of one another. Meanwhile Leonora continued to lobby for Max's release, calling on all the friends she could think of, including Roland Penrose, who wrote back to reassure her that he and Paul Éluard were doing all they could. Herbert Read was also petitioned to help.

Further assistance, certainly moral and also perhaps influential, poured in from an unlikely source: at her home in Lancashire, Maurie wrote that she 'was delighted to get your letter, & am trying everything

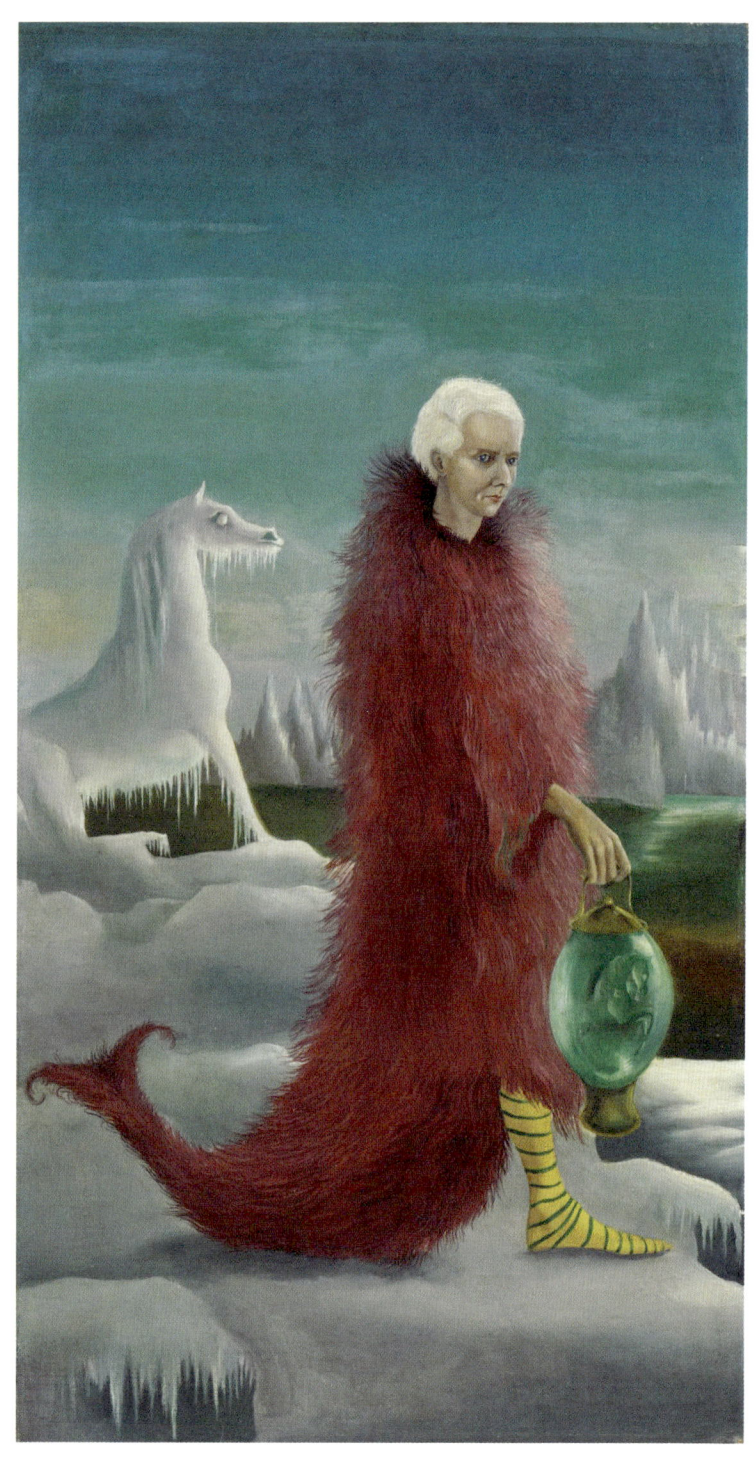

Portrait of Max Ernst, 1939

in my power to help you, when the Consul replies will send it on to you – it looks hopeful as he is taking his time'. She said that she was sending food – a plum cake, tins of sardines – and asked whether Leonora (still in Largentière at this point) would return to Les Alliberts if she had a companion; perhaps Joan Powell, who 'seems anxious to be with you'.[10]

At Christmas, there was good news: Max was released from the camp and returned to Leonora, who had gone back to Les Alliberts. Hugely relieved – but perhaps not convinced that their problems were over – the couple spent the next few months there together. Leonora wrote to Leonor about the meals she was preparing: a 'good dish' made out of tinned tuna and a sauce of tomatoes, onions, olives and cream, and a Bakewell tart with a recipe supplied by Maurie.

Perhaps the bas-relief and the paintings on the cupboards were finished by this point, because both Leonora and Max now turned to their canvases. She painted him and he painted her. His *Leonora in the Morning Light* shows her emerging into a forest clearing: she looks confident, in control. Her *Portrait of Max Ernst* shows him in a robe of rose-coloured fur that ends in a fish's tail; behind him is a white horse, Leonora's avatar, and it is frozen. Does this depict a feeling that had been gnawing at her for a while – that ultimately Max would, like her family before him, diminish rather than expand her potential? Was the thought already taking hold within her that the time would come when she would need to cast him off?

The prices later realized by these mirror-image portraits point up an ongoing issue in the art world: that work by women is consistently undervalued compared to work by men. Of course, Max was more famous than Leonora (although one could ask, why is an artist famous in the first place?), but even so it is hard to understand the hugely different figures involved when both paintings were sold after Leonora's death. Her portrait of him, sold to the National Galleries of Scotland in 2018, had a price tag of £560,000. His portrait of her – sold six years earlier, so it would be worth even more comparatively – went at auction for £6.3 million to a private collector.

Another fascinating element to the story of the Saint-Martin house is that Leonora left her entire bookcase there, with around 150 books in it. Some had clearly been sent over from Lancashire; they were childhood gifts, and are inscribed. Many are books that have long been associated with Leonora's art: Lewis Carroll, *Grimm's Fairy Tales*, *Irish Fairy Tales*, stories from Hans Christian Andersen, as well as *Moral Tales* by her erstwhile kinswoman Maria Edgeworth. *When*

Churchyards Yawn, a collection of ghost stories edited by Cynthia Asquith, was a present 'from Pat [her older brother] Xmas 1931', the same year the book was published. Other titles she seems to have bought in Paris, maybe at the original Shakespeare & Co. There is a book of Coleridge's poetry and novels by Poe, Trollope, Austen and the Brontës. T. S. Eliot sits alongside Goethe and Wilde.

The bookcase shows that even while Leonora was tucked away in a forgotten corner of France, she kept in touch with the things that had always mattered to her, especially ideas, literature and politics. There are the latest works by Daphne du Maurier, John Steinbeck and Evelyn Waugh – *Rebecca*, *Of Mice and Men* and *Vile Bodies* respectively, all published in 1938. And she was clearly a fan of the new *Penguin Parade* series, which consisted of short stories, poems and illustrations by contemporary writers published two or three times a year – she had volumes two to six, published between 1937 and 1939.

There are exhibition catalogues too, including the catalogue from the London surrealism exhibition of 1936, with the list of exhibits by Max. And there is evidence of how long-held many of Leonora's central beliefs were: a copy of *Buddhism: Its Birth and Disposal* by Caroline A. F. Rhys Davids, inscribed 'Leonora Carrington, Hazelwood, 1935'; and the American naturalist William Long's 1919 classic *How Animals Talk*. Long's work was seen as blurring the lines between the animal world and the human world, just as Leonora's did.

Max had once said that he and Leonora would stay in Saint-Martin 'if the world allows it' – and the time was coming when the world would no longer allow it. With hindsight, it seems almost reckless that the couple simply stayed put, waiting for the inevitable. Many years later, Leonora told author Rosemary Sullivan that she and Max had realized too late that they should have fled from France after his release. Their failure to do so, she suggested, was because they were clinging to an idea of a world whose disappearance they couldn't contemplate. 'We couldn't imagine a world other than Paris,' she said. 'You must remember what Paris was in those days, before the war. Paris was wonderful. Paris was freedom.'[11] They seem to have been unable to process how bad things might become. Leonora told Sullivan that Max found the term 'enemy alien' ridiculous and that he was always sure that in France, whatever happened, they'd be able to talk to people and find a way through.

In May 1940, the gendarmes returned to Les Alliberts. They had received reports from the village that Max had been sending light signals to the enemy, and he was to be returned to internment at Les Milles. This time, his departure was even more traumatic: he was handcuffed and taken from the house by a policeman with a gun. Leonora was distraught, as she later wrote in her memoir *Down Below*: 'I wept for several hours, down in the village; then I went up again to my house where, for twenty-four hours, I indulged in voluntary vomiting induced by drinking orange blossom water and interrupted by a short nap. I hoped that my sorrow would be diminished by these spasms, which tore at my stomach like earthquakes. I know now that this was but one of the aspects of those vomitings: I had real-ised the injustice of society, I wanted first of all to cleanse myself, then go beyond its brutal ineptitude.'[12] Her stomach, she continues, was the seat of society, the place in which she was united with all the elements of the earth. As ever with Leonora, everything was connected.

For three weeks she ate hardly anything, drank a little wine and worked on her vines, astonishing the locals with her strength. She seemed stronger than she had ever been. 'The more I sweated, the better I liked it, because this meant that I was getting purified.'[13] Despite Max's imprisonment and the events in Europe – Belgium and northern France had now been invaded by Germany – she 'had no fear whatsoever within me'.[14] She once told me that she knew, throughout this tumultuous period of war, that whatever else hap-pened, she would survive. She had always had a strongly developed intuition, and there were moments when she was aware of an aura or sixth sense about how things were going to play out. During that same three-week period, her home was invaded by soldiers who accused her of spying and threatened to shoot her on the spot: 'Their threats impressed me very little indeed, for I knew that I was not destined to die.'[15]

And then she had a visitor: Catherine Yarrow, a British artist she had known in Paris. Catherine was on her way to Spain with her Hungarian partner, Michel Lucas. The pair stayed at Les Alliberts, and Catherine tried to persuade Leonora to break free from Max in the same way she had broken free of her father. Leonora thought she was wrong – 'I think that she interpreted me fragmentarily, which is worse than not to interpret at all' – but in the end she gave in to Catherine's pleading to accompany her and Michel to Spain. In her mind was the thought that she would be able to do more for Max from Madrid than she could from rural France.

Leonora and Michel went to Bourg-Saint-Andéol to get a travelling permit. The gendarmes said they couldn't help, but again Leonora's intuition kicked in. 'We were unable to leave, yet I knew that we would leave the following day.'[16] There were debts to be settled at the Bar des Touristes, but Leonora had no money; instead she made the house over to its proprietor, with whom she and Max had built up a tab. Then she went back to Les Alliberts and spent the whole night sorting out what she would take with her. Her only luggage was a suitcase which bore the brand name REVELATION, and there was much that couldn't fit into it: paintings, letters, papers.

The following morning, the schoolmistress in Saint-Martin gave her the papers she needed to travel. Having opened the dovecote in the garden to release the birds, she got into Catherine's Fiat, sandwiched in the front between her and Michel. She now felt 'terribly anguished', because she knew there were unavoidable difficulties ahead. When the brakes jammed a few miles out of Saint-Martin, she saw it as echoing what was happening inside herself. 'I, too, was jammed within, by forces foreign to my conscious will, which were also paralysing the mechanism of the car. This was the first stage of my identification with the external world. I was the car. The car had jammed on account of me, because I, too, was jammed between Saint-Martin and Spain.'[17]

They drove through the night. Probably partly due to lack of sleep, Leonora was losing her grip on reality. She thought she could see legs and arms dangling from the trucks they were passing, and the road they travelled along was lined with coffins. It all stank, she wrote later, of death. They reached Perpignan at seven o'clock in the morning and went from there to the border town of Andorra. By this point Leonora was very disturbed. When she tried to walk, her body was 'jammed', just as the brakes had been. 'I realised that my anguish – my mind, if you prefer – was painfully trying to unite itself with my body; my mind could no longer manifest itself without producing an immediate effect on my body.'[18]

The solution, she found, was to immerse herself in the landscape. She walked into the mountains alone. At first she felt unable to negotiate the path, the rocks, the challenges, but after a few days it became easier. She made a kind of pact with the mountain, and then an agreement with the animals she found there: horses, goats, birds – today we might term it nature therapy. She found she could connect with animals that usually ran away from humans, including a herd of horses that galloped off when Catherine and Michel approached.

While this was going on, Michel was frantically sending telegrams to Harold Carrington in England, asking for his help to cross the Spanish border. Twice they tried to get into Spain without success. Then a priest – a Jesuit, Leonora recalled later – sent by her father made contact with them, handing over 'a mysterious and very dirty piece of paper' that allowed her and Catherine to cross the border. They had to leave Michel behind. The women drove to Barcelona, from where Leonora felt they should continue to Madrid as quickly as possible. She persuaded Catherine to abandon the Fiat, and the following day they took a train to the Spanish capital.

Meanwhile, the house they had left behind at Saint-Martin lay dark and shuttered with the sculptures inside growing dusty, the abandoned canvases piled up in a corner. It would be some months before Max, released from his prison camp, returned, and when he did he was distraught to find that his lover had gone. He didn't stay long in Saint-Martin after that. When he went, he took with him some of the paintings Leonora had left behind, including her self-portrait.

For some years afterwards, Les Alliberts remained the property of the publican to whom Leonora had sold it. In the mid-1950s it was sold again, to a family from Lyon who would use it as their holiday home for the next eight decades. It remains in their ownership to this day, so it is thanks to them that the art has survived almost entirely intact and there have been so few changes to the property. It has never been open to the public and there are no plans to change that; but the years the artist couple spent in Saint-Martin are remembered in the village. One of its streets is called Rue Max Ernst, and a reproduction of the bat mosaic from the Les Alliberts cellar floor can be seen in the village square.

I have been fortunate enough to visit the house on several occasions, including while researching this chapter. Leonora's spirit felt only a whisper away as I walked through the rooms where she lived and loved, painted and wrote. My first visit was in early May 2011; I hoped on that occasion to be able to report back to Leonora about the way the house looked. Sadly she died a few weeks later, before I had time to get to Mexico again. She herself had never returned; the day she closed the door and got into Catherine Yarrow's Fiat was the last time she saw Les Alliberts. She had not remained jammed, as she feared she might. She had moved on; but she had left a bit of her heart in Saint-Martin, and perhaps it remains there still.

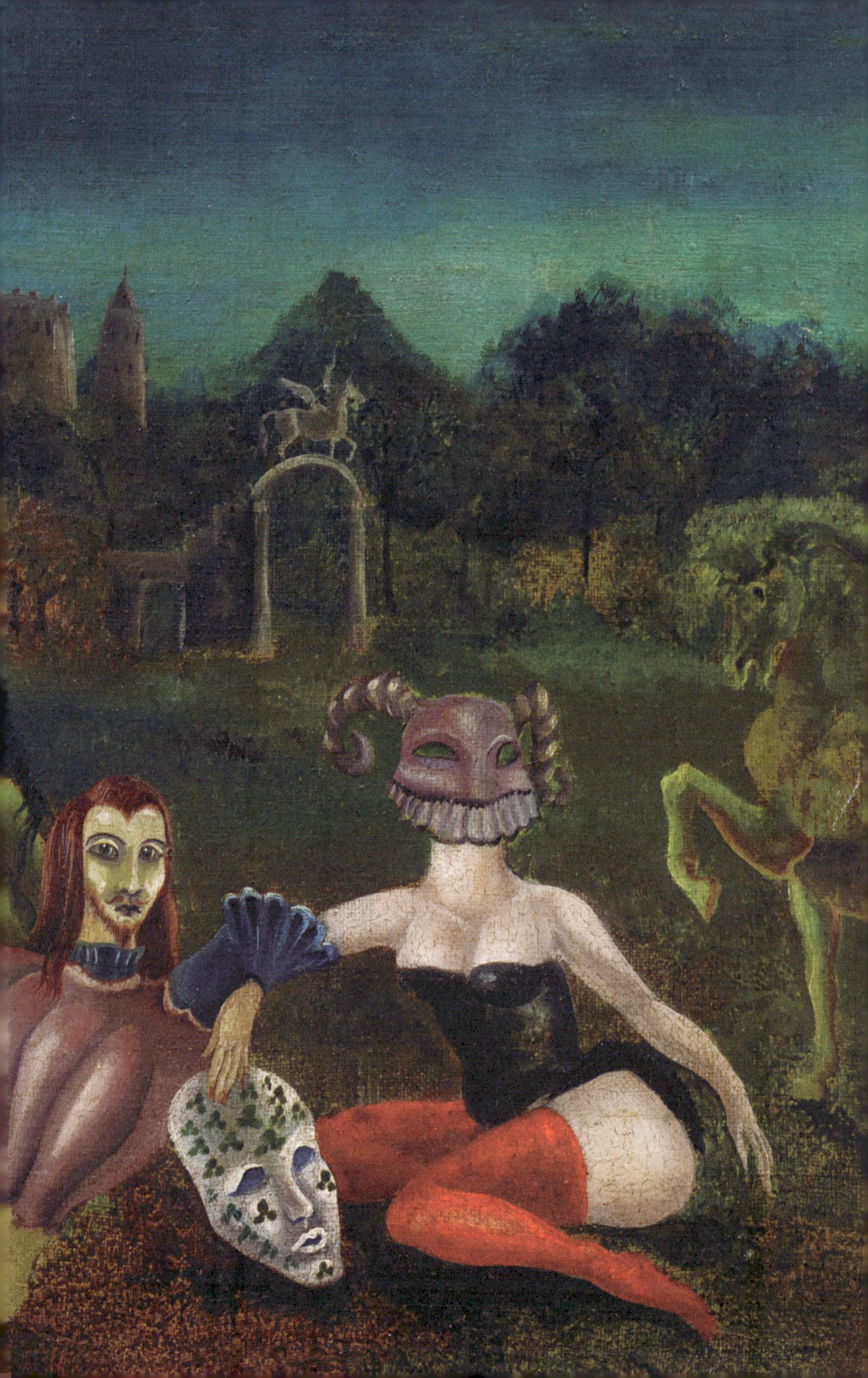

7

Santander and Lisbon

1940–1941

When she and Catherine reached Madrid in the summer of 1940, the main thing on Leonora's mind was finding a way to use her connections in Britain to secure Max's release. But whether or not this idea had ever been realistic, it's clear from her own account that her mental health was now too compromised for it to be possible. Although Catherine was outwardly supportive of the plan to help Max, her real priority was probably to get Leonora to a safe place so that family and friends could arrange for the care she needed.

As soon as they arrived, Leonora experienced the psychological breakdown she describes in *Down Below*: 'In the political confusion and the torrid heat, I convinced myself that Madrid was the world's stomach and I had been chosen for the task of restoring this digestive organ to health,' she writes. 'I believed that I was capable of bearing this dreadful weight and of drawing from it a solution for the world. The dysentery I suffered from later was nothing but the illness of Madrid taking shape in my intestinal tract.'[1]

She goes on to chronicle the appalling experience of being gang-raped by soldiers before being dumped in a park and taken by a policeman back to her hotel, where she spent the rest of the night taking cold baths and alternating between two nightgowns, one green, the other pink. How much of this account is what actually took place and how much is imagined, it's impossible to know. She also details a brief love affair with a doctor called Alberto: he 'was a perfect fool, and probably a scoundrel besides'.[2] By this point, Leonora had become convinced that she would somehow be able to alert Spain's ruler,

Down Below, detail, 1940

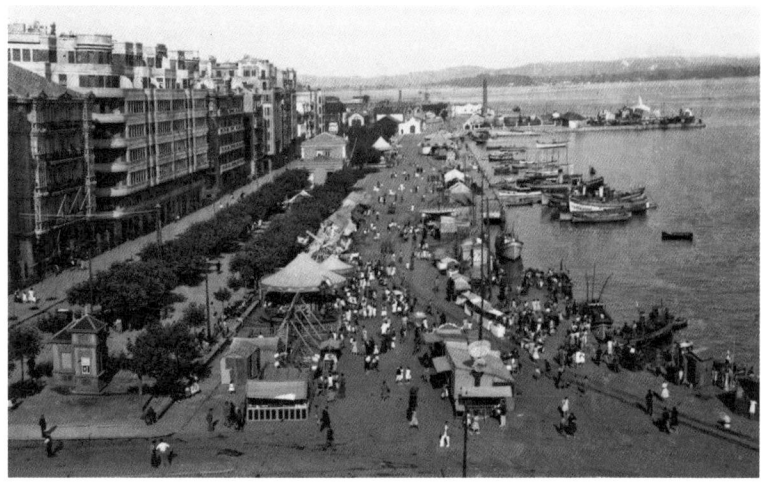

Santander, 1947. Photograph by Joaquín Araúna Agenjo

General Franco, to the dangers facing Europe; this would trigger a series of events that would turn the continent away from war.

A shadowy figure in the background was a businessman called Van Ghent, who was connected through work to Harold. Leonora didn't trust him – she didn't trust many people, with good reason – but when she denounced him to the head of ICI, on whose board Harold had a seat, her father called a doctor and had her admitted to a sanatorium run by nuns. He promised Leonora that she wouldn't be there for long; Alberto and another doctor would take her to the northern coast of Spain, to the seaside, where she could live happily.

Perhaps because she was so unwell, Leonora seems to have taken this story at face value, only realizing her mistake when she woke up in 'a tiny room with no windows on the outside, the only window being pierced into the wall to the right that separated me from the next room'.[3] The room held a cheap bedside table and wardrobe, a marble-topped table and a chair; through a glass door, she could see down a corridor. It was clearly a hospital of some kind, and her first thought was that the car in which she had been travelling had met with an accident. But then she found she was restrained, her hands and feet tied to the bed with leather straps. She was in Santander, in the place she would refer to for the rest of her life as 'the asylum': a psychiatric clinic run by a Dr Mariano Morales and his son, Dr Luis Morales.

After Leonora's death, I visited the Sanatorio Peña Castillo (Castle Rock Hospital), as the Morales hospital was correctly called. Reality

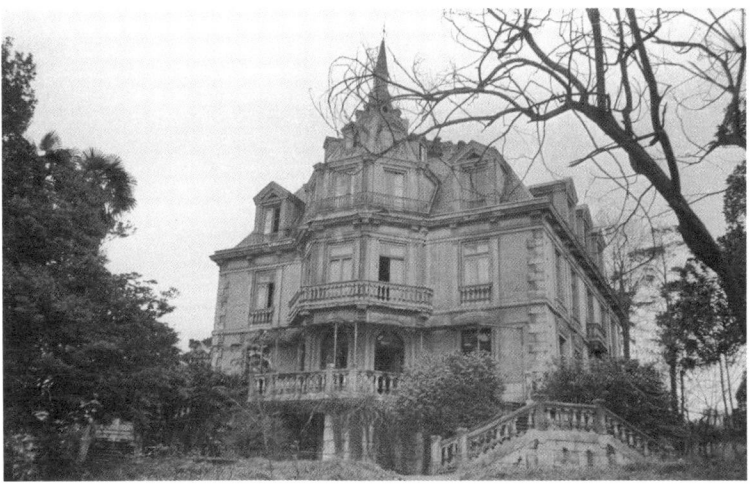

Sanatorio Peña Castillo, Santander, 1963. Photograph by Pablo Hojas Llama

presented a very different scene from the image I had conjured
up after listening to her account of the place. I'd imagined a grim-
looking, isolated building, perhaps with bars on the windows; in fact,
the clinic was pleasantly situated in rolling parkland about two miles
from the centre of Santander. Today it's in a suburb, but in the 1940s
it would have been on the city's outskirts.

Leonora had terrible experiences here. Not once or twice, but
three times, she was tied to a bed and given injections of Cardiazol,
a drug that induced seizures. It was a kind of precursor to electric
shock treatment, and she never forgot how terrifying it was. But
her surroundings were in direct contrast to her experience: in the
midst of the most desperate, degrading and dangerous part of her
struggle towards a different kind of life, she was surrounded by
beautiful gardens, flowers, a pond, fruit trees. Art historians have
pondered on whether Leonora converted the horror of what she
was going through into something bearable by reimagining the
space in which she found herself – but she didn't have to reimagine
it, because even as she descended into her own hell, outside the sun
was shining, the birds were singing and the mountains shimmered on
the horizon.

Leonora spent six months as a patient at the sanatorium. For
obvious reasons she was unable to create much art during this period,
but there are some sketches and a painting that directly reference her
time here. Her *Map of Down Below* (c. 1941) is a line drawing of 'the

asylum'; again, it has sometimes been assumed to be an imaginative representation of the layout. In fact, it is a very faithful sketch of the corner of the park where the sanatorium's main buildings were located. Approaching the Parque de Morales, as it is known today, along the main road from the centre of town, the first thing you see is an igloo-shaped stone building near the railings; this is quite clearly identifiable on Leonora's map, where she calls it the 'bower and cave'. Further along the road, again close to the railings, is another strange edifice, a stone structure that might once have been a small shrine. This corresponds with the sketched outline of a figure on the map (Leonora herself, perhaps) being shadowed by a larger, coffin-shaped object. Other mapped locations also correlate with what we know of the clinic; I have seen photographs of the radiography rooms, and those are recorded on the map too. From the spot where Leonora has written '4' and marked it in her key 'Apple trees and view of Costa Blanca and the valley', you can stand and look across at the valley and the mountains on the other side, although the apple trees are now gone.

So 'Down Below' is not, after all, a figurative construct, but the accurate plotting of an area of the sanatorium. In her memoir of the same name, Leonora explains that Down Below (*Abajo* in Spanish) was a hotel-like area of the clinic where people 'lived...very happily'.[4] Either they had been cured and were convalescing before their re-emergence into the outside world, or they were at the clinic on a different pretext from Leonora, who was a psychiatric patient. She certainly seems to have aspired to moving to Down Below, so perhaps at least some of the inhabitants had conditions that showed signs of improvement. Unfortunately for Leonora, at this point in her story things were about to get a lot worse: it was the eve of her first Cardiazol dose, an event she describes as 'the most terrible and blackest day in my life'.[5]

The irony of all this is that, despite the months Leonora spent in the 'asylum' and the horrific treatment forced on her, she was probably not suffering from any serious psychiatric condition. This, at least, seems to have been the view of Dr Luis Morales later in his career. On my trip to Santander I met Marisa Samaniego, a former teacher who knew Morales in his later life and spoke to him several times about Leonora. Morales told her that the two of them had kept in touch, by letter and even by phone, for some time after Leonora's departure. She even gave him one of her paintings, dedicated to him, as a leaving present. He kept it all his life.

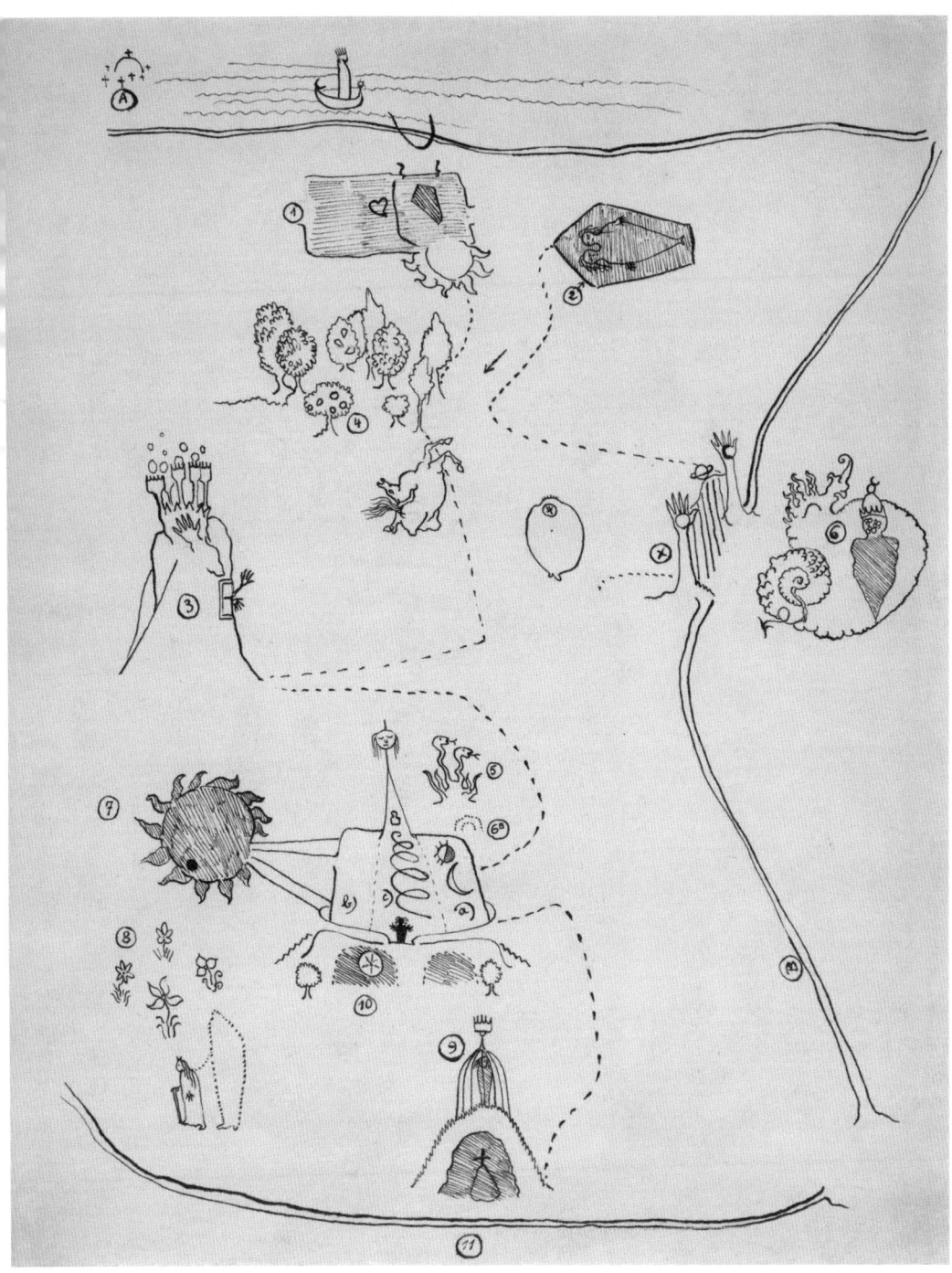

Map of Down Below, c. 1941

Fear, 1937–41

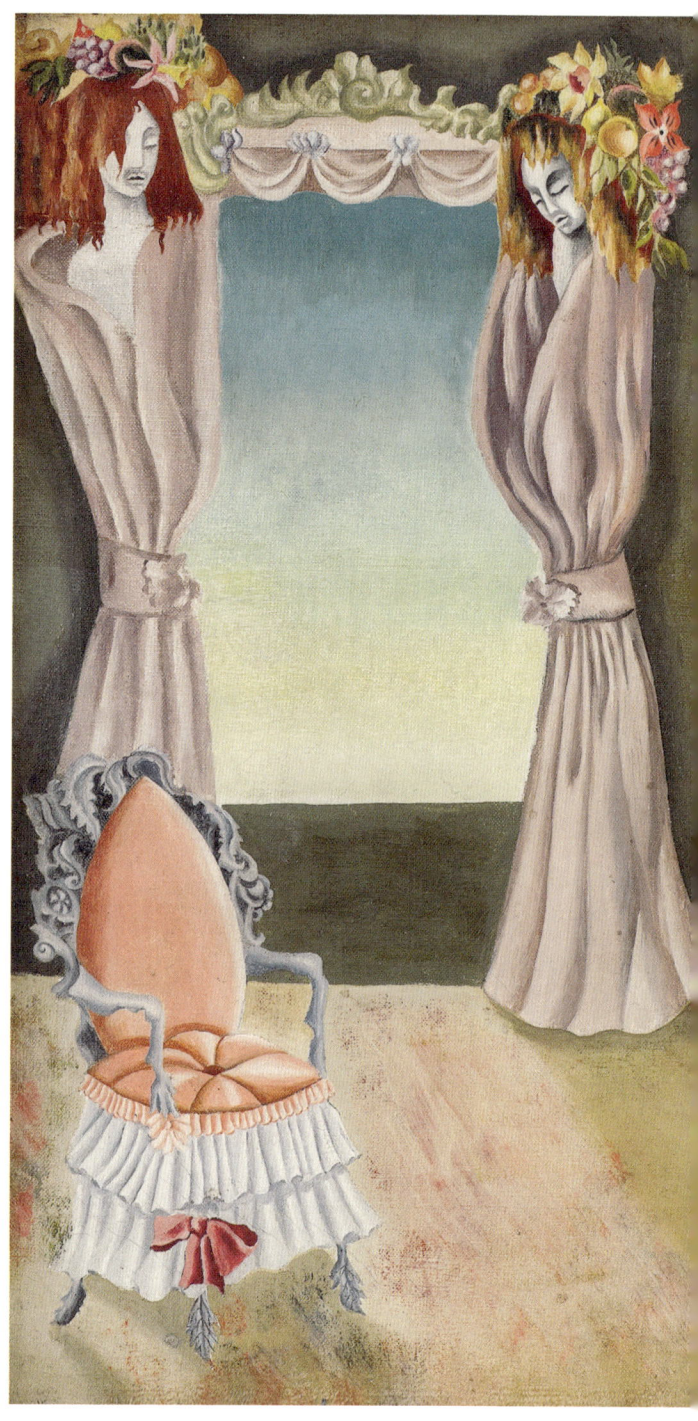

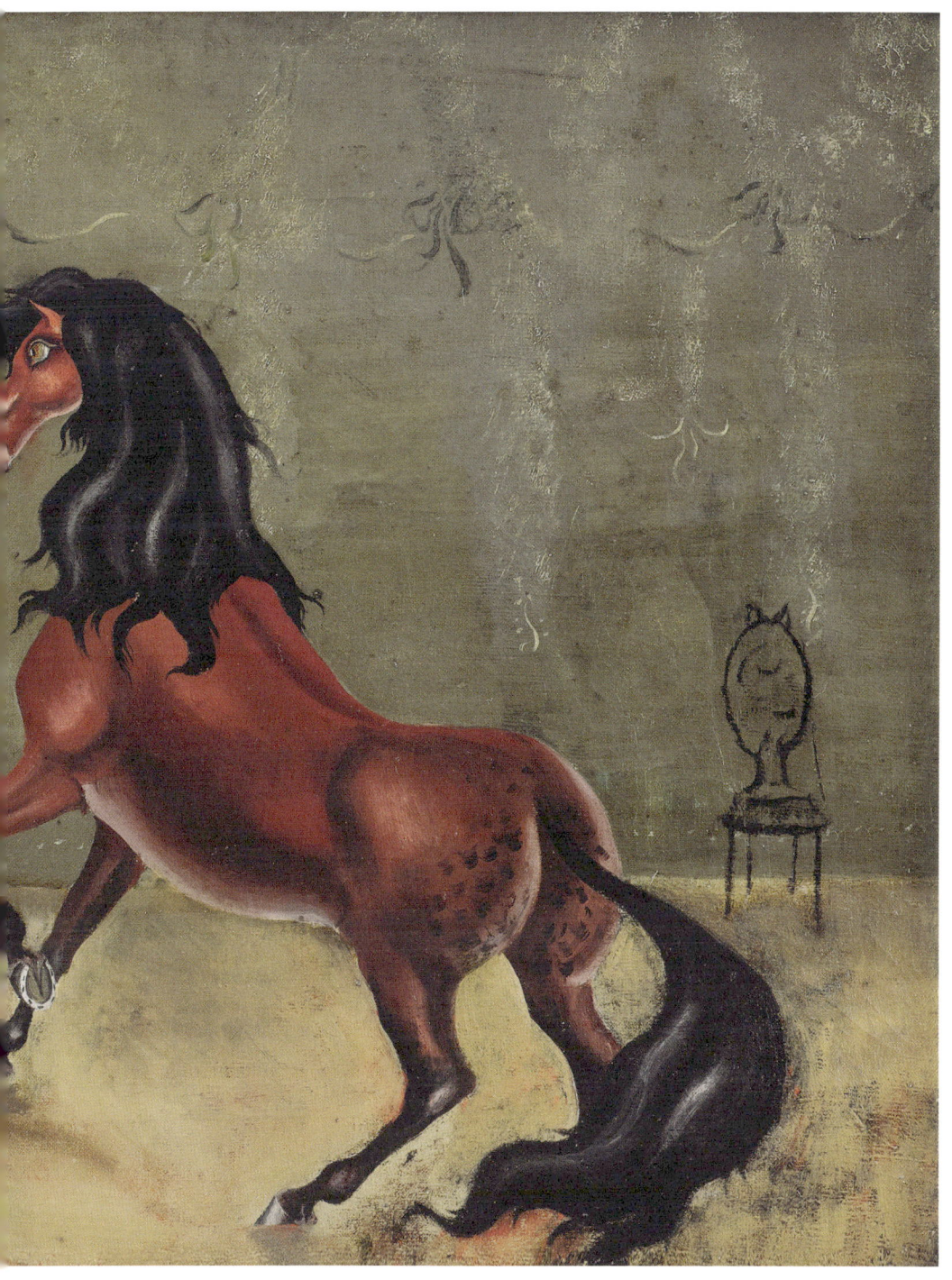

Samaniego explained that Morales later came to believe Leonora was not ill at all. 'He said to me, Leonora was not mad. I apologize to her. He said research done later in his life, during the 1970s and beyond, showed that he had made many mistakes with his patients, including Leonora.'[6] The art historian Susan Aberth makes the same point: '[Morales] wondered if Carrington, in 1941, was actually sane in her adaptation to society as it was at that time and if now she would even be classified as ill.'[7]

Leonora's account of her stay in Santander, dictated over the course of three days in 1943 to a doctor called Pierre Mabille and published in the surrealist journal *VVV* in New York the following year, is like her paintings: many worlds coexist in it, just as they do on her canvases. It is up to the reader of her words, as it is up to the viewer of her visual art, to decide which worlds to tap into, and to determine whether and how the different worlds connect with one another. All of Leonora's work – her writing and her painting, and later her tapestries and her sculpture – was driven by a need to make sense of the complications of life; not just her own life, but life in general (or perhaps the two are the same). So it's unsurprising that her experience over six months in the north of Spain was so formative, so fundamental to everything that would happen afterwards, that she found it necessary to unpack it in a painting called *Down Below* as well writing about it.

It seems remarkable that Leonora found it within herself to paint during her time in the asylum; and yet she did. She told her friend Salomon Grimberg, who has written about her and who curated an exhibition of her work in 2008, that she wrote to her family from Santander – the first time she communicated with them during her hospitalization, and perhaps the only time – asking if they could send some painting materials. 'Although she received no direct acknowledgment of her letter, she knew [her father] had received it when painting materials arrived. Despite their being of lesser quality than she would have preferred, she was grateful and began painting.'[8]

Down Below is an uncomfortable painting. The landscape is dark and menacing; the figures appear disconnected from one another, unsmiling, discombobulated. They are wearing clothes that make them look as though they have come from entirely different, unrelated landscapes. In the centre is a sexualized woman wearing red stockings and a black bodice, with a mask covering her face. She holds another mask in her hand, as though preparing to change personae. Beside her is an androgynous figure with a moustache, staring out at the viewer.

An all-white figure with breasts and a bird-like face is in profile behind, as well as another shadowy figure with breasts and dark hair. At the far right is another figure, apparently female, with long, dark hair; Susan Aberth takes this to be Leonora herself, but the face doesn't look like Leonora's. I wonder whether in fact all the creatures in the painting – including the horse that prances behind the other figures – represent different elements of Leonora. But whether just one of them is her or they all are, the dominant mood of the work is menacing, nightmarish. This was not a place where Leonora wanted to be, and it is not a place where we would want to be, either. The beauty of the surrounding park has closed in, in Leonora's mind; her focus is entirely on her internal struggles and the terrible ordeal she has to undergo. She must concentrate on one thing and one thing alone: survival.

Leonora's story, as has often been remarked, is as surreal as anything she wrote or painted, and it was in Santander that one of the most surreal moments of all took place. Because here, in the north of Spain, on board a warship (it has sometimes been recorded as a submarine but, as Leonora later admitted, that may have been an embellishment), there now appeared an unlikely visitor from Lancashire: Mary Kavanaugh, a.k.a. Nanny Carrington. She had been sent by Harold and Maurie in an attempt to persuade Leonora back to England, and to them. Years later, when we spoke about this extraordinary turn of events, Leonora was as incredulous about it as she had been at the time, and she always felt it reflected on her family that none of them had decided to make the trip. 'I don't think Nanny had ever been outside the British Isles before,' she told me. 'She certainly didn't speak any Spanish.'

But now Kavanaugh found herself in the north of Spain, hundreds of miles from home, on a continent at war, and charged with a bizarre mission. Leonora takes up the story in *Down Below*: 'She [Nanny] arrived in great exaltation, after a terrible fifteen-day journey in the narrow cabin of a warship. She had not expected to find me in an insane asylum and thought she was going to see the healthy girl she had left four years ago. I received her oddly and mistrustfully; she was sent to me by my hostile parents, and I knew that her intention was to take me back to them.'[9]

Nanny was nervous in Santander, Leonora reported. Part of her discomfort stemmed from jealousy, because another woman – a nurse Leonora referred to as Frau Asegurado (literally, the 'insurance' or 'keeper') – seemed to have taken her place by Leonora's side. Nanny

Down Below, 1940

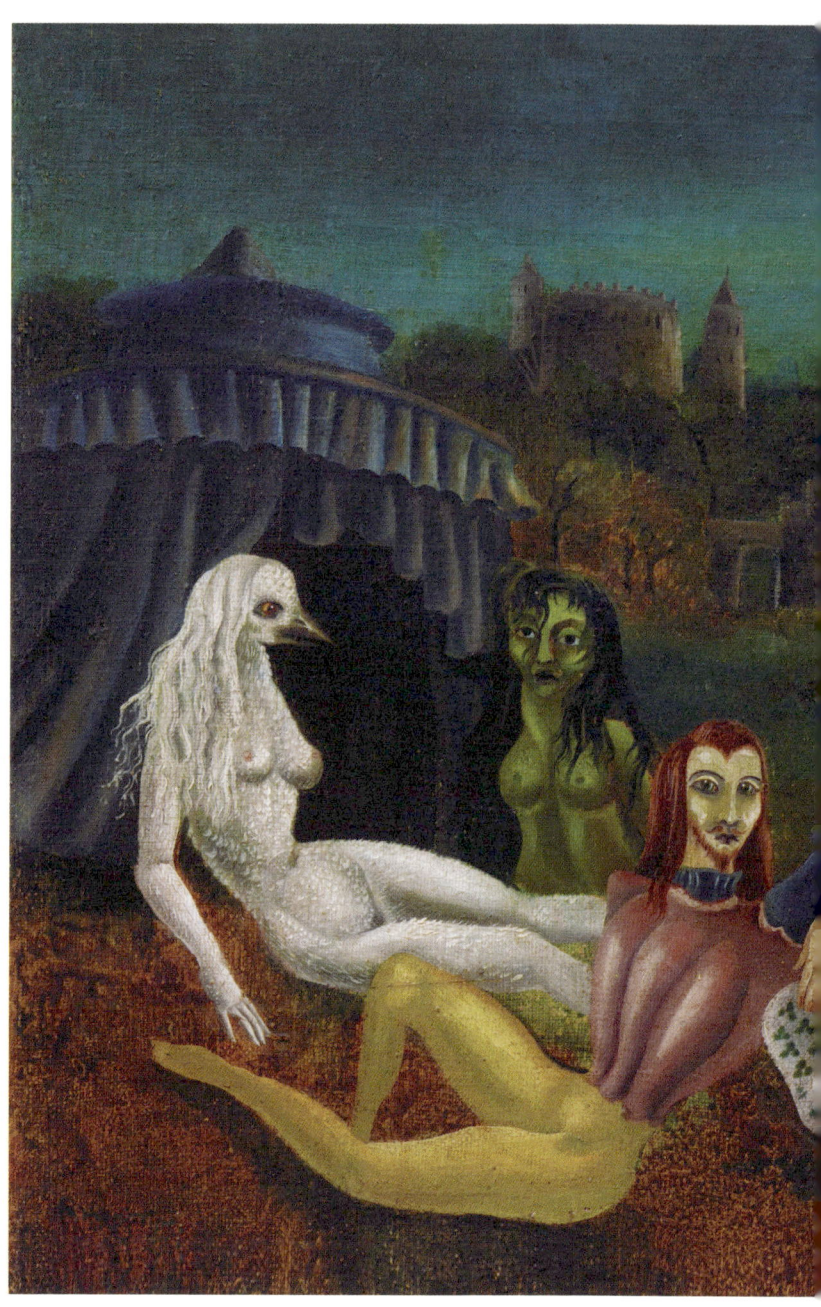

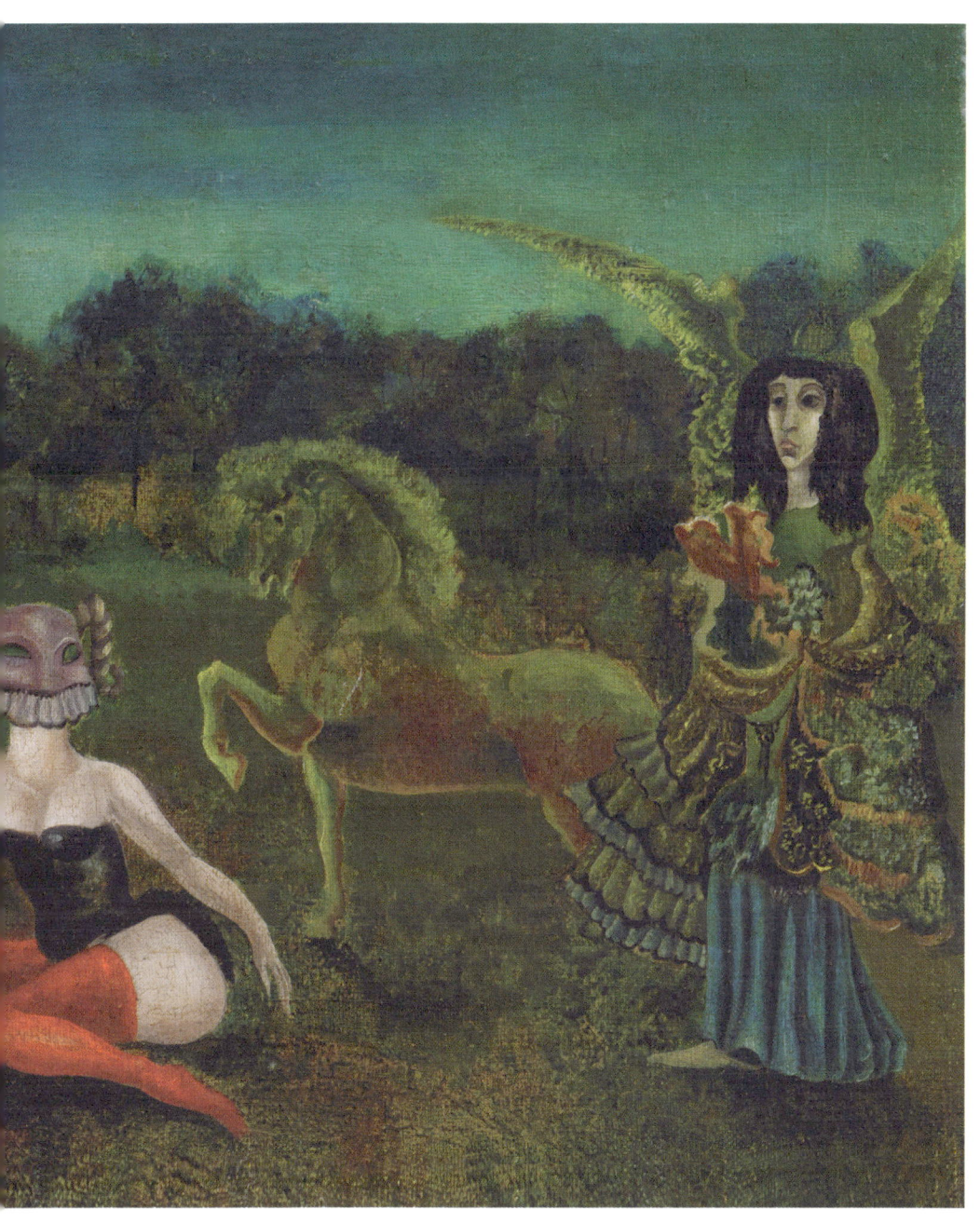

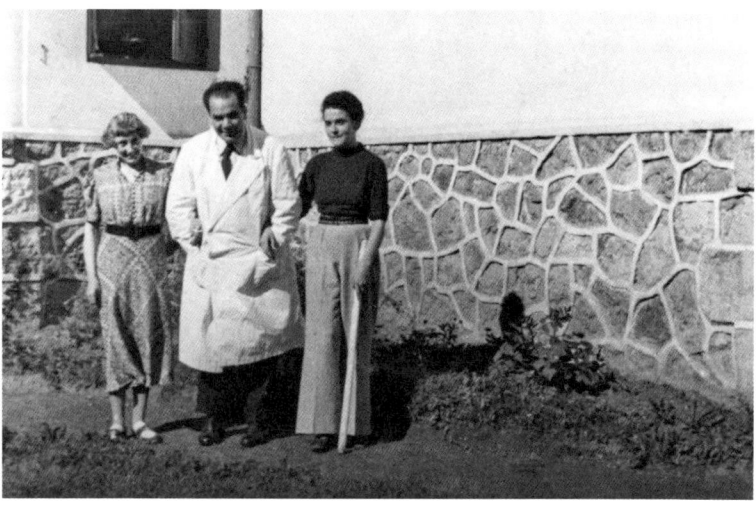

Photograph of Leonora Carrington with her nanny Mary Kavanaugh and Dr Morales at the sanatorium, Santander, 1941

was at the sanatorium to witness the third and final dose of Cardiazol administered to Leonora; horrified, she repeated again and again, 'What have they done to you...what have they done to you?' and wept beside her bed. Far from being touched by her sorrow, Leonora was exasperated by it, 'for I felt...that my parents were still trying to pull me back through her'.[10] Soon afterwards, having presumably realized that her mission was an impossible one, Nanny Carrington returned to England. Leonora suggests there was no farewell, but that she herself 'knew when she went away'.[11]

Leonora's eventual departure from the sanatorium is laced in mystery. By her own account, the pivotal figure was a cousin called Guillermo Gil, related via the Bamford family (of the heavy equipment company J. & C. Bamford, better known as JCB). Our family certainly are distantly related to the Bamfords, and there definitely was a Guillermo Gil, but he remains an elusive character in this tale. According to Leonora, he was a doctor working at the main hospital in Santander. His medical credentials enabled him to meet with her, after which he told her he would write to the British ambassador in Madrid to get her out. Which, according to Leonora, he did. 'They sent me to Madrid with Frau Asegurado, my keeper.'[12]

That was how, on the last day of 1940, Leonora and her nurse came to make the long journey by train from the north of Spain to its capital. There was a long delay, she recalled, in Avila, the town where Saint

Teresa (subject of a painting Leonora did in 1958) was born. The train had trucks full of sheep, and they were bleating from the cold: 'I'll remember the suffering sheep to my dying day,' wrote Leonora. 'It was like Hell.'[13]

They arrived in Madrid and checked into a large, expensive hotel. Harold Carrington had sought the help of business contacts who worked for ICI, and one of these men preyed on Leonora and tried to groom her as a sexual partner. One evening, over dinner, he told her that her family intended to place her in another sanatorium, this time in South Africa; if she wanted to avoid that, she could remain in Spain as his mistress. It was a terrible predicament and Leonora had no idea which way to choose. As they left the restaurant, there was a huge gust of wind and its metal sign fell down, narrowly missing her. In that instant, she decided: 'No. It's no.'

'It's going to be Portugal and then South Africa for you then,' the man said.[14]

But there was someone else in Madrid who would prove to be a true ally: Renato Leduc, a Mexican poet. Leonora had met him before, in Paris while she was living with Max, and probably never imagined she would see him again. But to kill time on one of those long Madrid afternoons, she and Frau Asegurado went to a tea dance, where she was astonished to see Renato across the room.

Like Leonora, he was passing through Madrid en route to Lisbon, from where he would be travelling by ship to New York. He filled her in on his story and she filled him in on hers; fortunately, Frau Asegurado didn't speak French, the language they conversed in. When you get to the Portuguese capital, Renato told her, find a way to get to the Mexican embassy; I'll be there, and I'll do my best to help you.

Happily for Leonora, Frau Asegurado was eventually dispatched back to Santander and she journeyed on to Lisbon alone, by train. For all that she dreaded the fate that supposedly awaited her – transportation to South Africa – somehow she did not think of disembarking at a station before Lisbon. She was already pinning her hopes on Renato: 'While still living in Paris, Ernst had invited Picasso to dine in our home, and he arrived with Leduc. I remember that as a gift, he brought me a Spanish wine boot. We dined and ended the evening dancing in a Cuban nightclub that Renato and Pablo had chosen. That is why it came to me that Renato could be my saviour.'[15]

In Lisbon she was met at the station by a delegation of business contacts sent by her father: two men who looked like policemen, and a hard-faced woman who told her they were passing her on to stay in Estoril, a few miles along the coast from Lisbon. There she would be put up in a lovely house with a woman who had been primed to look after her for a few days. 'You don't fight with such people. You have to think more quickly than they. So I said, "That will be lovely."'[16]

The following day, Leonora told her host in Estoril that she had realized the weather was going to be terrible for her hands, so she needed gloves – and also that she didn't possess a hat. Of course, said the woman, you must have a hat. They went back into central Lisbon. When they stopped at a café, Leonora, feigning illness, clutched her stomach and said she had to get to the bathroom. 'I had judged correctly: it was a café with two doors.'[17] She ran out of the back exit, hailed a taxi, jumped in and spoke the words that would alter the course of the rest of her life: 'Mexican embassy, *por favor*.'

When she arrived there a few minutes later, Renato was nowhere to be found. The staff suggested she should come back another time, but Leonora was adamant she had to wait for him to turn up, as she knew he eventually would. She told them the police were after her – 'Which was more or less true' – and they allowed her to stay.[18]

Eventually Renato appeared and introduced her to the Mexican ambassador, who, Leonora later remembered, was wonderful. He assured her that she was now on Mexican territory and no one, not even the English, could touch her.[19] On learning that she had Mexican sanctuary, Harold's business contacts and the woman in the Estoril house seem to have backed off. Leonora was given a room in a small hotel and began to spend a lot of time with Renato, whom 'I'd found...attractive when I first met him, and I still found him very attractive.'[20]

Renato was a charming man, only a few years younger than Max, with a romantic backstory. He had been a revolutionary fighter during the Mexican Civil War of 1910, serving as a telegraphist for the colourful rebel leader Francisco 'Pancho' Villa. After the war ended he abandoned plans to become a lawyer, instead joining the Mexican diplomatic service, and during the 1930s he was posted to Paris, where he befriended many of the surrealists. From the start he was sympathetic to Leonora's plight, and first floated the idea of helping to get her a visa to enter Mexico. But it quickly became clear that there was a simpler path – and it was one Leonora welcomed. 'He said, "We're going to have to get married. I know it's awful for both of us, as we don't believe in this sort of thing, but..."'.[21]

Lisbon at this point was crammed with refugees: rich and poor, Jewish and Christian, from countries right across Europe. All of them were intent on the same objective: getting across the Atlantic to the United States, where they would be safe from Hitler. But it wasn't the Führer that Leonora feared most. She would often say later that she had needed to escape from her own family just as urgently as from Hitler – and of the two, her family had seemed like the biggest threat.

In his novel *The Night in Lisbon* (1961), German writer Erich Maria Remarque sums up the mood of the city: 'The coast of Portugal had become the last hope of the fugitives to whom justice, freedom and tolerance meant more than home and livelihood. This was the gate to America. If you couldn't reach it you were lost....As usual in times of war, fear and affliction the individual human being had ceased to exist; only one thing counted: a valid passport.'[22]

Leonora was a great deal more privileged than many of the others huddled in the Portuguese capital waiting for passage, but like everyone else, her prize was a passport out. Now Renato had provided the possibility of that passport – and, as she was over twenty-one, she was free to marry him without her father's permission. Many years later, she described to me the fear she felt at this stage of her journey. She could almost taste the freedom for which she'd so long yearned, but she was desperately afraid that something beyond her control – perhaps a political development that brought Portugal into the war – would intervene, dashing her hopes.

She befriended an Englishwoman called Mary Ransome, who worked as a secretary in the city's British government passport office. They were staying in the same hotel. More than seventy-five years later, Mary described Leonora to me: 'She was extremely self-possessed, very ladylike, quite beautiful, and she had a quiet, dignified, level voice.' They had lots in common, including a convent boarding-school education; but there was also plenty, Mary remembered, that pointed up how different Leonora was from her. 'I came from a very straight background and it was pretty clear, from our earliest conversations, that she inhabited a quite different world from my own.' Leonora's life seemed 'very bohemian', and she told Mary about the extremely difficult time she'd had in Santander. 'She...was very tight-lipped about the asylum and how she'd been treated there; it was clear it had been a very hurtful and difficult time in her life.'[23]

While she waited to escape, Leonora had plenty of down time to fill. Mary remembered how the two of them would wander around the city, looking out at the sea and admiring the gardens, churches and Roman ruins. Lisbon today has changed much since the 1940s, but some things remain the same: the medieval castle of St George on a hilltop; the pastel-painted buildings; the yellow trams that shudder their way through the steep, narrow streets of Alfama, the city's original Moorish neighbourhood. There is the same food, always from the sea – shellfish, fish stew, grilled sardines – and the soulful fado music still curls out of bars and small sun-drenched squares, played by itinerant singing guitarists. The views out to sea are just as remarkable, especially from the hilltop in Alfama towards the horizon on which every refugee's eyes were once set: out west, towards America.

As they walked around the city, Leonora and Mary exchanged confidences and Leonora, of course, told Mary about Max. By now she had no idea what had become of him. She continued to feel guilty about having left him in France, and must at times have wondered whether he was even still alive. But then, one day while she was out walking alone, she saw his figure in the distance. Max too, it turned out, was in Lisbon.

Mary Ransome recalled, 'One day she [Leonora] came to find me and said, very calmly: "I've met Max." I was astonished, but she said it as though it was the most natural thing in the world. She didn't seem daunted or thrown off balance by it. She was always very level; it was momentous news, but she didn't seem excited or exhilarated by it – she took everything in her stride.'[24]

Mary's description says a great deal for how grounded Leonora was, because being back with Max could have changed everything. He was still very much in love with her; at least, that was the impression he gave to Peggy Guggenheim, who was now his lover. The pair had kindled their relationship in Marseilles while Max, having escaped from custody with the help of American writer Varian Fry and his Emergency Rescue Committee, was living at the Villa Air-Bel, Fry's safe house. They had fallen into an affair that initially, Peggy reported, was 'not serious'; but soon afterwards, she realized she had fallen in love with him.[25] Now, like so many others, they were planning to leave for America via Lisbon.

Peggy wasn't in the city yet when Leonora and Max met again, but her autobiography describes the moment when he told her what had happened. He was at the station to meet her when she arrived with her ex-husband Laurence Vail and their children, Pegeen and Sindbad. 'Max looked strange and, taking me by the arm, he said, "I have something awful to tell you." He walked me down the platform

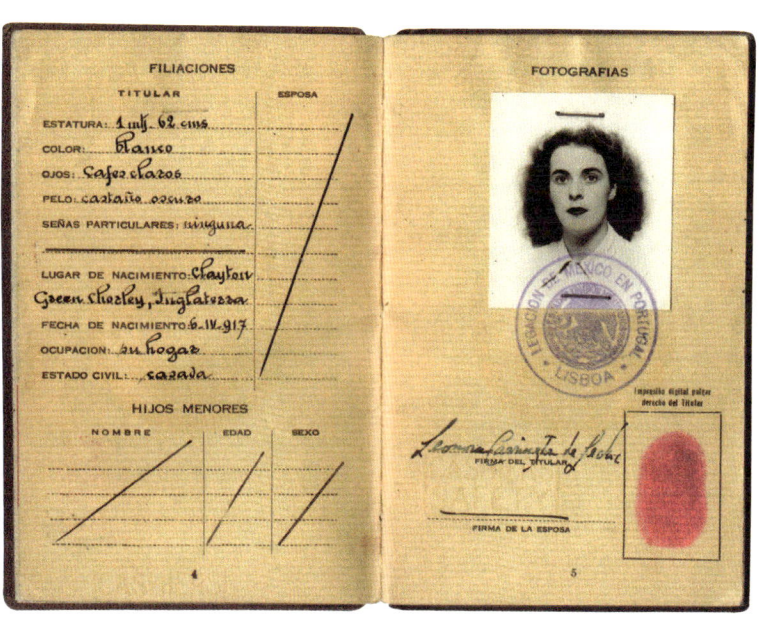

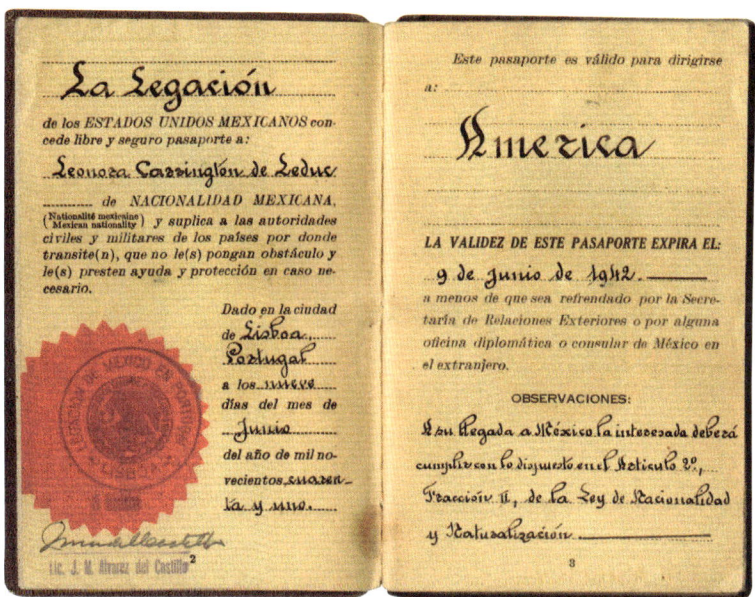

Passport of Leonora Carrington, 9 June 1941

and surprised me by saying, "I have found Leonora. She is in Lisbon." I felt a dagger go through my heart, but I pulled myself together and said "I am very happy for you." By this time I knew how much he loved her.'[26]

What followed next was a period Leonora always described as very weird, a time when she and Max were again in the same place, but in wildly different circumstances from those they had known two years earlier. Then, they had been lovers; now they each had a new partner. Then they had been mostly alone; now they were surrounded, not only by Peggy and Renato but also by Peggy's children, her ex-husband and his new wife and their children, and Renato's friends at the Mexican embassy.

Soon after meeting Max again, Leonora went ahead with her marriage to Renato. It took place on 26 May 1941 at the British Consulate General on the Rua de São Francisco Borja. Mary Ransome was there for the celebrations and recalled waiting in a café nearby with some Mexicans, friends of Renato: 'After the newlyweds emerged, we all went for lunch in the sunshine.'[27]

Peggy Guggenheim's memoir is characteristically honest and straightforward, and she writes frankly about this difficult period. For a while she saw very little of Max, who she knew was spending most of his days with Leonora; but Leonora's nights were spent with Renato. Peggy 'realized more than ever how much Max loved her'.[28] In her view, Leonora seemed unable to decide whether to stay with Renato or return to Max – and in fact, Peggy thought Leonora didn't really want either of them. Mary Ransome also had memories of this period, which she described to me as 'excruciating', although in her version it was Max who was doing the deciding.

Many years later, Leonora talked with me about what had happened between her and Max. She sometimes wondered, she said, whether the two of them would have stayed together if not for the war. I asked her what that period, when they were trying to decide their future, had been like. 'It wasn't as it is now,' she told me. 'It was wartime, emotional things weren't so important. You had to do what you had to do to survive, and to get out. Hitler was coming – we were all trying to get away from him.'[29]

At one point Leonora had to have an operation, and when Peggy visited her in hospital she was bowled over by her love rival's beauty. 'Her skin was like alabaster and her hair was rich in its black waviness; it swept all over her shoulders. She had enormous, mad, dark eyes with thick black brows and a tip-tilted nose. Her figure was lovely but she always dressed very badly, on purpose.'[30]

Renato, relates Peggy, was looking after Leonora like a father; Max, on the other hand, 'was always like a baby and couldn't be anyone's father'.[31] Peggy thought Leonora needed a father figure more than she needed anything else, to give her life some stability. She also recorded an odd occasion when Leonora 'brought Max to my room and seemed in some strange way to be giving him to me'.[32]

Soon after this, Peggy and Max moved to the seaside at Estoril (and resumed their sex life), but even then it seemed to Peggy as if Max was always waiting for Leonora to phone him. This, understandably, dragged her down. One day in Lisbon she bumped into Leonora at one of their favourite restaurants, the Leão d'Ouro. 'We had a terrible scene and I told her either to go back to Max, as he wanted nothing more than that, or to leave him in peace with me. She said that she only saw him out of pity and…that she certainly would leave him alone.'[33]

The truth was, as everyone involved knew, that Leonora's relationship with Renato was as convenient as Max's with Peggy. Renato was Leonora's passport out of Lisbon, and Peggy was Max's. As Leonora explained to me, it is impossible to imagine the emotional effects of being trapped in a war zone unless it happens to you. Exiting Europe was everything; love took second place. In any case, as Leonora's behaviour was hinting and as Peggy had already guessed, Leonora had moved on emotionally – even if she retained a fondness for Max, who was clearly still besotted.

At last, in July 1941, the paperwork was ready and passage was procured for Leonora and Renato on the SS *Exeter*, bound for New York. Peggy, Max and their large group were travelling on a Pan-Am Clipper, which would make the same journey in just twenty-four hours. Leonora and Renato left two days ahead of the others; during the crossing, the plane passed directly over their ship.

Leonora could not have been more pleased to get out. Everything in Europe 'reeked of death and evil', as she said later. 'Anything was better than going to South Africa or subjecting myself to the design of my family…I began a road without return.'[34]

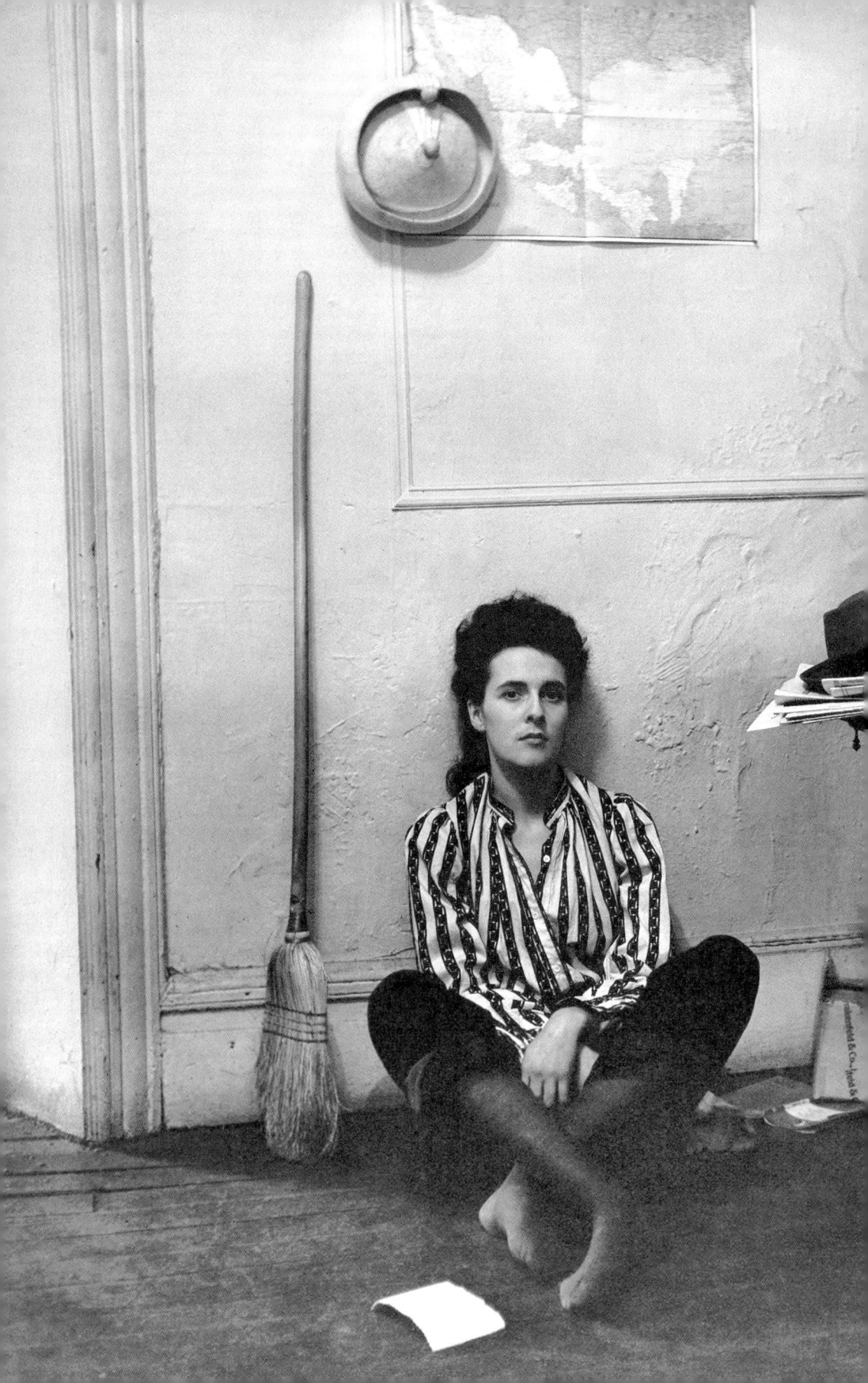

8
New York
1941–1942

If Peggy Guggenheim had believed that leaving Lisbon would be a means of separating Max from Leonora, she realized as soon as they reached New York that it hadn't worked. On their very first evening, in the restaurant where they had supper (accompanied by a detective, since Max was German and still had to be processed on Ellis Island), the first person they saw was Catherine Yarrow, the friend with whom Leonora had left Saint-Martin. Max became very upset. He knew Catherine had been instrumental in Leonora's decision to travel to Spain, and the shock he had felt on returning to Les Alliberts after his release and finding her gone was still fresh in his memory. He refused to shake hands with Catherine, and there was 'almost… a dreadful scene'.[1]

Peggy quickly made contact with André Breton, whom she had helped financially to leave Europe with his wife Jacqueline Lamba and their daughter, Aube. Breton, she recalled in her memoir, 'wanted to hear all about Max and our life in Lisbon and what had gone on between Leonora and Max. The report had gone around New York that Max would not leave Leonora in Lisbon, and that was why we had remained there so long. Breton did not gather that I was in love with Max. We talked a lot about Leonora and Max, and Breton confirmed my opinion that she was the only woman Max had ever loved.'[2]

Leonora and Renato arrived in New York by sea a few days later. They moved into an apartment on West 73rd Street provided for them by the Mexican government, for whom Renato would continue to work (Leonora seems never to have been entirely clear about what

Leonora Carrington in her Greenwich Village apartment, 1942.
Photograph by Hermann Landshoff

he did, but apparently it was something in the technical department of the tax office).[3] For her, as well as the relief of having finally put her family and Hitler behind her, this new chapter in New York represented a chance to reconnect with the artists she had known in Paris. 'I saw the Surrealists all the time. I saw a lot of Breton. Buñuel was there, and Masson was there....Everybody was there. And Duchamp was living at the time at Max and Peggy's. They had a mansion on Sutton Place.'[4]

Peggy's apartment was a hub for the group of exiles and there were many gatherings, parties and soirees, as well as a series of photoshoots of the Parisian artistic superstars reconvened in their New York setting. There had been a subtle but important shift in Leonora's status since the Paris days. Then, she had been included in the circle on account of her love affair with Max. Now she was part of the group on her own terms, recognized as the increasingly proficient artist she was becoming.

André Breton was the first to notice this. In early January 1942 he wrote to his friend Benjamin Péret, who was living in Mexico with his wife Remedios Varo, that the two 'most vital' people in New York were the Chilean painter Roberto Matta, and Leonora Carrington.[5] He and Leonora, he wrote, 'experienced a total degree of understanding'.[6] Even when she mocked him, laughing audibly when he tried to bring a surrealist meeting to order in a Greenwich Village bar as he had in the old days in Paris, he accepted the insult without comment.

It was Leonora's close friendship with Breton in this period that led her to create *Down Below*, one of her most important written works. All of her writing, she told me, was autobiographical, but many of the stories – like 'Little Francis' – were disguised, because there were others to consider as well as herself. *Down Below*, though, was different: it really concerned her alone, so she could be entirely frank about what had taken place. The only filter to truth was that sometimes, her perception of what was happening may have been somewhat different from objective reality.

Breton was fascinated by Leonora's memories of the asylum and wanted to publish an account of her time there in *VVV*, the surrealist magazine he had established in New York. In the end it was the surrealists' doctor, Pierre Mabille (whose escape from Europe Peggy had also financed), who persuaded her to write about it, arguing that setting the experience down would help liberate her from it. Leonora's attempts to do this, though, didn't work – and in fact she had made an

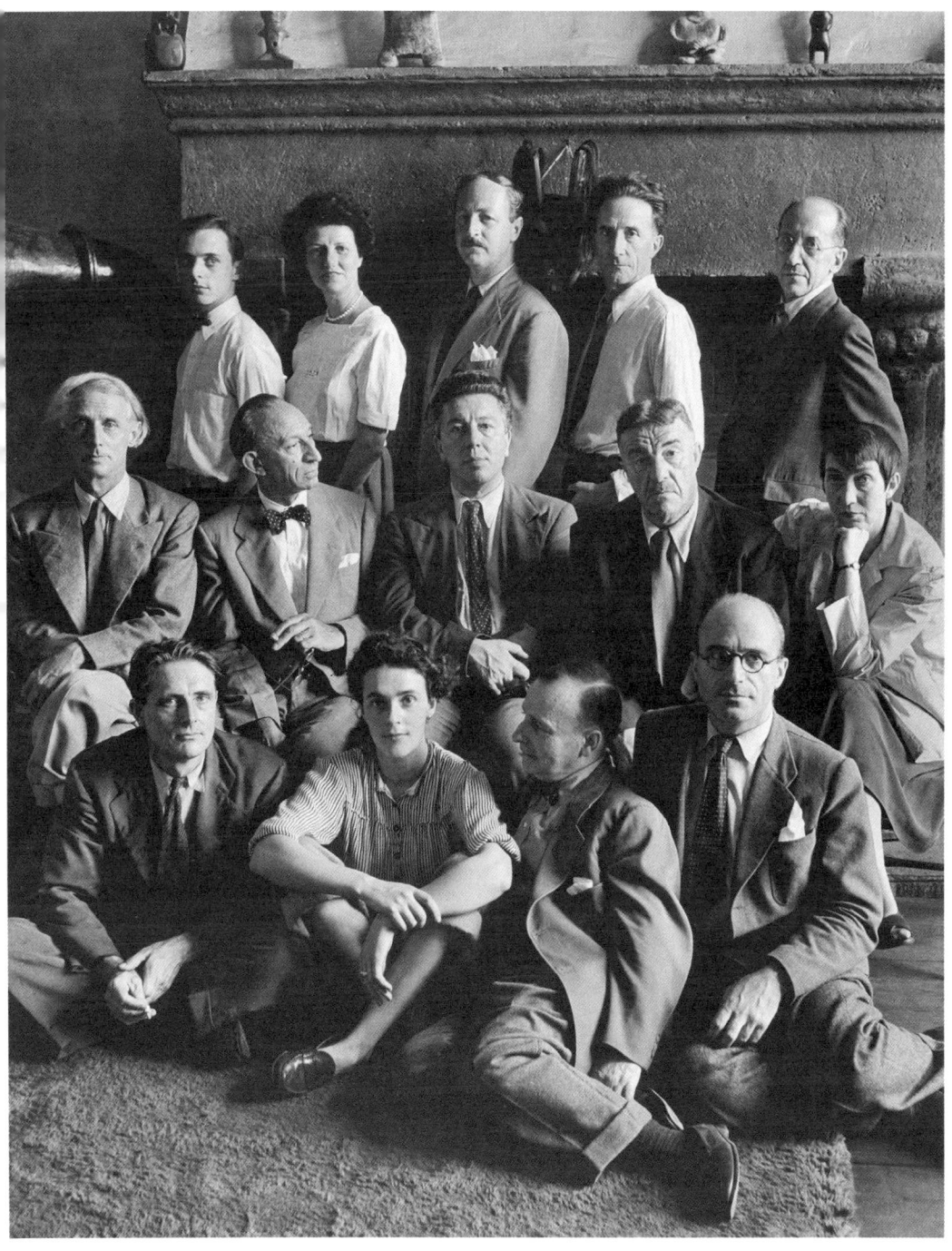

The Surrealists in Peggy Guggenheim's apartment, 1942. Photograph by Hermann Landshoff

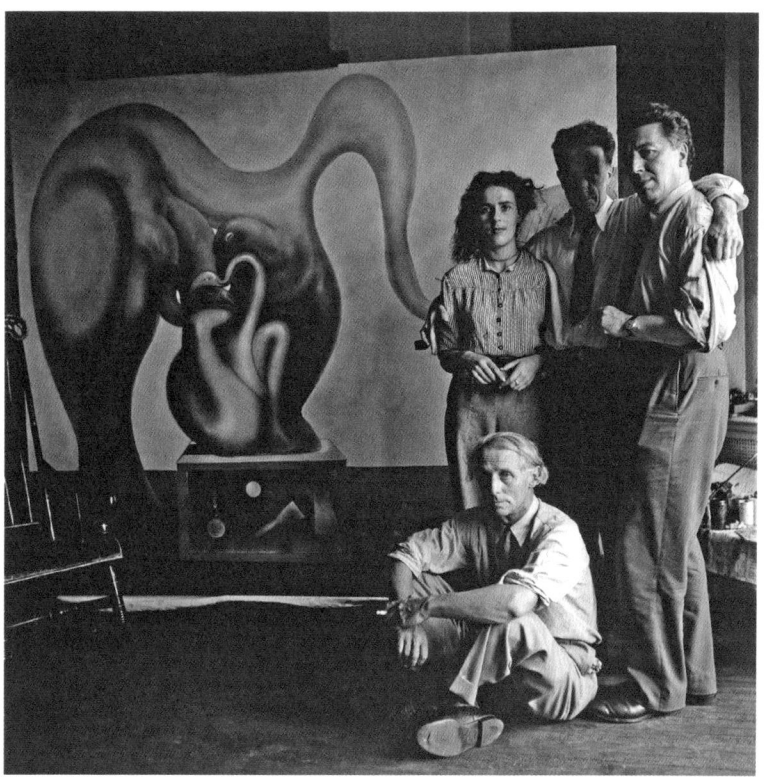

Max Ernst, Leonora Carrington, Marcel Duchamp and André Breton,
posing in front of Ernst's painting *Le surréalisme et la peinture* (1942), 1942.
Photograph by Hermann Landshoff

earlier attempt to write about it, which had also failed, and that manuscript had disappeared. Mabille came up with another idea. If Leonora
couldn't write it down herself, could she dictate her experiences to his
wife, Jeanne Megnen, who would transcribe them? This explains why
Down Below was originally written in French, Megnen's language, and
then translated for publication in *VVV*. It appeared in the fourth issue
of the magazine, in 1944, by which time Leonora was no longer in New
York. Breton wrote to Péret that he found it 'sensational'.[7]

Remembering what had happened in Spain, though, was only one
of the ways in which Leonora was making sense of her new situation.
She was also engaging properly again with painting. Her teacher from
the Kensington days, Amédée Ozenfant, was in New York, as was
one of her friends from his London academy, Stella Snead. Leonora
painted a portrait of Stella with her cats at around this time, but the

first painting she produced in the city was a more sinister work, *Garden Bedroom*. It can be seen as a companion piece to *Inn of the Dawn Horse*, her self-portrait begun in Paris and completed in the Ardèche; but where that earlier work is enigmatic and measured, this piece is chaotic and disturbing. It features a dishevelled Leonora, this time sitting astride the rocking horse. Her hair is splayed out around her head and she has a look of grim determination on her face. She is moving on, riding on: away from Europe and towards the better life she knows will one day be hers.

New York could have been the setting for that better life. In the eighteen months she spent there between the summer of 1941 and the winter of 1942/3, she was making a name for herself. Breton wasn't the only person to have noticed: the artist Hedda Sterne remembered her as 'simply the most beautiful creature...she went around in jodhpurs and boots – nobody was doing that. I remember a show, a Surrealist show...and at the opening night Leonora Carrington, when people didn't do that, came in a dress from a thrift shop, a high-necked lace dress. She looked absolutely beautiful.'[8] The dress sounds like the one in which Lee Miller photographed Leonor Fini at Saint-Martin the previous year; perhaps it had travelled to New York in the REVELATION suitcase. How interesting, too, that Leonora wore jodhpurs in real life, just as she does in *Self-Portrait/Inn of the Dawn Horse*.

Her art was going well: she was 'painting at her best'[9] one day in autumn 1941 when she had a visit from the Polish make-up entrepreneur Helena Rubinstein and one of her seven younger sisters, Manka. Helena bought a painting of five black dogs, and Manka asked if she could commission a work. They spoke for a while about Mexico, since Leonora had a Mexican husband and might one day be going there. Before they left, Helena offered Leonora two hundred dollars to paint a mural with a theme of her choice. Leonora was thrilled by the sales – the only problem, she realized once they had left, was that she had no idea where to acquire a canvas for a mural-sized painting.

Marc Chagall was one of the most successful artists in New York at the time, so Leonora decided to approach him to ask for help: could he loan her a canvas? Chagall looked at her paintings, refused to lend her a canvas, and left her with the patronizing comment that she should 'Keep painting, my little one, keep painting.' Fortunately, '[a]t the eleventh hour, Breton rescued the day by giving her one of his bed sheets, and she was able to paint the mural with Ernst, Duchamp, and Roberto Matta as assistants. Ernst momentarily shifted out of the

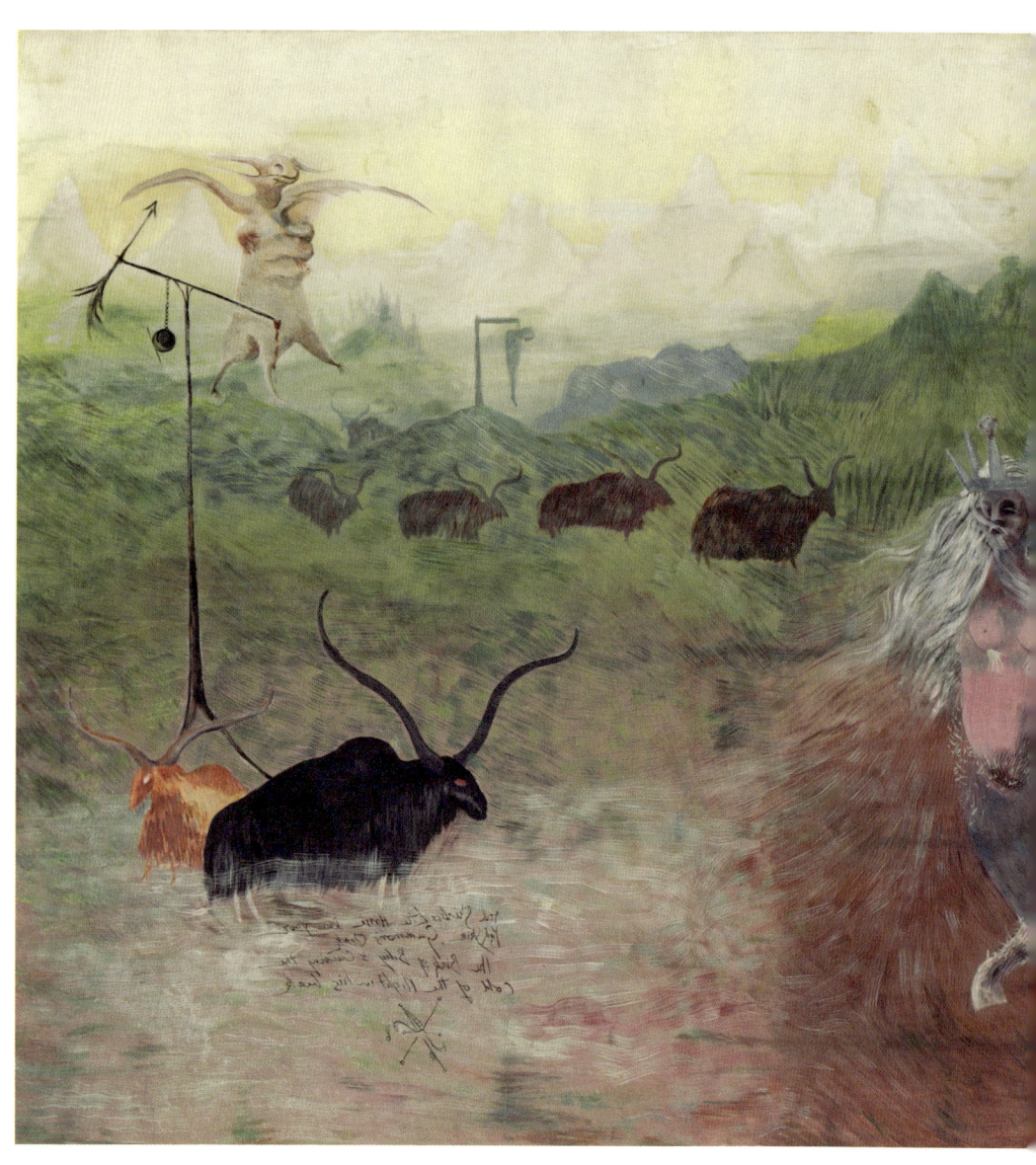

Leonora Carrington, in collaboration with Max Ernst, Marcel Duchamp
and Matta, *Summer*, 1941

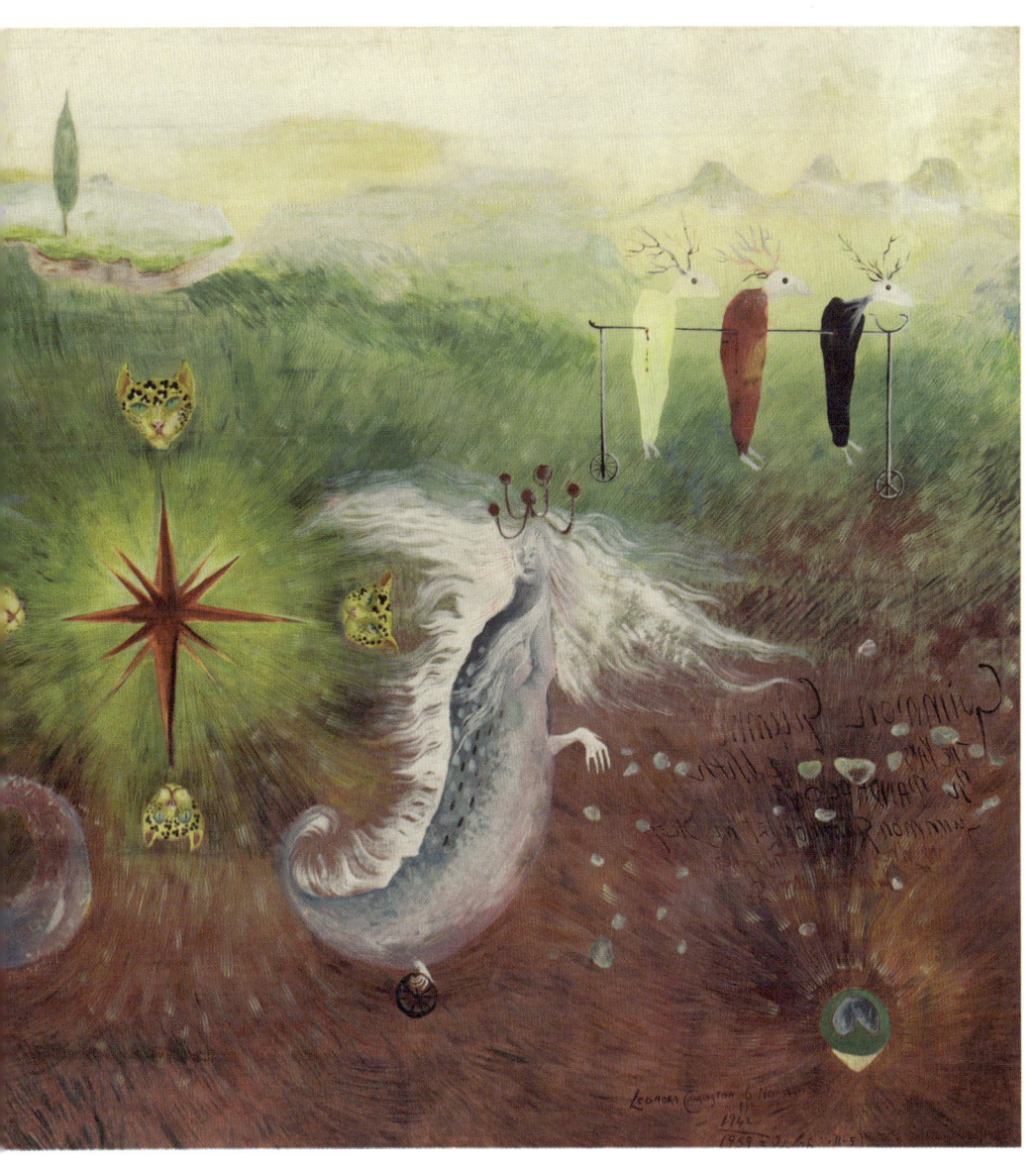

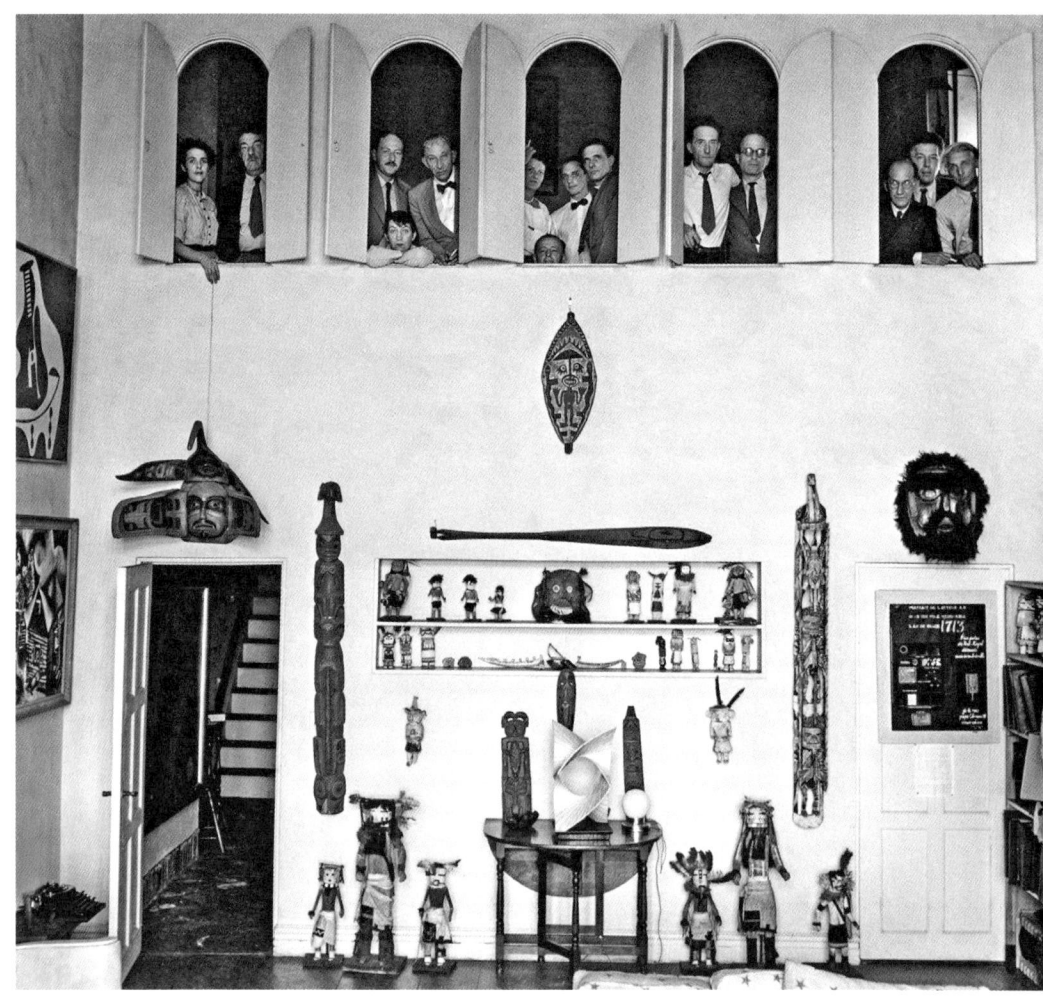

The Surrealists in Peggy Guggenheim's apartment, 1942.
Photograph by Hermann Landshoff

assistant mode and painted his signature bird in the upper left corner to complement the work. Carrington titled it "Summer". Manka loved it.'[10]

There were plenty of parties in New York at this time, and most of them took place in Hale House at 440 East 51st Street, the Sutton Place mansion Peggy Guggenheim had rented for herself, Max and her huge art collection. The biggest room was a space Peggy called 'the chapel' because it had 'a balcony above with five little windows overlooking [it]. Here five choirboys might well have sung Gregorian chants.'[11] Instead, she got the surrealists to pose for photographer Hermann Landshoff: fourteen of them are gathered in an image that also features a medley of Peggy's Native American artworks. No doubt they were there for one of the parties, at which she typically served whisky and potato chips. Peering out through the arched windows are Ozenfant, Duchamp, Berenice Abbott and Piet Mondrian. Peggy herself is in the centre. Perhaps she arranged the line-up, because Leonora and Max are as far from one another as possible – Leonora far left, Max far right. As she was honest enough to admit, Peggy was always keen to put distance between them.

The fact was, Max was still devoted to Leonora, and Peggy was acutely aware of it. In the days before the SS *Exeter* docked in New York he had been desperate to see his former lover again, and in the weeks that followed the two saw a lot of one another. They do not seem to have reignited their intimate relationship, though that was of little consolation to Peggy. She had already guessed that Max loved Leonora in a way he had never loved her – or, quite possibly, anyone else – and probably never would. Leonora, meanwhile, always confessed to being quite puritanical about relationships. She believed people should be together because they truly loved one another. She also admired Peggy greatly (indeed, the feeling was entirely mutual) and would have seen sleeping with Max again as a betrayal of her.

But she had another reason, too, to keep her distance physically from Max. Because what had begun as a marriage of convenience with Renato had matured into something more meaningful: if it wasn't true love, it was certainly sexually sparky, with a great deal of mutual affection. Leonora had also, as Peggy had noticed, come to depend on Renato as a kind of father figure in the same way she had first been drawn to Max. Peggy had rightly pointed out that Max was too much of a baby himself to be anyone's father – Renato, though, fulfilled Leonora's fantasies. When she needed someone to care for her, to put her first, to marry her and to get her to where she wanted to be, he was there; to the end of her life, she spoke about him warmly and with gratitude.

A series of letters discovered after Leonora's death, written to Renato while they were living together in the apartment on the Upper West Side, reveal her feelings towards him. One, written on 22 September 1941, is addressed to an absent Renato: he has gone missing, out with friends, and Leonora sounds desperate to have him back. 'I die slowly and painfully waiting to see you,' she writes (the letter is typed, in French). 'Come back soon. I love you, I want to sleep with you, I want to kiss you and lick you. I would give the cat, my hair and my left hand for you to come back.'

She goes on: 'Renato for the love of the devil, come home. If you're annoyed by this love, you need to know it's not convenient to fall in love with crazy women, we are all like that. I love you, I love you, I love you, I love you, I love you, I love you, I love you, I love you, I love you. I'm tortured, I'm in agony, I'm angry, I'm exaggerating.' She won't go to bed on her own, she says; but 'when you come back you will be calm, and you won't imagine the storm and sorrows I have endured'.[12]

Why is it rare, she asks in another letter, for people who are living together to write to one another? 'In writing, one becomes freer. I want to put the jewels of my personality before you.' But Renato has left her alone again – clearly, it's a pattern of behaviour that she loathes – and she says she is crying, becoming emotional…'pure female tricks to eat you better my child (as the wolf said to Little Red Riding Hood)'. And then comes this line: 'Every time I cry alone I put on the crown of a martyr…maybe it's the spoiled girl who cries in me then. Maybe I have to dismiss her – and how do I do that?'[13]

Some of these feelings are also played out in her short story 'Waiting'. It follows a conversation between two women: 'Margaret' ('her clothes were too long and her hair much too untidy, like someone saved from drowning') is Leonora. She tells a passing stranger, Elizabeth, that she is 'waiting for Fernando', who is forty-three (like Renato) and has blue-grey hair that Margaret loves. But she has become so sad waiting for him that she has no tears left. The two wander into Elizabeth's apartment, where Margaret realizes that Elizabeth and Fernando are lovers too. Perhaps the tale conflates her relationships with Max and with Renato at this point.

Leonora was divided between quite different lives in New York. Some of the time, she was a lovelorn wife pining for her husband to

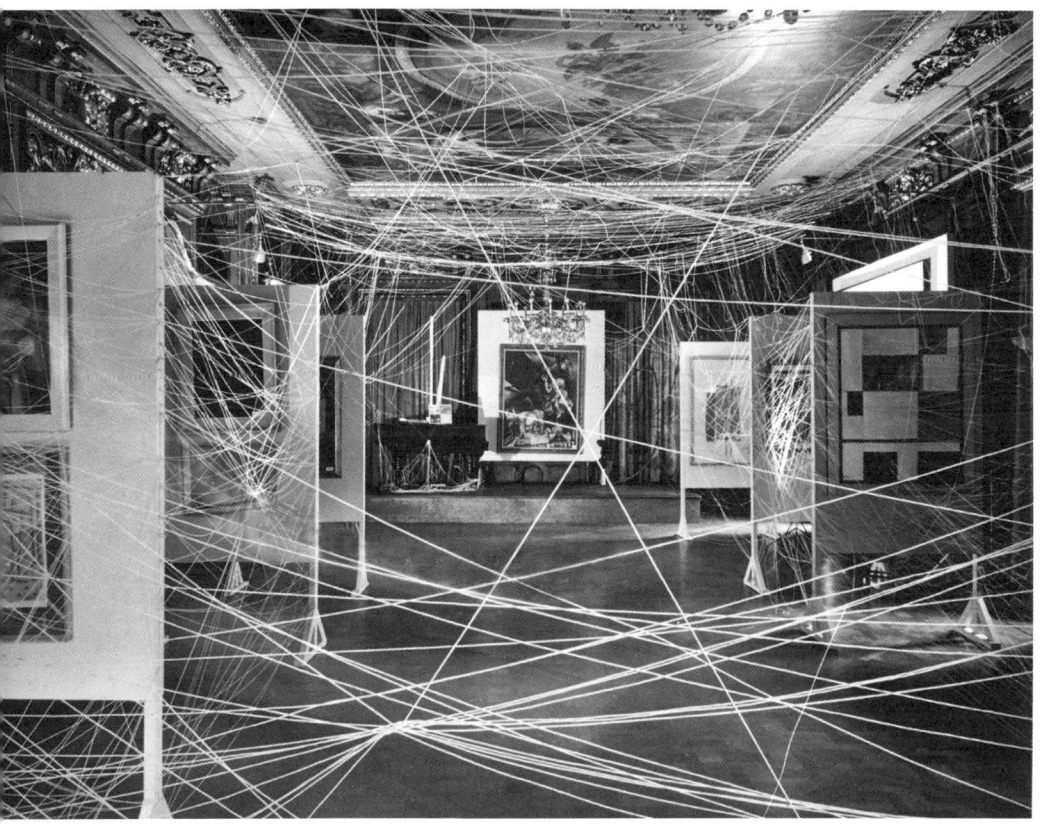

Installation view of 'First Papers of Surrealism' exhibition, showing Marcel Duchamp's
His Twine, 1942. Photograph by John D. Schiff

come home while he was out with his mates; other times she was
an up-and-coming surrealist superstar. Through the late summer
and autumn of 1942, she was central to a major exhibition of the
exiled group that took place at the Whitelaw Reid Mansion in mid-
town Manhattan between 14 October and 7 November. Billed as the
biggest ever surrealist exhibition in America, it aimed to convey
what the refugee artists had had to go through to get themselves
across the Atlantic. Leonora, who exhibited alongside Frida Kahlo,
Meret Oppenheim, Hedda Sterne, Remedios Varo and others, was
also heavily involved in creating a setting that spoke to the difficulties
of the artists. She helped weave a criss-cross web across the gallery;
the idea was to place barriers between the visitors and the work,
suggestive of the barriers its creators had encountered during their
long journeys.

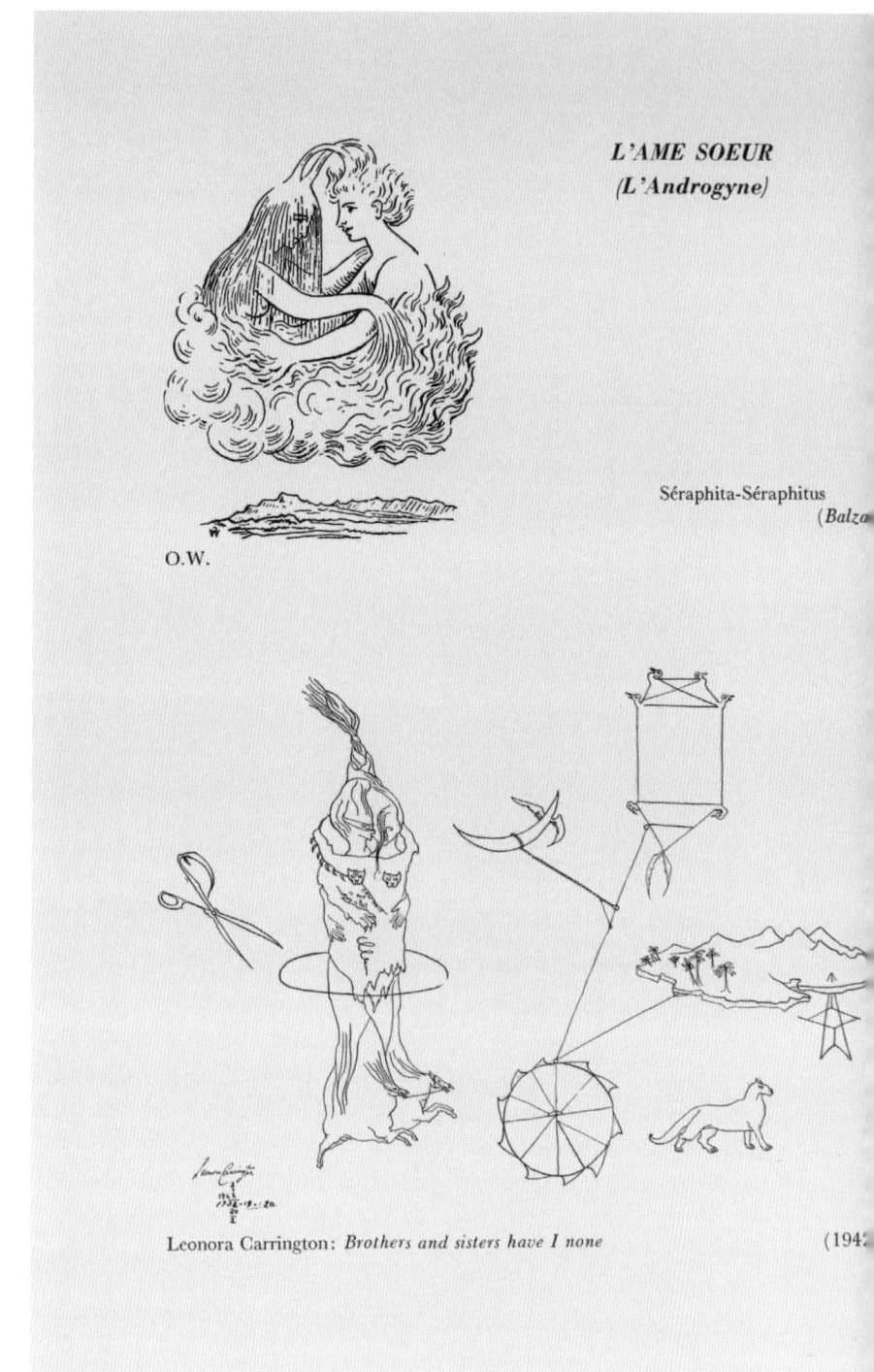

L'AME SOEUR
(L'Androgyne)

Séraphita-Séraphitus
(*Balz...*

O.W.

Leonora Carrington: *Brothers and sisters have I none*

(194...

Spread from 'First Papers of Surrealism' with Carrington's work
Brothers and Sisters Have I None, 1942

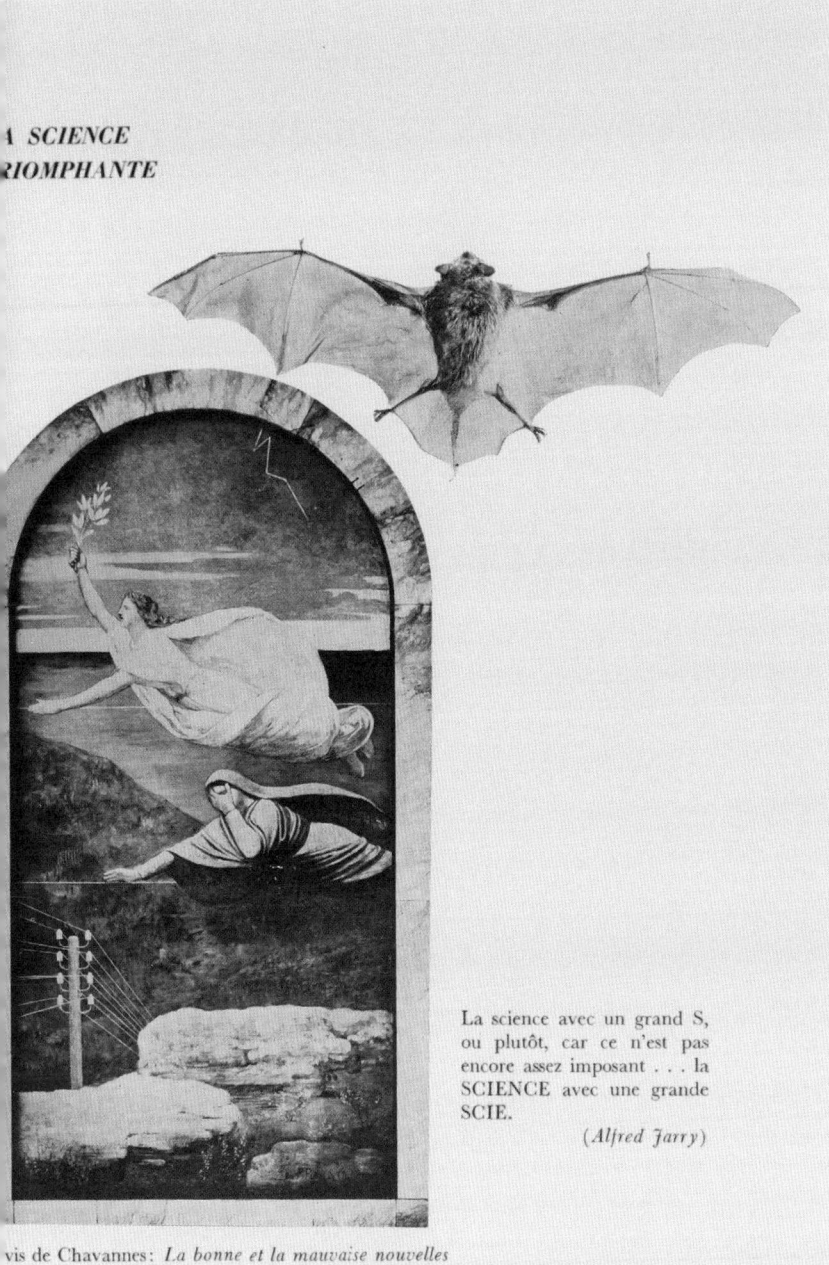

La science avec un grand S,
ou plutôt, car ce n'est pas
encore assez imposant . . . la
SCIENCE avec une grande
SCIE.

(*Alfred Jarry*)

vis de Chavannes: *La bonne et la mauvaise nouvelles*

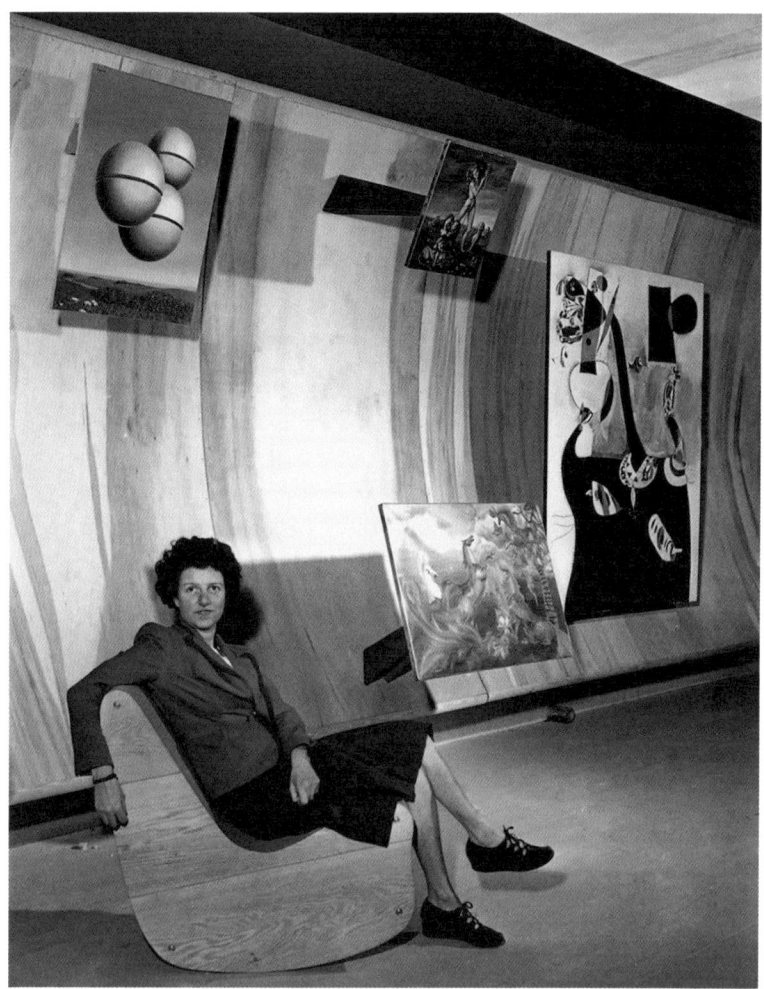

Peggy Guggenheim in her gallery Art of This Century, New York, 1942.
Exhibition design by Frederick Kiesler. Photograph by Berenice Abbott

Throughout all of this Max continued to betray his feelings for
Leonora in countless ways, and Peggy was acutely aware of all of them.
In France she had seen him paint Leonora's portrait over and over
again, but it was a long time before he painted Peggy. Now, in New
York, he would spend entire days with Leonora, something he never
did with Peggy. When Peggy asked Max to dedicate a book to her, he
wrote something cold, although she had seen the warmth with which
he had inscribed books to Leonora.

It couldn't go on, and it didn't. Just as Peggy was thinking of leaving Max, in the late autumn of 1941, Leonora decided to leave New

York and accompany Renato back to his native Mexico. That had long been the plan, although worries over money and the uncertainty of finding work in Mexico City had delayed their journey. The hiatus had given Leonora a chance to experience the life of an artist in New York City. It was fun, and interesting, and she was making headway in her career; but these were not her guiding stars. What mattered more to her was following her own intuition – and also playing out the adventure she had embarked on five years earlier when she left her family, and Britain, behind. Still feeling close to Renato, and believing that Mexico held adventures she could not yet imagine, she agreed to make the long trip by road with him and a group of other Mexican staff from the embassy.

Precisely when and where her final meeting with Max took place is not recorded. Neither of them ever spoke in detail about their feelings for one another, so the deepest story of their relationship remained with them, and they took it to their graves.

In New York, Peggy – who had married Max soon after Leonora's departure – was working hard on an exhibition to take place in the spring of 1943 at her gallery, Art of This Century. It would include the work of thirty women, including Leonora. Max helped her with the curation and when he suggested adding another artist, so that it became '31 Women', she readily agreed.

That, she later realized, was a mistake: the additional artist was Dorothea Tanning, for whom Max would eventually leave her. In her memoirs Peggy calls Dorothea 'vastly inferior to Leonora, who really was a creature of genius'.[14] The painter Buffie Johnson, also part of the New York group, observed that Peggy 'couldn't understand why Max fell for [Dorothea]. It seemed absolutely incredible, because Leonora Carrington was so marvellous.'[15] Leonora and Max would never meet again. He spent the rest of his life with Tanning, and died in 1976 at the age of eighty-four.

'Do you believe that the past dies?' Elizabeth asks Margaret, in Leonora's story 'Waiting'. Yes, says Margaret. But only if the present cuts its throat.

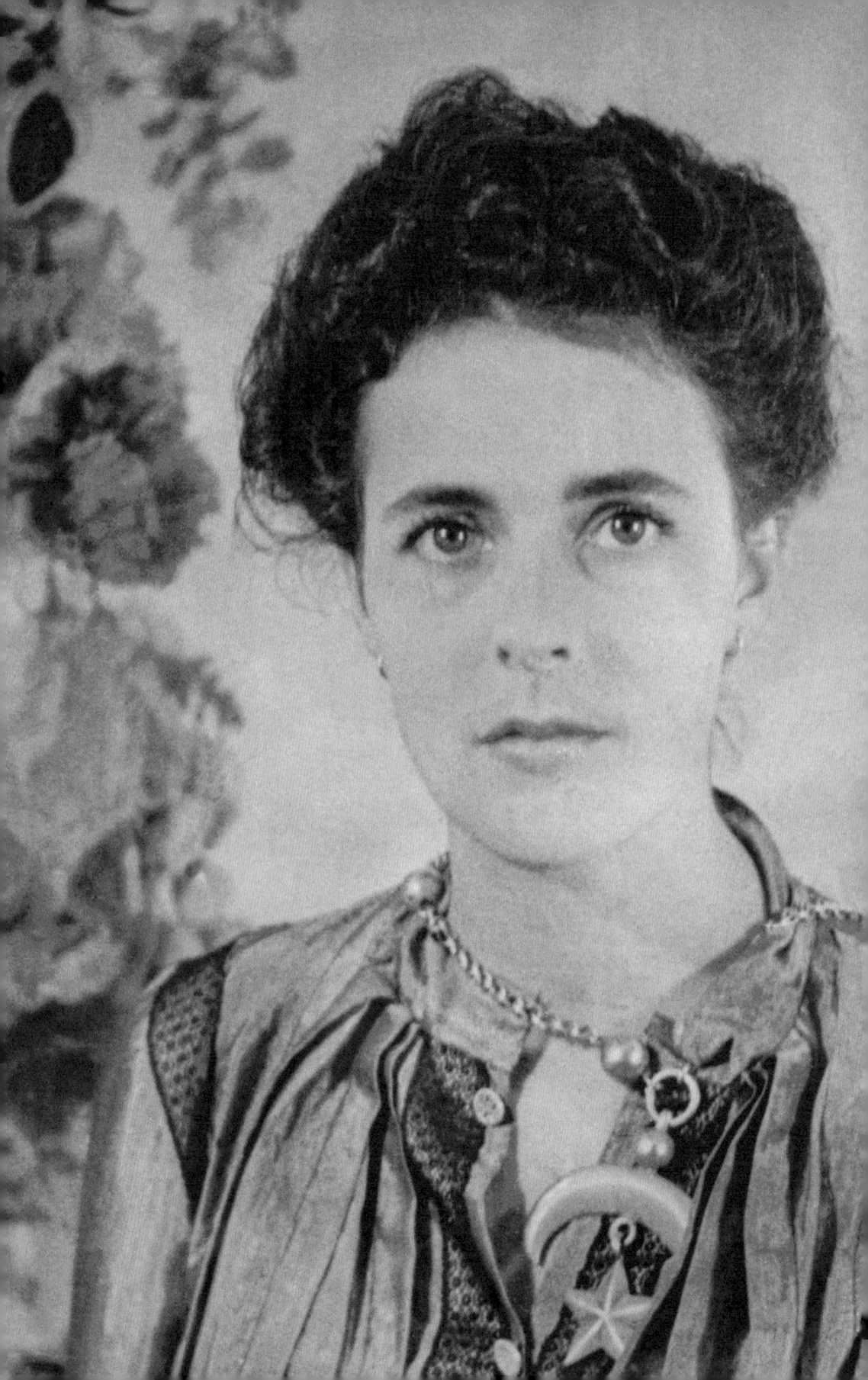

9
Mexico
1942–1968

By 1942 Leonora had already experienced many fresh horizons, but her arrival in Mexico introduced her to a landscape quite unlike anything she had seen before: more exotic, more colourful, more dramatic and more remote. She and Renato had travelled by car from New York, crossing the border at Nuevo Laredo on the Rio Grande in Tamaulipas. It seemed, she remembered later, 'a totally new world. It had a feeling of the Orient…there were still people (at that time) going around on horses and with big hats.'[1]

They were travelling in a convoy with other diplomats, along roads that wound up mountains and down valleys, through rainforests and pine woods, past groves of orchids and plains of cacti. There were lush fields of mangoes, melons and the papayas that Leonora would enjoy for breakfast to the end of her life; there were vast, dry canyons and broad, tree-fringed rivers. It must have been immediately clear to her that her new country was a place of contrasts: abundant meadows of flowers gave way to miles of bare aridity before the landscape returned again to the colours of poinsettias, dahlias and marigolds.

And then, eventually, they arrived in Mexico City, the oldest city in North America, along roads that had once been causeways connecting the ancient Aztec island of Tenochtitlan with the mainland. Mexico City in 1942 was much smaller than it is today – it had a population of around 2 million, compared with the current figure of around 21 million – but it was still huge in 1940s terms. The city centre might have been reminiscent of Madrid and Santander but for the most part, the whole place smelled, looked and sounded very different from

Leonora Carrington in Mexico

anywhere Leonora had previously lived. The scent of stone-ground maize filled the air, along with the slapping sound of it being shaped into tortillas on street-corner griddles; there were wafts of acrid tobacco and dust and bad drains, of strong coffee and charcoal fires.

Ornate colonial buildings lined the streets around the Zócalo, the central square where the men of the Old World battled against the men of the New in the Mexican–American war of 1847. Nearby, sweeping through the heart of the city, was the wide boulevard of the Paseo de la Reforma, planned by the archduke-turned-emperor Maximilian and named after the upheaval that led to his death by firing squad in 1867. In the large park called Chapultepec there were ancient ahuehuete trees that had been tall even in the days of the 15th-century poet king Nezahualcoyotl, and amid the flower stalls of the Alameda was a huge neoclassical monument to the 19th-century reformer Benito Juárez.

Mexico City was already a melting pot of people from a wide variety of different heritages. As well as Indians, whose traditional roots stretched into the distant past, there were Spaniards, Creoles, Africans. Many were Catholic – the Spanish missionaries had done their work well, and more than 96 per cent of Mexicans were of their faith – but the Roman dogma had become intertwined with the beliefs of the Maya peoples, the Aztecs and the pagans, belief systems that predated Christianity. This mixing up of ideas and spirituality fascinated Leonora; later, it would inspire her 1963–64 mural *El mundo mágico de los mayas (The Magical World of the Maya)*. There were women wearing huipils, a standard outer garment for more than a thousand years; elaborately embroidered costumes from Tehuantepec; and the ubiquitous rebozo, an all-purpose shawl serving as head covering, shoulder wrap, baby sling and shopping bag.

Leonora and Renato settled into an apartment in the Mixcoac neighbourhood to the south of the city. Renato soon took up with the many friends he had not seen during his long sojourn in Europe and, just as she had often been in New York, Leonora was left alone. At least now there were plenty of new things for her to see. One of her favourite pastimes was walking around the market a few streets away from where they lived. 'One of the activities that I liked best was going to the market; it was fantastic to discover chipotle chile or the maguey worms,' she remembered.[2] It was the beginning of a fascination with markets, what they represented as well as what they were, that would remain with her for the rest of her life.

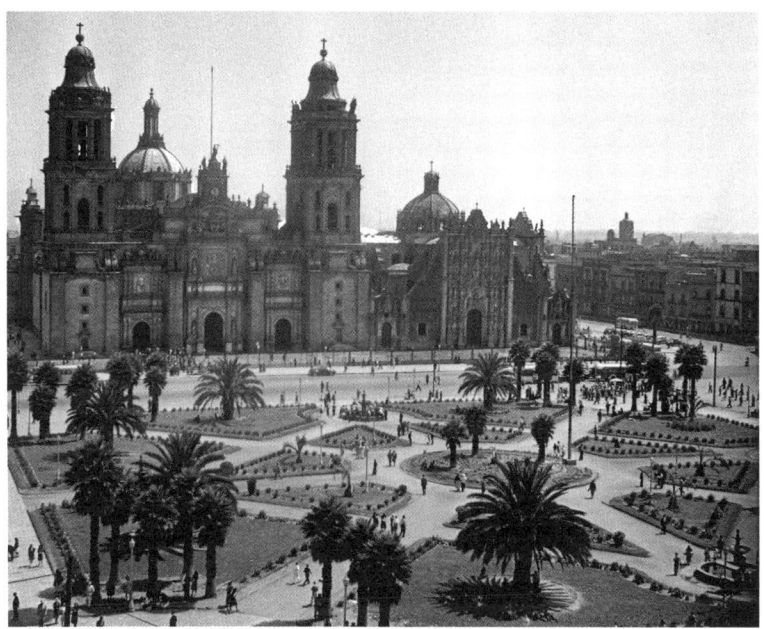

Zócalo, Mexico City, *c.* 1941–43

Today, the markets of Mexico City remain one of the places where the fantastical meets the everyday. To experience their magic and their madness is to begin to appreciate the centuries of life and history that are layered into the fabric of the place. While I was visiting her many years later Leonora encouraged me to spend time, as she had, exploring the markets. I went one day to Sonora, a huge, crowded place whose sights, sounds and general air of outright chaos summed up for me, as they had for her, so many facets of the country.

One place she had specifically told me to visit was the area where herbs were sold, most of them hanging up dried, to be mixed into tinctures with water when you got them home. There were holy medals and rosaries, fans and books, shells and whips. Music blared out the entire time, and babies cried; I stood mesmerized by a wall at least three metres high loaded with masks and monsters, skeletons, faces, colours, feathers, maracas, toys and more. Nearby was a stall selling models of the reverse-saint skeleton known as the Santa Muerte, complete with cigarette and glass of tequila in hand; they ranged from tiny to life-sized.

But visiting the market and walking around the city, absorbing though it was, didn't take up all of Leonora's time. With Renato increasingly pulled into his old life, she began to make contact with other Europeans who, like her, had fled the continent because of the war. Mexico had an 'open door' policy under the government of President Lázaro Cárdenas, and this led to Spaniards, Hungarians, Italians, Germans and Swiss nationals gathering in Mexico City, many of them artists and writers. Leonora, of course, was not officially a refugee – she was in Mexico as the wife of a Mexican. But her marriage to Renato, though it had its moments of genuine love, affection and excitement, had originally been one of convenience, and now that he was neglecting her Leonora decided to strike out on her own. The relationships she formed around this time would become some of the

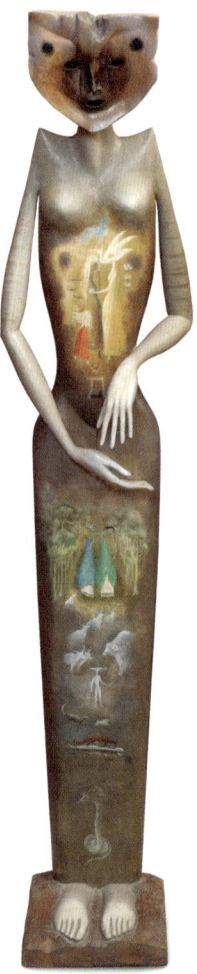

Cat Woman (La Grande Dame), 1951

longest-lasting and most significant of her life, helping her to flourish both as an artist and as a human being.

One of these new friends was Remedios Varo, a Spanish artist who was married to the French poet Benjamin Péret. Leonora had first met the couple in Paris, but it was here in Mexico that she and Remedios became close. This friendship opened the door to many others, including with the French artist Alice Rahon, the Austrian painter Wolfgang Paalen and the Swiss photographer Eva Sulzer. Through this group Leonora would also get to know Hungarian photographer Kati Horna, with whom she would have one of the longest-lasting friendships of her life, and Kati's partner José Horna, a Spanish craftsman with whom Leonora would collaborate on sculptures including *Cat Woman (La Grande Dame)* and the Cuna. And she would also meet the person with whom she would come to have the most lasting connection of all: another Hungarian photographer, Emerico 'Chiki' Weisz, who was to become her second husband.

Along with Remedios and Benjamin, Chiki had arrived in Mexico in October 1942 aboard the *Serpa Pinto*. Raised in a Jewish family in Budapest, six years Leonora's senior, he had endured an impoverished childhood; for a time his mother, by then widowed, was so poor she had to have him cared for in an orphanage. This episode in his life would become the basis for one of Leonora's short stories, 'The Stone Door', in which an orphan boy called Zachariah dreams about meeting a young English girl from a much more privileged background. In the story the pair realize they are soulmates, and as in Leonora's fiction, so in her life. With Chiki – a photographer who had worked alongside his and Kati's childhood friend Endre Ernő Friedmann, better known as the war photographer Robert Capa – Leonora felt she could embark on a shared lifetime.

Before this, though, came an amicable separation from her first husband, Renato; although passion had undoubtedly infused their relationship at times, it was clear that it wasn't going to work for the long haul. Having moved out of their shared apartment, Leonora went to live with Remedios and Benjamin in the house they rented in the district of San Rafael, on a street called Gabino Barreda. It was a tumbledown building with a French window for a door, holes in the walls and rodents in the kitchen, but its art collection was second to none. The walls were covered with original works by Picasso, Ernst and Tanguy, picked up by the émigrés during their journey through France towards Mexico.

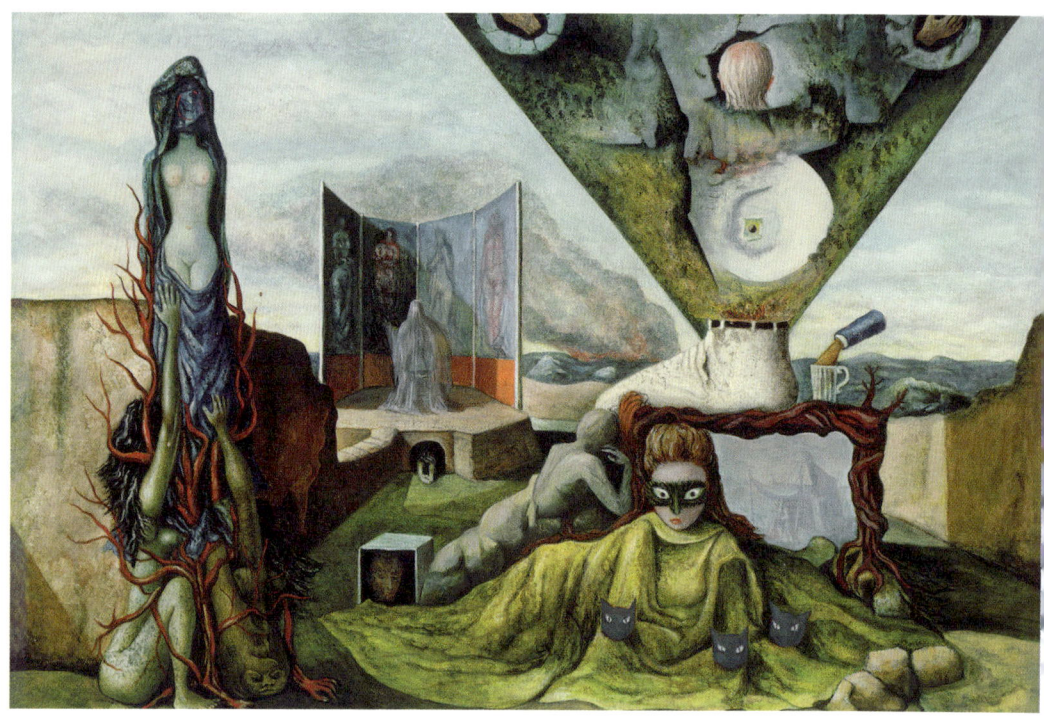

Gunther Gerzso, *Los días de la calle Gabino Barreda (The Days of Gabino Barreda Street)*, 1944

Something of the wild and surreal mood of the house is captured in *Los días de la calle Gabino Barreda (The Days of Gabino Barreda Street)*, a 1944 painting by Gunther Gerzso, a Mexico-born artist who had been raised partly in Switzerland. He was part of the circle that centred on the Gabino Barreda Street house: other figures for whom it was a focal point included Remedios's former husband Gerardo Lizárraga, Esteban Francés and Miriam Wolf, as well as the Hornas. Centre stage in Gerzso's painting is a figure clearly identifiable as Remedios, draped in a green cloth with several cats – she was always surrounded by cats – dotted around her. Nearby is Leonora, her face obscured but her hair betraying her identity. Her hands, entwined with red thorns, hold aloft a mannequin that is perhaps also herself. Behind all of this is the sea over which the group has travelled, and the fire of the war they have escaped burns on the horizon. It is a painting about journeys and migration, about art and danger, about influences old and new.

By the beginning of 1946, Leonora was pregnant. She and Chiki quickly married: they held a party afterwards at the Hornas' house on

Calle Tabasco. The group gathered around a small fountain that Kati and José's daughter Norah still has today, in her own garden on the other side of Mexico City. Most of the key members of the group were in attendance: Gerzso, Varo, Péret, Wolf, the Hornas and Lizárraga. Leonora –young, composed, confident and excited was at the beginning of a significant new stage of her life. Having spent so much of her youth with people with whom she felt no affinity – her family, her teachers and classmates – she is at last part of a group with whom she feels entirely at home. Though she was twice a bride, she never wore the traditional gear; maybe the early days of ball gowns in London had put her off that sort of dressing up forever. Her outfit for her marriage to Chiki was a tailored suit over a blouse, and a pair of drop pearl earrings that she still wore when I knew her many decades later.

According to Inés Amor, who ran the Galería de Arte Mexicano – the most important Mexico City gallery of contemporary art, and the first one in the country to represent Leonora – the European incomers led a bohemian existence. They kept themselves to themselves, and within their circle 'Leonora was like a queen in her court...beautiful and interesting, everyone was...attracted to her personality although later on, they would end up fighting with her. Among the refugees from Hungary, she found the man who would become her husband: Weisz. [He] told me one day: "I was born to protect Leonora, and I couldn't prevent her from being how she is."'[3] Amor's take on the situation alludes to the difficulty many people (including Amor herself) had in maintaining a good relationship with Leonora. Her falling-out with her family might have been the most seismic altercation of her life, but it was certainly not the only one – and often, the people with whom she fell out were the very ones who (like Amor) could be most helpful to her. The comment Amor remembers from Chiki hints at this same character trait, the fact that Leonora could sometimes seem like her own worst enemy. Once crossed, she was often adamant she would not patch up a relationship. My diary of a visit to her in spring 2009 records a conversation we had about getting older. She says: 'It's a bore. You need people.' I say: 'But we all need people, don't we?' And Leonora replies: 'Yes, we do need people,' as though it's a complete revelation to her.

Amor explains that the European group was never part of the established Mexican circle of artists, and that there was a certain amount of mutual suspicion between them. These were the days when art in Mexico was dominated by *los tres grandes*: Diego Rivera, David

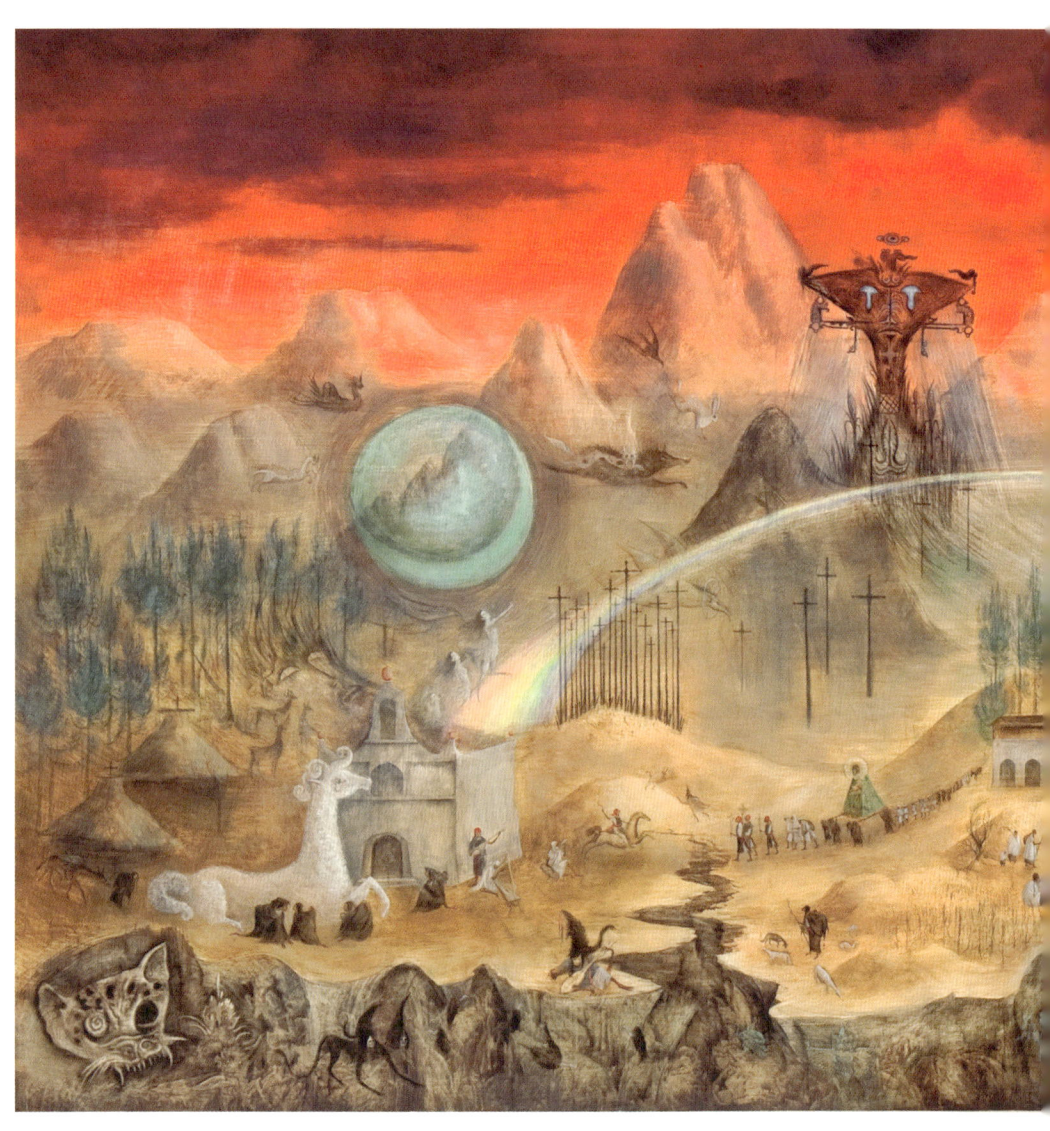

El mundo mágico de los mayas (The Magical World of the Maya), 1963–64

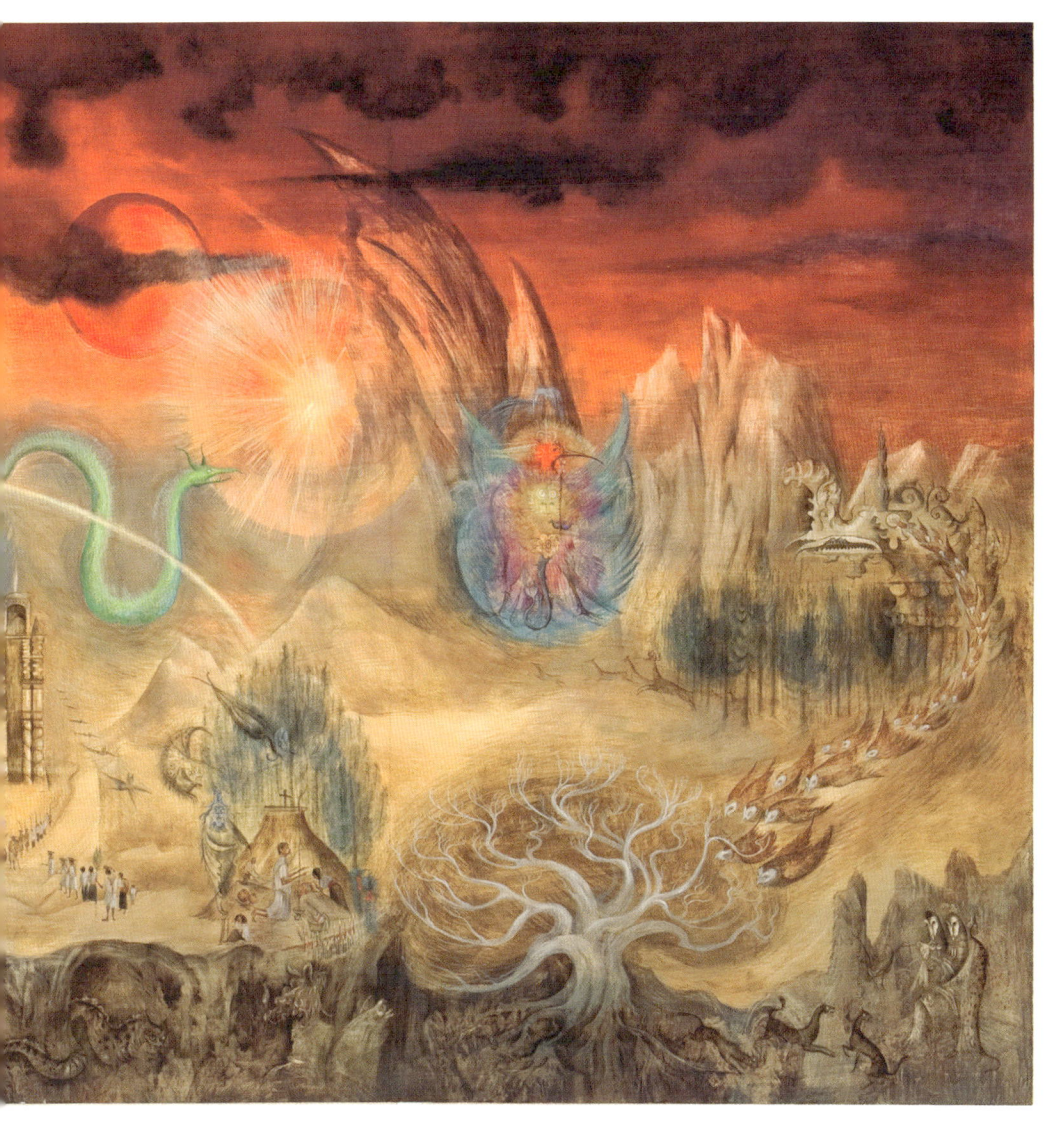

Alfaro Siqueiros and José Clemente Orozco. Frida Kahlo, Rivera's wife, was a struggling painter whom nobody would have thought to bracket with this group; of course, she would go on to become arguably the most famous female painter the world has known, and certainly more significant than *los tres*. Leonora would always remember her meetings with Kahlo, who, impacted by her increasingly fragile health, was painting on a canvas suspended over her bed. While Mexican artists tended to focus on the recent history of their country, Amor says, the exiles were more fascinated with Mexico's nature, landscape and pre-Columbian art: 'Except for the Spaniards, the other Europeans always continued to be foreigners in the country.'[4]

Leonora certainly became knowledgeable about Mexican muralism and in the early 1960s she would paint her own mural, *El mundo mágico de los mayas*, but she was clear that this didn't involve associating herself with the Mexican school. 'I was not interested in a social message in painting and my mural was totally foreign to that discourse,' she explained.[5] Explanations were not something she gave often; she was always very clear that for her, elucidation was neither necessary nor possible, because she believed that art spoke to people in the deepest part of their psyche. She warned me not to try to rationalize or intellectualize it. The way to understand paintings, she said, was to tune in to one's own feelings about a work: 'You're trying to intellectualize something desperately, and you're wasting your time. That's not a way of understanding, to make into a kind of mini-logic – you'll never understand by that road.'[6]

The Mexican muralists were not surrealists and understandably they eschewed a European-centric art movement, but surrealism had already made a mark on the country in two ways. In 1938, André Breton – to whom Leonora was close at various points in her life, and whom she always called 'the headmaster of surrealism' – travelled to Mexico to take part in a series of lectures as part of a tour that had already taken him to Barcelona, London and Prague. As the story goes, he arrived at the port of Veracruz with his wife Jacqueline and their daughter Aube, only to find the organizers had forgotten he was coming and no one was there to meet them. The Bretons arranged their own transport to Mexico City and André made his way to the university where the lecture was to be held – only to find it locked up and silent. Perplexed, he went to a nearby cantina to ponder what to do next. While he was there, a man with a gun walked into the bar and shot one of his fellow drinkers. You invited me here to talk about surrealism, he told his

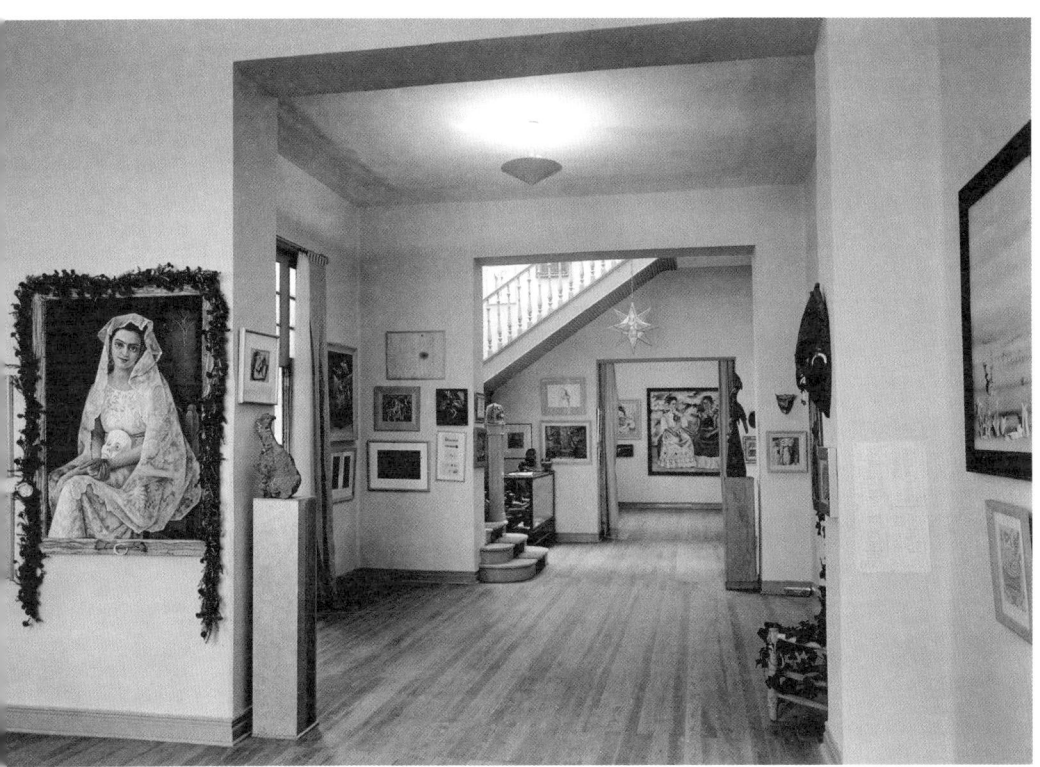

Installation view of the Exposición Internacional del Surrealismo, 1940

listeners a few days later once the confusion was sorted out – but really, there was no need. Mexico, as he often said afterwards, was the most surreal country on Earth.

Breton's new-found fascination with Mexico, where he was a guest of the Riveras and became a champion of Kahlo's work (claiming her as a 'surrealist discovery'), led to another significant moment in the movement's Mexican history: an International Exhibition of Surrealism in the capital in 1940. This show, held at Amor's Galería de Arte Mexicano, promised to be a high point of the year for Mexico's *artísticas*: the guest list, published in a newspaper, included the words 'all Mexico'. The invitations were 'burnt' – singed along their edges – and the catalogue promised 'clairvoyant watches', 'perfume of the Fifth Dimension' and 'Radioactive Frames'.[7]

Reviews were mixed: one said the show had nothing of the deep-felt or fiery qualities that might be expected of surrealism, and that the movement, having become fashionable, was now dead. Others noted

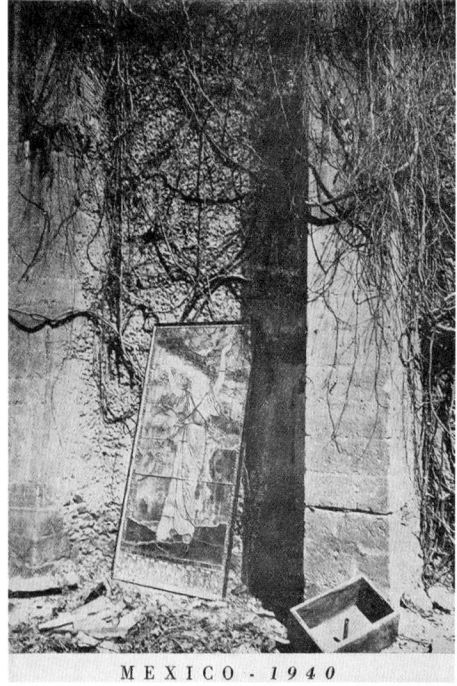

MEXICO · *1940*

Manuel Álvarez Bravo, cover of Exposición Internacional del Surrealismo
exhibition catalogue, Galería de Arte Mexicano, Mexico City, 1940

that there were few if any genuine surrealists among the Mexican
exhibitors. Certainly Kahlo, who had two pieces in the exhibition
(*The Two Fridas*, 1939, and *The Wounded Table*, 1940), had always been
ambivalent about the movement and her part in it. 'I never knew I
was a Surrealist,' she said cuttingly, 'til André Breton came to Mexico
and told me I was. The only thing I know is that I paint because I need
to, and I paint always whatever passes through my head, without any
other consideration.'[8]

Kahlo's biographer Hayden Herrera has an interesting take on why
surrealism didn't take off in Mexico as Breton and the other organizers of the show – Wolfgang Paalen and the poet César Moro – had
hoped. One obstacle, she says, was the dominance of the muralist
movement, with its commitment to realism. But 'another impedi-
ment...lay in the fact that Mexico had its own magic and myths and
thus did not need foreign notions of fantasy. The self-conscious search

for subconscious truths that may have provided European Surrealists with some release from the confines of the rational world and ordinary bourgeois life offered little enchantment in a country where reality and dreams are perceived to merge and miracles are thought to be daily occurrences.'[9] In other words: Mexico didn't need surrealism, and surrealism couldn't have Mexico.

But Mexico did have Leonora Carrington. In 1956 – four years after Kahlo's death – Rivera praised Leonora's work: 'Mexico has the good fortune that among us live three women painters who undoubtedly are among the most important women artists in the world: Remedios Varo – ah, how the painting of that woman enchants me! – Leonora Carrington and Alice Rahon.'[10]

In Mexico, Leonora, along with Varo and Kati Horna, would reinvent surrealism. 'There was an inner circle and they were the people we were closest to: Remedios, Kati and José,' says Gabriel Weisz Carrington, Leonora's eldest son. 'We almost lived together, in a way. We would have lunch together and supper together, and parties together. It was like an extended family – and we had no connection with our actual families.' His father Chiki's family had mostly been wiped out by the Holocaust, and Chiki never returned to Hungary – indeed, having arrived in Mexico in the early 1940s, he never left the country again. 'And we had no connection with my mother's family for years and years.'[11]

Mexico brought Leonora a sense of joy and security that was entirely new to her. During her first pregnancy, in 1946, she wrote to Pierre Matisse, Henri's son and her gallerist in New York: 'As you no doubt know I am married again & entirely happy & perhaps for the first time in my life living in peace.'[12] She was creating a new family: after her marriage to Chiki there were two sons in quick succession, Gabriel and Pablo. Motherhood had a huge impact on her, in ways she had not expected. 'I had no idea what the maternal instinct is. I had no idea that I was going to be more or less possessed by it,' she remembered later. 'I'd seen no signs of it before my sons were born, but it appeared out of the depths...'[13]

Leonora created what was probably her finest work during the late 1940s and early 1950s, beginning with *Amor che move il sole et l'altre stelle* (The Love that Moves the Sun and the Other Stars), painted on the eve of her first child's birth. It shows a golden light being transported in a dreamlike procession, with colours reminiscent of the Florentine paintings she had so enjoyed during her time in Italy. Transport is central, too, in her 1944 work *Chiki, ton pays* (Chiki, Your Country), a magnificent painting of jewel-like colours that shows her pregnant self and Chiki driving towards their new life, amid a landscape of fantastical creatures and occasions. Atop the magical pod transporting them across the sky is a tiny, nest-like world; this is the world Leonora always carries with her, and it is the world in which she and Chiki will raise their children. They are taking their own world and their own reality with them towards Mexico. Their new country will influence Leonora's life and her work, but so much of what she will go on painting, right through her long life, is already right there with her. As her friend Edward James, whom she had met on a beach in Acapulco in 1944, wrote: 'it is...surprising that no really Mexican characteristics have ever appeared in her art. One awaited more "mexicanidad" from her.'[14]

The following year she painted another masterpiece, *The House Opposite*, again in the colours of the 16th-century greats and with more than a nod to the Renaissance predellas she had seen. The painting takes the form of a kind of doll's-house cutaway, in which different women (all, perhaps, Leonora) are at different stages of life and having different experiences. In the very centre is a girl with a white rocking horse sitting in despair on a forest floor; in a room below, a girl is running into the picture carrying a bird. The energy flows between the rooms, and indeed the figures appear to move freely between floors and through ceilings. As so often, Leonora is exploring boundaries, and this painting showcases that exploration more than most. Where is the boundary, she seems to be asking, between a human being and a tree? Where does a woman stop and a horse begin? What is the boundary between humans and nature, between men and women, between earth and water (one room seems to be on the seabed) – between life and death? Today we are hyper-aware of the interconnectedness of everything; but Leonora was already depicting that interconnectedness in her work eighty years ago.

She herself remembered that she had 'painted so beautifully when I was pregnant';[15] and through the early weeks and months of sleep-deprived parenthood she worked on, remembering later that she would paint with a baby in one hand and a brush in the other. It wasn't just about creativity: the small family relied on the money Leonora was making through her sales. She was no longer receiving any funds from her family in England, and Chiki didn't earn enough as a jobbing photographer to keep them all. Money was tight, as evidenced by her description of the cramped apartment on Avenida Álvaro Obregón in

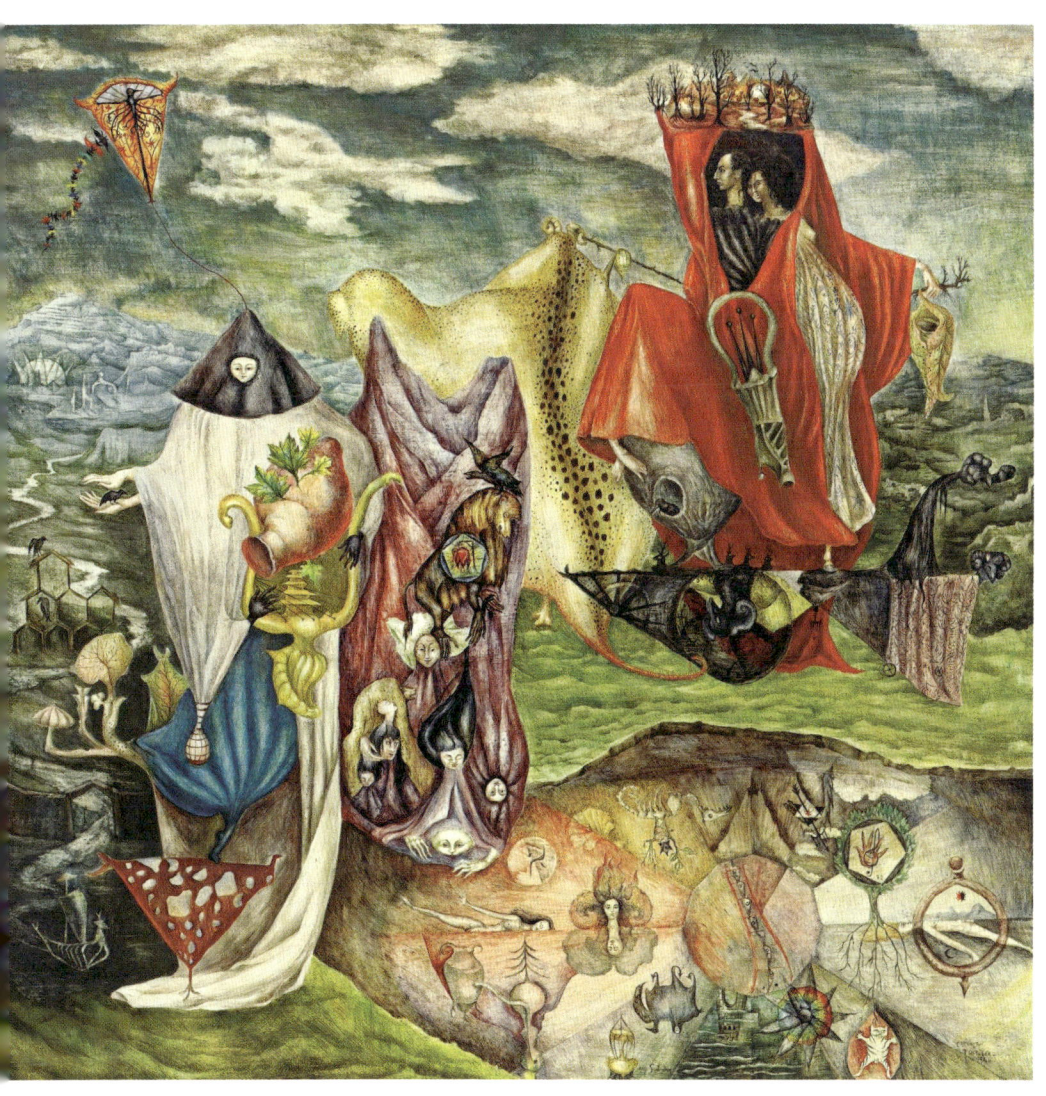

Chiki, ton pays, 1944

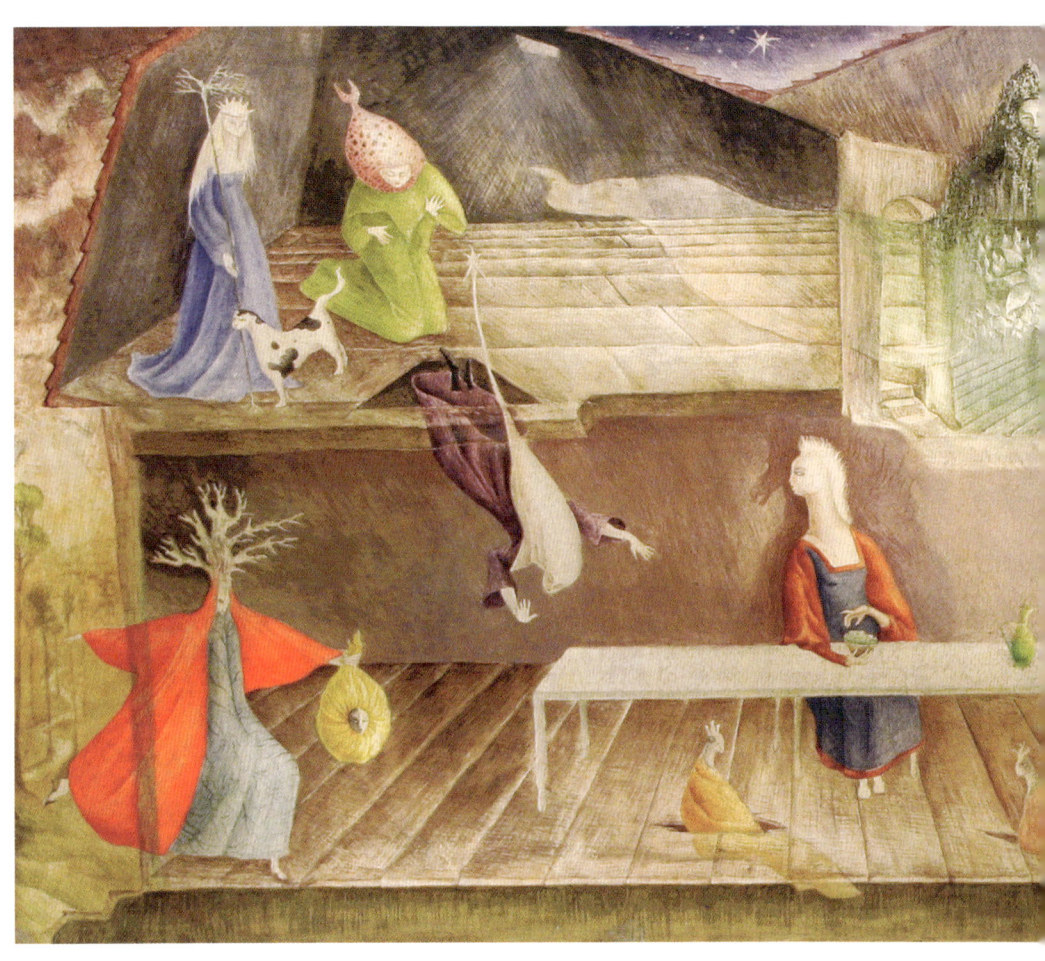

The House Opposite, 1945

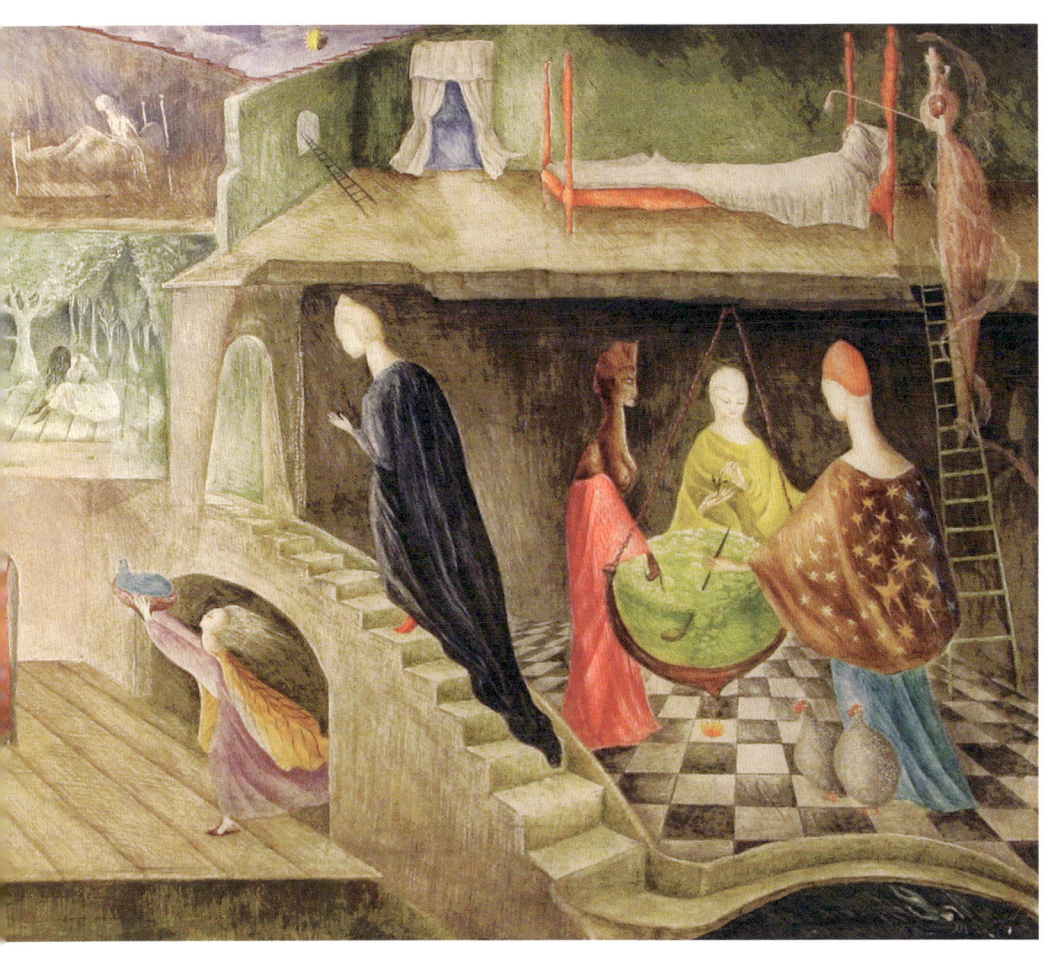

the Roma area of Mexico City, where she and Chiki were living with Gabriel. 'There are no panes hardly left in the windows…I can hardly move in the studio & have to jump over things as I bought another easel for 2 pesos (!!!) rather rickety but it works…it [the studio] is so full of things that one would have to be an acrobat to paint.'[16]

Soon after the birth of her second son, Leonora wrote that she had 'had to sell the picture called *Tuesday* to Edward James for six hundred dollars because I had to have this money to be able to take a Nanny for the baby otherwise I wouldn't have time to work during the summer. Up til now I've looked after him myself and it doesn't leave much time for anything else.'[17] In another letter she mentions that she has sold *The Giantess/Guardian of the Egg*, her 1947 painting of a giant goddess guarding an egg that represents the future of humankind, for £500, 'being in need at the time'.[18]

The births of her children unsettled Leonora and for a while she appears to have toyed – perhaps not entirely seriously – with the idea of returning to Europe, and even to England. One has to wonder what was in her mind when, in 1946, she decided to call her first-born child Harold after the father she would never see again (the baby was always known by his second name, Gabriel). But as ever, that 'Harold' was a sign of blurred boundaries: Leonora had left her family, yes, but she was clearly not immune to the bonds of kinship – as she demonstrated when I arrived at her house in 2006 and was welcomed in.

In 1947 her mother Maurie, who despite everything had continued to support her as much as possible, wrote to Pierre Matisse thanking him for sending the catalogue of an exhibition of Leonora's work he had held in New York. 'We miss her desperately and long for the time when she can come home again,' she said. When Pablo was born, Maurie made the long journey from Lancashire to Mexico City to be with her daughter, and this perhaps led to Leonora's homesickness. 'I have a hankering to return to England…the family have bought Hazelwood & only my mother and father live there now. It tempts me beyond reason to rest in an organised household. This will probably blow over as most of my England nostalgias do,' she wrote to Edward James.[19]

James was about to go to England at this point, and Leonora asks him in her letter to tell her all about it. 'Don't forget to let me know how you find England. The things that interest me most are food questions for the baby, heating possibilities etc. etc. & possibility of war. Apparently I have quite a lot of money in England & tell me how

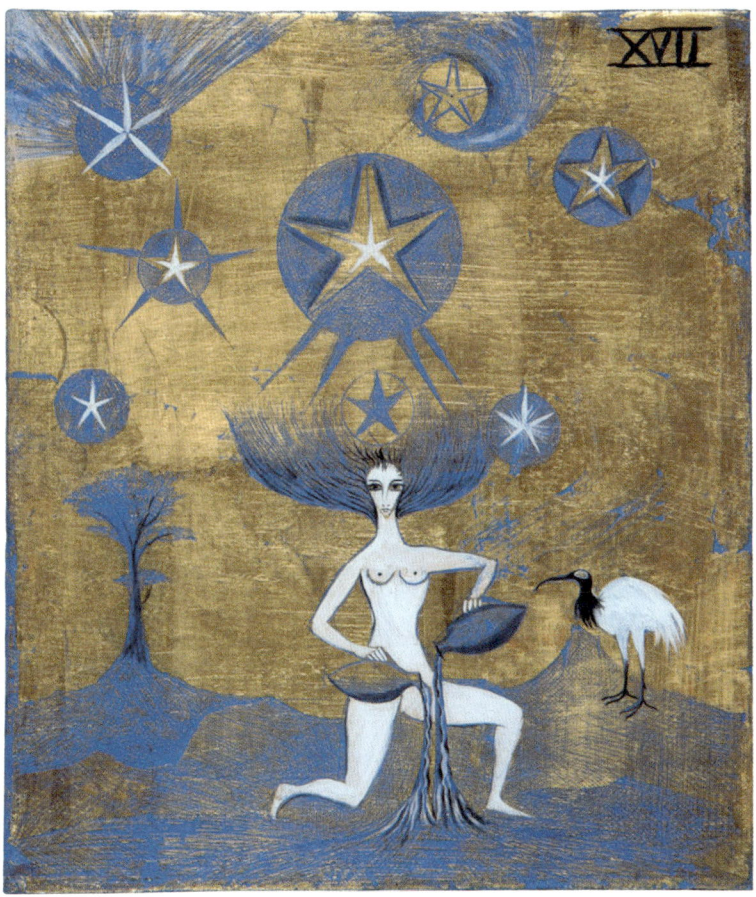

The Star, c. 1955

far that helps for living conditions? What would be the possibilities of Chiki finding work?' She ends: 'Don't hesitate to say if you advise staying in Mexico,' and signs the letter: 'From all four of us, Leonora.'[20]

On 2 February (presumably 1948) she wrote to 'Mr O'Higgins' (the Mexican artist Pablo O'Higgins), asking him to pass on to James that she and Chiki had found a new home she called 'absolutely perfect'. This was the house at 194 Calle Chihuahua that would be her base for the next sixty-three years, until her death in 2011. It was on 'a quiet street with trees on each side. The house is very old & was built by campesinos who were intelligent enough not to get an architect… there are 3 floors – the third floor has 3 rooms only they haven't got doors or windows, these communicate with a large terrace which will

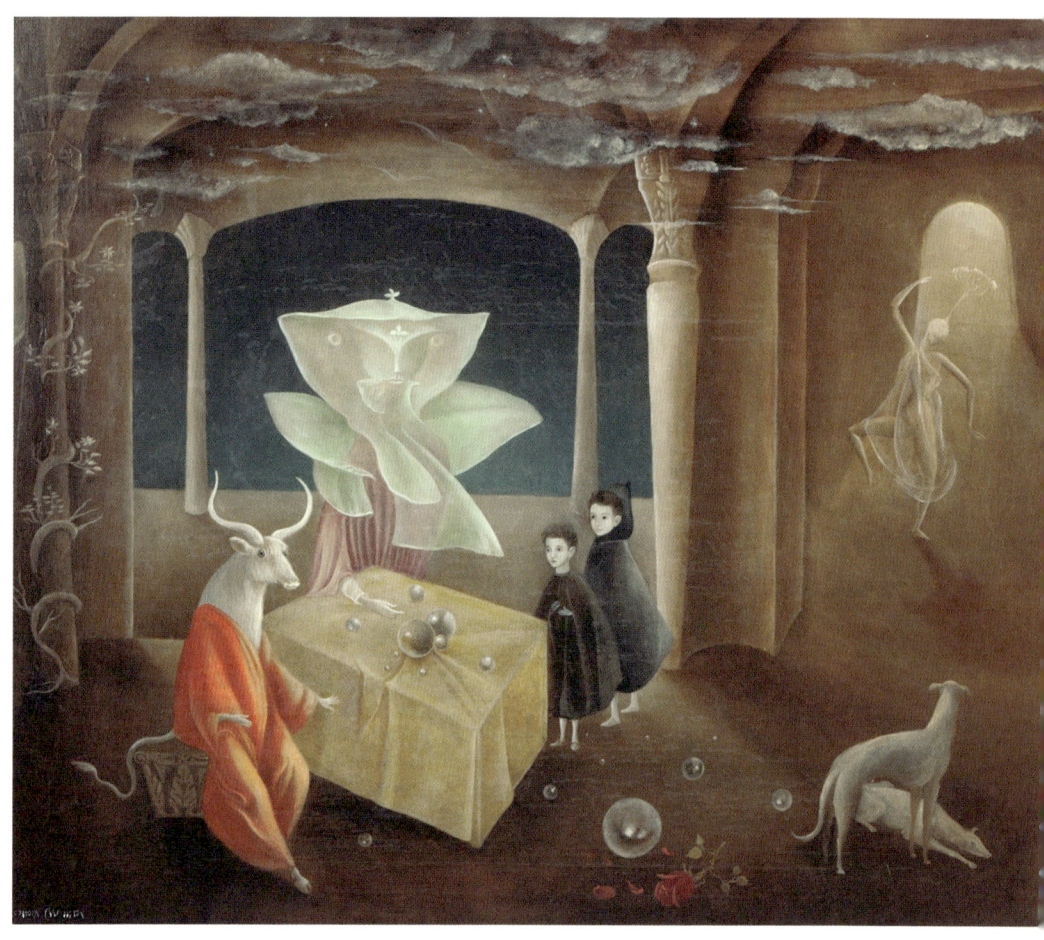

And Then We Saw the Daughter of the Minotaur!, 1953

do for the washing. The floor below is the main floor and communicates with the top by a wooden ladder. There is another terrace which communicates with the kitchen & below by another ladder. The studio is beautiful & we are putting in a fireplace. The room will be divided by the blue curtain which is now in the bedroom here. There are two yards which will be gardens including a large sand heap.' She writes that she will plant grass and orange trees and geraniums, and there will be room for four or five cats and a dog.[21]

Colonia Roma, where the house is located, is an area to the southwest of Mexico City's historic centre. It was built by middle-class professionals, particularly those who arrived from Europe, early in the 20th century; there are still ornate mansions with French windows

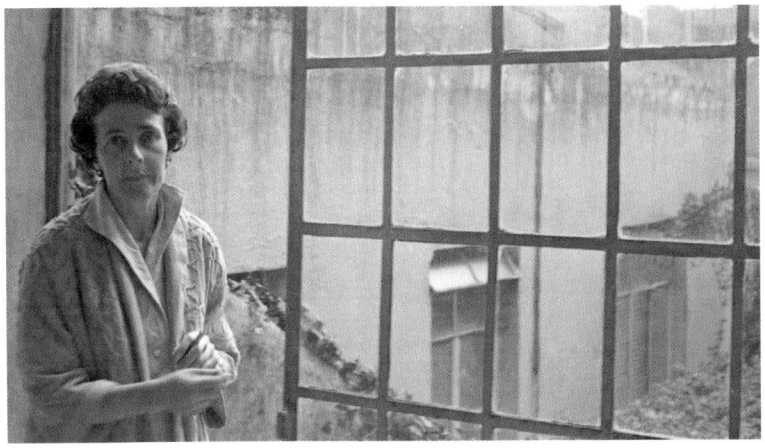

Leonora Carrington in her home in Mexico, *c.* 1960. Photograph by Nacho López

and grand front gates behind which passers-by can glimpse courtyards with fountains, open-air staircases and wrought-iron balustrades. The area never felt, and still doesn't feel, pristine – it has always seemed edgy, interesting. It feels like a place of great potential, where there is much to discover.

The house at 194 Chihuahua was to become that world Leonora had painted atop her carriage in *Chiki, ton pays*: it would be her kingdom, a place where she felt safe enough to raise her children and where she found the space to paint. It would also be the unofficial headquarters of the friends she came to see as her family, Remedios Varo and Kati Horna. By now, Kati and José had a daughter they named Norah; when she was a child, she remembered later, Leonora always delighted in telling her why that was. 'She would tell me: "So...you were just born, and you were absolutely violet-coloured. I had to run around the entire neighbourhood to find a doctor who would help us, who would save your life and transform you into the beautiful, pink-coloured baby who would smile every time she saw me and reach out her little hand."'[22]

Like Gabriel, Norah remembers how closely the group lived. 'Coexisting was easy and also, a way of collaborating on shared fantasies they would make real in my father's workshop or my mother's darkroom, where the smells of wood, paintings, whiting, film developer and hot chocolate with churros intermingled. And they made us very happy, Leonora with her gaiety and talent, Chiki with his patience and care, my mother with her generosity, my father with his childlike spirit, and all of them with their poets' souls.'[23]

Leonora was painting plenty, and she also worked with José on several pieces that combine his exquisite craftsmanship with her delicate, dreamy brushwork. The best example is the crib or *cuna* they made for Norah; the way she remembers it is testament to the fact that the art they were making was rooted in their real lives. This was art for living, not for museums or galleries. 'I loved to gaze at the fairy with her star and the animals who followed her, and the sails reminiscent of a pirate ship on top and fairies, underneath.'[24] Her father also made her a dolls' house, for which Leonora created pieces of furniture and dolls out of papier-mâché; one Christmas, she gave her a castle with a horse's head. There were puzzles with drawings by Aunt Remedios, and photo albums of flowers created by Kati.

For Leonora in particular, but also for Remedios and for Kati, there was a special liberation in being the women they were, in the place they now were. So far away from the conventions of their homelands, they were able to reinvent themselves – and also, as white, educated Europeans, they had far more choices and greater privilege than the vast majority of Mexican women. It is said that Frida Kahlo once spoke of the artistic incomers as 'those European bitches'; if so, it may have been her jealousy speaking. There were demands and expectations on Frida that Leonora, Remedios and Kati never had to cope with, and of course none of the European women were married, as Frida was, to men whose art was widely seen to eclipse theirs. Leonora, in fact, had already glimpsed what this sort of partnership was like when she had been with Max: she could see the danger that he would forever be regarded as the giant and she as the novice.

Unlike *los tres grandes*, whose work was rooted in the big political issues of life, *las tres europeas* found artistic sustenance close to home; in fact, they often found it within the home. The kitchen especially was a place of magic and alchemy, a place where ideas were brewed as readily as tea. For Leonora, Remedios and Kati, the house was fundamental, and much of their life together took place within the kitchen, that hidden domestic space where women's lives have so often been confined. And yet for this group it was anything but confinement: they made the kitchen into a room where they could be exactly what they wanted to be, a place where they were truly free.

Edward James was a frequent visitor to the house at 194 Calle Chihuahua and his descriptions are among the best we have of those days. He was particularly struck, he wrote, by the studio: 'I have consistently observed…that the quality of the art which one finds in a studio is almost unfailingly in inverse ration to the luxury of the premises,' he wrote in 1948. Given that, 'Leonora Carrington's studio had everything most conducive to make it the true matrix of true art. Small in the extreme, it was an ill-furnished and not very well lighted room. It had nothing to endow it with the title of studio at all, save a few almost worn-out paint brushes and a number of gesso panels set on a dog-and-cat-populated floor, leaning face averted against a whitewashed and peeling wall. The place was a combined kitchen, nursery, bedroom, kennel and junk-store. The disorder was apocalyptic: the appurtenances of the poorest. My hopes and expectations began to swell...'[25]

Pedro Friedeberg, a Mexican artist who was often at the house during the 1950s and '60s, described its ambience in a manner that, despite evidently employing some dramatic licence, is both entertaining and insightful. A typical day, he wrote, involved the arrival of 'three Lacandon Indians...waiting for an audience with the master, who is in the midst of gathering materials for *El mundo mágico de los mayas* [the mural Leonora painted at her house, destined for a room in the city's new Museum of Anthropology]. Meanwhile, 'in the salon upstairs, María Félix [a Mexican film star] is already sitting on a very high stool in riding jodhpurs and with her breasts bared, posing for the portrait Leonora is making of her.' Downstairs, the cook accidentally short-circuits the electric oven, which explodes and scares two cats that are asleep nearby. 'At this point, Gaby [Gabriel, Leonora's eldest son] enters with one of his axolotls, and María's assistants flee in terror. Meanwhile, the cobras of Edward James...slowly climb the stairs, while on the telephone he shouts like a lunatic at his veterinarian, who is in Managua, Nicaragua, that the rattlesnakes...have not ovulated in six months...' In the neighbouring room, Leonora's younger son Pablo is listening to jazz, interrupted by the crying of the cook's baby. Through a window onto the patio, two figures can be seen making their way slowly down the spiral staircase from the roof: these are Chiki and Aldous Huxley, an occasional visitor to the house when in Mexico, who at this stage is almost blind. 'Leonora doesn't turn a hair and continues to smoke constantly as she paints La Doña [Félix], who tells her one of her customary anecdotes...from atop a dusty bookcase, the Siamese cats watch the whole thing.'[26]

Then the doorbell rings: it is flowers from Sofía Bassi, a Mexican painter who would later serve a prison sentence for her involvement in the murder of her son-in-law. Leonora looks at the flowers and then

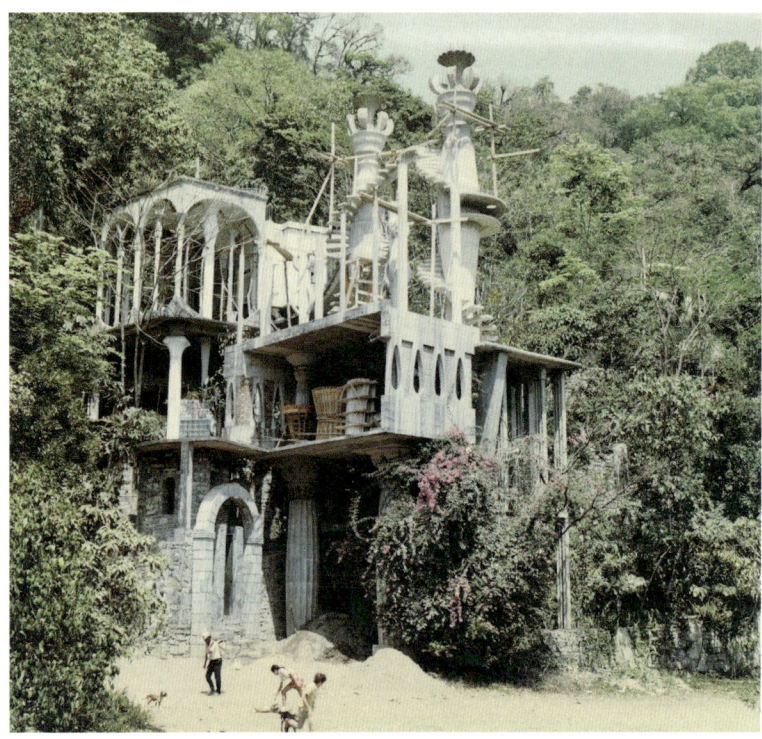

La Cinematografia under construction at Las Pozas, Xilitla, *c.* 1960

throws them immediately into the trash bin. 'Don't they know I hate cut flowers?' she shouts.[27]

Life in Mexico in the 1940s, '50s and '60s brought Leonora great joy. She was enjoying the family she had created – all the more because of the family she had left behind – and she was painting because it was her lifeblood as well as her living. Her relationship with Edward James was both personal and professional; the two were close friends, and they communicated with a kind of honesty that would be more common between siblings. From the early 1960s onwards, Edward had a new project in Mexico that took up a lot of his time and attention. He had purchased some land near a small town called Xilitla in the central part of the country and was busy creating first an orchid garden and then, after bad weather killed all the plants, a concrete sculpture garden. Leonora would visit Las Pozas (as the site became known) at least once, making the ten-hour car journey with Edward and his friend and project manager, Plutarco Gastélum. At Plutarco's house, El Castillo, Leonora painted a mural of a creature who many people thought was reminiscent of her descriptions of Edward himself.

In 1963 the friends were devastated by two deaths, both unexpected. First, in April, José Horna died; then, in October, Remedios Varo, seemingly of a heart attack. Both had only been in their fifties. It was a terrible time for the close-knit circle – of the three couples who made up the centre of the group, only Leonora and Chiki remained.

Leonora and Kati, already close, became even closer after this. Leonora had recently acted as a model for a project of Kati's called *Ode to Necrophilia*, published in a new anti-establishment magazine called *S-nob*, which gave Kati's work a boost. The series of photographs shows Leonora lying on a bed; in another image she is smoking, in the middle of a room, wearing a bra and holding an umbrella. The pictures show pleasure, suffering and death, personified by the presence of a white mask, intertwined. They echo Kati's earlier work during the Spanish Civil War, when she had documented disillusion, loss and displacement.

In 1968 came another shocking event, one which would change the course of Leonora's life yet again. In the run-up to the Olympic Games, which were due to begin in Mexico City that October, troops opened fire on a student demonstration in the Plaza de las Tres Culturas, killing an unknown number of students. Leonora's sons were university students at the time. She was appalled, and attended a number of activist meetings in the wake of the outrage. When she was denounced to the authorities as an agitator, she decided to leave Mexico for the US and ended up in New Orleans, where she stayed for a while until it seemed safe to return to Mexico City. The shocking events that precipitated this journey, and the time she spent in the US, opened the way to a new chapter in her life.

Leonora was now aged fifty-one, and a whole new series of adventures beckoned.

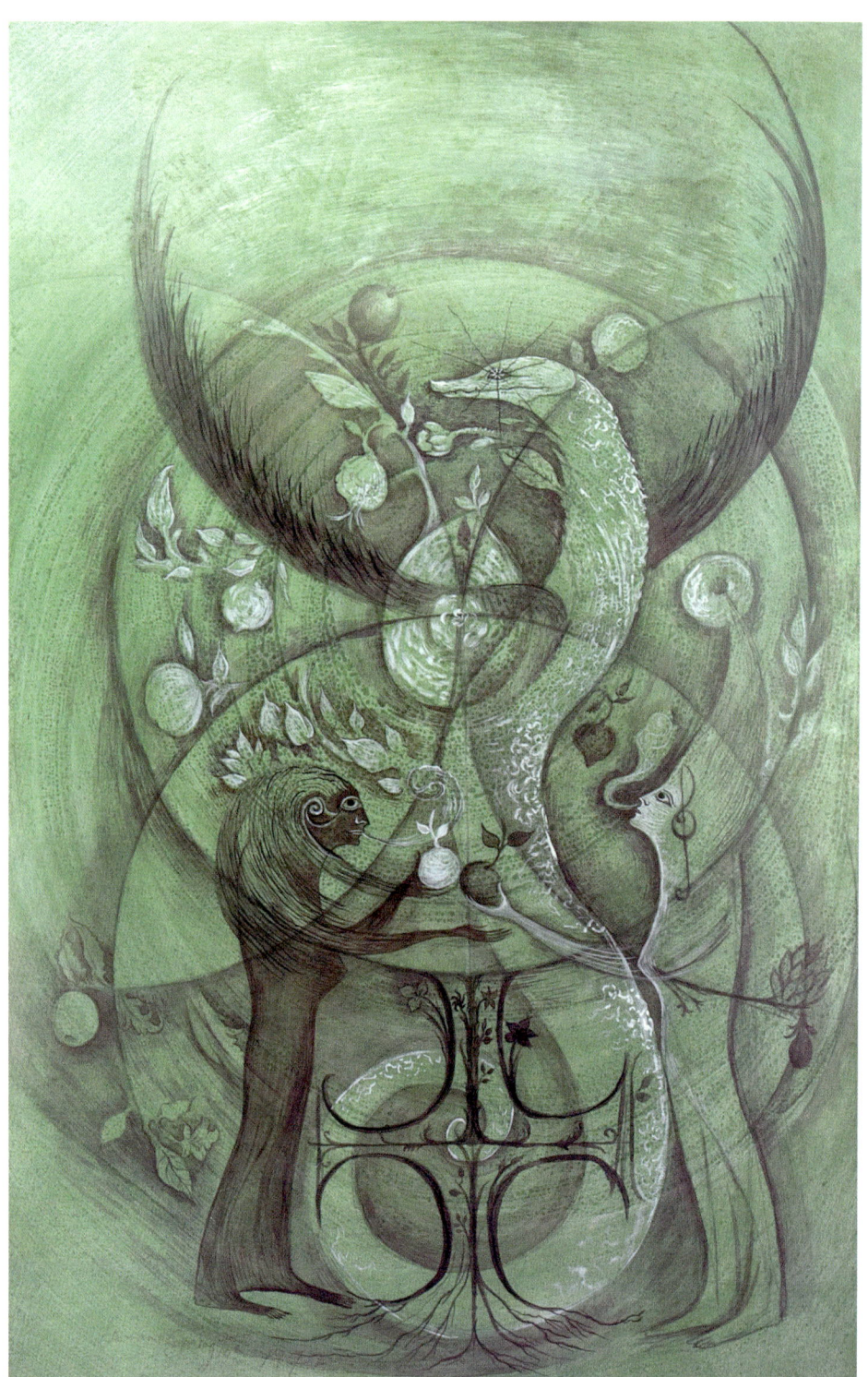

10
New York and Chicago
1968–1992

We used to talk, sometimes, about where Leonora would go back to if she could travel again; where she might live if she was starting afresh. Often, New York was the place she mentioned. In her fifties, her sixties and her seventies it became somewhere she could live easily, where she could be curious and explore life in the way she wanted to.

There was a freedom in New York that appealed to her. She made friends there – not influential friends, just people she liked and wanted to be around. Leonora was actually very bad at making influential friends: the more 'useful' someone might be, the more likely she was to fall out with them or fail to connect with them. She was the antithesis of a social gold-digger; she wanted authenticity, and she knew that interesting people come from all walks of life.

She didn't go out of her way to hang out in art galleries, but sometimes there were shows on that she wanted to see. She enjoyed walking the streets, connecting with the world around her and finding the best way of being herself in the post-child-rearing phase of her life. She lived in the moment, always open to an unexpected turn on which everything else could hinge. She was a searcher, and New York was a great city to search in.

Chiki was not part of her travels. Having seen his birth family all but destroyed by the Second World War, he was not inclined to leave Mexico. The country that had given him a second chance seemed the safest place to be, so he stayed put, but he in no way interfered with Leonora's decision to go away. Although they were often apart during the 1970s and '80s, in many ways he remained her anchor, certainly

Mujeres Conciencia, 1972

to Mexico. When she eventually returned there it was to be with him, and a 1992 BBC *Omnibus* documentary portrays them as an affectionate pair, by then in their seventies, who held one another's hands when crossing the street. Chiki was still alive when I first visited Leonora, in 2006; he died the following year at the age of ninety-five.

By 1971 Leonora was spending a lot of time in America. In the summer of that year she met a woman to whom she would remain close for the rest of her life, and who would prove an unrivalled ally. Gloria Orenstein, whom I got to know through Leonora in Mexico City, is an exotic and magical creature like Leonora herself. She first heard of Leonora when, as a postgraduate student, she was writing a dissertation on surrealism, and she wrote to her in Mexico telling her about her research. Leonora replied to say that she was not remotely interested in academia, but she was very interested in learning more about why women in New York were burning their bras. Could Gloria explain what was going on?

The two began to correspond. They sent one another postcards, pictures, jokes – and when Gloria first saw Leonora's paintings, they immediately brought 'something alive for me'.[1] Still, though, there seemed no way for them to meet in person – until one day in July 1971 when, sitting at her kitchen table in Manhattan, Gloria decided to 'invoke the universe' to enable her to meet Leonora. 'I said: if I can't go to Mexico, let Mexico come to me,' she remembers. At that precise moment, the phone rang, and she answered it to hear a deep voice say: 'This is Leonora Carrington. I'm in New York and I'd like to meet you.'

When they got together later that day, the first thing Leonora did was to make the sign of the horns with her fingers – something she continued to do from time to time in the years I knew her. It's a gesture with a variety of meanings, and Leonora liked its symbolism of nonconformity, of going against the tide, even of devilishness. Gloria told her about the strange circumstances around her phone call, to which Leonora replied that she wasn't remotely surprised by the story.

During the first evening these two friends ever spent together, feminism was one of the main topics they discussed. Leonora, Gloria recalls, wanted to know all about the American women's movement, and when Gloria told her that Betty Friedan, author of *The Feminine Mystique*, would be speaking the following evening to the National Organization of Women, Leonora said straight away that she wanted to attend. This they did, and a few days later they also managed to meet

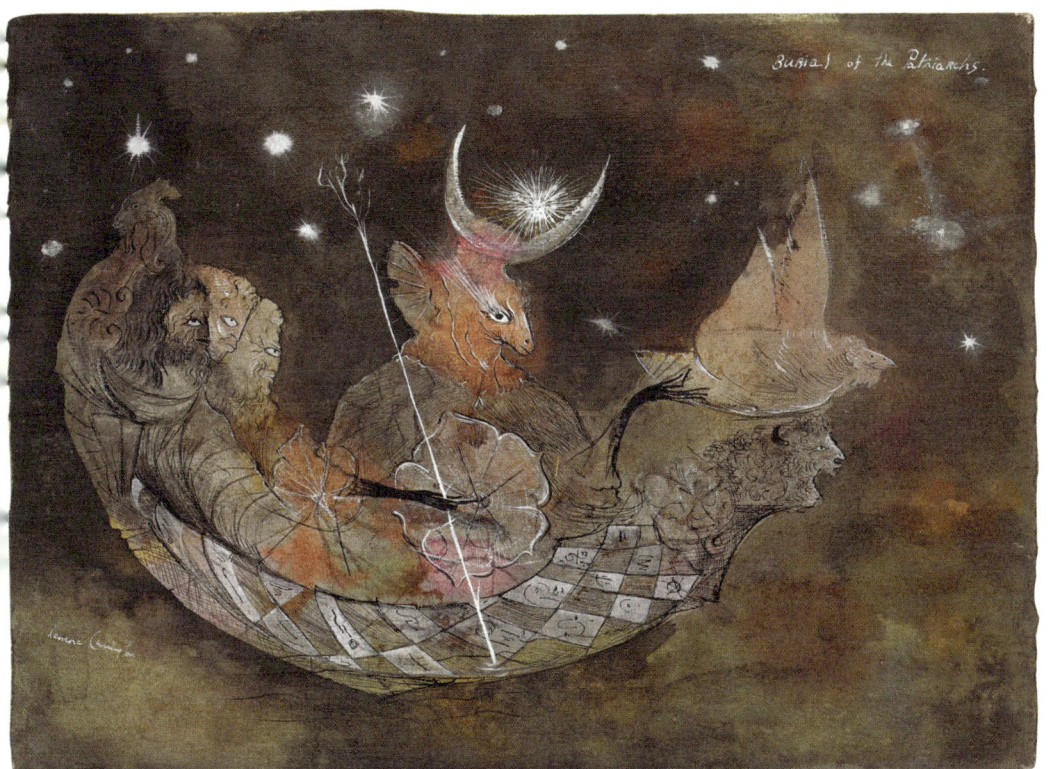

Burial of the Patriarchs, c. 1963

with Friedan and her fellow activist Jacqueline Ceballos. Leonora told them she hoped to help set up a women's movement in Mexico – no small task, given that it has long been one of the most macho countries on the planet.

Other than an artist, Leonora's natural instinct had always been, and would continue to be, to avoid being labelled anything with an *ist* at the end of it. That sentiment extended to 'surrealist' for certain; but if there was one exception, she'd probably have made it for 'feminist'. Equality was an obvious truth for her at a time when not everyone agreed. She told one of her friends, the Mexican journalist Elena Poniatowska, that her favourite date in all of history was 'one that has not happened yet: the fall of patriarchy that will take place in the 21st century'.[2] Her 1963 painting *Burial of the Patriarchs* shows three confused-looking bearded men being rowed on a gondola by an elegant horse-woman with white moon-horns. The men are huddled together at one end of the boat. It is clear who is in control.

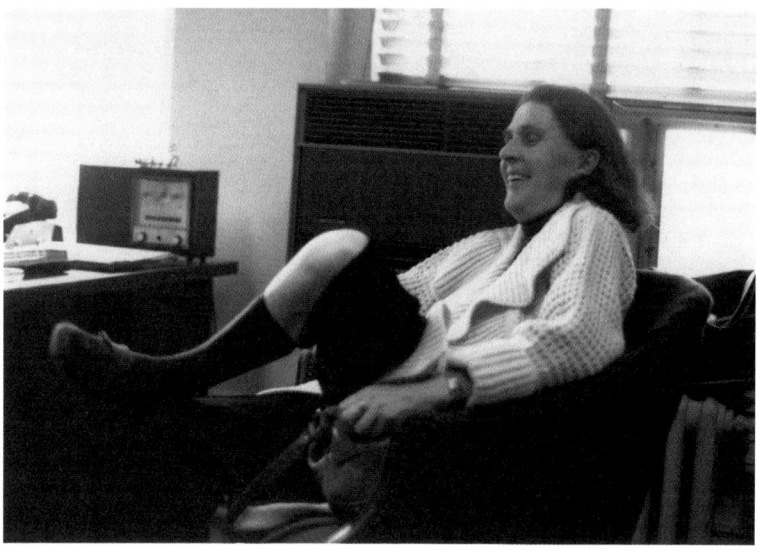

Leonora Carrington during an interview with Joanne Pottlitzer,
New York, 1976

In 1972, back in Mexico for a spell, Leonora designed a poster for
the emerging women's liberation movement. Whitney Chadwick has
credited her with being one of its founders.[3] The poster image, entitled
Mujeres Conciencia (Awakened Women) 'represents the New Eve (the
liberated woman) standing next to the giant serpent as she returns
the fruit of knowledge to the Old Eve (the subjugated woman), and in
doing so, rejects the patriarchal myth of her sinful nature given as cause
for her expulsion from the Garden of Eden. It is a reminder to women
everywhere to be conscious and to have conscience to restore the original vision of the goddess to avoid further destruction of the planet.'[4]
This was not, of course, Leonora's first foray into eco-feminism; the
aforementioned painting *The Giantess/Guardian of the Egg*, from 1947,
is powerful evidence of her early engagement with these ideas.

It was to this theme of the 'last egg', the final hope for humankind
on Earth, that Leonora would return in New York. The other person
present at her first supper with Gloria Orenstein on that evening in
1971 was a mutual friend of theirs, a theatre director called Joanne
Pottlitzer. She was already taking an interest in a play Leonora had
written, *Opus Siniestrus*, subtitled 'The Story of the Last Egg'. 'She
[Leonora] wanted to show that the salvation – or transformation –
of our planet lies in the hands of women,' Pottlitzer has written.[5] She

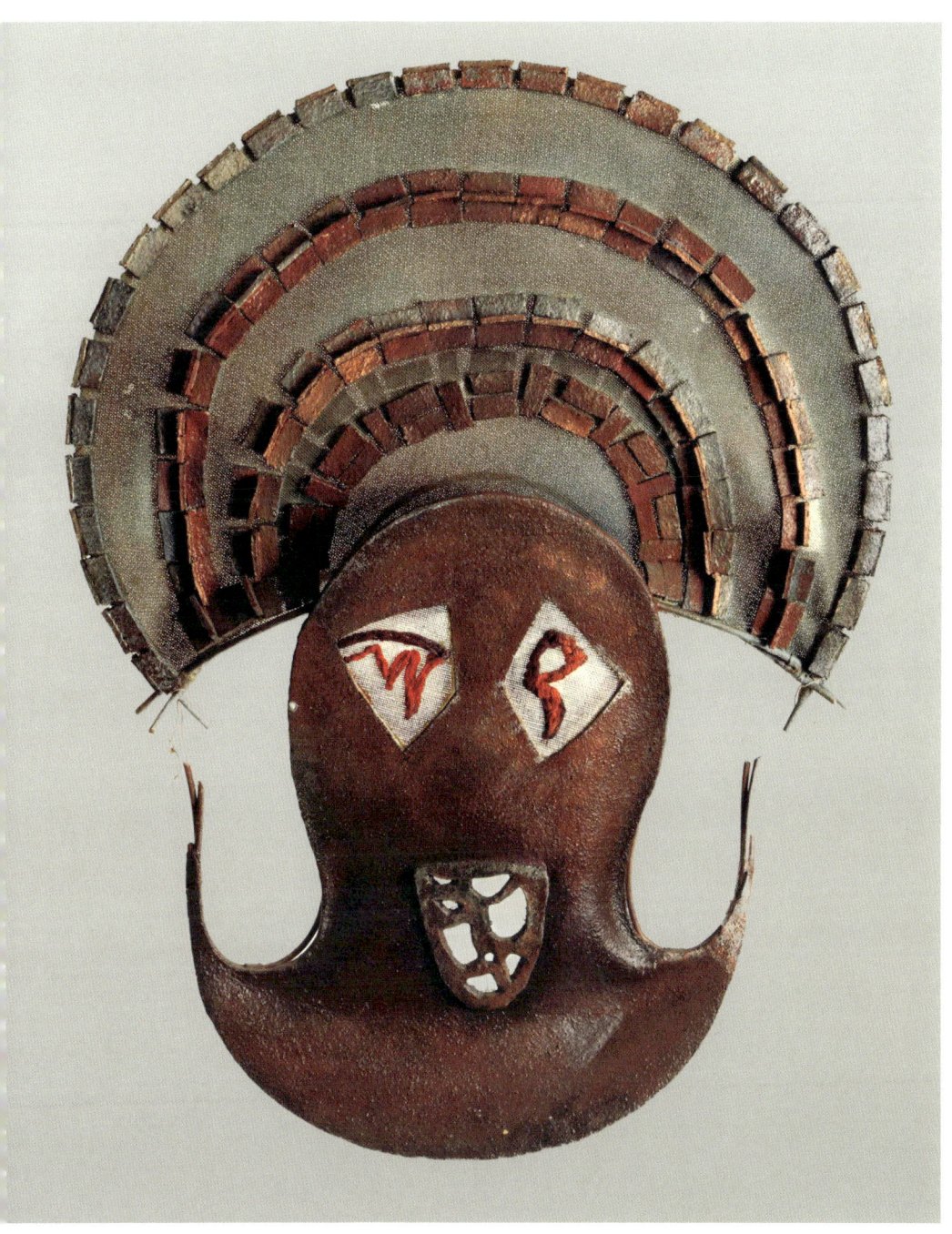

Mask for the play *Opus Siniestrus*, 1976. Designed by
Leonora Carrington, crafted by Jane Stein and Vita Giorgi

goes on to quote Leonora directly, from one of their conversations: 'If we take the Earth as a prototype and look at the mess the human species has made of it, we see conflict between man and woman, when they should be complementing one another.'[6]

Like *The Hearing Trumpet*, *Opus Siniestrus* is wild and wacky, a humour-filled romp punctuated with thoughtful nuggets of lasting truth. It's the story of a world in which all the women have died save one, an obese woman of eighty, the ex-madam of a brothel. She has possession of the last surviving human egg, and she holds the future of the planet in her hands. The egg has long symbolized not only hope, fertility and the future, but also balance between the broader picture and the individual focus. In *Down Below* Leonora describes it as 'the macrocosm and the microcosm, the dividing line between the Big and the Small'.[7] In one scene in the play, a voice is heard coming from a dark spiral that sucks everything into it: what Leonora seems to have been describing was the black hole of cosmology.

Pottlitzer approached the Guggenheim Museum in New York, whose spiral layout made it particularly apt as a possible site for a stage production of *Opus Siniestrus*. Leonora began to design the masks and props, and auditioning began for fifteen actors to play the forty-five roles. Funding, though, was slow to come in, which meant that sadly, in 1978, the project was abandoned. It was a source of deep disappointment to all involved. Perhaps, though, its opening night is still to come. '*Opus Siniestrus* is an incredible piece of theatre that still deserves a full production: its themes and the issues it touches on – women's issues, war, guns, violence, reverence for money, cut-throat capitalism, patriarchal power – are as relevant today as they were in the '70s, perhaps even more so,' wrote Pottlitzer in 2018.[8]

While in New York Leonora lived mostly in rented apartments. Her untitled painting of the apartment where she was staying in around 1980 shows a studio basement flat with a steep staircase down from a balcony, three windows on the left wall, and an unmade bed in the centre of the room. It seems to be a place of little light and the overall impression is of drabness, greyness. Leonora's shoes are beside the bed; her pink nightshirt, which brings the only hint of colour into the piece, hangs against the wall. There is no furniture save a chair; there are no pictures on the walls, no books, no paints, no easel. It's a very different painting from most of Leonora's work – the antithesis of the magical worlds that usually inhabit her canvases. Maybe she was painting what she told Joanne Pottlitzer, which was that she was

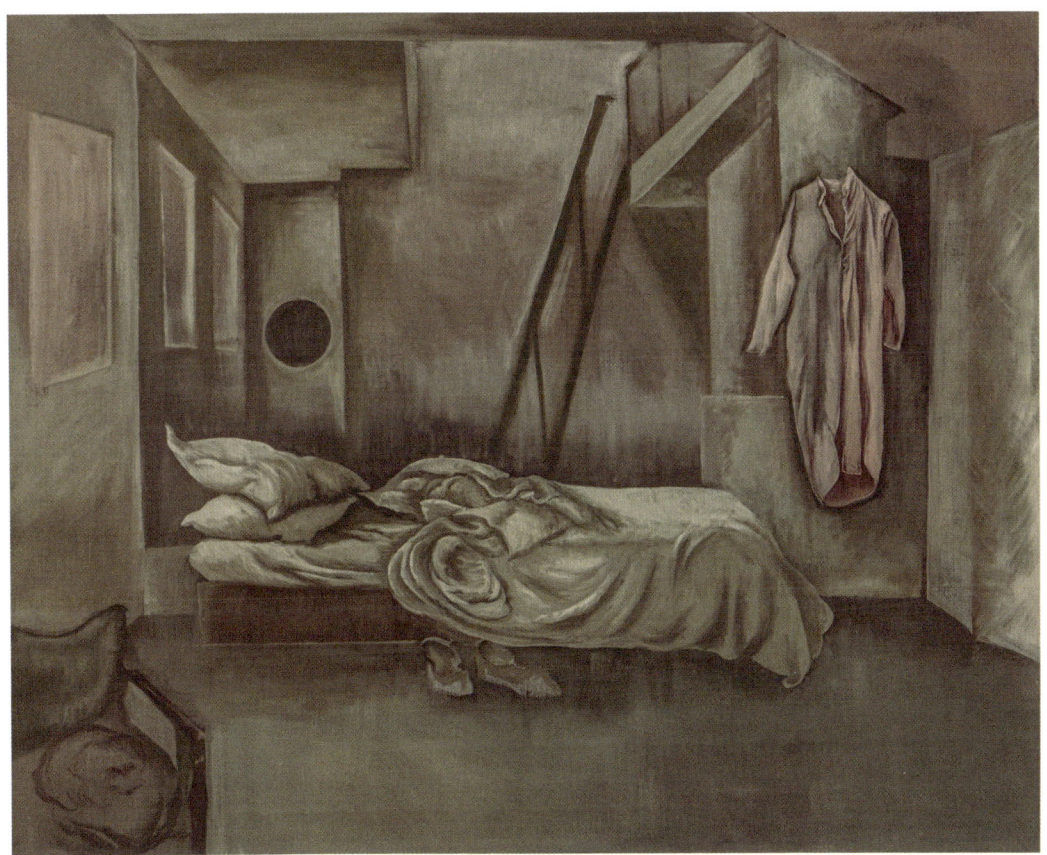

Untitled, c. 1980. The apartment where Carrington lived in New York City in the 1970s and 1980s

'an ordinary woman. And an ordinary woman is the territory from where one begins any kind of work.'[9]

Salomon Grimberg remembers Leonora in 'a tiny basement apartment opposite Gramercy Square'.[10] The eponymous hotel on that square would later become famous as the base used by musicians including the Beatles, Bob Marley and the Rolling Stones when they were playing in New York. Leonora was proud to have got there first: she loved the park, she told me, and there were 'lots of old ladies living there at the time'.

Leonora never seemed like an old lady herself. There was an agelessness about her, a resolve within her that was timeless and strong. But she had long been fascinated by later life, and though like most people she didn't relish being physically challenged by age, she was more curious about the state of the second half of life than she was

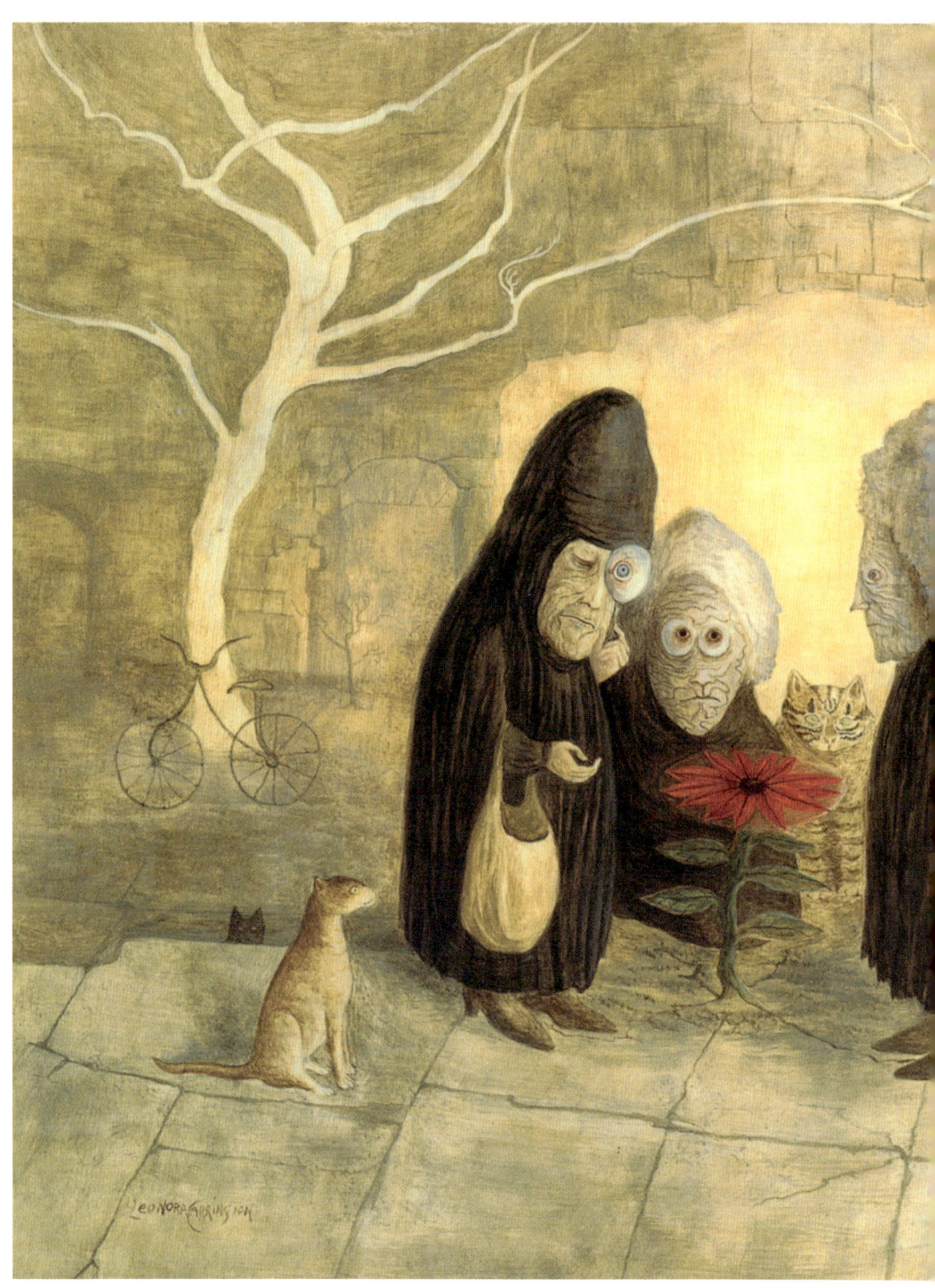

Kron Flower, 1987

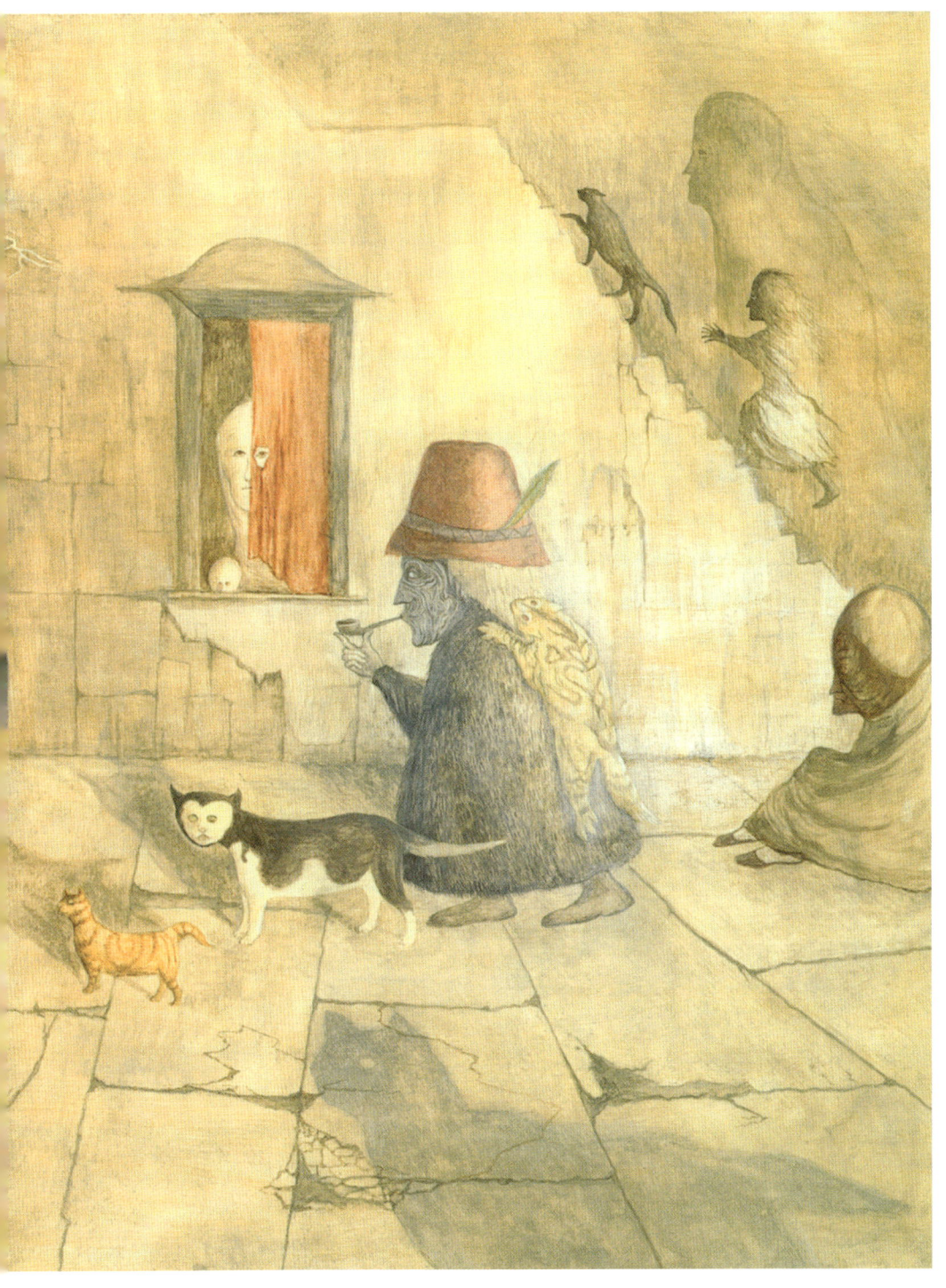

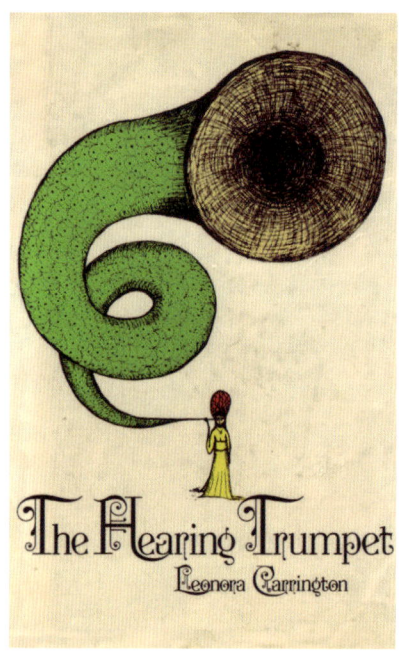

Cover of Leonora Carrington's *The Hearing Trumpet*, 1976,
artwork by Pablo Weisz Carrington

afraid of it. From the late 1970s more and more of her paintings feature elderly figures, usually female; and she had already written, many years earlier, *The Hearing Trumpet*, her novella about a fantastical old age. It has remained in print ever since and in 2009 the *Guardian* named it as one of the '1,000 novels everyone must read'.[11]

In New York, she could be anonymous. Not that she was famous – in fact, she was not at all known during her time in the city – but as an Englishwoman in Mexico she was always going to stand out, whereas in Manhattan she was just another face in the crowd. She was signed up with a New York gallery, but she sold few paintings and often had to survive on very little money. She told me she sometimes ate ice cream because it was the cheapest way of getting calories inside her. One of the books I noticed on her shelf in Mexico City was called *How to Survive in New York on a Dollar a Day*.

In the wider world, though, her work was beginning to register during the 1970s and '80s. Part of this was down to Gloria, who wrote in 1975 that she had been surprised to find, on first encountering Leonora's work, that 'I had never seen any of these paintings before in any of the books on Surrealism, nor had I ever come across any monographic study of her work. In fact, as I began to search through the literature of the Surrealist movement I could find only casual or anecdotal reference to her, and most of what I did find seemed to me to be completely outdated.'[12] Gloria realized that the art world needed to be brought up to date on the existence of Leonora as an artist in her own right, not merely a woman who had once been the young muse, lover or appendage of an older, established male artist.

The women surrealist artists of Gloria's acquaintance had experienced an identity crisis as they grew older – they had left the *femme-enfant* ideal of the male gaze behind and emerged as mature practitioners in their own right. Leonora and her friends had also developed a new way of being surrealists; she herself was not remotely interested in the 'who's in and who's out' culture, or the pattern of arguments, falling-outs and obsession with hierarchy that had characterized the movement's male-dominated Paris days. The group in Mexico City of which she was a part, along with Remedios Varo and Kati Horna, might have looked like a backwater, a periphery – but in truth it was a frontier. Frida Kahlo, painting between delivering her important husband's lunches as he created his murals a few decades earlier, would have understood. None of these women cared about the male rules of surrealism; they weren't even interested in being surrealists. Leonora, like Frida, was simply painting her own reality in all its glorious, multi-layered complexity.

If Gloria raised the alarm about women surrealists and their place in history, it was Whitney Chadwick who a few years later put them into the canon. Her landmark book *Women Artists and the Surrealist Movement* (1985) was controversial: some of the women she was writing about, including Meret Oppenheim, felt they were being ghettoized. But Chadwick's riposte was that the playing field for men and women was fundamentally unfair. She examined the idea of the muse: it was, she said, like an albatross round the neck of the woman artist, 'difficult to ignore but of no help in forging a personal identity as an artist'.[13] Asked how she felt about the surrealist identification of woman and muse, Leonora had responded with a single word: 'Bullshit.'

Chicago had long had a thriving surrealist group – some of those at its centre had known Breton in Paris in the 1960s – and Leonora's name was very familiar to them. Which is why Gina Litherland, one of their number, remembers how astonished she was to answer the phone one day to her friend Franklin Rosemont, who with his wife Penelope had helped found the group, and learn that Leonora Carrington had moved to the city and was living in a residential area called Oak Park. 'It was like hearing Picasso had moved in round the corner,' she said.[14] Leonora was there to be close to her younger son, Pablo, who had become a doctor and was now working in a Chicago hospital. He and his wife, Wendy, had two young sons; Leonora had her own apartment in a building called the Oak Park Arms.

She was still spending time in Chicago as late as 1991; the academic and writer Peter Conrad went there to interview her for the *Observer* magazine that year, to coincide with a show of her work at London's Serpentine Gallery. In his piece, Conrad described where she lived as 'a down-at-heel, incongruously Gothic apartment block, decorated with spurious crests and second-hand heraldic props, frowning at a cheery average suburban street'. Her apartment was small and bare with a smattering of Mexican cacti, sacred Taoist texts and a papier-mâché mermaid. 'She has none of her own paintings: the only signs of creative brewing and stewing are a French cooking apron slung over an empty easel and a pile of clear plastic boxes meant for storing food which contain tubes of paint: the witch's oils, as Coleridge called them.'[15]

Litherland and the Rosemonts got to know Leonora well in Oak Park during the 1980s. Penelope remembers her as 'a true artist, always creating something. But when you went to visit her at the apartment there was nothing on the walls. She kept all her work in her bedroom – but if you got her to show you what she was working on, there was always something new, something different and inventive.'[16] Leonora's concern for the environment is what most impressed itself on Penelope. Leonora was a committed supporter of a local group called Earth First!, and she especially liked the most radical part of their agenda, which was essentially a call for urban rewilding – again, significantly ahead of its time. It was about 'dismantling...highways, malls and other cement-blighted areas and letting wilderness take over'. Meeting a raccoon in an alley in Oak Park was, said Penelope, one of the highlights of Leonora's time in Chicago.

Penelope also remembers that Leonora was keen on what the group called their 'Surrealist Survival Kits'; these were 'a collection of poetic, magical, talismanic objects, along with images and other "Surrealist things"'. A kit might include a feather, a pebble, a piece of glass, some verses from a poem. 'The purpose of these kits is to offset the destructive facts of daily life, to pull us through the hardest times, to reawaken our sense of wonder and to renew our capacity for reverie and revolt.'[17] For Penelope, it spoke to Leonora's wider vision of the world: 'tentative, playful, humorous, generous, adventurous, egalitarian, non-dogmatic, the opposite of conventional either/or thinking'.

Chicago was a serendipitous stopping-off point for Leonora. As with everywhere else, she got there by chance, but the fog of fate cleared to reveal a purpose that was enriching, leading her on to new ideas and fresh horizons. She always seemed to thrive in situations where she had to start afresh; she was the antithesis of the kind of person who clings to long-term friendships and well-worn paths. She made a virtue of finding herself in a new environment, surrounded by people she hadn't known previously, who spoke of things she hadn't encountered before. In Chicago, as elsewhere, the friends with whom she spent her time were drawn from a wide range of ages, stages and backgrounds. She was always keen to listen, and to learn.

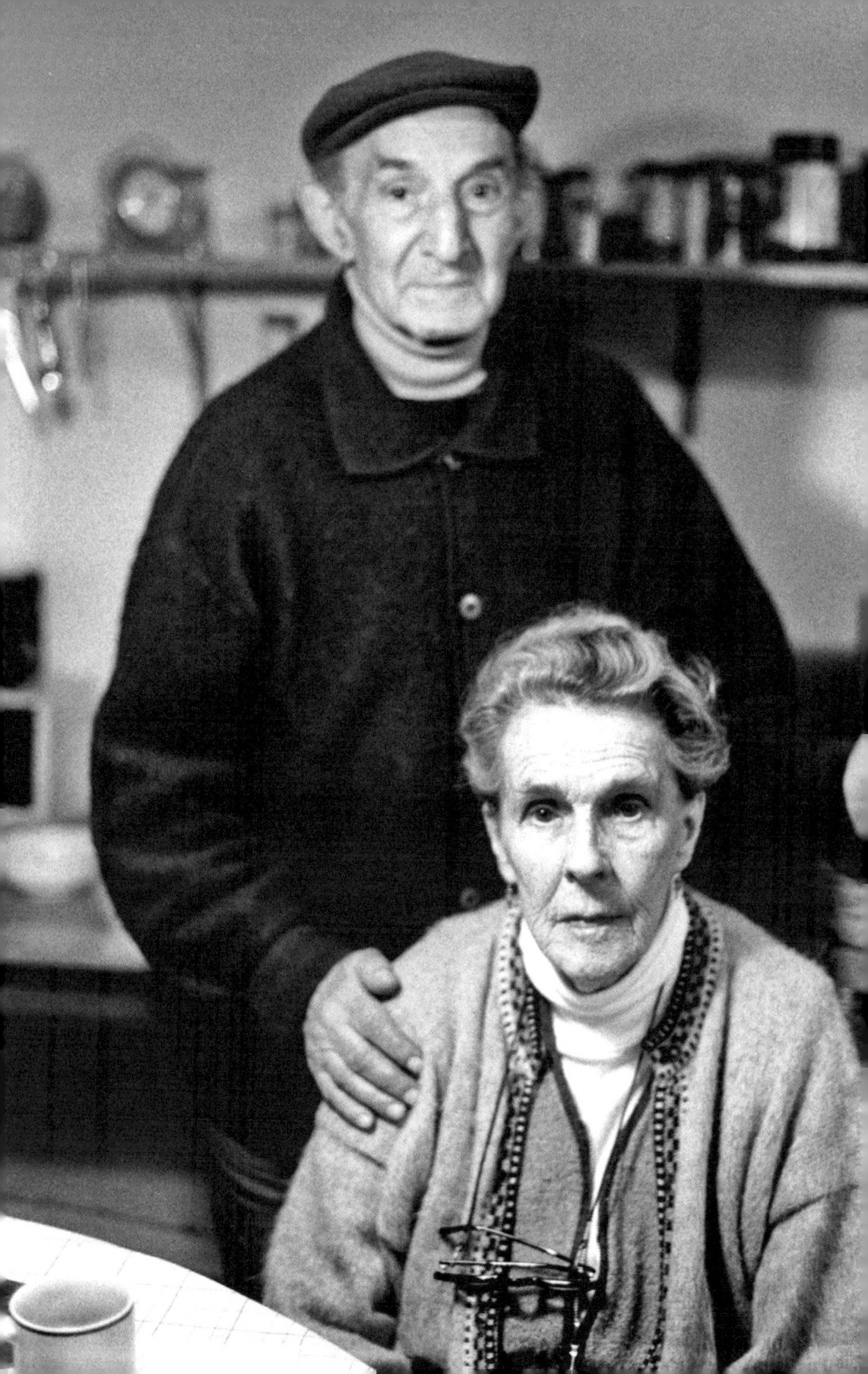

11
Mexico City
1992–the present

Every time I left Leonora's house, the thought at the front of my mind was: will I ever be here again? I had visited her first in the autumn of 2006; from spring 2007 I went to see her in Mexico City twice a year, usually in spring and autumn.

She was eighty-nine when I met her, and death was something we often talked about. Thinking about it, Leonora's work is packed with references to dying; unsurprising, when you consider her abiding interest in boundaries. What more important boundary is there for any human being, any living creature? Her honest appraisal of where she was – all she knew for sure, she used to say, was that she was a female human animal, and that she would one day die – meant the idea of death seemed very present.

So every time I got into the taxi that would take me from her home in Roma Norte to the Aeropuerto Benito Juárez for the long flight back to Britain, I'd always wonder: had we just had our final goodbye?

In September 2010, we had. Leonora seemed on good form. The previous year she'd had a fall, and I'd thought she might not make a full recovery. But she had, and how: that September trip she was a little slower, but still lively and curious, and we had lots of fun. Waiting for her in 2011, though, was a lung condition that advanced to pneumonia, and in the evening of 25 May she died. Her funeral took place the following day, so there was no possibility of getting there. Instead I watched the Mexican TV news online: the hearse carrying her coffin sped through the streets of Mexico City, trying to get clear of the TV camera people on their motorbikes. If Leonora and I had been watching it together, we would probably have found it funny.

Chiki Weisz and Leonora Carrington in their home in Mexico, 1998

I travelled to Mexico again the following year and visited the British cemetery, where I laid flowers on Leonora's grave. By then it had a white headstone, with words from her sons chiselled into it. From Gaby: *I will always look into your eyes*. From Pablo: *Like a strong blinding light of imagination you came and you left us*.

I continued to spend time in Mexico; maybe not quite as regularly as when Leonora was alive, but I usually went there twice a year. I did not return to 194 Calle Chihuahua at all during these visits. Pablo and Wendy were sometimes in residence, but our trips never coincided. So although I sometimes walked along the street and even once met her housekeeper, Yolanda, on the pavement, I didn't step over the threshold into Leonora's kingdom again.

But exactly ten years on from her death, in May 2021, I found myself back in her kitchen. Eerily, it was just as I remembered it. The same pots and pans were hanging by the sink; the spice jars, labelled in her handwriting, were on the shelves, and the postcards including some pictures of the royal family, much commented upon by journalists and visitors over the years (someone had drawn a balaclava on the face of Prince Charles), were still taped to the kitchen cupboards. A Liberty oilcloth covered the round table that dominated the room, just as it always had. Leonora's woollen cardigan and small black bag were hanging over the chair where she always sat; on the table were her teacup, a pile of letters and even a half-smoked cigarette in an ashtray.

It felt, arriving in that room, as though Leonora had just popped next door – to use the bathroom, perhaps, or to nip upstairs to fetch her bottle of tequila from the top shelf in her wardrobe where she always kept it. Instantly I was back in her world. I half expected to hear her voice as she came into the room behind me: 'Ah, so you're back. What's been happening? Would you like a cup of tea?'

What I was experiencing was an intricate, exhaustive recreation and reimagining of Leonora's house, similar to that of Frida Kahlo's home, the Blue House, after her death in 1953. The Blue House is across town in the neighbourhood of Coyoacán; it's one of Mexico City's most popular tourist attractions. Could Leonora's house prove equally successful? Visitors would soon be welcomed into its rooms – but first, for a whole fortnight, I would have it virtually to myself, to remember the days we had spent here together and to ponder what the house-museum, officially now known as the Casa Estudio Leonora Carrington, would add to her legacy.

The recreation was carried out by the Metropolitan Autonomous University of Mexico (UAM), who had purchased the house from Leonora's family. Under their guidance it has been presented exactly as it appeared during the final years of her life. The project cost £3 million, and, as at Kahlo's Blue House, it contains a huge wealth of objects that belonged to Leonora: her tables and chairs, sofas and coffee tables, beds and kitchen cupboards; her desk and typewriter; studies of her work on the walls; and everywhere, pieces of her sculpture. In the dining room, the large, disused range she bought decades ago is festooned with yellow Post-it notes with telephone numbers in Leonora's handwriting. Upstairs, her books line the walls of the sitting room, just as they did in her lifetime – contemporary novels by the authors she loved (Ian McEwan, Doris Lessing and Margaret Atwood among them) nestle up against tomes on the interests that informed her art: the occult, Gnosticism, Kabbalah, tarot, herbalism and shamanism.

Leonora was fascinated by belief systems, and often immersed in a particular one. She told the Rosemonts in Chicago that Gnosticism was the religion she loved best; but she had 'dabbled', she said, in many others. As she explained to Penelope Rosemont: 'Most mothers worry about their children joining some "cult" but with me it has always been just the opposite, my sons are always worried about which crackpot group their mother is going to join next.'[1] Another friend, the French Canadian artist Alan Glass, remembered that she 'had different interests in different periods. She had her "alchemy period" in the 1940s and 1950s. Then came the Ouspensky group, but also Tibetan Buddhism.' With Alan she had gone to visit a Tibetan monastery in Canada; on another occasion, with Edward James, she went to the Kagyu Samye Ling Buddhist monastery in Dumfries, Scotland. Later, Alan recalled, her interests in feminism and ecology came to the fore. She wasn't afraid to change what she believed: 'When I met her she had a lot of birds in cages, but not long after, she detested keeping animals imprisoned.' She also, he said, 'mixed everything: Kabbalah, Tantric Buddhism, alchemy and Celtic culture'.[2]

Leonora herself once said that no religion or sect had ever fully convinced her, but that 'the closest thing [that did] was Tibetan Buddhism. In this religion one followed practices that were intellectually satisfying, and in another way their beliefs are extraordinary. But I have always remained on the frontier of this sort of thing: I was always interested in discovering something that corresponded to my experiences. That is what I was really doing.'[3]

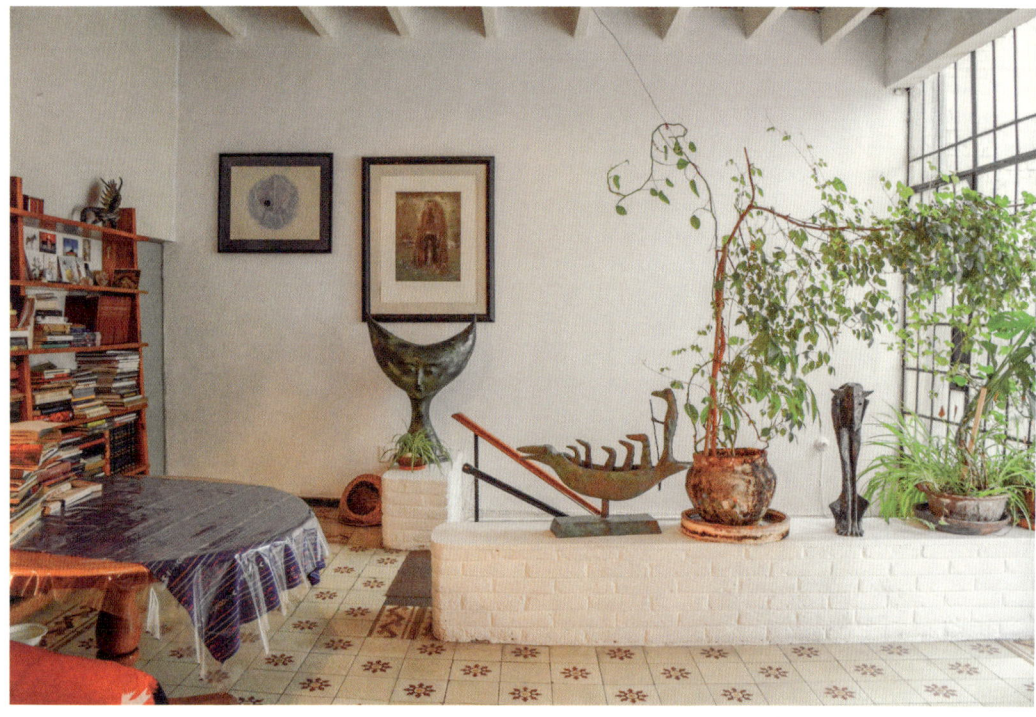

Interior of Casa Estudio Leonora Carrington, Mexico City

Other books in Leonora's collection celebrate the work of her friends: the photography of Lee Miller and Kati Horna, the art of Remedios Varo and Gunther Gerzso, the poetry of Nobel laureate Octavio Paz. And then there are the books about the animals she loved: *Birds with Human Faces* and *The Book of Owls*. And *Expert Obedience Training for Dogs*, though I'm not sure that was ever deployed to best effect with Yeti, her Maltese terrier.

Yeti was a late addition to the household, arriving in 2009. For a while before that, Leonora had been talking about getting a puppy. It seemed an ambitious undertaking for a woman in her nineties and I thought it was unlikely she'd go through with it. But then Yeti appeared, a gift from a friend. From then until the end of her life, they would be constant companions. Yeti enriched Leonora's life in innumerable ways; she was her ally and her consolation in those final years, as death nudged ever closer.

In all, the house at 194 Calle Chihuahua contains 8,600 objects that belonged to Leonora. Many of them are strikingly intimate, particularly those in her first-floor bedroom, which is off an outside corridor

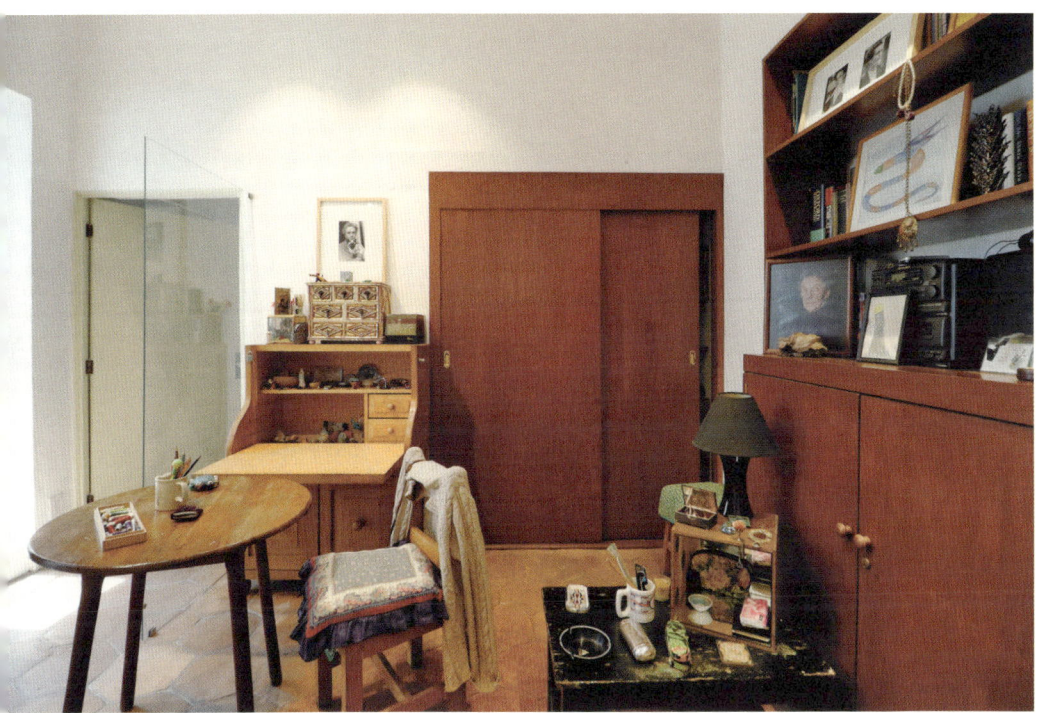

Interior of Casa Estudio Leonora Carrington, Mexico City

and a few steps from her studio. This room was never a public space during her lifetime: it was her sanctuary. Sometimes she would ask me to sit there with her, beside her bed, while she rested in the afternoon, drifting in that state between wakefulness and sleep so valued by the surrealists. One time, when I was sure she was sleeping, she suddenly sat bolt upright and exclaimed: 'Why do you think there have been so few women artists through history, when there have been so many women writers?'

In her wardrobe hang the clothes in which I remember her, mostly grey and black jumpers, cardigans and trousers; on the bedside table, her spectacles and telephone remain. And in the bathroom, most touchingly of all, is her lipstick and make-up. Even into old age, Leonora set great store by looking as good as possible. She bathed each morning and always enjoyed the feeling of being dressed and ready for the day.

Her bedroom illustrates, in the starkest possible way, Leonora's natural frugality. She was not someone for whom creature comforts rated highly; it was always the interior elements of life that excited

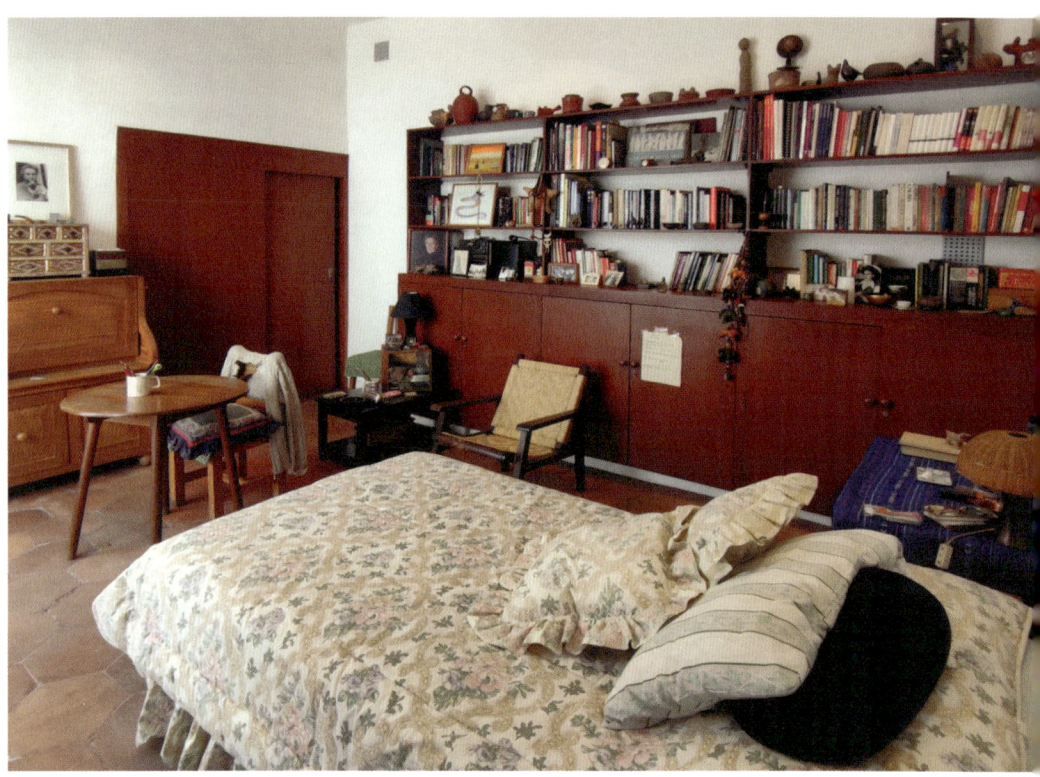

Bedroom in Casa Estudio Leonora Carrington, Mexico City

and interested her. She slept in a narrow single bed. The floor, like the other floors in the house, was tiled. There was a bookcase, a coffee table and a rattan chair or two, and a tiny bedside lamp on a small table. It was functional, like all the spaces in her life. She was proud of her home, proud of what it represented, and every aspect of it was congruent with the world she believed in. It wasn't showy or demonstrating anything except the individual she was and the family who surrounded her. At home she was looking neither for validation of her status nor physical luxury; what she cared about was feeling safe – at least, as safe as she believed it was possible to feel – and being authentic. 194 Calle Chihuahua represented Leonora's kingdom, her lair, her place of refuge.

One of the highlights of the Casa Estudio for many visitors is the studio, the engine room of Leonora's art. It's on the first floor, a few steps from her bedroom, across an outdoor patio. The studio wasn't in use during the time I knew her but it was a place where we'd sometimes sit and chat. Leonora felt the spirits of the other worlds she could connect with were particularly strong in the studio; on at least one occasion, I remember us heading up there only for her to decide, at the door, that the aura wasn't good. There were spirits there she didn't want to encounter; we headed back down to the kitchen, where I think she always felt safest.

The studio has a blue-tiled floor and whitewashed walls, which on the facing wall support wooden shelves filled with the detritus of the artist: brushes, pencils, pots, glue. On a coatstand there's a brown overall and a yellow and orange pinny. It looks more like a kitchen apron than an artist's apron, but then, for Leonora, painting was very like cooking; she often remarked on the similarities between the two. For her the kitchen and the studio were parallel spaces and, as she told me when we first met, painting for her was a need, not a choice. She likened it to going into the kitchen in search of food. Her process of creating paint, using the tempera method beloved of the Renaissance artists, involved mixing egg yolk with powdered pigments, and on another shelf those powders are stored in small glass bottles.

There is also a mirror here, mounted on a triangular wooden frame. Leonora's friend Eva Marcovich remembers that they would use it to experiment with what it was possible to see, and what remained hidden. Leonora told Eva that it was important to look at the empty spaces as well as the objects. 'We performed many exercises, noting how the appearance of things is quite limited and informs us only of certain elements of reality, because there are many other realities and ways to approach them.' Leonora had, said Eva, 'that gaze, that capacity to be able to cross thresholds and to be able to touch deeper and deeper elements, figures, situations and environments that most people could not see.'[4]

The studio was certainly not the only place on the premises where she created art. Indeed, I would be surprised if there was any part of the house where she didn't at some point paint, sculpt or draw. She painted *El mundo mágico de los mayas* in the sitting room. The preliminary sketches for that piece were made in Chiapas in southern Mexico, where she spent time across a six-month period in 1963, travelling sometimes by bus via Oaxaca to Tuxtla Gutiérrez and then by horse or mule, at other times taking the train to Veracruz. In Chiapas she stayed in the town of San Cristóbal with Swiss anthropologist Gertrude Blom, who introduced her to a whole range of elements of traditional life in the region, including the *curanderos* or healers. Many

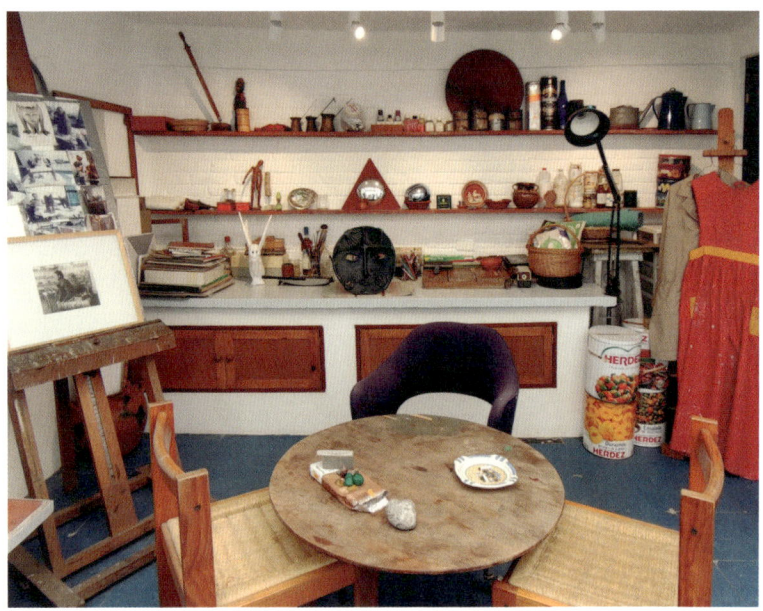

Studio in Casa Estudio Leonora Carrington, Mexico City

of the ideas of Maya heritage were on her wavelength, especially the belief that every human being has an animal companion, a familiar, who remains with them throughout their life.

The mural is a fabulous achievement, incorporating many of the different worlds on which Leonora's work always focused. The world of traditional beliefs brushes up against the Christianity of the Spanish missionaries; the world of the dead, the underworld of the earth and the tree roots, lies visible and alive just below the orange expanse of the land. There, humans are interspersed with animals – some tiny, others outsize. A volcano-red sky meets the peaks of the mountains and the glow of the sun, while on the right of the canvas a flock of owls swoop magnificently into the frame.

During the time I knew Leonora, her garage was serving as a work-room for her sculpture, and that was the only work she was involved in. There was a burgeoning of pieces from her in the final years of her life; in many ways, sculpture was an ideal medium for her in her nineties. She was able to focus on the sorts of figures that had peopled her paintings for so long, and which now came to life in three dimensions. Although Leonora's painting and her writing will be her lasting legacy, her sculpture adds a new and interesting dimension to her oeuvre.

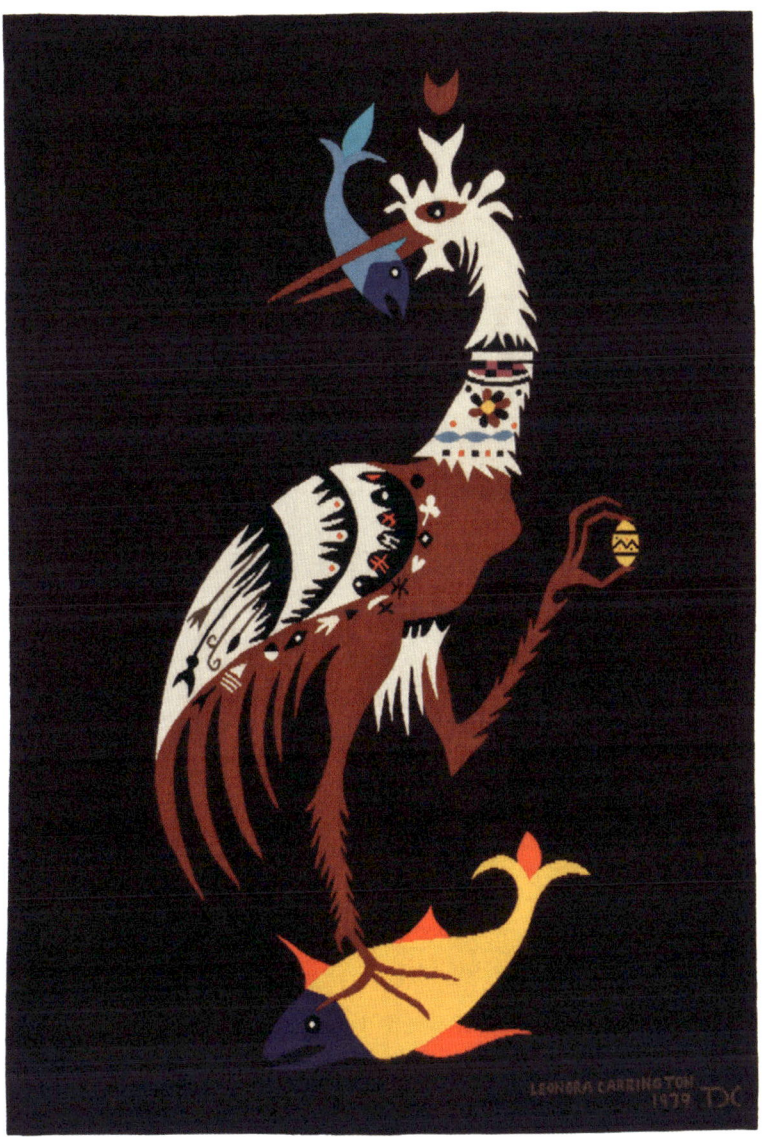

Bird with Fish, 1979

Later life wasn't the first time she had engaged with sculpture. During the 1950s in particular she had experimented with a wide range of media, including tapestry and embroidery. In a similar vein to *La Cuna*, the crib she created with José Horna for his little daughter Norah, Leonora's polychrome wood sculpture *Cat Woman* (page 154) is one of her finest pieces of three-dimensional work. It dates from 1951

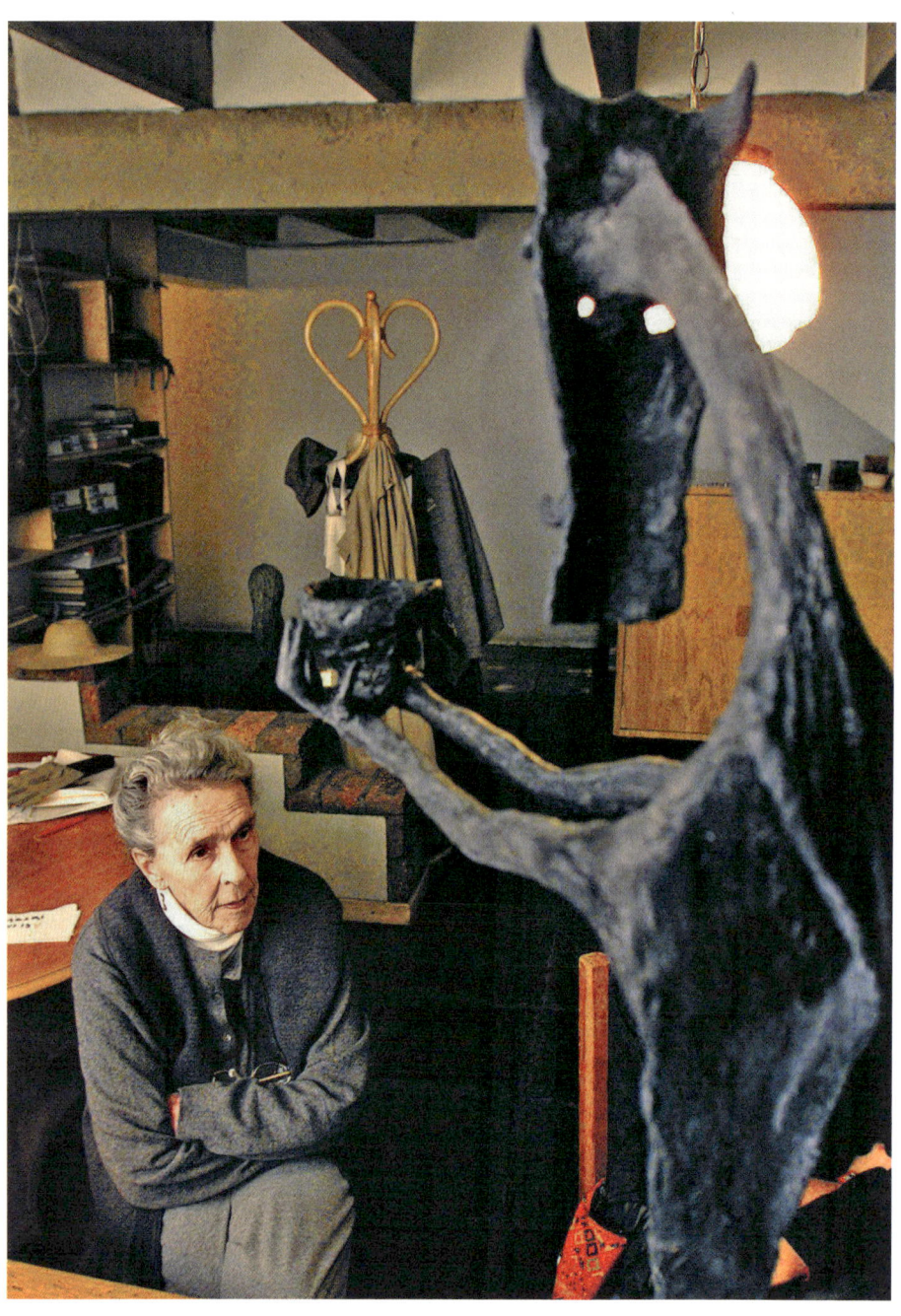

Leonora Carrington with her sculpture *La Virgen de la Cueva*, 2000

and, like the *cuna*, features a series of delicately executed paintings on the skirt and abdomen of the female figure.

One of the most interesting elements of being with Leonora in the years when I knew her was that the time of our friendship corresponded exactly with her real-life 'Hearing Trumpet' era. In the novel of that name her protagonist, Marian Leatherby, is ninety-two. I spent Leonora's ninety-second birthday with her in Mexico City; it was a low-key affair. We went out for lunch with Gabriel, her eldest son, and his wife Paty. They were not a family to make a huge deal of a birthday – Leonora received a paperback book about how to cope with memory loss, and was thrilled with it. Short-term memory loss was becoming a problem in her later years, although she was always able to recall the events of longer ago (which wasn't necessarily a consolation, since she wanted to be able to talk about the present moment more than the 1930s).

Leonora had written *The Hearing Trumpet* in her forties although it wasn't published until later in her life, and there are a number of similarities between the way she lived at 194 Calle Chihuahua in the years I knew her, and the life Marian leads in the novel. Leonora's attitude to life in her nineties was certainly Marian-esque. Like Marian, her senses continued to be acute, although rheumatism had bent her skeleton as it had her protagonist's: 'This does not prevent me taking a walk in clement weather [and] I consider that I am still a useful member of society and I believe still capable of being pleasant and amusing when the occasion seems fit.'[5] Marian's diet – mashed vegetables, chocolate, bread – was exactly the sort of food Leonora was eating, with the addition at 194 Calle Chihuahua of *pollo* (chicken) and *frijoles* (beans).

Like 194 Calle Chihuahua, the house Marian shared with the son who was about to deposit her in an old people's home was located in a residential area of the city and had a small garden. There was a house-keeper like Yolanda (named Rosina in the book), a cactus plant and, right outside Leonora's bedroom door as outside Marian's, a back yard. Like Marian, Leonora only needed to open the door to enjoy the morning sun or the evening stars.

In the final years of her life, Leonora's circle naturally contracted. She became more selective about whom she wanted to spend time with; as Elena Poniatowska put it, 'the door that leads to Leonora is narrow. Few are the chosen ones. Leonora, at times, laments her solitude, yet she refuses to abandon it.'[6] Elena recalled that Leonora's favourite place to eat was Sanborn's, a diner chain ubiquitous in

The Magdalens, 1986

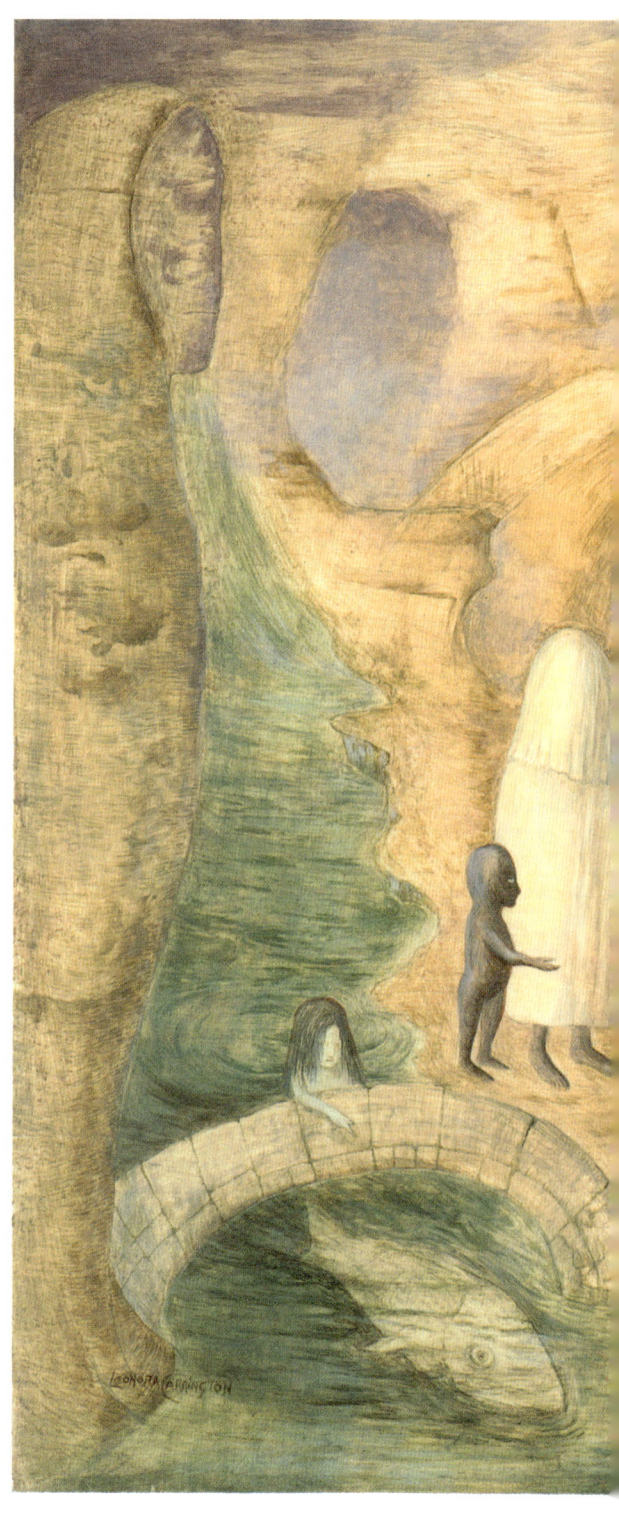

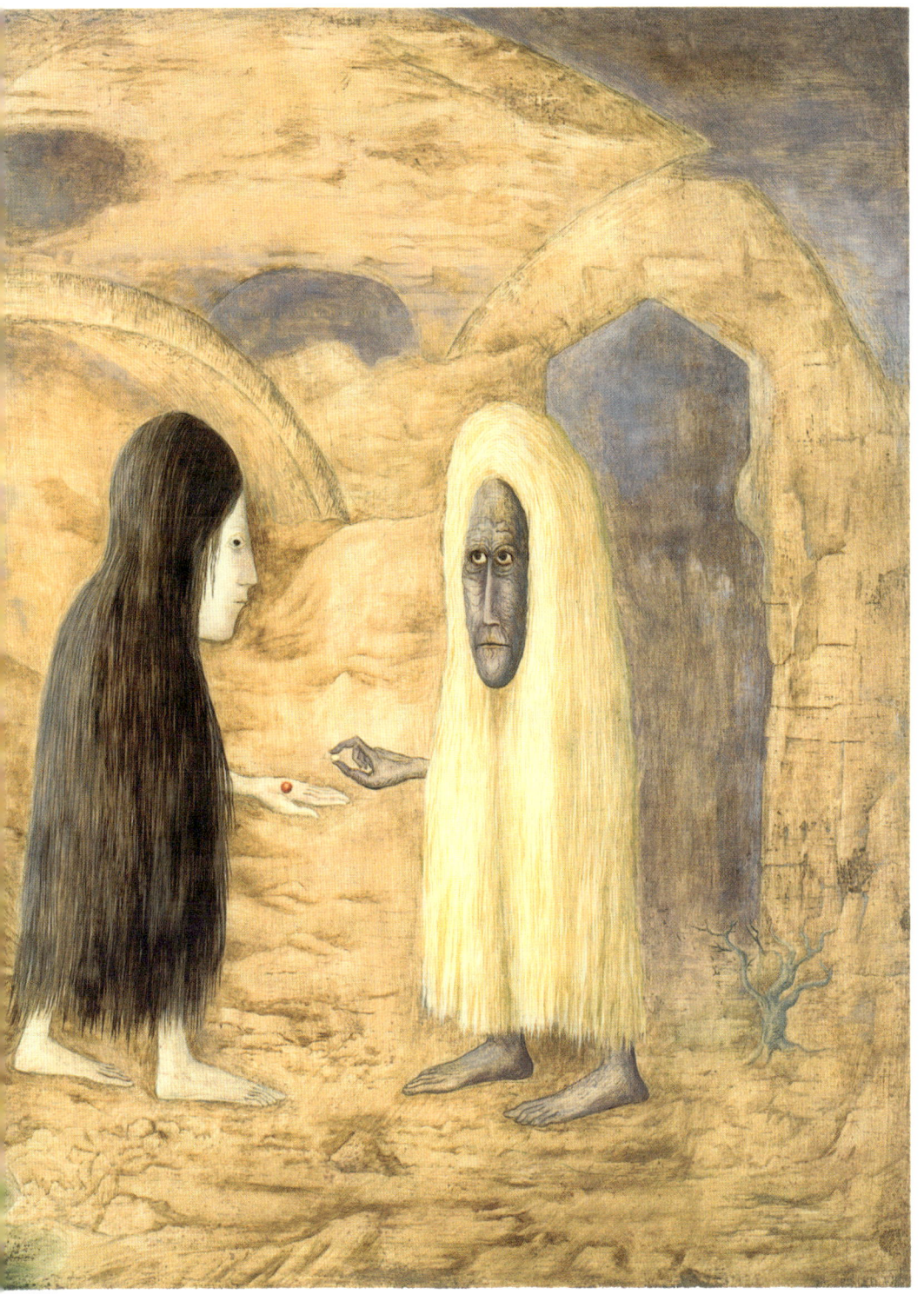

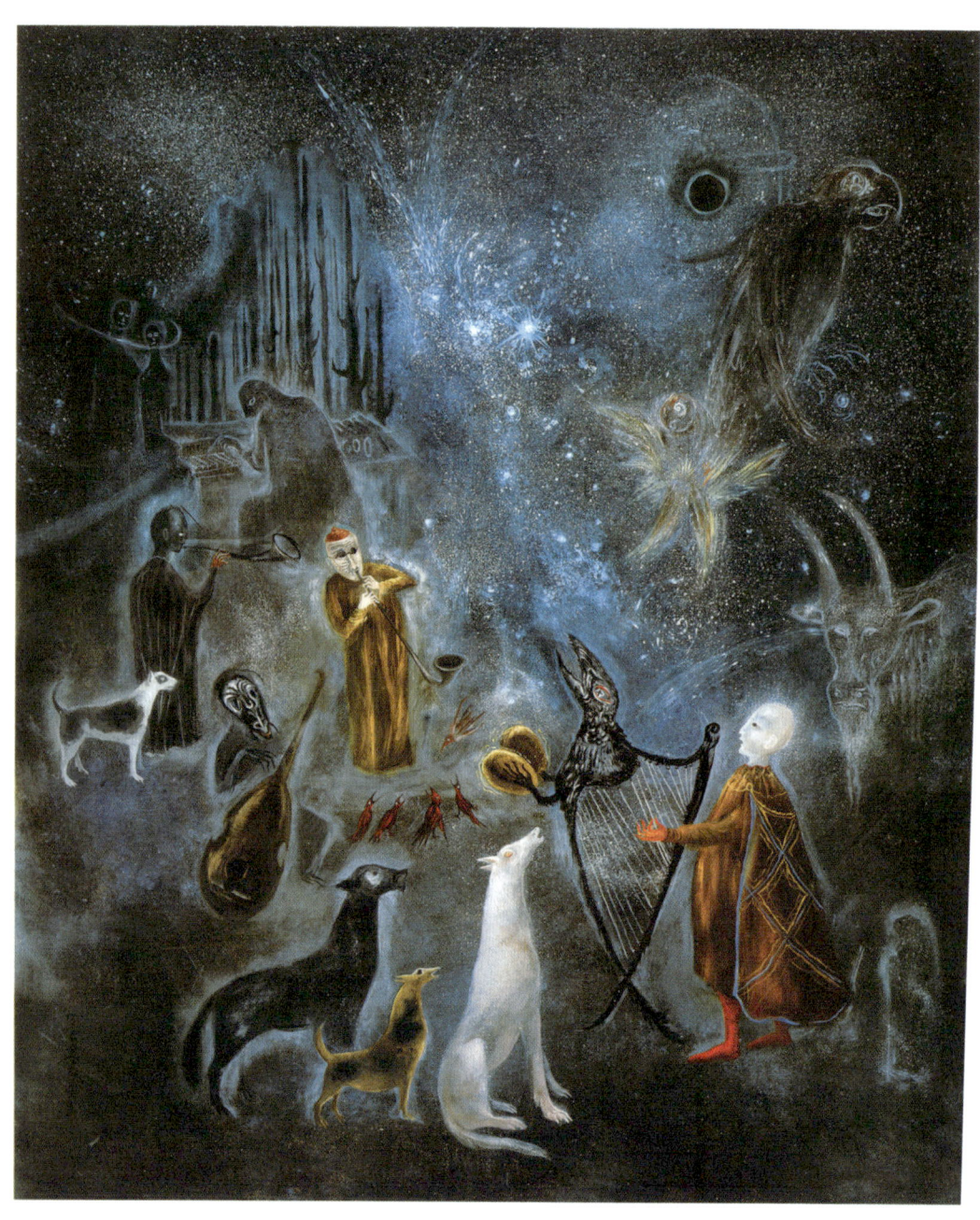

Q Symphony, 2002

Mexico. Its closest branch was a five-minute walk from her house; I often ate there with Leonora too. 'The waitresses there know her and what table she prefers. Before she asks for the menu, they have already brought her the usual; eggs à la Mexicana. She doesn't even finish the small portion of refried beans on the side.'[7] Occasionally we walked down to the Avenida Álvaro Obregón and ate at the upmarket Casa Lamm. At Sanborn's I never witnessed her being approached by a fan; it's a busy fast-food restaurant, catering more for Mexicans than for tourists or American residents. But at Casa Lamm, located within a small arts centre, she was sometimes approached by people who recognized her and wanted to say hello, to ask for an autograph or to take a photograph with her (she didn't like being photographed, so the answer to that request was usually no).

Death remained, as it had always been, a preoccupation. Leonora spoke about it often and she discussed it with interviewers, already feeling its shadow in her sixties and seventies. In 1991, she told Paul De Angelis that death was what worried her above all else, but also that she believed humanity's attitude towards it was misguided. Death, like dreams, put people (and indeed animals) into a different space. 'I think that to reach an understanding about death first we must understand the distinct places that exist within us, and dreams are one of these places,' she said.[8] In 2003, she told Sylvia Cherem that she was in 'the process of learning to die'.[9]

One afternoon in Mexico City, we spoke about death for many hours. But when I arrived to see her the next day, she was already waiting at the door because she had important news to impart. 'I had the most extraordinary dream – I dreamt I was dead. Can you imagine it, to dream you are dead? I was dead, and I was swimming through this water, I was under the water. And I suddenly realized that it felt all right. It felt safe...it felt free. I wasn't frightened. In fact, to my surprise I found I was rather enjoying it.'

When I think of Leonora now, I imagine her swimming through the waters of another world, and I hope very much that she is enjoying it. Perhaps ironically, the death she so feared has brought, in her case, a rebirth on this earth as well as that possible reincarnation elsewhere. Leonora's legacy was in its infancy when she died in 2011, but today her fame is growing beyond anything she could have imagined. We used to joke about how her work would be reproduced on mugs and T-shirts, tea towels and fridge magnets: yet today I have those mugs, I own that T-shirt, those tea towels are in my kitchen drawer and my fridge is festooned with those magnets. Even though Leonora didn't really like the commercialization of art in this way, I think she would have been secretly pleased that her work is now popular enough to have spawned the creation of these products.

There was certainly recognition of her achievements and her contribution during her lifetime. She was awarded the OBE in 2000, and there were many exhibitions in the US, Mexico and even the UK, including the major 1991 Serpentine Gallery show. The same year, an important show of her work entitled 'Leonora Carrington: The Mexican Years', was held at the Mexican Museum in San Francisco. She lived to see a 2010 exhibition that I co-curated at Pallant House Gallery in Chichester, 'Surreal Friends', which focused on her relationship with Remedios Varo and Kati Horna. It was the first time Leonora's work had been exhibited in her home country for twenty years.

Interest has risen to a new level since her death. In January 2012, less than a year after she died, her work had a significant showing as part of a landmark exhibition titled 'In Wonderland: The Surrealist Adventures of Women Artists in Mexico and the United States', co-organized by the Los Angeles County Museum of Art and the Museo de Arte Moderno in Mexico City. Since then, there have been individual shows of Leonora's work at Tate Liverpool, at the Irish Museum of Modern Art in Dublin, and in New York. The year 2018 saw the most extensive and important exhibition ever of her work, 'Magical Tales', at Mexico City's Museum of Modern Art – this was curated by Tere Arcq, and Stefan van Raay who also worked on the Pallant House show. They did a superb job of bringing together so many elements of Leonora's output: alongside some of her greatest paintings there were tapestries and sculpture, masks and stage sets. Particularly important were pieces of her work that had rarely or never been seen before, notably her remarkable paintings of tarot cards (page 169), and a fabulous screen with a 'cold' side whose colours were blues and greys, and a 'warm' side bursting with yellows, oranges and reds.

Fascination with Leonora's work continues to grow. The title of the Venice Biennale in 2022, 'The Milk of Dreams', was taken from her children's book, published after her death. At the time of writing, plans are under way for a major exhibition in Denmark and Spain, introducing her to yet more audiences. Museums and galleries around the world have been snapping up her paintings to hang on their walls: in Rotterdam, the Museum Boijmans Van Beuningen acquired 1947's *Again the Gemini are in the Orchard*, and in Edinburgh the Scottish

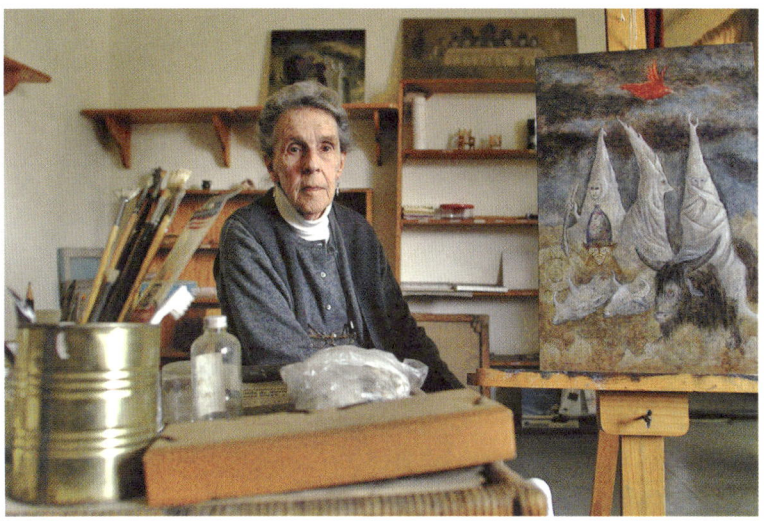

Leonora Carrington at home, 2000

National Galleries bought the *Portrait of Max Ernst* of a few years earlier. In 2022, *Self-Portrait/Inn of the Dawn Horse* was chosen as the lead
image for a major exhibition on surrealism at Tate Modern and could
be seen plastered across the tube stations of London.

What is the reason for such a remarkable surge in popularity and
critical attention? The answer, it seems to me, is that Leonora's work
connects so forcefully, so remarkably, with the issues of our present
time. She was a visionary: she saw into the future, as much as she saw
into other worlds that surround us. So much of what preoccupies the
wider world today was already preoccupying her in the 1940s and even
earlier. Feminism, ecology; spirituality outside of organized religion;
the ability of nature to heal us; and especially the interconnectedness
of everything: these fascinated Leonora, and now they are at the fore-
front of everyone's mind.

And so death has been not an ending but a new beginning for
Leonora. Her physical presence is gone, but she often feels not far
away at all, in one of those other worlds from which we are separated
only by the flimsiest of veils. Her spirit and her artistic legacy are one.
She lives on through them, and will continue to do so as long as the
themes of her work continue to resonate in this world of ours. And
that is likely to be for a very long time indeed.

Notes

Chapter 1

1 *Omnibus: Leonora and the House of Fear*, BBC documentary, 1992.
2 Leonora Carrington, *The Hearing Trumpet* (Penguin, 2005), p. 13.
3 Leonora Carrington, *The House of Fear* (Virago, 1989), pp. 30–1.
4 Leonora Carrington, conversation with the author, 2009.
5 'Illustrated Particulars, with Plan and Conditions of Sale...of Crookhey Hall Estate' (1926).
6 Whitney Chadwick, *Women Artists and the Surrealist Movement* (Thames & Hudson, 2021), p. 252.
7 Independently minded, feminist women do seem to run in my family. The first Leonora, my great-aunt who became a Sister of Charity, once challenged the authority of the archbishop – something that was unheard of for a nun in early 20th-century Ireland. A cousin, Ethel Moorhead (1869–1955) was one of Scotland's first and most militant suffragettes; and her sister Alice (1868–1910) was one of the first female doctors to practise in Scotland.
8 Leonora Carrington, childhood notebooks.
9 *Omnibus: Leonora and the House of Fear*.

Chapter 2

1 Barry Guise and Pam Brook, *The Midland Hotel: Morecambe's White Hope*, p. 103.
2 *Ibid*. p. 59.
3 Gabriel Weisz Carrington, *The Invisible Painting: My Memoir of Leonora Carrington* (Manchester University Press, 2021), p. 25.
4 Leonora Carrington, *The Hearing Trumpet* (Penguin, 2005), p. 15.
5 *Ibid*. p. 15.
6 *Ibid*. p. 16.
7 Robert de Trafford was not related to Leonora, although he was my great-great-uncle via my grandmother's family, the Mostyns, who were close friends of the Carringtons. It was through this friendship that my grandparents met, during a summer visit my grandfather George made to stay with his sister Maurie. The Mostyns lived in the next village, Clifton Hill, and my grandmother Miriam was their eldest daughter. When George and Miriam married at St James's Church, Spanish Place, London in 1931, Leonora's brother Arthur was a page boy.
8 The word 'fishes' for the pupils dates back to a time when New Hall School was at Liege, now in Belgium, and girls from Catholic families were sent there in secret to be educated. To keep their cover, the captain who ferried them across would say he was expecting 'a consignment of fish' whenever a boatload of children were on their way.
9 My information on New Hall comes from two sources: *Fishy Tales* (a book of living memories collected from the school community) and *New Hall and its School* by Tony Tuckwell. I am indebted to Stella Beer, archivist at New Hall School, for her help with these sources.
10 Tuckwell, *New Hall and its School*, p. 162.
11 Leonora Carrington, childhood notebooks, private collection.
12 Leonora quoted in Susan Aberth, *Leonora Carrington: Surrealism, Alchemy and Art* (Lund Humphries, 2004), p. 18.
13 Silvia Cherem, 'Eternally Married to the Wind: Interview with Leonora Carrington', in *Leonora Carrington: What She Might Be* (Dallas Museum of Art, 2008), p. 24.
14 *Ibid*. p. 25.
15 Marina Warner, 'Leonora Carrington's Spirit Bestiary; or the Art of Playing Make-Belief', in *Leonora Carrington: Paintings, Drawings and Sculptures 1940–1990* (Serpentine Gallery, 1991), p. 16.
16 Mentioned in a letter from Edward James to Leonora Carrington (1948) and quoted in *Leonora Carrington: Magical Tales* (Instituto Nacional de Bellas Artes, 2018), p. 155.
17 Adam Hogg, 'Testimonio', in *Leonora Carrington: Magical Tales*, p. 400.
18 Paul De Angelis, 'Interview with Leonora Carrington', in *Leonora Carrington: The Mexican Years, 1943–1985* (University of New Mexico Press, 1991), ed. Patricia Draher, p. 34.
19 Leonora Carrington, childhood notebooks, private collection.
20 Carrington, *The Hearing Trumpet*, pp. 59–60.

Chapter 3

1 Leonora Carrington, *The Hearing Trumpet* (Penguin, 2005), p. 65.
2 *Ibid*. p. 64.
3 'First Court of the Season', *The Times*, 29 March 1935.
4 Silvia Cherem, 'Eternally Married to the Wind: Interview with Leonora Carrington', in *Leonora Carrington: What She Might Be* (Dallas Museum of Art, 2008), p. 26.
5 Paul De Angelis, 'Interview with Leonora Carrington', in *Leonora Carrington: The Mexican Years, 1943–1985* (University of New Mexico Press, 1991), ed. Patricia Draher, p. 34.
6 Leonora Carrington, 'The Debutante', in *The House of Fear: Notes from Down Below* (Virago, 1989), p. 44.
7 Herbert Read, introduction to the International Surrealist Exhibition catalogue (1936), p. 13.
8 De Angelis, 'Interview', p. 34.
9 *Omnibus: Leonora and the House of Fear*, BBC documentary, 1992.
10 Alan Powers, *Serge Chermayeff: Designer, Architect, Teacher* (Riba Publications, 2001), p. 90.
11 De Angelis, 'Interview', p. 34.
12 *Ibid*. p. 34.
13 *Ibid*. p. 34.
14 Ozenfant Academy of Fine Arts prospectus, from the collection at 2 Willow Road.
15 *Ibid*.
16 Adam Hogg, 'Testimonio', in *Leonora Carrington: Magical Tales* (Instituto Nacional de Bellas Artes, 2018), p. 400.
17 De Angelis, 'Interview', p. 36.
18 *Ibid*. p. 36.

Chapter 4

1 Antony Penrose (ed.), *The Surrealists in Cornwall: The Boat of Your Body* (Falmouth Art Gallery, 2004), n.p.
2 Eileen Agar, *A Look at My Life* (Methuen, 1988), p. 120.
3 Leonora Carrington, conversation with the author, 2006.
4 Agar, *A Look at My Life*, p. 133.
5 Carrington, conversation with the author, 2006.
6 Agar, p. 133.
7 Quoted in Joanna Moorhead, *The Surreal Life of Leonora Carrington* (Virago, 2019).
8 Paul Éluard, 'The Last Letter to Roland Penrose',

© the artist's estate. Translated from the French by Roland Penrose and quoted in *The Surrealists in Cornwall*, n.p.
9 Paul De Angelis, 'Interview with Leonora Carrington', in *Leonora Carrington: The Mexican Years, 1943–1985* (University of New Mexico Press, 1991), ed. Patricia Draher, p. 36.

Chapter 5

1 Paul De Angelis, 'Interview with Leonora Carrington', in *Leonora Carrington: The Mexican Years, 1943–1985* (University of New Mexico Press, 1991), ed. Patricia Draher, p. 36.
2 Stefan van Raay, 'The Young Artist', in *Leonora Carrington: Magical Tales* (Instituto Nacional de Bellas Artes, 2018), p. 36.
3 Joanna Moorhead, 'Leonora and Me', *Guardian*, 2 January, 2007.
4 Leonora Carrington, conversation with the author, February 2008.
5 Whitney Chadwick, 'The Two Leonors', in *Leonora Carrington: Magical Tales*, p. 58.
6 Carrington, conversation with the author, February 2008.
7 Van Raay, 'The Young Artist', p. 36.
8 Peggy Guggenheim, *Out of This Century: Confessions of an Art Addict* (André Deutsch, 1979), Kindle loc. 3782.
9 *Ibid*. loc. 3070.
10 Whitney Chadwick, 'Leonora Carrington: Evolution of a Feminist Consciousness', *Woman's Art Journal* 7, no. 1 (Spring/Summer 1986), p. 38.
11 Silvia Cherem, 'Eternally Married to the Wind: Interview with Leonora Carrington', in *Leonora Carrington: What She Might Be* (Dallas Museum of Art, 2008), p. 32.
12 Vincent Bouvet and Gerard Durozoi, *Paris Between the Wars: Art, Style and Glamour in the Crazy Years* (Thames & Hudson, 2010), p. 256.
13 Moorhead, 'Leonora and Me'.
14 Cherem, 'Eternally Married to the Wind', p. 31.
15 Jimmy Ernst, *Notes from a Not-So-Still Life* (St Martin's Press, 1984), p. 109.

Chapter 6

1 'Little Francis', in Leonora Carrington, *The House of Fear: Notes from Down Below* (Virago, 1989), p. 76.
2 *Ibid*. p. 79.
3 Joanna Moorhead, *The Surreal Life of Leonora Carrington* (Virago, 2019), p. 93.
4 Paul De Angelis, 'Interview with Leonora

Carrington', in *Leonora Carrington: The Mexican Years, 1943–1985* (University of New Mexico Press, 1991), ed. Patricia Draher, p. 36.

5   Whitney Chadwick, 'The Two Leonors', in *Leonora Carrington: Magical Tales* (Instituto Nacional de Bellas Artes, 2018), p. 60.

6   *Ibid.* p. 60.

7   *Ibid.* p. 60.

8   *Ibid.* p. 61.

9   *Ibid.* p. 62.

10 Letter from Maurie to Leonora, undated, discovered in the house at Les Alliberts by the author, 2011.

11 Rosemary Sullivan, *Villa Air-Bel* (Harper Perennial, 2007), p. 13.

12 Leonora Carrington, *Down Below* in *In the House of Fear: Notes from Down Below* (Virago, 1989), p. 164.

13 *Ibid.* p. 165.

14 *Ibid.* p. 165.

15 *Ibid.* p. 165.

16 *Ibid.* p. 166.

17 *Ibid.* p. 167.

18 *Ibid.* p. 168.

Chapter 7

1   Leonora Carrington, *Down Below* in *In the House of Fear: Notes from Down Below* (Virago, 1989), p. 170.

2   *Ibid.* p. 174.

3   *Ibid.* p. 177.

4   *Ibid.* p. 188.

5   *Ibid.* p. 191.

6   Marisa Samaniego, conversation with the author, November 2021.

7   Susan Aberth, *Leonora Carrington: Surrealism, Alchemy and Art* (Lund Humphries, 2004), p. 46.

8   Salomon Grimberg, 'Travelling toward the Unknown, Leonora Carrington Stopped in New York', in *Leonora Carrington: Magical Tales* (Instituto Nacional de Bellas Artes, 2018), p. 78.

9   Carrington, *Down Below*, p. 201.

10 *Ibid.* pp. 207–8.

11 *Ibid.* p. 208.

12 Postscript to *Down Below*, as told to Marina Warner, p. 210.

13 *Ibid.* p. 211.

14 *Ibid.* p. 212.

15 Silvia Cherem, 'Eternally Married to the Wind: Interview with Leonora Carrington', in *Leonora Carrington: What She Might Be* (Dallas Museum of Art, 2008), p. 35.

16 Postscript to *Down Below*, p. 212.

17 *Ibid.* p. 212.

18 *Ibid.* p. 213.

19 *Ibid.* p. 213.

20 *Ibid.* p. 213.

21 *Ibid.* p. 213.

22 Erich Maria Remarque, *The Night in Lisbon: A Novel* (Random House, 2014), p. 4.

23 Mary Ransome Dittrich, conversation with the author, summer 2017.

24 *Ibid.*

25 Peggy Guggenheim, *Out of This Century: Confessions of an Art Addict* (André Deutsch, 1979), Kindle loc. 4006.

26 *Ibid.* loc. 4108.

27 Dittrich, conversation with the author, summer 2017.

28 Guggenheim, *Out of This Century*, loc. 4143.

29 Leonora Carrington, conversation with the author, September 2008.

30 Guggenheim, *Out of This Century*, loc. 3069.

31 *Ibid.* loc. 4147.

32 *Ibid.* loc. 4134.

33 *Ibid.* loc. 4160.

34 Cherem, 'Eternally Married to the Wind', p. 36.

Chapter 8

1   Peggy Guggenheim, *Out of This Century: Confessions of an Art Addict* (André Deutsch, 1979), Kindle loc. 4274.

2   *Ibid.* loc. 4325.

3   Salomon Grimberg, 'Travelling toward the Unknown, Leonora Carrington Stopped in New York', in *Leonora Carrington: Magical Tales* (Instituto Nacional de Bellas Artes, 2018), p. 72.

4   Paul De Angelis, 'Interview with Leonora Carrington', in *Leonora Carrington: The Mexican Years, 1943–1985* (University of New Mexico Press, 1991), ed. Patricia Draher, p. 38.

5   Jaime Moreno Villarreal, 'The Greater the Shadow, the Greater the Luminescence', in *Leonora Carrington: Magical Tales*, p. 102.

6   *Ibid.* p. 102.

7   *Ibid.* p. 106.

8   Quoted in Jacqueline Bograd Weld, *Peggy: The Wayward Guggenheim* (New York, 1986), p. 227.

9   *Ibid.* p. 227.

10 The quotes and events around this mural are in Grimberg, 'Travelling toward the Unknown', and are informed by an interview with Manka Rubinstein in 1987.

11 Guggenheim, *Out of This Century*, loc. 4475.
12 Letter from Leonora Carrington to Renato Leduc, 22 September, 1941, as seen in 'Leonora Carrington: Magical Tales' at the Museum of Modern Art in Mexico City, 2018.
13 *Ibid*.
14 Guggenheim, *Out of This Century*, loc. 4851.
15 Weld, *Peggy*, p. 295.

Chapter 9

1 Paul De Angelis, 'Interview with Leonora Carrington', in *Leonora Carrington: The Mexican Years, 1943–1985* (University of New Mexico Press, 1991), ed. Patricia Draher, p. 38.
2 Silvia Cherem, 'Eternally Married to the Wind: Interview with Leonora Carrington', in *Leonora Carrington: What She Might Be* (Dallas Museum of Art, 2008), p. 40.
3 Inés Amor, in *Leonora Carrington: Magical Tales* (Instituto Nacional de Bellas Artes, 2018), p. 134.
4 *Ibid*. p. 134.
5 Cherem, 'Eternally Married to the Wind', p. 40.
6 One such conversation is part of the Tate film *Leonora Carrington: Britain's Lost Surrealist* (2015).
7 Hayden Herrera, *Frida: A Biography of Frida Kahlo* (Harper Perennial, 2002), p. 255.
8 *Ibid*. p. 254.
9 *Ibid*. p. 256.
10 Quoted in Janet A. Kaplan, *Remedios Varo: Unexpected Journeys* (Abbeville Press, 2000), p. 133.
11 Gabriel Weisz Carrington, conversation with the author, March 2022.
12 Letter from Leonora Carrington to Pierre Matisse dated 23 March [1946], Matisse Collection, Morgan Library, New York.
13 De Angelis, 'Interview', p. 40.
14 Edward James on Leonora Carrington, 1975, reproduced in *Leonora Carrington: Paintings, Drawings and Sculptures 1940–1990* (Serpentine Gallery, 1991), p. 41. James was well known as a patron and friend to numerous surrealists.
15 Letter from Leonora Carrington to Edward James, 1 August [1946], Edward James Foundation archive, Sussex.
16 Letter from Leonora Carrington to Edward James, 11 November [n.d.], Edward James Foundation archive, Sussex.

17 Letter from Leonora Carrington to 'Miss Vivano' (who probably worked for Pierre Matisse), 12 April [n.d.], Pierre Matisse collection, Morgan Library.
18 *Ibid*.
19 *Ibid*.
20 Letter from Leonora Carrington to Edward James, 6 August [1947], Edward James Foundation archive, Sussex.
21 *Ibid*.
22 *Ibid*.
23 Norah Horna, 'Testimonio' in *Leonora Carrington: Magical Tales* (Instituto Nacional de Bellas Artes, 2018), p. 406.
24 *Ibid*. p. 408.
25 Edward James, draft 'Introduction' to the exhibition catalogue for Leonora Carrington's exhibition at the Pierre Matisse Gallery, New York, 1948, Edward James Foundation archive, Sussex.
26 Pedro Friedeberg, 'Testimonio', in *Leonora Carrington: Magical Tales* (Instituto Nacional de Bellas Artes, 2018), p. 418.
27 *Ibid*. p. 418.

Chapter 10

1 From the short film *Gloria's Call*, dir. Cheri Gaulke (2019).
2 *Leonora Carrington: What She Might Be* (Dallas Museum of Art, 2008), p. 86.
3 Whitney Chadwick, 'Leonora Carrington: Evolution of a Feminist Consciousness', *Woman's Art Journal* 7, no. 1 (Spring/Summer 1986).
4 Salomon Grimberg in *Leonora Carrington: What She Might Be*, p. 86.
5 Joanne Pottlitzer, 'An "Ordinary" Exorcist', in *Leonora Carrington: Magical Tales* (Instituto Nacional de Bellas Artes, 2018), p. 347.
6 *Ibid*. p. 347.
7 Leonora Carrington, *Down Below* in *In the House of Fear: Notes from Down Below* (Virago, 1989), p. 175.
8 Pottlitzer, 'An "Ordinary" Exorcist', p. 363.
9 *Ibid*. p. 365.
10 Grimberg in *Leonora Carrington: What She Might Be*, p. 90.
11 '1000 novels everyone must read: the definitive list', *Guardian*, 23 January, 2009.
12 Gloria Feman Orenstein, 'Art History and the Case for the Women of Surrealism', *Journal of General Education* 27, no. 1 (Spring 1975), p. 31.

13 Whitney Chadwick, *Women Artists and the Surrealist Movement* (Thames & Hudson, 1985).

14 Gina Litherland, conversation with the author, 2018; from postscript to Joanna Moorhead, *The Surreal Life of Leonora Carrington* (Virago, 2019), p. 287.

15 Peter Conrad, 'Leonora, the Last of the Surrealists', *Observer Magazine*, 8 December, 1991.

16 Penelope Rosemont, conversation with the author, 2018.

17 Penelope Rosemont, 'A Revolution in the Way We Think and Feel: Conversations with Leonora Carrington', in Ron Sakolsky (ed.), *Surrealist Subversions* (Autonomedia, 2002), pp. 184–90.

Chapter 11

1 Penelope Rosemont, conversation with the author, 2018; from postscript to Joanna Moorhead, *The Surreal Life of Leonora Carrington* (Virago, 2019), p. 290.

2 Alan Glass, 'Testimonio', in *Leonora Carrington: Magical Tales* (Instituto Nacional de Bellas Artes, 2018), p. 421.

3 Paul De Angelis, 'Interview with Leonora Carrington', in *Leonora Carrington: The Mexican Years, 1943–1985* (University of New Mexico Press, 1991), ed. Patricia Draher, p. 42.

4 Eva Marcovich, 'Testimonio', in *Leonora Carrington: Magical Tales*, p. 435.

5 Leonora Carrington, *The Hearing Trumpet* (Penguin, 2005), p. 1.

6 Elena Poniatowska, 'Testimonio', in *Leonora Carrington: Magical Tales*, p. 455.

7 *Ibid*. p. 455.

8 De Angelis, 'Interview', p. 34.

9 *Leonora Carrington: What She Might Be* (Dallas Museum of Art, 2008), p. 43.

Further Reading

Aberth, Susan L., *Leonora Carrington: Surrealism, Alchemy and Art*, Farnham: Lund Humphries, 2004

Aberth, Susan L. and Tere Arcq, *The Tarot of Leonora Carrington*, Somerset: Fulgar Press, 2020

Allmer, Patricia, ed., *Angels of Anarchy: Women Artists and Surrealism*, exhib. cat. Manchester: Manchester City Art Gallery and Prestel, 2009

Carrington, Gabriel Weisz, *The Invisible Painting: My Memoir of Leonora Carrington*, Manchester: Manchester University Press, 2021

Leonora Carrington, exhib. cat. Dublin: Irish Museum of Modern Art, 2013

Leonora Carrington, exhib. cat. Copenhagen: Arken and Fundación Mapfre, Madrid, 2022

Leonora Carrington: Magical Tales, exhib. cat. Mexico City: Museo del Palacio de Bellas Artes/Museo de Arte Moderno, 2018

Leonora Carrington: The Story of the Last Egg, exhib. cat. San Francisco: Gallery Wendi Norris, 2019

Leonora Carrington: The Talismanic Lens, exhib. cat. San Francisco: Frey Norris Gallery, 2007

Leonora Carrington: What She Might Be, exhib. cat. Dallas: Dallas Museum of Art, 2008

Carrington, Leonora, *Down Below*, New York: The New York Review of Books, 2017

Carrington, Leonora, *The Hearing Trumpet*, Harmondsworth: Penguin Classics, 2005

Carrington, Leonora, *The House of Fear: Notes from Down Below*, London: Virago, 1989

Carrington, Leonora, *The Milk of Dreams*, New York: The New York Review of Books, 2013

Carrington, Leonora, *The Seventh Horse and Other Stories*, London: Virago, 1989

Carrington, Leonora, introduction by Kathryn Davis, *The Complete Stories of Leonora Carrington*, St Louis, MO: Dorothy Project, 2017

Chadwick, Whitney, *The Militant Muse*, London and New York: Thames & Hudson, 2017

Chadwick, Whitney, *Women Artists and the Surrealist Movement*, London and New York: Thames & Hudson, 1985

Draher, Patricia, ed., *Leonora Carrington: The Mexican Years 1943–1985*, exhib. cat. San Francisco: The Mexican Museum/University of New Mexico Press, 1991

Ernst, Jimmy, *Notes from a Not-So-Still Life*, New York: St Martin's Press, 1984

Fort, Ilene Susan and Tere Arcq, eds, *In Wonderland: The Surrealist Adventures of Women Artists in Mexico and the United States*, exhib. cat. Los Angeles: Los Angeles County Museum of Art and DelMonico Books, 2012

Guggenheim, Peggy, *Out of This Century: Confessions of an Art Addict*, London: Andre Deutsch, 2005

Kaplan, Janet A., *Remedios Varo: Unexpected Journeys*, New York: Abbeville Press, 2000

Penrose, Antony, *The Surrealists in Cornwall*, exhib. cat. Falmouth: Falmouth Art Gallery, 2004

Remarque, Erich Maria, *The Night in Lisbon: A Novel*, London: Random House, 2014

Schlieker, Andrea, ed., *Leonora Carrington: Paintings, Drawings and Sculptures 1940–1990*, exhib. cat. London: Serpentine Gallery, 1991

Sullivan, Rosemary, *Villa Bel-Air: World War II, Escape, and a House in Marseille*, New York: Harper Collins, 2007

Surreal Friends: Leonora Carrington, Remedios Varo and Kati Horna, exhib. cat. Farnham: Lund Humphries/Pallant House Gallery, 2010

Weber, Ronald, *The Lisbon Route: Entry and Escape in Nazi Europe*, Chicago: Ivan R Dee, 2011

Acknowledgments

Much of this book has been researched 'on the road'. I have spent the last couple of years revisiting the places and spaces in the life of Leonora Carrington, in the hope of piecing together the story of how they influenced her art. I am indebted to the many people in the locations Leonora once inhabited, who have been so generous, welcoming and sharing their knowledge with me.

I began where Leonora's life began, and indeed where my own life began: in Lancashire, where her father, and later my father who was his nephew, were mill owners. Crookhey Hall, Leonora's first childhood home, is now a school. The head Samantha Lea showed me around and explained how the layout has stayed the same and how it has changed, since Leonora's day. At the schools Leonora attended I was given a great deal of assistance by, at St Mary's Ascot, the alumnae director Cathy Leneghan, and at New Hall (School), Stella Beer, as well as the principal Katherine Jeffrey and her PA Beatrice Stoddard.

I spent a week at Hazelwood Hall, Leonora's home when she was a teenager, with my husband Gary Smith, who gamely agreed to a holiday there in the interests of my research. In London, where Leonora was an art student after her disastrous season as a debutante, I was very grateful for the help of Sophie Clarke, collections and house officer for the National Trust at 2 Willow Road, Hampstead, one-time home of Ernő Goldfinger, and also Steve Reynolds at Highpoint, where Leonora met Max Ernst for the first time in 1937, at the Goldfingers' flat.

Tony Penrose, son of Lee Miller and Roland Penrose, has been as kind as ever in helping me with the story of the time Leonora spent with his parents in Cornwall and later in France. In Saint-Martin-d'Ardèche, I am indebted to Albert Neyron, who generously allowed me to properly investigate the house in the South of France where Leonora and Max had their idyllic summer. I would also like to thank Henry Eliot and Andrea Rangecroft for their companionship on that leg of the research, as we were also making a podcast for Henry's series *On The Road With Penguin Classics*.

In Lisbon, I am so grateful to historian Inês Fialho Brandão, who spent time with me both in central Lisbon and in Cascais, where she filled me in on vital information about Leonora's life, including helping to find the house where Leonora lived with her partner Renato Leduc (sharp-eyed readers who have also read my Virago book on Leonora might have noticed that I now realize the house she inhabited in Lisbon was in a different place from where I first understood it was). Also in Lisbon, Edward Godfrey and Mark Crathorne of the British Historical Society of Portugal were kind and welcoming. In Santander, the support of Soledad San Luis was invaluable, as was the time we spent with Marisa Samaniego, who knew Dr Luis Morales from the sanatorium where Leonora was held.

In Mexico City, where the house in which Leonora lived for more than sixty years has now become a museum and a centre for research into her life, I received the warmest of welcomes from Alejandra Osorio Olave, its then director. Also in Mexico, Catherine Petitgas was a wonderful supporter of this work; and indeed, without the assistance of both Alejandra and Catherine, this book would not have been written. Thank you also to Leonora's sons, for their friendship, their kindness and their support – Gabriel and his wife Paty, and Pablo and his wife Wendy.

From New York, Leonora's great friend Gloria Orenstein is my guide from afar, always cheering me on and reminding me so much of Leonora's spirit. Susan Aberth, too, has been a huge moral support, for which I send many thanks. Also in the US, thank you as ever to the uber-knowledgeable Salomon Grimberg.

The enthusiasm, kindness and experience of the team at Thames & Hudson have been invaluable, and in particular I would like to thank Julie Bosser, Peter Burgess, Mohara Gill, Nikos Kotsopoulos, Camilla Rockwood and Roger Thorp.

My family, as ever, have been supportive of what they regard as my slightly mad obsession with my cousin's life. But, I believe they are as proud as I am of Leonora, and of what her art represents. Gary, our daughters Rosie, Elinor, Miranda and Catriona, and my mother Doris – thank you for reading my work, for asking questions, and for caring about what I am passionate about.

And finally, wherever she now is, thank you to Leonora. Our friendship changed my life, and I hope you would be happy with the work I continue to do, with the aim of sharing your art more widely, and helping to make it better known.

Credits

All artworks are by Leonora Carrington unless otherwise stated. All artworks by Leonora Carrington © Estate of Leonora Carrington/ARS, NY and DACS, London 2023.

Dimensions of works are given in centimetres and inches, height before width.

2, 6 Hermann Landshoff, Leonora Carrington, 1942. Münchner Stadtmuseum. Sammlung Fotografie/Archiv Landshoff. Photo Scala, Florence/bpk, Bildagentur für Kunst, Kultur und Geschichte, Berlin. Photo © 2022 Münchner Stadtmuseum **12** Photograph of Leonora as a child. Consejo Leonora Carrington AC, Mexico **14** View of Clayton-le-Woods village, 1900s. Photo Chronicle/Alamy Stock Photo **15** Crookhey Hall, exterior. Crookhey Hall School, Lancaster **16** *Bird Bath II*, 1978. Acrylic on canvas board, 71 × 56 (28 × 22). Private collection. Courtesy Gallery Wendi Norris, San Francisco **18–19** *The Inventory*, 1956. Oil on canvas, 29 × 39.5 (11½ × 15⅝). Private collection. Photo Christie's Images Limited **20, 21** Crookhey Hall, interior. Crookhey Hall School, Lancaster **22–23** *Night Nursery Everything*, 1947. Oil on masonite, 58 × 80 (22⅞ × 31½). Private collection **25** *Neighbourly Advice*, 1947. Tempera on masonite, 25.4 × 38.1 (10 × 15). Private collection. Photo Christie's Images/Bridgeman Images **26–27** *Crookhey Hall* (1947), 1987. Lithograph, 61 × 91.4 (24⅛ × 36). Edition of 50. Courtesy RoGallery, Long Island City **28** Photograph of Leonora and children. Consejo Leonora Carrington AC, Mexico **29** Leonora as a child with her brother Gerard and dog, 1926. Collection of Joe Carrington. **30–31** *The Bird Men of Burnley*, 1970. Oil on canvas, 44.5 × 66 (17½ × 26). Private collection. Courtesy Gallery Wendi Norris, San Francisco **32** St Patrick's Church, Moate. National Library of Ireland, Dublin. The Lawrence Photograph Collection. Photo Robert French **34–35** *Grandmother Moorhead's Aromatic Kitchen*, 1975. Oil on canvas, 79 × 124.5 (31⅛ × 49⅛). The Charles B. Goddard Center for Visual and Performing Arts, Ardmore. Photo The Charles B. Goddard Center for Visual and Performing Arts **38, 48** *Nunscape in Manzanillo*, 1956. Tempera on masonite, 100 × 150 (39⅜ × 59⅛). Private collection **41** Morecambe Bay. Photo Nicky Beeson/Alamy Stock Photo **42** Leonora Carrington with her brothers Gerard and Arthur, her uncle George Moorhead and her nanny Mary Kavanaugh at Hazelwood Hall. Collection of the author **44** *The Hour of the Angelus*, 1949. Tempera on panel, 61 × 92 (24⅛ × 36¼). Private

Collection. Photo Christie's Images, London/Scala, Florence **46** Students at the New Hall School, Chelmsford. Courtesy New Hall School, Chelmsford **50–51** *Green Tea*, 1942. Oil on canvas, 61 × 76.2 (24 × 30). The Museum of Modern Art, New York. Gift of the Drue Heinz Trust (by exchange). Courtesy Gallery Wendi Norris, San Francisco **52** Attributed to Edizione Brogi, The Uffizi and Palazzo Vecchio, Florence, late 19th century. Rijksmuseum, Amsterdam **56** Leonora as a debutante and her mother Maurie, *c.* 1935. Private collection **60** Exhibition announcement, International Surrealist Exhibition, New Burlington Galleries, London, 1936. The Metropolitan Museum of Art, New York. Gift of Friends of the Thomas J. Watson Library **61** Interior view of the International Surrealist Exhibition, New Burlington Galleries, London, 1936. National Galleries of Scotland **64 (left)** Highpoint One. Photo akg-images/A.F. Kersting **64 (right)** Amédée Ozenfant with Ursula Goldfinger outside the Ozenfant Academy of Fine Arts, London. National Trust. Photo National Trust (Sophie Clarke) **65** Poster advertising the Max Ernst exhibition at The Mayor Gallery, with Max Ernst's work *The Chinese Nightingale* (1920), 1937. Courtesy The Mayor Gallery, London. Ernst © ADAGP, Paris and DACS, London 2023 **66** Max Ernst, *Two Children Are Threatened by a Nightingale*, 1924. Oil with painted wood elements and cut-and-pasted printed paper on wood with wood frame, 69.8 × 57.1 (27½ × 22½). The Museum of Modern Art, New York. Ernst © ADAGP, Paris and DACS, London 2023 **67** Anna Riwkin, Max Ernst, 1933. Moderna Museet, Stockholm. Photo Anna Riwkin/Moderna Museet **68** Roland Penrose, Four women asleep (Lee Miller, Ady Fidelin, Nusch Éluard and Leonora Carrington), Lambe Creek, Cornwall, 1937. Roland Penrose © Lee Miller Archives, England 2023. All rights reserved. www.leemiller.co.uk **70** Lee Miller, Lambe Creek, Cornwall, 1937. © Lee Miller Archives, England 2023. All rights reserved. www.leemiller.co.uk **71** Roland Penrose, Lambe Creek Cottage, Lambe Creek, Cornwall, 1937. Roland Penrose © Lee Miller Archives, England 2023. All rights reserved. www.leemiller.co.uk **73** Lee Miller, E. L. T. Mesens, Max Ernst, Leonora Carrington and Paul Éluard, Lambe Creek, Cornwall, 1937. © Lee Miller Archives, England 2023. All rights reserved. www.leemiller.co.uk **75** Lee Miller, Nusch Éluard, E. L. T. Mesens, Leonora Carrington and Max Ernst, Lambe Creek, Cornwall, 1937. © Lee Miller Archives, England 2023. All rights reserved. www.leemiller.co.uk **78, 87** *Self-Portrait/Inn of the Dawn Horse*, *c.* 1937–38. Oil on canvas, 65 × 81.3 (25⅝ × 32⅛). The Museum of Modern Art, New York. The Pierre and Maria-Gaetana Matisse Collection, 2002 **81** Eugène

Atget, Rue Jacob 12, Paris, *c*. 1910. Musée Carnavalet, Histoire de Paris **84–85** *The Horses of Lord Candlestick*, 1938. Oil on canvas, 61 × 93.3 (24⅛ × 36¾). Private collection, US. Photo courtesy of Mary-Anne Martin Fine Art, New York **86** Max Ernst on a rocking horse, Paris, 1938. Max Ernst Museum Brühl des LVR **89** Invitation card, International Exhibition of Surrealism, Paris, 1938. Private collection **90** Raoul Ubac, photograph of Max Ernst and Joan Miró mannequins at the International Exhibition of Surrealism, Paris, 1938. Musée d'Art Moderne, Paris. Photo Paris Musées, musée d'Art moderne, Dist. RMN-Grand Palais/image ville de Paris. Ubac © ADAGP, Paris and DACS, London 2023. Ernst © ADAGP, Paris and DACS, London 2023. Miró © Successió Miró/ADAGP, Paris and DACS London 2023 **91, 92** Inside pages from Leonora Carrington's *La maison de la peur*, with Max Ernst illustrations, 1938. Published by H. Parisot, Paris. Beinecke Rare Book and Manuscript Library, Yale University Library, New Haven. Ernst © ADAGP, Paris and DACS, London 2023 **94, 107** Max Ernst, *Leonora in the Morning Light*, 1940. Oil on canvas, 66 × 82.3 (26 × 32½). Private collection. Ernst © ADAGP, Paris and DACS, London 2023 **98** Leonora Carrington's home at Saint-Martin-d'Ardèche, exterior. *World of Interiors*, February 2018 issue. Photo Tim Beddow, *World of Interiors* © Condé Nast. Ernst © ADAGP, Paris and DACS, London 2023 **99** Leonora Carrington's home at Saint-Martin-d'Ardèche, exterior. Photo the author. Ernst © ADAGP, Paris and DACS, London 2023 **100–1** Saint-Martin-d'Ardèche interior, with Max Ernst work on the wall. *World of Interiors*, February 2018 issue. Photo Tim Beddow, *World of Interiors* © Condé Nast. Ernst © ADAGP, Paris and DACS, London 2023 **102** Photographer unknown, Leonora Carrington and Leonor Fini with friends at Saint-Martin-d'Ardèche, 1939. Private collection **103** Lee Miller, Leonora Carrington at Saint-Martin-d'Ardèche, 1939. © Lee Miller Archives, England 2023. All rights reserved. www.leemiller.co.uk **104** Saint-Martin-d'Ardèche interior with work by Leonora Carrington. *World of Interiors*, February 2018 issue. Photo Tim Beddow, *World of Interiors* © Condé Nast **105** Saint-Martin-d'Ardèche interior with work by Leonora Carrington. *World of Interiors*, February 2018 issue. Photo Tim Beddow, *World of Interiors* © Condé Nast **108** *Portrait of Max Ernst*, 1939. Oil on canvas, 50.3 × 26.8 (19⅞ × 10⅝). Scottish National Gallery of Modern Art, Edinburgh. National Galleries of Scotland. Purchased with assistance from the Henry and Sula Walton Fund and the Art Fund, 2018 **114, 124–25** *Down Below*, 1940. Oil on canvas, 40 × 59.7 (15¾ × 23⅝). Private collection. Courtesy Gallery

Wendi Norris, San Francisco **116** Archive photograph of Santander city, 1947. Fondo Joaquín Araúna Agenjo. Photo © City of Santander. Documentation Center of the Image of Santander/Joaquín Araúna Agenjo. With the assistance of the City of Santander **117** Archive photograph of Sanatorio Morales Santander, 1963. Fondo Pablo Hojas Llama. Photo © City of Santander. Documentation Center of the Image of Santander/Pablo Hojas Llama. With the assistance of the City of Santander **119** *Map of Down Below*, *c*. 1941. Ink on paper, 32.4 × 25.1 (12¾ × 9⅞). Harvard Art Museums/Fogg Museum. Margaret Fisher 1986 Fund. Photo President and Fellows of Harvard College **120–21** *Fear*, 1937–41. Oil on canvas, 33.3 × 46 (13⅛ × 18⅛). Private collection. Courtesy Di Donna Galleries, New York **126** Photograph of Leonora Carrington with her nanny Mary Kavanaugh and Dr Morales at the sanatorium, Santander, 1941. Archivo Patricia Leduc Romero **131** Leonora Carrington's passport, 9 June 1941. Archivo Patricia Leduc Romero **134** Hermann Landshoff, Leonora Carrington in her Greenwich Village apartment, 1942. Münchner Stadtmuseum. Sammlung Fotografie/Archiv Landshoff. Photo Scala, Florence/bpk, Bildagentur für Kunst, Kultur und Geschichte, Berlin. Photo © 2022 Münchner Stadtmuseum **137** Hermann Landshoff, The Surrealists in Peggy Guggenheim's apartment, 1942 Münchner Stadtmuseum. Sammlung Fotografie/Archiv Landshoff. Photo Scala, Florence/bpk, Bildagentur für Kunst, Kultur und Geschichte, Berlin. Photo © 2022 Münchner Stadtmuseum **138** Hermann Landshoff, Max Ernst, Leonora Carrington, Marcel Duchamp and André Breton, posing in front of Ernst's painting *Le surréalisme et la peinture* (1942), 1942. Münchner Stadtmuseum. Sammlung Fotografie/Archiv Landshoff. Photo Scala, Florence/bpk, Bildagentur für Kunst, Kultur und Geschichte, Berlin. Ernst © ADAGP, Paris and DACS, London 2023 **140–41** Leonora Carrington, in collaboration with Max Ernst, Marcel Duchamp and Matta, *Summer*, 1941. Oil on cotton bedsheet, 2.3 × 3.6 m (7 × 12 ft). Tel Aviv Museum of Art. Ernst © ADAGP, Paris and DACS, London 2023. Duchamp © Association Marcel Duchamp/ADAGP, Paris and DACS, London 2023. Matta © ADAGP, Paris and DACS, London 2023 **142** Hermann Landshoff, The Surrealists in Peggy Guggenheim's apartment, 1942. Münchner Stadtmuseum. Sammlung Fotografie/Archiv Landshoff. Photo Scala, Florence/bpk, Bildagentur für Kunst, Kultur und Geschichte, Berlin. Photo © 2022 Münchner Stadtmuseum **145** John D. Schiff, Installation view of First Papers of Surrealism exhibition, showing Marcel Duchamp's *His Twine*,

1942. Philadelphia Museum of Art. Gift of Jacqueline, Paul and Peter Matisse in memory of their mother Alexina Duchamp. Courtesy of the Philadelphia Museum of Art Archives. © Association Marcel Duchamp/ADAGP, Paris and DACS, London 2023 **146–47** Spread from First Papers of Surrealism exhibition catalogue with Leonora Carrington's work *Brothers and Sisters Have I None*, 1942. Published by Coordinating Council of French Relief Societies, Inc., New York. Private collection **148** Berenice Abbot, Peggy Guggenheim in her gallery Art of This Century, 1942. Exhibition design by Frederick Kiesler. Photo AP/Shutterstock. Fini © ADAGP, Paris and DACS, London 2023. Kiesler © Austrian Frederick and Lillian Kiesler Private Foundation. Magritte © ADAGP, Paris and DACS, London 2023. Miró © Successió Miró/ADAGP, Paris and DACS London 2023. **150** Leonora Carrington in Mexico. West Dean College of Arts and Conservation **153** Zócalo, Mexico City, *c.* 1941–43. Private collection **154** *Cat Woman (La Grande Dame)*, 1951. Carved and polychrome wood, height *c.* 202 (79⅝). Private collection **156** Gunther Gerzso, *Los días de la calle Gabino Barreda (The Days of Gabino Barreda Street)*, 1944. Oil on canvas, 46.6 × 61 (18⅜ × 24⅛). Private collection. Gerzso © DACS 2023 **158–59** *El mundo mágico de los mayas (The Magical World of the Maya)*, 1963–64. Casein on wood, 213 × 457 (83⅞ × 180). Museo Nacional de Antropología, Mexico. Photo Schalkwijk, Dist. RMN-Grand Palais/image Schalkwijk Archive **161** Installation view of the Exposición Internacional del Surrealismo, Galería de Arte Mexicano, Mexico City, 1940. Courtesy Galería de Arte Mexicano, Mexico City. Work by Kahlo and work by Rivera © 2023 Banco de México Diego Rivera Frida Kahlo Museums Trust, Mexico, D.F./Artists Rights Society (ARS), New York **162** Manuel Álvarez Bravo, cover of Exposición Internacional del Surrealismo exhibition catalogue, Galería de Arte Mexicano, Mexico City. Courtesy Archivo Manuel Álvarez Bravo, SC, Mexico **165** *Chiki, ton pays*, 1944. Oil, tempera and ink on canvas, 89.5 × 90.2 (35¼ × 35⅝). Private collection **166–67** *The House Opposite*, 1945. Tempera on board, 33 × 82 (13 × 32⅜).West Dean College of Arts and Conservation **169** *The Star*, *c.* 1955. Oil and gold leaf on board, 16 × 14 (6⅜ × 5⅝). Private collection **170** *And Then We Saw the Daughter of the Minotaur!*, 1953. Oil on canvas, 60 × 70 (23⅝ × 27⅝). The Museum of Modern Art, New York. Gift of Joan H. Tisch (by exchange). Courtesy Gallery Wendi Norris, San Francisco **171** Nacho López, Leonora Carrington in her home in Mexico, *c.* 1960. Instituto Nacional de Antropología e Historia, Mexico. Secretaría de Cultura – INAH – Mexico. Reproducción Autorizada por el Instituto

Nacional de Antropología e Historia **174** La Cinematografía under construction at Las Pozas, Xilitla, *c.* 1960. West Dean College of Arts and Conservation **176** *Mujeres Conciencia*, 1972. Gouache on cardboard, 75 × 49 (29⅝ × 19⅜). Private collection. Courtesy Gallery Wendi Norris, San Francisco **179** *Burial of the Patriarchs*, *c.* 1963. Watercolour, gouache and pen and ink on paper, 25.4 × 35.6 (10 × 14⅛). Private collection **180** Leonora Carrington during an interview with Joanne Pottlitzer, New York, 1976. Photo Joanne Pottlitzer **181** Designed by Leonora Carrington, crafted by Jane Stein and Vita Giorgi, Mask for the play *Opus Siniestrus*, 1976. Mesh, acrylic, felt, cane, stamen, wood, and thread. 78.7 × 58.4 × 10.2 (31 × 23 × 4). Courtesy Gallery Wendi Norris, San Francisco **183** *Untitled* (Apartment where Leonora lived in New York City in the 1970s and 1980s), *c.* 1980. Oil on canvas, 62 × 79 (24½ × 31⅛). Private collection **184–85** *Kron Flower*, 1987. Tempera on panel, 61 × 101 (24⅛ × 39⅞). Private collection **186** Cover of Leonora Carrington's *The Hearing Trumpet*, 1976. Artwork by Pablo Weisz-Carrington. Private collection **190** Chiki Weisz and Leonora Carrington in their home in Mexico, 1998. Photo Marion Kalter/akg-images **194, 196, 198** Casa Estudio Leonora Carrington, Universidad Autónoma Metropolitana, Mexico **195** Casa Estudio Leonora Carrington, Universidad Autónoma Metropolitana, Mexico. Photo Tania Victoria/ Secretaría de Cultura de la Ciudad de México **199** *Bird with Fish*, 1979. Wool tapestry, 188 × 129.5 (74 × 51). Private collection **200** Leonora Carrington with her sculpture *La Virgen de la Cueva*, 2000. Photo Daniel Aguilar/Reuters/Alamy Stock Photo **202–3** *The Magdalens*, 1986. Tempera on wood panel, 61 × 76.2 (24⅛ × 30). Private collection. Courtesy Gallery Wendi Norris, San Francisco **204** *Q Symphony*, 2002. Acrylic on cardboard, 92 × 76 (36¼ × 30). Private collection **207** Leonora Carrington in her home, 2000. Photo Daniel Aguilar/Reuters/Alamy Stock Photo

Extracts from Leonora Carrington's *Down Below* and *Little Francis* reproduced by kind permission of *The New York Review of Books*.

Extracts from Leonora Carrington's letter to Pierre Matisse reproduced by kind permission of The Morgan Library & Museum, MA 5020, United States.

Extracts from Edward James's letters reproduced by kind permission of West Dean College, part of the Edward James Foundation

Index

Page references in *italics* indicate illustrations;
   LC = Leonora Carrington.

'31 Women' exhibition (1943), 149

Abbott, Berenice, *142*, 143; photograph of
   Peggy Guggenheim, *148*
Aberth, Susan, 122, 123
Agar, Eileen, 72, 76
Agenjo, Joaquín Araúna, photograph by,
   116
Alberto (doctor), 115, 116
Les Alliberts *see* Saint-Martin-d'Ardèche
Álvarez Bravo, Manuel, cover of Surrealism
   catalogue, *162*
Amor, Inés, 157, 160, 161
Angelico, Fra, 57
Aragon, Louis, 72
Arcq, Tere, 206
Argomedo, Paty (LC's daughter-in-law),
   201
Arnside, 39–40
The Art of this Century, New York, *148*, 149
Asegurado, Frau (nurse), 123, 126, 127
Askew, Kirk, 53
Atget, Eugéne, photograph of Rue Jacob, *81*

Bamford family, 126
Bard, Joseph, 72, 76
Bassi, Sofía, 173
BBC, *Omnibus: Leonora and the House of Fear*
   (documentary), 178
Beddow, Tim, photographs of Saint-Martin-
   d'Ardèche, *98*, *100–101*, *104*, *105*
Bellmer, Hans, 107
Black Bess (pony), 49
Blackwell, Ursula *see* Goldfinger, Ursula
Blom, Gertrude, 197
Blunt, Anthony, 70
Breton, André, 72, 80, 81, 82, 88, 93, 135, 136, 138,
   138, 139, 160–61, 162
Breton, Aube, 135, 160
Buddhism, 110, 193
Buñuel, Luis, 136

Café de Flore, Paris, 81, 82
Capa, Robert (Endre Ernő Friedmann), 155
Carrington, Arthur (LC's brother), 25, 36, *42*
Carrington, Arthur (LC's grandfather), 13
Carrington, Gerard (LC's brother), 25, 29, 32, 36, *42*
Carrington, Harold (LC's father): arrest warrant
   for Ernst, 69–70; background, 13, 58–59;
   business acquaintances, 43, 62, 116, 127, 128;
   career, 13, 33, 39, 59; character, 86; daughter's
   escape to Spain, 113; daughter's relationship with
   Ernst, 67, 69–70; daughter's schooling, 43, 47,
   54; daughter's stay in sanatorium, 116, 122, 123;
   family holidays, 53; homes, 21, 37, 39; marriage, 14,
   32; plan for daughter's journey to South Africa,
   127–28; plans for daughter's future, 57–59;
   relationship with daughter, 59, 79–80, 86–87,
   168; religion, 32
Carrington, Leonora: adolescence, 38–55, *42*,
   46; apartment in Chicago, 10, 187–89, 193;
   apartment in Greenwich Village, *134*, 135–36, *183*;
   apartment in Paris (Rue Jacob 12), 80, *81*, 87, 127;
   apartment with Chiki in Mexico City (Avenida
   Álvaro Obregón, Roma), 164–68; apartment
   with Leduc in Mexico City (Mixcoac), 152;
   appearance (*see also* photographs of), 42–43,
   132–33, 139, 157, 195; arrival in Mexico City, *150*,
   151–52; art training, 47, 48, 62–64; artistic
   legacy, 205–7; artistic talent, 36; awarded OBE,
   206; belief systems, 110, 152, 193, 198; and bells,
   43–46, 95–96; bird imagery, 15–17, 33, 40; birth,
   13, 14; book collection, 109–10, 186, 193, 194;
   breakdown in Spain, 112, 115, 116; 'Candlestick'
   pseudonym, 21, 83; cats, 156, 173; childhood, *12*,
   13–37, *28*, *29*; cooking (*see also* kitchens), 59, 83,
   109, 197, 201; correspondence, 106, 107, 122,
   144, 168–70, 178; cut flowers, 173–74; death
   and burial, 191–92; death as theme, 191, 198,
   205, 207; as debutante, *56*, 57–60, 62; departure
   for Paris, 79–80; destroyed portrait, 106; dogs,
   29, 59, 194; domestic imagery (*see also* kitchens),
   24, 33, 172; drug treatment (Cardiazol), 117,
   118–22, 126; ecology, 188, 193, 207; embroidery,
   199; exhibitions, 145, 149, 168, 188, 206;
   fantastical imagery, 33, 36, 41, 153, 162–64;

feminism, 29–32, 93, 178–82, 193, 207; finances, 97, 112, 149, 164–69, 186; finishing schools, 49–54; flight from Europe to America, 127–29, 133; flight from France to Spain, 110, 111–13, 115, 135; flight from Mexico to New Orleans, 175; in Florence, 49–53; French language, 95, 138; friendships, 53, 72, 77, 102, 106, 155–57, 171–75, 177, 194; frottage, 65; grandchildren, 8, 188; home in Mexico City (194 Calle Chihuahua, Colonia Roma) (*see also* Casa Estudio Leonora Carrington museum), 7–9, 11, 24, 169–74, *171*, *190*, 192, 201, *207*; homesickness for England, 168–69; horse motif (*see also* rocking horses), 21, 49, 83, 89–93, 99, 109, 172, 179; humour, 49, 81; hunting imagery, 21; imagination, 13, 21, 41, 62, 83; interest in alchemy, 193; interviews with, 7, 9–10, 52–54, 59, 62, 83, 160, *180*, 188, 205; journey from Santander to Madrid, 126–27; journey to Mexico, 139, 148–49; kitchens (*see also* cooking), 33, 172, 192, 197; later apartments in New York, 182–83; love of markets, 55, 152–53; masks, *181*, 182, 206; meetings with Kahlo, 160; as model for Horna's *Ode to Necrophilia*, 175; mythology, 28–29, 162–63; nickname (Prim), 8, 14; notebooks, 49, 54, 89; and nuns, 37, 43, 46–48, 116; nursery, 20, 24–29, 36; old age, 17, 157, 183–86, 191, 195–96, 198–201; operation in Lisbon, 132–33; passport, 129, *131*; and patriarchy, 80, 91, 179, 180, 182; photographs of, *2*, *6*, *12*, *28*, *29*, *42*, *46*, *56*, *68*, *73*, *75*, *102*, *103*, *126*, *134*, *137*, *138*, *142*, *143*, *150*, *171*, *180*, *190*, *200*, *207*; pony, 21, 49; portraiture, 53; predellas, 53, 164; pregnancies, 156, 163–68; privilege, 57, 79, 129, 172; psychological imagery, 24; recognition in later life, 186–87, 206; recognition in Mexico, 163, 205; recognition in New York, 136–39, 145; relationship with Chiki (Emerico) Weisz, 155, 163, 164–68, 169, 173, 177–78, *190*; relationship with father, 59, 79–80, 86–87, 168; relationship with Max Ernst, 69–77, 79, 80, 81, 83–86, 88, 93, 105, 106, 132, 133, 135, 143, 148, 149, 172; relationship with Renato Leduc, 128–29, 132, 133, 135–36, 143–45, 148–49, 152, 154; relationship with Surrealism, 25, 33–36, 69, 76, 82; religion (*see also* belief systems), 13, 14, 15, 43, 48, 193; rocking horses, 24, *86*, 87–88, 139, 164; sales of paintings, 21, 83, 109, 139, 164, 168, 186; schooling (*see also* art training; finishing schools), 37, 43–49, *46*; screen paintings, 206; sculpture, 155, 172, 198–99, 206; self-imagery, 15, 104; shared house in Mexico City (Gabino Barreda, San Rafael), 155–56; sign of the horns, 178;

smoking, 173, 175, 192; spirituality (*see also* belief systems), 24, 152, 207; storytelling, 28–33, 53; studios, 168, 170, 172–73, 195, 196–97, *198*, *207*; swearing, 54; tapestries, 199, 206; tarot card paintings, *169*, 206; tempera, 53, 197; tequila, 8, 153, 192; treatment in Santander psychiatric clinic, 11, 116–26, *117*, *126*, 129, 136; voice, 7, 129, 178; women's liberation movement, *176*, 179–80; writing, 10, 24, 93, 136; zoo visits, 59–60
WORKS: *Again the Gemini are in the Orchard*, 206; *Amor che move il sole et l'altre stelle (The Love that Moves the Sun and the Other Stars)*, 163; *Bird Bath II*, 15–17, *16*; *The Bird Men of Burnley*, *30–31*; *Bird with Fish*, 199; *Brothers and Sisters Have I None*, 146–47; *Burial of the Patriarchs*, 179, *179*; *Cat Woman (La Grande Dame)* (sculpture), *154*, 155, 199–201; *Chiki, ton pays* (Chiki, Your Country), 164, *165*, 171; *Crookhey Hall*, 24–25, *26–27*; *La Cuna* (Norah's crib), 155, 199; 'The Debutante' (story), 59–60; *Down Below*, *114*, 117–18, 122–23, *124–25*; *Down Below* (memoir), 111, 115, 118, 123, 136–38, 182; *Edwardian Hunt Breakfast*, 21; *Fear*, *120–21*; *Garden Bedroom*, 139; *The Giantess/Guardian of the Egg*, 168, 180; *Grandmother Moorhead's Aromatic Kitchen*, 32–33, *34–35*; *Green Tea*, *50–51*; *The Hearing Trumpet* (novella), 17, 41–43, 54–55, 57, 58, 186, *186*, 201; *The Horses of Lord Candlestick*, 21, 83, *84–85*; *The Hour of the Angelus*, *44–45*, 46; *The House Opposite*, 24, 53, 164, *166–67*; 'The House of Fear' (story), 17, 89–93; *The Inventory*, *18–19*; *Kron Flower*, *184–85*; 'Little Francis' (story), 82, 95, 97, 105, 136; *The Magdalens*, *202–3*; *Map of Down Below*, 117–18, *119*; *The Meal of Lord Candlestick*, 83; 'The Milk of Dreams' (book), 206; *Mujeres Conciencia* (poster, Awakened Women), *176*, 180; *El mundo mágico de los mayas* (mural, *The Magical World of the Maya*), 152, *158–59*, 160, 173, 197–98; mural at El Castillo (Plutarco Gastélum's house), 174–75; *Neighbourly Advice*, 24, *25*; *Night Nursery Everything*, *22–23*, 24; *Nunscape in Manzanillo*, *38*, *48*; *The Old Maids*, 24; *Opus Siniestrus* (play), 180–82, *181*; *Portrait of Max Ernst*, *108*, 109, 207; *Q Symphony*, *204*; *The Star*, *169*; artworks in Saint-Martin-d'Ardèche home, 97, 98–99, 104, *104*, *105*; 'The Stone Door' (story), 155; *Self-Portrait/Inn of the Dawn Horse*, 24, *78*, 87, 87–88, 139, 207; *Summer* (with Ernst, Duchamp and Matta), 139–43, *140–41*; *And Then We Saw the Daughter of the Minotaur!*, *170*; *Tuesday*, 168; *Untitled*, 182–83, *183*; *La Virgen de la Cueva* (sculpture), *200*; 'Waiting' (story), 144, 149; *A Winter Fairy Tale*, 53

Carrington, Maurie (Moorhead, LC's mother):
  background, 14, 25, 28, 59; daughter's 'coming
  out', *56, 57*, 58–60; daughter's relationship
  with Ernst, 62, 67, 69, 79–80, 106; daughter's
  schooling, 47; daughter's stay in sanatorium,
  123; daughter's visits, 41; family holidays, 53,
  57; family relationship to author, 7; financial
  assistance to daughter, 97; letters to daughter,
  107–9; marriage, 14, 32; religion, 14; social
  status, 20, 58; storytelling, 28; visit to daughter in
  Mexico, 168; visit to daughter in Paris, 106
Carrington, Pat (LC's brother), 25, 36, 110
Carrington, Thomas (LC's great-grandfather), 59
Carrington and Dewhurst (textile company), 13
Casa Estudio Leonora Carrington, Mexico City
  (museum), 192–97, *194, 195, 196, 198*
Casa Lamm (restaurant), 205
Catholicism, 13, 14, 32, 152
Ceballos, Jacqueline, 179
Celtic history, 29, 41, 193
Chadwick, Whitney, 80–81, 83, 93, 106, 180, 187
Chagall, Marc, 139
Chelsea School of Art, 62
Cherem, Silvia, 52, 205
Chermayeff, Serge, 62, 69
Chiapas, southern Mexico, LC's travels to, 197–98
Chicago, LC's apartment in (Oak Park Arms), 10,
  187–89, 193
Cimabue, 52–53
Clayton-le-Woods, 13, *14*
Cologne, 80, 86
Conrad, Peter, 188
Cornwall *see* Lambe Creek, Cornwall
Country Life, 40
Crookhey Hall, 11, 13, 14, *15*, 15–29, *20, 21*, 33–37,
  43, 49, 87

Dalí, Salvador, 72, 77, 80, 88
De Angelis, Paul, 205
Duchamp, Marcel, 88, 136, *138, 142*, 143; *His Twine*,
  145; *Summer* (with Carrington, Ernst and Matta),
  139–43, *140–41*

Earth First! (group), 188
Edgeworth, Maria, 29–32; 'Essay on the Noble
  Science of Self-Justification', 32
Éluard, Nusch (Maria Benz), *68*, 72, 74, *75*, 76
Éluard, Paul, 72, *73*, 76, 88, 93, 107; 'The Last Letter
  to Roland Penrose', 77
Ernst, Jimmy (Hans-Ulrich, son of Ernst), 67, 93, 97
Ernst, Louise, 67

Ernst, Marie-Berthe, 65, 67, 82, 93, 97
Ernst, Max, 60, 62; background, 65–67; first
  meeting with LC, 11, 65–67; imprisonment and
  release, 106–11, 113, 115, 130; Mayor Gallery
  exhibition (1937), 65, *65*, 69–70, 104–5;
  photographs of, *67, 73, 75, 86, 138, 142, 143*;
  relationship with Breton, 82; relationship with
  Gala, 72; relationship with Guggenheim, 82–83,
  130–33, 135, 143, 148–49; relationship with LC,
  69–77, 79, 80, 81, 83–86, 88, 93, 105, 106, 132,
  133, 135, 143, 148, 149, 172; reunion with LC in
  Lisbon, 130–32; in Saint-Martin-d'Ardèche
  (Les Alliberts), 95, 96, 97, 102, 105, 106, 110,
  113, 135; and the Surrealists, 67, 88, 93; works in
  Mexico, 155
  WORKS: artworks in Saint-Martin-d'Ardèche
  home, 97, 98–99, *99*, *100–101*, 104–5; *L'Ange
  du foyer*, 99; *Leonora in the Morning Light*, *94, 107*,
  109; *La maison de la peur* illustrations, *91, 92*;
  preface to 'The House of Fear', 91–93; *Summer*
  (with Carrington, Duchamp and Matta), 139–43,
  140–41; *Le surréalisme et la peinture*, *138*; Surrealist
  mannequin, 88, *90*; *Two Children Are Threatened
  by a Nightingale*, 62, *66*
Exposición Internacional del Surrealismo (1940),
  161, 161–62, *162*

Félix, María, 173
Fidelin, Ady, *68*, 71–72, 74
Fini, Leonor, 80–81, 102, *102*, 105, 106, 139
'First Papers of Surrealism' exhibition (1942), 145,
  145, 146–47
Fleming, Ian, 64
Florence, LC's stay in, 49–53, *52*
Francés, Esteban, 156
Franco, General Francisco, 116
Friedan, Betty, 178–79
Friedeberg, Pedro, 173
Fry, Varian, 130

Gala (Elena Diakonova, Éluard, then Dalí),
  72, 76, 77
Galería de Arte Mexicano, Mexico City, 157, *161*,
  161–62, *162*
Galerie des Beaux-Arts, Paris, 88–89, *89, 90*
Gastélum, Plutarco, 174–75
Gerzso, Gunther, 156, 157, *194*; *Los días de la calle
  Gabino Barreda (The Days of Gabino Barreda
  Street)*, 156, *156*
Gil, Guillermo, 126
Gill, Eric, 39

Giorgi, Vita, mask for *Opus Siniestrus*, *181*
Glass, Alan, 193
Gnosticism, 193
Goldfinger, Ernő, 64–65
Goldfinger, Ursula (Blackwell), *64*, 64–65
Grimberg, Salomon, 122, 183
Grünewald, Matthias, 83
Guardian, 7, 186
Guggenheim, Peggy, 82–83, 132–33, *142*, 143, *148*, 149; relationship with Ernst, 82–83, 130–33, 135, 143, 148–49; Surrealists in apartment of (Sutton Place mansion), 136, *137*, *142*, 143; '31 Women' exhibition (1943), 149
Guggenheim Jeune, Paris, 83
Guggenheim Museum, New York, 182

Hazelwood Hall, 11, 37, 39–43, *42*, 55, 69, 87, 168
Herrera, Hayden, 162
Highpoint One, Highgate, London, *64*, 64–65
Hitler, Adolf, 67, 74, 81, 86, 129, 132
Hogg, Adam, 53
Horna, José, 155, 156–57, 163, 171, 172, 175
Horna, Kati, 155, 156–57, 163, 171, 172, 175, 187, 194, 206; *Ode to Necrophilia*, 175
Horna, Norah, 157, 171–72
Huxley, Aldous, 173; *Eyeless in Gaza*, 59

Ignatius, Mother (Beveridge), 47–48
International Exhibition of Surrealism, Paris (1938), 88–89, *89*, *90*
International Surrealist Exhibition, London (1936), *60*, 60–62, *61*, 69, 72, 110
Irish Museum of Modern Art, 206

James, Edward, 164, 168, 172, 173, 174–75, 193; Las Pozas house, 174, *174*
Johnson, Buffie, 149

Kahlo, Frida, 145, 160, 161, 162, 163, 172, 187, 192
Kavanaugh, Mary (Nanny Carrington), 25–29, 32, *42*, 123–26, *126*
Kiesler, Frederick, exhibition design, *148*

Lamba, Jacqueline, 135, 160
Lambe Creek, Cornwall, *68*, *70*, 70–77, *71*, *73*, *75*
Landshoff, Hermann, photographs by, *6*, *134*, *137*, *138*, *142*, 143
Leduc, Renato, 127–29, 132, 133, 135–36, 143–45, 148–49, 151–55
Lisbon, 127–33; crossing to New York from, 127–29, 133; LC's marriage to Leduc in, 127, 128–29, 132, 133; LC's operation in, 132–33; LC's reunion with Ernst in, 130–32; war refugees, 129
Litherland, Gina, 187–88
Lizárraga, Gerardo, 156, 157
Llama, Pablo Hojas, photograph by, *117*
London, 57–67, 69; Highpoint One, Highgate, *64*, 64–65; LC exhibition, 188, 206; LC's art training in, 62–64, *64*; Surrealism in, *60*, 60–62, *61*, 69, 72, 110
Los Angeles County Museum of Art, 206
López, Nacho, photograph of LC by, *171*
Lubetkin, Berthold, 64
Lucas, Michel, 111–12, 113

Mabille, Pierre, 122, 136–38
Madrid, LC's escape to, 111, 113, 115, 127
La maison de la peur ('The House of Fear'), 91, *91*, *92*
Man Ray, 71, 72, 88
Mandiargues, André Pieyre de, 106
Marcovich, Eva, 7, 197
Masson, André, 136
Matisse, Pierre, 163, 168
Matta, Roberto, 136; *Summer* (with Carrington, Ernst and Duchamp), 139–43, *140–41*
Mawson, Thomas, 42
Maya culture, 198
Mayor Gallery, Mayfair, 65, *65*, 69–70, 104–5
Megnen, Jeanne, 138
Mendelsohn, Erich, 62
Mesens, E. L. T. (Édouard), 72, *73*, *75*
Metropolitan Autonomous University of Mexico (UAM), 193
Metropolitan Museum of Art, New York, 24
Mexican Museum, San Francisco, 206
Mexico, 33–36, 151–75; art scene in, 157–60, 172; LC's journey to, 139, 148–49; LC's travels to Chiapas, 197–98; muralism, 160, 162; recognition of LC in, 163, 205; women's liberation movement, *176*, 179–80
Mexico City: author's visits, 7–11, 13, 49, 53–54, 72, 76, 153, 157, 191–92, 201–5; Casa Estudio Leonora Carrington (museum), 192–97, *194*, *195*, *196*, *198*; LC's apartment with Leduc in (Mixcoac), 152; LC's arrival in, *150*, 151–52; LC's first apartment with Chiki (Avenida Álvaro Obregón, Roma), 164–68; LC's flight to New Orleans from, 175; LC's home in (194 Calle Chihuahua, Colonia Roma) (*see also* Casa Estudio Leonora Carrington museum), 7–9, 11, 24, 169–74, *171*, *190*, 192, 201, *207*; LC's later years in, *190*, 191–207, *200*, *207*;

markets of, 152–53; shared house in (Gabino Barreda, San Rafael), 155–56; Tlatelolco massacre (1968), 175; Zócalo, *153*

Michelangelo, 52

Midland Hotel, Morecambe, 39–40

Miller, Lee, *68*, 70–71, 72, 102, 194; photographs at Lambe Creek, Cornwall, *70*, *73*, 74, *75*, 76–77; photographs at Saint-Martin-d'Ardèche, 102, *103*, 139

Miró, Joan, 80; Surrealist mannequin, *90*

Moate, County Westmeath, Ireland, 14, 32, *32*, 33

Mondrian, Piet, *142*, 143

Monte Carlo, 57

Moore, Henry, 72

Moore, Irina, 72

Moorhead, George (LC's uncle, author's grandfather), 14, *42*

Moorhead, Henry (LC's grandfather), 29, 32, 33

Moorhead, Leonora (Sister Mary Monica, Aunt Leo, LC's aunt), 14

Moorhead, Mary Monica (Somers, LC's grandmother), 29–33

Morales, Dr Luis, 116, 118–19

Morales, Dr Mariano, 116, *126*

Morecambe Bay, 40, *41*; Midland Hotel, 39–40

Moro, César, 162

Museo de Arte Moderno (Museum of Modern Art), Mexico City, 206

Museum Boijmans Van Beuningen, Rotterdam, 206

Nash, Paul, 76

National Galleries of Scotland, 109, 206

Nazism, 86

New Burlington Galleries, London, *60*, 60–62, *61*, 69, 72, 110

New Hall School, Chelmsford, 37, 43–47, *46*

New Orleans, LC's flight to, 175

New York: crossing to, 127–29, *131*, 133, 135; LC's apartment in Greenwich Village, *134*, 135–36, *183*; LC's exhibitions in, 149, 168, 206; LC's first stay in, 135–49; LC's later travels to, 177–86; recognition of LC in, 53, 136–39, 145; Surrealist exiles in, 136, *137*, *138*, 139, *142*, 143, 145

Obrist, Hans Ulrich, 10

Observer, 188

O'Higgins, Pablo, 169–70

Oppenheim, Meret, 106, 145, 187; *Object (Breakfast in Fur)*, 80

Orenstein, Gloria, 178–79, 180, 186–87

Orozco, José Clemente, 160

Ouspensky group, 193

Ozenfant, Amédée, 62–63, *64*, 138, *142*, 143

Ozenfant Academy of Fine Arts, London, 62–64, *64*

Paalen, Wolfgang, 155, 162

Palazzo Vecchio, Florence, 52

Pallant House Gallery exhibition (2010), 206

Paris, 79–93; books bought by LC in, 110; Café de Flore, 81, 82; LC at finishing school in, 54; LC's arrival in, 79–80; LC's departure from, 93; LC's first meeting Leduc in, 127; LC's published work in, 89–93; Rue Cassoni billet, 54; Rue Jacob 12 apartment, 80, *81*, 87, 127; Simon family extended stay, 54–55

Paz, Octavio, 194

Penrose, Antony, 76

Penrose, Beacus, 70

Penrose, Miss, 49, 53

Penrose, Roland, 70–71, 72, 74, 76, 102, 107; photographs at Lambe Creek, Cornwall, *68*, *71*

Péret, Benjamin, 136, 138, 155, 157

Picasso, Pablo, 77, 80, 81, 127, 155; *Femme assise sur fond jaune et rose, II – Portrait de femme*, 72

Poniatowska, Elena, 179, 201–5

Pottlitzer, Joanne, *180*, 180–83

Powell, Joan, 53–54, 65, 102, *102*, 109

Powell, Philip, 102, *102*

Raay, Stefan van, 206

Rahon, Alice, 155, 163

Ransome, Mary, 129–30, 132

Ravilious, Eric, *Day and Night*, 39

Read, Herbert, 61, 107; *Surrealism*, 62

Remarque, Erich Maria, *The Night in Lisbon*, 129

Renaissance art, 49–53, 63, 163, 164

Rivera, Diego, 157, 161, 163

Riwkin, Anna, photograph of Ernst, *67*

Rosemont, Franklin, 187–88, 193

Rosemont, Penelope, 187–89, 193

Rubinstein, Helena, 139

Rubinstein, Manka, 139–43

St Mary's School, Ascot, 47–49

Saint-Martin-d'Ardèche (Les Alliberts, home), 11, 95–113, *98*, *102*, *103*, 139; artwork by Carrington and Ernst in, 97, 98–99, *99*, *100–101*, *104*, 104–5, *105*

Samaniego, Marisa, 118–22

Sampson, Miss, 54
Sanatorio Peña Castillo, Santander (Morales), 11, 116–26, *117*, *126*, 129, 136
Sanborn's (restaurant), 201–5
Santander, 115–26, *116*; Sanatorio Péna Castillo (Morales), 11, 116–26, *117*, *126*, 129, 136
Sassetta, 53
Schiff, John D., exhibition photograph by, *145*
Second World War, 74, 106, 111, 132, 133
Serpentine Gallery, London, 188, 206
Sicily, 57
Sienese School, 53
Silverdale, 39
Simon, Lucien, 54–55
Simon family, 54–55
Siqueiros, David Alfaro, 157–60
Snead, Stella, 63, 138–39
S-nob (magazine), 175
Spectator, The, 70
Stalin, Josef, 106
Stein, Jane, mask for *Opus Siniestrus*, *181*
Sterne, Hedda, 139, 145
Stonyhurst College, 36, 43
Sullivan, Rosemary, 110
Sulzer, Eva, 155
Surrealism: in Chicago, 187–88; and Irish culture, 33–36; LC's relationship with, 25, 33–36, 69, 76, 82; literature on LC, 186–87; in London, 60, 60–62, *61*, 69, 72, 110; manifestos, 82; Ernst's relationship with, 67, 88, 93; in Mexico, 82, 160–63, *161*, *162*, 187; in New York, 80, 136, 139, 143, 145; in Paris, 71–72, 81–82, 88–89, *89*, *90*; 'Surrealist Survival Kits', 188; *VVV* (journal), 122, 136–38; women artists, 72, 80, 93, 145, 187
Swift, Jonathan, *Gulliver's Travels*, 60
Switzerland, 53

Tanguy, Yves, 155
Tanning, Dorothea, 139
Tate Liverpool, 206
Tate Modern, 207
Teresa, Saint, 126–27
The Times, 58
Toyen (Marie Čermínová), 88
Trafford, Father Robert de, 43
Trotsky, Leon, 93, 106
Tuatha Dé Danann, 29
Tzara, Tristan, 105–6

Ubac, Raoul, exhibition photograph by, *90*
Uccello, Paolo, 52
Uffizi, Florence, 49–52, *52*

Van Ghent (in Madrid), 116
Varo, Remedios, 88, 136, 145, 155–57, 163, 171, 172, 175, 187, 194, 206
Veneziani, Federico, 106
Venice Biennale (2022), 206
VVV (Surrealist journal), 122, 136–38

Ward, Mary, 47
Warner, Marina, 53
Waterhouse, Alfred, 15
Weisz, Emerico 'Chiki' (LC's husband), 155, 163, 164–68, 169, 173, 177–78, *190*
Weisz, Wendy Hauser (LC's daughter-in-law), 188, 192
Weisz Carrington, Gabriel (Gaby, LC's son), 40–41, 163, 168, 173, 192, 201
Weisz Carrington, Pablo (LC's son), 24, 41, 163, 168, 173, 188, 192; cover of *The Hearing Trumpet*, *186*
Weld, Sister Mary Dismas (headmistress), 46, *46*
Westwood House, 13, 14
Whitelaw Reid Mansion, New York (1942), 145, *145*
Winkie (pony), 49
Wolf, Miriam, 156, 157

Yarrow, Catherine, 111–13, 115, 135
Yeti (LC's dog), 194
Yolanda (LC's housekeeper), 8, 192, 201